D1689923

Kageneck
Deutsch-amerikanisches Begriffslexikon
U.S.-German Comparative Dictionary

U.S.-German Comparative Dictionary of Direct Investment
Real Estate, Taxes, Corporate Law

With Sample Agreements

By

KARL-ERBO GRAF KAGENECK
Munich–New York

With the Support of

MICHAEL PRINZ ZU LÖWENSTEIN
Frankfurt

ALBERT P. BEHLER
New York

CHRISTOPHER B. PRICE
New York

GEORG VON WERZ
Munich

C. H. BECK'SCHE VERLAGSBUCHHANDLUNG
Munich 1998

Deutsch-amerikanisches Begriffslexikon Direktinvestitionen
Immobilien, Steuern, Gesellschaftsrecht

Mit Formulierungsmustern für Verträge

Von

KARL-ERBO GRAF KAGENECK
New York–München

unter Mitarbeit von

MICHAEL PRINZ ZU LÖWENSTEIN
Frankfurt

ALBERT P. BEHLER
New York

CHRISTOPHER B. PRICE
New York

GEORG VON WERZ
München

C. H. BECK'SCHE VERLAGSBUCHHANDLUNG
München 1998

Die Deutsche Bibliothek – CIP-Einheitsaufnahme

Kageneck, Karl-Erbo:
Deutsch-amerikanisches Begriffswörterbuch Immobilienrecht und
Immobilienbesteuerung : mit Formulierungsmustern für Verträge / von
Karl-Erbo Graf Kageneck. Unter Mitarb. von Michael Prinz zu
Löwenstein. - München : Beck, 1998
  Parallelsacht.: US-German comparative dictionary of real property and
related tax law
  ISBN 3-406-42399-X

ISBN 3 406 42399 X

Satz: Jung Satzcentrum, Lahnau
Druck: C. H. Beck'sche Buchdruckerei, Nördlingen
Gedruckt auf säurefreiem, alterungsbeständigem Papier
(hergestellt aus chlorfrei gebleichtem Zellstoff)

Contents/Inhaltsverzeichnis

Preface VII
Vorwort IX

Abbreviations
Abkürzungen XI

English Language Index
Verzeichnis der englischsprachigen Begriffe XV

German-American Encyclopedia
Deutsch-amerikanisches Lexikon 1

Sample Agreements
Formulierungsmuster für Verträge 171

German Sample Agreements (in Translation)
(Musterverträge nach deutschem Recht in englischer
Übersetzung) 173
1. Real Property Purchase Agreement:
   Purchase and Sale of an Office Building
   (Grundstückskaufvertrag: Geschäftsgrundstück mit
   Bürogebäude) 175
2. Office Lease Agreement
   (Gewerberaummietvertrag) 183

U.S. Sample Agreements
(Musterverträge nach dem Recht der USA) 197
3. Purchase and Sale Agreement
   (Grundstückskaufvertrag) 197
4. Form of Agreement of Lease
   (Gewerblicher Mietvertrag, ausführliche Fassung) 219
5. Form of Agreement of Lease, Basic Version
   (Gewerblicher Mietvertrag, einfache Fassung) 303

Preface

Publications about the laws of other countries often contain large amounts of unnecessary information because the educated reader already „knows" much of the information. He correctly assumes that most legal issues of his home jurisdiction exist likewise in foreign jurisdictions, and that many of these issues have similar answers.

The purpose of this booklet is to give the reader an overview over U.S. and German real property laws and related tax, companies and business laws, as well as practices and market trends. The book provides „net" information by focusing on important conceptual differences between U.S. and German laws and usage. Any reader with some knowledge of U.S. property laws and the real estate business will thus be able to quickly grasp important legal and business concepts of the real estate business in Germany. He will also be able to better advise German, and possibly other European investors in the U.S. by pointing out the relevant differences in legal concepts and answers.

Terms which are simply translated without annotation have the same or a substantially similar meaning. Differences between them are generally too insignificant to warrant discussion in this booklet. Terms which are followed by annotations usually cannot be translated literally. They are conceptually different, sometimes materially. The same applies to translations marked with a „~", indicating the approximate meaning of laws or institutions not to be found in the jurisdiction of the target language. When, for example, the German „Abfallgesetz" is more or less literally translated as „Waste Removal Act", the reader should bear in mind that there is no such Act in the U.S.

German real estate law is similar in concept and in many details to the real estate laws of several other continental European (civil code) countries, such as France, Switzerland, Austria, Italy, Spain, and some Eastern European countries. Of course, the reader cannot assume that a specific rule described in this booklet will in fact apply in other European countries.

The book also addresses a few important differences in other legal areas, such as commercial and corporate law.

Preface

The purpose of this booklet is not to provide the reader with significant detail. The sole objective is to alert him of the existence of certain important differences between U.S. and German legal concepts and to depict the essence of those differences without describing every applicable detail.

Vorwort

Publikationen zum Recht anderer Länder enthalten über weite Strecken Informationen, die dem vorgebildeten Leser wenig Nutzen bringen, da er die Informationen zum großen Teil schon „kennt". Er vermutet nämlich richtigerweise, daß nicht nur die meisten Rechtsfragen seines Heimatrechts auch in der fremden Rechtsordnung existieren, sondern daß auch die Mehrzahl der Antworten bzw. Praktiken einander gleichen oder ähneln.

Sinn dieses Büchleins soll es sein, dem Praktiker und dem versierten Immobilieninvestor mit möglichst wenig Text möglichst viel Information über das fremde Immobilienrecht und das damit zusammenhängende Steuerrecht sowie über Marktgepflogenheiten und Trends zu vermitteln. Dabei wird auf Zitate weitgehend verzichtet, unter anderem weil das U.S.-Immobilienrecht Landesrecht ist. Die Unterschiede im Recht der Einzelstaaten sind jedoch meist gering. Wo sie fundamentaler Natur sind, wird im Text darauf hingewiesen.

Der Leser kann davon ausgehen, daß Begriffe, denen keine Anmerkungen folgen, im amerikanischen und deutschen Recht weitgehend die gleiche Bedeutung haben bzw. daß Unterschiede im Detail zu unerheblich sind, um im Rahmen dieses Büchleins Erwähnung zu verdienen. Bei den mit Anmerkungen versehenen Begriffen bestehen meist nennenswerte Unterschiede. In diesen Unterschieden liegt die eigentlich interessante Information für den grenzüberschreitenden Investor. Sie zu kennen, bedeutet für den Kenner des deutschen Immobilienrechts, daß er auch im U.S.-Immobilien- und Immobiliensteuerrecht weitgehend bewandert ist. Umgekehrt kann er den amerikanischen Investor in Deutschland schneller und gezielter beraten, da er ihn auf die relevanten Unterschiede direkt hinweisen kann.

Das Wörterbuch verweist auch auf einige wichtige Unterschiede in anderen Rechtsgebieten, z. B. dem Gesellschafts- und Handelsrecht.

Dieses Büchlein will keinerlei Anspruch auf Vollständigkeit erheben, da es sich bewußt auf die wichtigeren Begriffe und auf die Darstellung der wesentlichen Unterschiede beschränkt.

Abbreviations / Abkürzungen

(All Agencies, Courts or Acts referred to below are Federal.
Alle erwähnten Behörden, Gerichte und Gesetze sind solche des Bundes.)

AbfG	Abfallgesetz (Waste Removal Act)
AfA	Absetzungen für Abnutzung (Depreciation Deductions)
AGBG	Gesetz zur Regelung des Rechts der Allgemeinen Geschäftsbedingungen (General Business Terms Act)
AktG	Aktiengesetz (Stock Corporation Act)
AuslandsInvG	Auslandsinvestmentgesetz (Foreign Investment Companies Registration and Tax Act)
AO	Abgabenordnung (Tax Procedure Act)
BauNVO	Baunutzungsverordnung (Building Use Ordinance)
BauGB	Baugesetzbuch (Federal Building Code)
BauO	Bauordnung (State Building Codes)
BeurkG	Beurkundungsgesetz (Notarization and Acknowledgement Act)
BewG	Bewertungsgesetz (General Tax Assessment Act)
BFH	Bundesfinanzhof (Supreme Tax Court)
BGB	Bürgerliches Gesetzbuch (Civil Code)
BGH	Bundesgerichtshof (Supreme Civil and Criminal Court)
BVerfG	Bundesverfassungsgericht (Supreme Constitutional Court
BImSchG	Bundesimmissionenschutzgesetz (Clean Air Act)
BVerwG	Bundesverwaltungsgericht (Supreme Administrative Court)
CERCLA	Comprehensive Environmental Response, Compensation and Liability Act of 1980 (U.S.)
ChemG	Chemikaliengesetz (Chemical Substances Act)
DBA	Doppelbesteuerungsabkommen (Double Taxation Treaty)
EGBGB	Einführungsgesetz zum Bürgerlichen Gesetzbuch (Introductory Act to the Civil Code)

Abbreviations / Abkürzungen

ErbbauRVO	Erbbaurechtsverordnung (Statutory Ground Lease Regulations)
ErbStG	Erbschaftsteuer- und Schenkungsteuergesetz (Estate and Gift Tax Act)
EstDV	Einkommensteuer-Durchführungsverordnung (Income Tax Regulations)
EStG	Einkommensteuergesetz (Income Tax Act)
FIRPTA	Foreign Investment in Real Property Tax Act (Gesetz zur Besteuerung von U.S. Immobilienveräußerungen durch Steuerausländer)
GBO	Grundbuchordnung (Deed Registry Act)
GewO	Gewerbeordnung (Business License Act)
GewStG	Gewerbesteuergesetz (Trade and Business Tax Act)
GG	Grundgesetz (German Constitution)
GmbH	Gesellschaft mit beschränkter Haftung (Limited Liability Company)
GmbHG	GmbH-Gesetz (Limited Liability Companies Act)
GrEStG	Grunderwerbsteuergesetz (Real Property Transfer Tax Act)
GrundstücksVG	Grundstücksverkehrsgesetz (Agricultural and Forest Lands Sales Act)
HGB	Handelsgesetzbuch (Commercial Code)
HOAI	Honorarordnung für Architekten und Ingenieure (Architectural and Engineering Fees Regulations)
HUD	Housing and Urban Development (U.S.-Bundesbehörde für Städteplanung und Hausbau)
IRC	Internal Revenue Code (Allgemeines U.S.-Steuergesetzbuch)
IRS	Internal Revenue Service (Bundesamt für Finanzen)
KAGG	Gesetz über Kapitalanlagegesellschaften (Investment Companies Act)
KG	Kommanditgesellschaft (Limited Partnership)
KGaA	Kommanditgesellschaft auf Aktien (Partnership Limited by Shares)
KO	Konkursordnung (Bankruptcy Code)
KStG	Körperschaftsteuergesetz (Corporate Income Tax Act)
MaBV	Makler- und Bauträgerverordnung (Brokers' and Developers' Regulation)
MHG	Miethöhegesetz (Rent Level Act)

Abbreviations / Abkürzungen

MwSt	Mehrwertsteuer (Value-Added Sales Tax)
OHG	Offene Handelsgesellschaft (Registered General Partnership)
REIT	Real Estate Investment Trust (U.S.-Kapitalanlagegesellschaft für Immobilien)
RIC	Regulated Investment Company (U.S.-Kapitalanlagegesellschaft für Wertpapiere)
StBauFG	Städtebauförderungsgesetz (Urban Renewal Act)
StGB	Strafgesetzbuch (Penal Code)
TzWrG	Teilzeit-Wohnrechtegesetz (Time Sharing Act)
UCC	Uniform Commercial Code (Modell-Handelsgesetzbuch)
UmwStG	Umwandlungssteuergesetz (Restructuring of Companies Taxation Act)
VAG	Versicherungsaufsichtsgesetz (Insurance Companies Act)
VerglO	Vergleichsordnung („Chapter 11" Procedure Act)
VwGO	Verwaltungsgerichtsordnung (Administrative Court Procedure Code)
VOB	Verdingungsordnung für Bauleistungen (General Conditions for Contractors)
VStG	Vermögensteuergesetz (Networth Tax Act)
WährG	Währungsgesetz (Currency Act)
WEG	Wohnungseigentumsgesetz (Condominium Act)
ZPO	Zivilprozeßordnung (Civil Procedure Code)
ZVG	Zwangsversteigerungsgesetz (Foreclosure Sales Act)

English Language Index
Verzeichnis der englischsprachigen Begriffe

Abandon – Besitzaufgabe; Dereliktion; Eigentumsaufgabe
Abode – Aufenthalt → Beschränkt Steuerpflichtige
Acceleration Clause → Fälligkeitsklausel
Acceptance → Abnahme
Accrual Basis → Betriebsvermögensvergleich
Accumulated Earnings Tax → Thesaurierung
Acknowledgement → Notar → Notarielle Beurkundung
Acquisitions → Fusionskontrolle → Unternehmensübernahmen
Acts of God – Höhere Gewalt
Adequate Protection → Absonderung
Adverse Possession – Ersitzung → Buchersitzung
Advertising – Werbung → Vergleichende Werbung
Affirmative Action → Anstellung und Kündigung
Agricultural Land → Grundstücksverkehrsgesetz
Air Conditioning – Klimatisierung → Umlagen
Air Rights → Luftraum
Amortization – Tilgung
Amortized Mortgage → Eigentümergrundschuld
Amortizing Loan – Tilgungsdarlehen
Antitrust → Fusionskontrolle → Wettbewerbsverbot
Appraisal – Wertgutachten
Appropriation – Aneignung
Appurtenant Chattels → Zubehör
Arbitration – Schiedsverfahren
Architects → Architekten
Architectural Plans → Architektenpläne
„**As Is**" → „Wie es steht und liegt"
Assessed Value → Einheitswert
Assessment → Steuererklärung → Bewertung
Asset Backed Securities → Verbriefung → Pfandbrief → Hypothekenbank
Asset Management → Grundstücksverwaltung
Assumption of Mortgage → Übernahme der Hypothek

English Language Index / Verzeichnis der engl. Begriffe

At Risk Rule → Negatives Kapitalkonto → Kapitaleinlage → Verlustzuweisungsgesellschaft
Attachment – Arrest; Beschlagnahme
Authority – Behörde; Vollmacht
Automatic Stay – Konkursbeschlag

Bank Secrecy → Bankgeheimnis
Bankruptcy → Konkurs
Bankruptcy Trustee – Konkursverwalter → Vergleichsverwalter
Basis – Buchwert
Bidding → Geringstes Gebot
Blanket Mortgage – Gesamthypothek
Board of Directors → Aufsichtsrat
Bona Fide → Guter Glaube
Boundaries → Grundstücksgrenzen
Branch Profits Tax – Niederlassungssteuer → Quellensteuer für Betriebsstättengewinn
Breach – Vertragsbruch
Broker → Makler
Builder Bond – Erfüllungsbürgschaft
Building and Loan Association → Bausparkassen
Building Authority → Baubehörde
Building Law → Baurecht
Building Code → Bauordnung
Building Distance – Bauwich; Abstandsflächen
Building Engineers → Architekten
Building Ground Risks → Baugrundrisiko
Building Permit → Baugenehmigung
Building Restrictions – Baubeschränkungen
Bulk Sale → Vermögensübernahme → Betriebsübergang
Business License → Gewerbeerlaubnis
Business Start-up Expenses → Anlaufkosten

Cancellation → Löschung
Capital Contribution → Kapitaleinlage
Capital Gain → Veräußerungsgewinn → Spekulationsgewinn
Capital Gain Holding Periods → Spekulationsfrist
Capital Loss → Veräußerungsverlust → Spekulationsverlust
Cancellation of Debt → Forderungsverzicht
Cash Basis – Einnahmen-Ausgaben-Überschuß

English Language Index / Verzeichnis der engl. Begriffe

Casualty Loss → Abbruchkosten
Certificate of Occupancy → Gebrauchsabnahmeschein
Chapter 11 → Vergleich
Charitable Foundation → Stiftung
Chattel – Bewegliches Vermögen
Chattel Mortgage → Pfandrecht
Check-The-Box Regulations → Hybride Gesellschaftsformen
Chemical Substances Act – Chemikaliengesetz → Umweltschutz
Citizenship → Staatsangehörigkeit
City Plan – Flächennutzungsplan
Civil Procedure → Zivilprozeß
Clean Air Act – Immissionenschutzgesetz
Clean Water Act – Wasserhaushaltsgesetz → Umweltschutz
Closed End Fund – Geschlossener Fonds
Closing → Auflassung
Coinsurance → Versicherung
Collateral – Sicherheiten
Commercial Mortgage Backed Securities → Pfandbrief → Verbriefung → Hypothekenbank
Commercial Property – Gewerbeobjekt
Commercial Zone – Gewerbegebiet
Commitment Fee – Bereitstellungsprovision
Common Areas – Gemeinflächen → Verkehrssicherungspflicht
Common Elements – Gemeinflächen
Completion Bond – Erfüllungsbürgschaft
Condemnation → Enteignung → Sozialbindung des Eigentums
Condominium → Wohnungseigentum
Consolidated Tax Returns → Organschaft → Dividendenbesteuerung
Construction Loan – Baudarlehen
Construction Period Interest → Bauzeitzinsen
Constructive Dividend → Verdeckte Gewinnausschüttung
Consumer Price Index → Lebenshaltungskostenindex
Contamination → Altlasten
Contingency Fees → Anwälte
Continuity of Enterprise → Betriebsübergang → Vermögensübernahme
Contractor – Unternehmer → Verdingungsordng f. Bauleistungen
Contributions of Property → Sacheinlagen
Contributory Negligence – Mitverschulden

English Language Index / Verzeichnis der engl. Begriffe

Conversion → Umwandlung (von Wohnraum)
Corporate Income Tax – Körperschaftsteuer → Einkommensteuer
Correction of Deed Registry → Grundbuchberichtigung
County Recorder → Grundbuch → Öffentlicher Glaube
CPI → Lebenshaltungskostenindex
Custom – Gewohnheitsrecht

Damages – Schadenersatz
Debtor in Possession → Vergleich → Vergleichsverwalter
Deductibility – Abzugsfähigkeit → Verlustausgleich
Deed Registry → Grundbuch → Öffentlicher Glaube
Deed of Trust → Hypothek
De-Facto Merger → Betriebsübergang → Vermögensübernahme
Defects – Mängel → Wie besichtigt
Deferral of Gain → Übertragung stiller Reserven
Deletion → Löschung
Demolition → Abbruchkosten
Deposit Insurance → Einlagensicherung
Depreciation – Abschreibungen → Absetzungen für Abnutzung → Sonderabschreibungen
Developer – Bauherr; Bauträger
Development Freeze – Bausperre → Veränderungssperre
Development Plans – Bauleitpläne
Director → Aufsichtsrat
Discharge of Debt → Forderungserlaß
Discount – Disagio → Geldbeschaffungskosten
Discrimination → Anstellung und Kündigung
Dismissals → Anstellung und Kündigung
Dispossess Proceedings – Räumungsklage
Dividends → Dividendenbesteuerung → Schachtelprivileg
Dividends received deduction → Schachtelprivileg → Einkommensteuer → Körperschaftsteuer
Division → Teilung
Domicile – Sitz; Wohnsitz → Beschränkt Steuerpflichtige
Dominant Tenement – Herrschendes Grundstück → Grunddienstbarkeit
Downpayment → Anzahlung
Due-on-Sale Clause → Sofortige Fälligkeit

English Language Index / Verzeichnis der engl. Begriffe

Earnings and Profits – Verwendbares Eigenkapital
Earnings Stripping → Gesellschafterfremdfinanzierung
Easement – Dienstbarkeit → Grunddienstbarkeit
Easement by Prescription – Ersitzung → Buchersitzung
Easement in Gross – Beschränkt Persönliche Dienstbarkeit
Easement of Necessity – Notweg
East Germany → Privatisierung → Sonderabschreibungen → Verlustzuweisungsgesellschaft
Electricity – Strom → Umlagen
Eminent Domain → Enteignung → Sozialbindung des Eigentums
Employees → Anstellung und Kündigung
Employee Stock Ownership → Mitarbeiteroptionen
Encroachment → Überbau
Encumbrances – Lasten; Belastungen
Environmental Crimes Act – Umweltkriminalitätsgesetz → Umweltschutz
Environmental Impact Act – Umweltverträglichkeitsgesetz → Umweltschutz
Environmental Liability Act – Umwelthaftungsgesetz → Umweltschutz
Environmental Procedure Regulations – Umweltverwaltungsrecht → Umweltschutz
Environmental Protection → Umweltschutz → Bundeswaldgesetz
Escalations – Mietsteigerungen → Mietanpassung → Lebenshaltungskostenindex
Escrow Account – Anderkonto
Estate Tax → Erbschaftsteuer
Estoppel Letter – (not customary in German transactions / keine deutsche Entsprechung)
Eviction – Räumungsklage
Exchange → Tausch
Exclusive Agency → Alleinauftrag
Executor – Testamentsvollstrecker
Expatriation Rules – Wegzugsbesteuerung → Beschränkt Steuerpflichtige
Expropriation → Enteignung → Sozialbindung des Eigentums

Fair Market Value – Verkehrswert
False Entries → Grundbuchberichtigung
FAR – Geschoßflächenzahl

English Language Index / Verzeichnis der engl. Begriffe

Federal Taxes – Bundessteuern → Steuern
Fee Simple – Eigentum
Fiduciary – Treuhänder
Finance Costs → Geldbeschaffungskosten
Fire – Gebäudebrand
Firing → Anstellung und Kündigung
FIRPTA → Immobilienholding
Fixed-Price Contract → Pauschalpreisvertrag
Fixed Rate Interest – Festzins
Fixtures → Wesentlicher Bestandteil
Floating Rate – Variable Zinsen
Floor-to-Area Ratio – Geschoßflächenzahl
Force Majeure – Höhere Gewalt
Foreclosure → Zwangsvollstreckung
Foreclosure Auction → Geringstes Gebot
Foreign Companies → Juristische Personen → Quellensteuer für Betriebsstättengewinn → Veräußerungsgewinn
Foreign Losses → Negative Ausländische Einkünfte
Foreign Real Estate Investors → Ausländische Immobilieninvestoren
Forest Land → Bundeswaldgesetz → Grundstücksverkehrsgesetz
Foundation → Stiftung
Fractional Interest – Bruchteil
Fraudulent Conveyances Act – Anfechtungsgesetz → Konkursanfechtung
Freeze → Veränderungssperre
Freeze-Out → Abfindungsangebot → Unternehmensübernahmen
Fund – Fonds
Fund-of-Funds → Dachfonds → Kapitalanlagegesellschaft
Future Advances under Mortgage → Höchstbetragshypothek
Future Interests → Anwartschaft
Futures → Warentermingeschäft

General Conditions for Contractors → Verdingungsordnung für Bauleistungen
General Contractor – Unternehmer → Verdingungsordnung für Bauleistungen
General Partner – Komplementär
General Partnership – BGB Gesellschaft → Offene Handelsgesellschaft

English Language Index / Verzeichnis der engl. Begriffe

General Terms and Conditions → Allgemeine Geschäftsbedingungen
Gift Tax – Schenkungsteuer → Erbschaftsteuer
Good Faith → Guter Glaube → Öffentlicher Glaube
Goodwill → Firmenwert
Grantor Trust → Stiftung
Green Card → Aufenthaltsgenehmigung
Ground Lease → Erbbaurecht
Guaranty → Bürgschaft

Hazardous Waste – Sondermüll
Heating – Heizung → Umlagen
Height Density – Geschoßflächenzahl
Hidden Defects – Verborgene Mängel → Wie es steht und liegt
Hidden Reserves – Stille Reserven → Übertragung stiller Reserven
Highest Bid – Meistgebot
Hiring → Anstellung und Kündigung
Historical Monument – Denkmal
Hobby Losses – Liebhaberei → Gewinnerzielungsabsicht → Verlustzuweisungsgesellschaft
Holding Period → Spekulationsfrist
Home Mortgage Interest → Hypothekenzinsen für Eigenheim
Home Owners' Association – Eigentümergemeinschaft
Home Ownership → Grundförderung
Homestead → Pfändungsschutz
Hotel Management → Hotelpacht (-betreiber)
Hunting Rights → Jagdrecht
Hybrid Entities → Hybride Gesellschaftsformen

Immigration – Einwanderung → Aufenthaltsgenehmigung → Staatsangehörigkeit
Incentive Stock Options → Mitarbeiteroptionen
Income Tax → Einkommensteuer
Indexing → Wertsicherungsklausel → Mietanpassung → Lebenshaltungskostenindex
Indirect Tax Credit → Dividendenbesteuerung
Industrial Park – Gewerbepark
Industrial Zone – Industriegebiet
Inheritance Law → Erbrecht

English Language Index / Verzeichnis der engl. Begriffe

Inheritance Tax → Erbschaftsteuer
Insolvency → Konkurs → Vergleich
Installment → Ratenzahlung
Intangibles – Immaterielle Wirtschaftsgüter → Firmenwert
Interest – Zinsen
Interstate Highways → Bundesstraßen
Interstate Land Sales Full Disclosure Act → Öffentliche Plazierung
Intrusion → Überbau
Invasion → Überbau
Investment Adviser → Anlageberater
Investment Company → Kapitalanlagegesellschaft

Joint and Several Liability – Gesamtschuldnerisch
Joint Tenancy – Gesamthandseigentum → Teilung
Judicial Sale – Zuschlag → Geringstes Gebot
Junior – Nachrangig → Rang → Verkäuferhypothek
Juridical Persons → Juristische Personen

Labor Court → Anstellung und Kündigung
Land Charge → Grundschuld
Landlord and Tenant Law – Mietrecht
Landmark – Denkmal
Latent Defects – Verborgene Mängel → Wie es steht und liegt
Lawyers → Anwälte
Lease – Miete
Leasehold Estate (long-term) → Dauerwohnrecht
Leasehold Mortgage → Beleihung des Mietrechts
Leases survive property sale → Kauf bricht nicht Miete
Leasing – Leasing → Sale-Lease-back
Legal Defect – Rechtsmangel
Legal Fees → Anwälte
Letter of Credit → Bürgschaft
Letter of Intent – Absichtserklärung
Letter Ruling → Verbindliche Auskunft
Liability Insurance → Haftpflichtversicherung
Life Estate – Nießbrauch
Life Insurance → Lebensversicherung
Limited Liability Company → Kommanditgesellschaft → Hybride Gesellschaftsformen

English Language Index / Verzeichnis der engl. Begriffe

Limited Liability Partnership → Partnerschaftsgesellschaft → Hybride Gesellschaftsformen
Limited Partnership → Kommanditgesellschaft
Liquidated Damages → Vertragsstrafe
Lis Pendens → Vormerkung
Local Taxes – Gemeindesteuern → Steuern
Loss Carry-Back – Verlustrücktrag → Verlustabzug
Loss Carry-Over – Verlustvortrag → Verlustabzug
Losses → Verlustausgleich
Lot – Flurstück; Parzelle
Low Income Housing → Gemeinnütziger Wohnungsbau

Maintenance → Erhaltungsaufwendungen → Mietanpassung
Management Board → Vorstand; Geschäftsführung
Manufactured Homes → Fertighäuser
Market Value – Verkehrswert
Master Lease – Generalmietvertrag
Master Plan – Flächennutzungsplan
Mechanic's Lien → Bauhandwerkerhypothek
Memorandum of Understanding – Absichtserklärung
Merger → Unternehmensübernahmen → Fusionskontrolle → Abfindungsangebot
Merger Control → Fusionskontrolle
Merger of Interests → Eigentümergrundschuld
Metering – Ablesen → Umlagen
Metes and Bounds → Grundstücksgrenzen
Minerals → Bodenschätze
Minority Shareholders → Abfindungsangebot → Unternehmensübernahmen
Mixed-Use Zone – Mischgebiet
Modular Homes → Fertighäuser
Mortgage → Hypothek → Höchstbetragshypothek → Grundschuld
Mortgage attaches to ... → Haftungsgegenstände
Mortgage-Backed Annuity – Rentenschuld
Mortgage-Backed Security → Pfandbrief → Hypothekenbank
Mortgage Bank → Hypothekenbank
Mortgage Bond → Pfandbrief → Hypothekenbank
Mortgage Points – Damnum → Geldbeschaffungskosten
Municipal Bonds → Kommunalobligationen → Hypothekenbank

English Language Index / Verzeichnis der engl. Begriffe

Municipal Services → Anschluß und Benutzungszwang
Mutual Fund – Fonds → Kapitalanlagegesellschaft
Mutual Savings Banks → Bausparkassen

Nationality → Staatsangehörigkeit
Naturalization – Einbürgerung → Staatsangehörigkeit → Aufenthaltsgenehmigung
Negative Pledge → Verbot der weiteren Belastung
Negotiable Mortgage → Verkehrshypothek → Grundschuld
Net Lease – Nettomiete
Net Worth Tax → Vermögensteuer
NOL – Verlustabzug; Verlustvortrag; Verlustrücktrag
NOL Trafficking → Mantelkauf
Non-Compete → Wettbewerbsverbot
Nonconforming Use – Vorbelastung
Non-Recourse → Objekthaftung
Non-Renewable Lease → Zeitmietvertrag
Non-Resident Aliens → Beschränkt Steuerflichtige
Nonvoting Stock – Stimmrechtslose Aktien → Vorzugsaktien
Notary (Public) → Notar
Nuclear Power Act – Atomgesetz → Umweltschutz
Nuisance – Immissionen

Obligations Law → Abstraktionsprinzip
Officers → Vorstand
Open-End Fund – Offener Fonds
Operating Cost – Betriebskosten → Mietanpassung
Outlying Areas → Außenbereich
Overage Rent – Umsatzmiete
Owner's Mortgage → Eigentümergrundschuld
Ownership – Eigentum

Parcel – Flurstück; Parzelle
Parent Subsidiary → Dividendenbesteuerung
Parking – Parkplätze; Stellplätze → Garagenablösung
Participating Loan – Partiarisches Darlehen
Partition → Teilung
Partner Loans → Gesellschafterfremdfinanzierung
Party Wall – Grenzmauer
Passing of Title → Eigentumsübergang

English Language Index / Verzeichnis der engl. Begriffe

Passive Activity Loss → Verlustausgleich → Verlustzuweisungsgesellschaft
Pension Funds → Pensionskassen
Percentage Rent – Umsatzmiete
Performance Bond – Erfüllungsbürgschaft
Personal Holding Company → Thesaurierung
Personal Property – Bewegliches Vermögen → Zubehör
Personal Servitude – Reallast
Piercing the Corporate Veil → Durchgriffshaftung
Plat – Parzellierungsplan
Points – Damnum → Geldbeschaffungskosten
Possession – Besitz
Power – Vollmacht
Power of Sale → Vollstreckbare Urkunde
Preemptive Right → Vorkaufsrecht → Gemeindliches Vorkaufsrecht
Preemptive Stock Rights → Bezugsrechte → Sacheinlagen
Preferential Transfer – Gläubigerbenachteiligung → Konkursanfechtung
Preferred Return → Gewinnvorab
Preferred Stock → Vorzugsaktien
Pre-Merger Filings → Fusionskontrolle
Prepayment Penalty – Vorfälligkeitsentschädigung
Preservation Ordinance – Erhaltungssatzung
Priority → Rang
Priority Notice → Vormerkung
Private Placement – Privatplazierung → Öffentliche Plazierung
Privatization → Privatisierung
Property Dealer → Gewerblicher Grundstückshändler
Property Insurance → Sachversicherung
Property Law → Abstraktionsprinzip → Numerus Clausus im Sachenrecht
Property Lines → Grundstücksgrenzen
Property Management → Grundstücksverwaltung
Public Offering → Öffentliche Plazierung
Public Service → Erschließung → Anschluß und Benutzungszwang → Erschließungsaufwand
Public Utilities → Anschluß und Benutzungszwang
Purchase Money Mortgage → Verkäuferhypothek
Purchase of Real Property → Grundstückskauf
Purchase Option – Ankaufsrecht

English Language Index / Verzeichnis der engl. Begriffe

Quitclaim Deed → Zugesicherte Eigenschaften

Rating → Junk Bonds
Real Estate Investment Fund – Immobilienfonds → Kapitalanlagegesellschaft
Real Estate Investment Trust → Kapitalanlagegesellschaft
Real Estate Prices → Immobilienpreise
Real Estate Settlement Procedures Act → Verbraucherkreditgesetz
Real Property Holding Corporation → Immobilienholding
Real Property Law → Immobilienrecht
Real Property Tax → Grundsteuer
Real Property Transfer Tax → Grunderwerbsteuer
Recapture → Spekulationsgewinn → Veräußerungsgewinn
Receivership – Zwangsverwaltung
Recorder of Deeds → Grundbuch → Öffentlicher Glaube
Recording – Eintragung; Grundbucheintragung → Öffentlicher Glaube
Recording Requirement → Buchungszwang → Spezialitätsprinzip
Recourse → Objekthaftung
Redemption – Rückkauf → Eigene Aktien
Redevelopment Area – Sanierungsgebiet
Reforestation → Bundeswaldgesetz
Reg D Offering → Öffentliche Plazierung
Register of Deeds → Grundbuch → Öffentlicher Glaube
Regulated Investment Company → Kapitalanlagegesellschaft
Rehabilitation Expenditures → Erhaltungsaufwendungen
Related Taxpayers → Angehörige
Remainders → Anwartschaft
Renewal Option – Verlängerungsoption
Renovation Expenditures → Erhaltungsaufwendungen
Rent Stabilization – Mieterschutz → Kündigungsschutz → Berechtigtes Interesse → Soziales Mietrecht
Rent Control → Mietpreisbindung
Rental Expenses → Werbungskostenpauschale
Rental Income → Vermietung und Verpachtung
Rentals – Mieten
Reorganisation/Conversion – Umwandlung → Umwandlung, Gesellschaftsrecht → Tausch
Reorganisation Plan – Vergleichsvorschlag → Vergleich
Repairs → Erhaltungsaufwendungen

English Language Index / Verzeichnis der engl. Begriffe

Replacement Costs – Wiederherstellungkosten; Wiederbeschaffungskosten
Repossession → Rückerwerb
Representations → Zugesicherte Eigenschaften
Residence Permit → Aufenthaltsgenehmigung
Resident Taxpayers → Beschränkt Steuerpflichtige
Residential Area → Wohngebiet
Residual Value – Wiederverkaufswert
Restraint of Alienation – Verfügungsbeschränkung → Sofortige Fälligkeit
Restraint of Trade → Wettbewerbsverbot → Fusionskontrolle
Retail Sales → Mehrwertsteuer
Retaining of Earnings → Thesaurierung → Dividendenbesteuerung
Reunification → Privatisierung
Reversions → Anwartschaft
Review Rights → Grundbucheinsicht
Right of First Refusal → Vorkaufsrecht → Gemeindliches Vorkaufsrecht
Right of Redemption → Einstellung der Zwangsversteigerung
Right of Way – Wegerecht
Risk of Loss → Gefahrübergang
Ruling → Verbindliche Auskunft

Safe Condition → Verkehrssicherungspflicht
Sale – Leaseback → Sale – Lease-back
Sale of Business → Betriebsübergang
Sales Agent → Handelsvertreter
Sales Tax – Umsatzsteuer → Mehrwertsteuer
Savings and Loan Banks → Bausparkassen
Savings Banks → Sparkassen
Second Mortgage – Nachrangig → Rang → Verkäuferhypothek
Securities Exchange Act – Wertpapierhandelsgesetz → Fusionskontrolle
Securitization → Pfandbrief → Hypothekenbank → Verbriefung
Security Interest → Pfandrecht
Seizing – Beschlagnahme
Seller Financing → Verkäuferhypothek
Separation of Units → Abgeschlossenheit
Sequestration – Beschlagnahme
Servient Tenement – Belastetes Grundstück → Grunddienstbarkeit

English Language Index / Verzeichnis der engl. Begriffe

Sewage – Abwasser → Umlagen
Shares for Property → Sacheinlagen
Short-term Capital Loss → Spekulationsverlust
Short-term Capital Gain → Spekulationsgewinn → Spekulationsgeschäft
Silent Partnership – Stille Gesellschaft → Hybride Gesellschaftsformen
Sinking Fund Loan – Tilgungsdarlehen
Small Business Stock → Übertragung stiller Reserven
Social Housing → Sozialer Wohnungsbau
Soil Contamination – Bodenverschmutzung → Altlasten
Special Depreciation → Sonderabschreibungen
Special Exception → Ausnahmegenehmigung
Specific Performance → Erfüllung
Special Use → Ausnahmegenehmigung
Stand-by Fee – Bereitstellungsprovision
Standard Deduction → Werbungskostenpauschale
Start-up Expenses → Anlaufkosten
State Highways – Landstraßen
State Taxes – Ländersteuern → Steuern
Statute of Limitations – Verjährung
Statute of Frauds → Schriftform → Notarielle Beurkundung → Notar
Statutory Liens – Gesetzliche Pfandrechte → Bauhandwerkerhypothek
Stock Dividend → Freianteile
Stock Options → Mitarbeiteroptionen
Stock Redemption → Eigene Aktien
Subcontractor – Subunternehmer → Verdingungsordnung für Bauleistungen
Subdivision – Parzellierung
Sublease → Untermiete
Subordinated – Nachrangig → Rang → Verkäuferhypothek
Subordination → Rangvorbehalt → Eigentümergrundschuld
Subpart F Taxation → Außensteuergesetz
Subrogation → Eigentümergrundschuld
Subscribed Capital → Kapitaleinlage
Subtenant – Untermieter → Untermiete
Surety → Bürgschaft
Survey – Vermessung → Grundstücksgrenzen

English Language Index / Verzeichnis der engl. Begriffe

Takeover – Übernahme → Eigene Aktien → Unternehmensübernahme → Fusionskontrolle
Tax Accounting → Steuerbilanz
Tax Assessment → Steuererklärung
Tax Consolidation → Organschaft → Dividendenbesteuerung
Tax Credit → Steuergutschrift → Anrechnungsmethode
Tax Credit Method → Anrechnungsmethode
Tax Deferral of Gain → Übertragung stiller Reserven
Tax Exemption – Steuerbefreiung
Tax-Free Exchange → Tausch → Sacheinlagen
Tax-free Reorganization → Umwandlung → Tausch
Tax Losses → Gewinnerzielungsabsicht → Negatives Kapitalkonto
Tax Recapture → Spekulationsgewinn → Veräußerungsgewinn
Tax Return → Steuererklärung
Tax Shelter – Abschreibungsgesellschaft → Gewinnerzielungsabsicht → Negatives Kapitalkonto → Verlustzuweisungsgesellschaft
Taxes → Steuern
Tenancy in Common – Bruchteilsgemeinschaft → Teilung
Tenant Fixtures – Scheinbestandteile → Wesentlicher Bestandteil
Terminal Value – Wiederverkaufswert
Termination of Residential Leases → Berechtigtes Interesse → Mieterschutz → Kündigungsschutz
Terms and Conditions → Allgemeine Geschäftsbedingungen
Thin Capitalization – Unterkapitalisierung → Durchgriffshaftung
Timber → Bundeswaldgesetz
Time of the Essence → Vollzug(szeitpunkt)
Time Sharing – Time Sharing → Teilzeit-Wohnrechtegesetz
Title – Eigentum
Title Insurance → Grundbuch → Öffentlicher Glaube
Tourists → Aufenthaltsgenehmigung
Trade and Business Tax → Gewerbesteuer
Trade or Business → Gewerbebetrieb
Treasury Stock → Eigene Aktien
Trespass – Besitzstörung; Hausfriedensbruch
Trust – Treuhandschaft → Stiftung
Truth in Lending Act → Verbraucherkreditgesetz

UCC → Handelsgesetzbuch
Undivided Interest – Ideeller Anteil
Unfair Competition – Unlauterer Wettbewerb

English Language Index / Verzeichnis der engl. Begriffe

Unfriendly Takeovers → Unternehmensübernahmen
Unions → Gewerkschaften
Urban Renewal Area – Sanierungsgebiet
Usage – Gewohnheitsrecht
Useful Life → Betriebsgewöhnliche Nutzungsdauer
Usufruct – Nießbrauch; Reallast
Usury – Wucher
Utilities – Versorgungsunternehmen → Umlagen

Vacancy → Leerstand
Vacation Home → Ferienwohnung
Value-Added Tax → Mehrwertsteuer
Variable Rate – Variable Zinsen
Variance – Befreiung → Dispens
VAT → Mehrwertsteuer
Visa → Aufenthaltsgenehmigung
Voidable Preference – Schiebungsanfechtung Absichtsanfechtung → Konkursanfechtung
Voidance → Konkursanfechtung
Volatility → Immobilienpreise

Warranties → Zugesicherte Eigenschaften
Warranty – Gewährleistung; → Wie besichtigt → Zugesicherte Eigenschaften
Warranty Deed → Zugesicherte Eigenschaften
Waste Oil Act – Altölgesetz → Umweltschutz
Waste Removal Act – Abfallgesetz → Umweltschutz
Water – Wasser → Umlagen
Wear and Tear – Abnutzung
Will → Testament
Withholding Taxes → Abzugssteuern → Dividendenbesteuerung
Wooded Lands → Bundeswaldgesetz
Work Permit – Arbeitserlaubnis → Aufenthaltsgenehmigung
Workers' Co-determination – Mitbestimmung → Aufsichtsrat
Workers' Council – Betriebsrat → Anstellung und Kündigung
Wraparound Mortgage → Verkäuferhypothek
Write Down → Wertberichtigung
Write Off → Wertberichtigung
Writing → Schriftform → Notarielle Beurkundung → Notar

English Language Index / Verzeichnis der engl. Begriffe

Yield → Rendite

Zerobonds → Zerobonds
Zoning Law → Baurecht
Zoning Ordinance → Bebauungsplan
Zoning Restrictions – Baubeschränkungen

German–U.S. Encyclopedia
Deutsch–amerikanisches Lexikon

Abbruchkosten   Demolition Cost

The cost of partial or full demolition (Abbruchkosten) and the remaining basis of the demolished structure (Restbuchwert) can generally be expensed under German tax law, irrespective of the cause of the demolition. The demolition costs are deductible expenses (Werbungskosten), and the write-off of the remaining basis gives rise to a deduction for extraordinary depreciation, § 7 Para. 1 and 4 EStG (Absetzung für außergewöhnliche technische Abnutzung).

If, however, the demolition occurs within three years after the purchase of the property, a rebuttable presumption exists that demolition was planned. In such case, no deduction is allowed, but the demolition cost may be added to the basis of a newly erected structure. If, however, the old building was substantially obsolete at the time of purchase, the demolition cost and remaining basis must generally be added to the (non-depreciable) basis of the land.

In den USA sind die Abbruchkosten und der Verlust des Restwerts eines Gebäudes nur im Schadensfall (casualty loss) abzugsfähig. In allen anderen Fällen gehören diese Kosten bzw. Werte zu den Anschaffungskosten (basis) des Landes und nicht zu den Herstellungskosten des neuen Bauwerks.

Abfallgesetz   ~ Waste Removal Act

Abfindungsangebot   Freeze-Out

Under German corporate law, no freeze-out exists. Minority shareholders who do not tender their shares after a successful acquisition or merger, or who insist on getting shares in the surviving entity, may not be forced to accept cash. While they may take the risk of remaining a sleeping minority forever, they may sometimes extract large ransoms because, under the elaborate German Stock Corporation Act (AktG), they can become a nuisance for management.

Abgeschlossenheit / ~ Separation of Units

Unter dem Recht Delawares und einiger anderen Einzelstaaten kann ein Mehrheitsaktionär, sofern er durch Kauf oder Fusion in den Besitz fast aller Aktien (typischerweise mindestens 90%) einer anderen Gesellschaft gekommen ist, den ausstehenden Aktionären ein Barabfindungsangebot machen, das diese annehmen müssen. Streiten können sich die Parteien dabei nur über die notfalls durch Gutachten festzustellende Abfindungshöhe, aber nicht mehr über die Frage, ob eine angemessene Abfindung angenommen werden muß.

Abgeschlossenheit   ~ Separation of Units

For any property to be converted into condominium ownership (→ Wohnungseigentum), the declaration of condominium (Teilungserklärung) must show the exact boundaries (→ Grundstücksgrenzen) of each unit (Sondereigentum, or Teileigentum for commercial space) and the common areas (Gemeinflächen). Germany has more extensive and burdensome building code regulations (baupolizeiliche Vorschriften; → Bauordnung) than the United States, relating to fire and noise protection, accessibility, day light and other matters. These rules make the separation (Teilungsfähigkeit) and conversion of most residential properties impossible or economically difficult (→ Umwandlung von Wohnraum).

Auch in den USA ist notwendiger Bestandteil der Teilungserklärung (declaration of condominium) die Festlegung der exakten Grenzen einer jeden Einheit (unit) von den Gemeinflächen (common areas). Die Teilungsfähigkeit (separation) amerikanischer Wohnimmobilien ist einfacher als in Deutschland, da die baupolizeilichen Vorschriften (buildingcode provisions) weniger einschneidend sind. Jedoch gibt es in einigen Städten, wie z. B. New York, umfangreiche Regeln zur Durchführung der → Umwandlung, inklusive der erforderlichen Abstimmung durch die Mieter, der Registrierung bei der zuständigen Landesbehörde und ähnliches mehr.

Ablösungsrecht   Right of Redemption

As in the U.S., a German debtor has an equitable right of redemption. He can avoid the foreclosure sale of mortgaged property by paying off the creditor before the judicial sale (Zuschlag), § 1142 BGB. Also, similar to U.S. law, the mortgagor may not grant the lender a deed-in-lieu-of-foreclosure and waive regular foreclosure proceedings before the underlying claim has become due and payable, § 1149 BGB. German law does not, however, provide for an additional post-foreclosure right of redemption.

Abnahme / Acceptance

Wie in Deutschland kann der Schuldner auch in der amerikanischen Zwangsversteigerung den Verlust des Sicherungsguts abwenden, indem er vor dem Zuschlag (judicial sale) die Forderung des betreibenden Gläubigers befriedigt. Dieses Abwendungsrecht heißt equitable right of redemption.

In etwa der Hälfte der U.S.-Einzelstaaten gibt es darüber hinaus ein statutory right of redemption. Dieses erlaubt es dem Schuldner oder anderen durch Vollstreckungsmaßnahmen Betroffenen, innerhalb eines gewissen Zeitraums nach Zuschlag das Eigentum zurückzuerwerben, und zwar durch nachträgliche Zahlung in Höhe des Meistgebots inklusive Versteigerungskosten an das Versteigerungsgericht. Dieses Rückerwerbsrecht gilt meist für ein Jahr nach dem Zuschlag, in manchen Staaten jedoch nur für zwei Monate, in anderen Staaten für zwei Jahre. Das statutory right of redemption entwickelte sich zum Schutz von Bauern, die durch eine schlechte Ernte ihren Hof verloren und durch eine gute Ernte im darauffolgenden Jahr eine neue Startmöglichkeit erhalten sollten. In Einzelstaaten, die kein statutory right of redemption kennen, sieht das Gesetz häufig vor, daß zwischen Abgabe des Meistgebots und Zuschlag genügend Zeit eingeräumt wird, um dem Schuldner eine letzte Möglichkeit der Befriedigung des betreibenden Gläubigers zu geben.

Eine Form der vollstreckbaren Urkunde in den USA ist die deed-in-lieu-of-foreclosure. Jedoch darf auch im U.S.-Recht nicht von vorneherein vereinbart sein, daß das Grundstück im Verzugsfall an den Gläubiger verfällt. Es muß grundsätzlich im Wege der Zwangsvollstreckung verwertet werden, es sei denn der Schuldner verzichtet im späteren Verlauf auf sein Ablösungsrecht.

Es gibt nur noch wenige Einzelstaaten, in denen die altmodische Form der „strict foreclosure" unter gewissen Umständen möglich ist. Diese erlaubt es dem Hypothekengläubiger, das Grundstück im Verzug in sein Eigentum zu überführen, ohne nachfolgende Zwangsversteigerung bzw. ohne die Pflicht, einen etwaigen Mehrerlös aus dem Verkauf oder der Versteigerung dem Schuldner auszuzahlen.

Abnahme   Acceptance

In Germany, before acceptance, contractors have the burden of proving the absence of construction defects. Upon acceptance, the burden of proof shifts to the developer who will have to show the existence of defects. In addition, the risk of loss passes (→ Gefahrübergang) to the developer once he accepts the work.

Abnutzung / Wear and Tear

If the General Conditions for Contractors (→ Verdingungsordnung für Bauleistungen; VOB) apply, acceptance is deemed to take place in certain cases through the lapse of time. The VOB also provide that the risk of loss passes to the developer upon completion of each project phase (Bauabschnitt), even if there has been no acceptance. These two, and certain other reasons, make it advisable for developers in some cases to exclude the applicability of some or all of the VOB standards.

In den USA gelten ähnliche Regeln wie in Deutschland. Meist nimmt der Architekt des Bauherrn den fertigen Bau ab. Für verdeckte Mängel, die nicht feststellbar sind, bleibt jedoch der Bauunternehmer auch nach Abnahme haftbar. Der Unternehmer gewährleistet in der Regel auch vertraglich die Mängelfreiheit des Baus.

Abnutzung	**Wear and Tear**
Abschreibungen (→ Absetzungen für Abnutzung)	**Depreciation**
Abschreibungsgesellschaft	**Tax Shelter**
Absetzungen für Abnutzung	**Depreciation**

German tax law provides for straight-line (lineare AfA, § 7 Para. 4 EStG) and accelerated (degressive AfA, § 7 Para. 5 EStG) depreciation. The applicable depreciation method and the useful life depend on the construction date of the property. Buildings which were erected after 1925 have a useful life of 50 years, i. e. they are depreciated at two percent per annum. Buildings whose construction dates back before 1925 have a useful life of 40 years. Industrial or commercially used buildings for which building permits were sought after March 1985, may be depreciated straight line over 25 years.

Accelerated depreciation under § 7(5) EStG is now available only for residential properties which were built by the taxpayer or acquired by him within the fiscal year of completion. The present depreciation rates for buildings developed after 1995 are five percent for the first seven years, 2.5 percent for the next six years and 1.25 percent for the balance of the years. Accelerated depreciation can be taken for the entire year, even if the property is purchased shortly before year end.

Switching between straight-line and accelerated depreciation methods is not allowed.

German tax law also has certain special depreciations (→ Sonderabschreibungen) which are added to the regular depreciation. The best known recent example of Sonderabschreibung is the optional 50% write-off of newly constructed properties in Eastern Germany, which was sharply reduced at the end of 1996. Similar to U.S. tax law, German fiscal authorities generally allocate about 80% of a property's cost to the building, 20% to the land. There are, of course, exceptions to this rule, always depending on the individual case.

Lastly, immediate write-downs exist under § 7 Para. 1 and 4 EStG for permanent damage to a building, or demolition (→ Abbruchkosten).

(The above represents a cursory overview over the extensive depreciation rules applicable to German real property.)

In den USA können Gebäude nur noch linear abgeschrieben werden, und zwar nach Sec. 168(c) IRC Wohngebäude in 27,5 Jahren, gewerbliche Bauten in 39 Jahren. Auch in den USA gilt die Faustregel, daß mindestens 20% der Anschaffungskosten auf das Land entfallen.

Absichtsanfechtung   ~ Voidance

(→ Konkursanfechtung)

Absichtserklärung   Letter of Intent
Memorandum of Understanding

Absonderung   ~ Adequate Protection

Secured claims are given preferred treatment (abgesonderte Befriedigung) in a German insolvency proceeding, § 4 KO (→ Konkurs; → Vergleich). This is not dissimilar from U.S. insolvency laws. However, there is an important conceptual difference: Under German law, a secured creditor can principally force the sale of his collateral. He is entitled to 100% of the proceeds except to the extent they exceed his claim. Section 82(2) VerglO expressly provides that the filing for bankruptcy protection by the debtor does not in any way affect the claims of lienholders. It can generally be said that German bankruptcy law primarily protects the creditors and attempts to preserve the debtor's assets for the benefit of the creditors and to ensure their orderly distribution or liquidation.

Germany is in the process of a major insolvency law reform. The new law will take effect in 1999. The protection of small and unsecured creditors, such as subcontractors in the real estate industry, has been quoted as one of the reasons for the reform (→ Konkurs; → Bauhandwerkerhypothek).

Abstandsflächen / Building Distance

In den USA gilt die besicherte Forderung im Konkurs des Schuldners von vornherein nur bis zur Höhe des Verkehrswertes des Sicherungsguts als besichert, ein soweit logisch zwingender Gedanke. Der Verkehrswert des Sicherungsguts wird vom Konkursgericht oder durch Gutachter festgestellt und nicht, wie in Deutschland, durch Versteigerung. Liegt der Nominalwert der Forderung über dem geschätzten Verkehrswert des Sicherungsguts, wird der überschüssige Teil der Forderung als gewöhnliche nicht bevorrechtigte Konkursforderung behandelt (unsecured non-priority claim), Sec. 506(a) Bankruptcy Code. Daher entscheidet in den USA häufig nicht der aus dem Verkauf des Sicherungsgegenstandes erzielte Erlös über die Höhe der Sicherheit, sondern ein Wertgutachten.

Tendenziell werden dabei der Schuldner bzw. andere nichtbesicherte Gläubiger begünstigt, auf Kosten des besicherten Gläubigers. Im amerikanischen Insolvenzrecht steht das finanzielle Überleben des Gemeinschuldners über den berechtigten Interessen der Gläubiger. Sofern der Gemeinschuldner einen realistischen Vergleichsvorschlag (reorganization plan) vorlegt, wird das Gericht die Gläubiger, auch besicherte Gläubiger, häufig zum → Vergleich zwingen, und sei es durch „cram down" der besicherten Gläubiger (secured creditors), d. h. Stundung von Amortisationszahlungen und Herabsenken der Zinsen.

Grundsätzlich gilt für den unterbesicherten Pfandrechtsgläubiger zwar die „absolute priority rule", derzufolge nachrangige Gläubiger oder Eigentümer nichts erhalten können, solange der vorrangige Gläubiger nicht vollständig befriedigt ist. Stimmt jedoch die Mehrheit der nachrangigen Gläubiger für den Vergleichsvorschlag (reorganisation plan) des Gemeinschuldners, wird das Gericht diesen in aller Regel genehmigen. Selbst ohne Zustimmung der Gläubiger erhält der Schuldner manchmal die Zustimmung des Gerichts, wenn er im Rahmen der Reorganisation das Einschiessen neuer Eigenmittel anbietet. Diese „new value" Durchbrechung des „absolute priority" Grundsatzes hat sich bei den Gerichten zunehmend durchgesetzt.

Abstandsflächen   Building Distance

Abstraktionsprinzip   ~ Property Interests are abstract

German law distinguishes conceptually between obligatory rights (Schuldrechtliche Ansprüche) and property interests (Dingliche Rechte). The invalidity or voidability of an agreement does not automatically affect the validity of a property interest that may have been created in executing the agreement. While this principle represents a fundamental difference between civil-law and common-law countries, it is, for the most part, a difference in methodology only, not in actual results.

Dem amerikanischen Recht ist das deutsche Abstraktionsprinzip fremd, demzufolge die Unwirksamkeit des schuldrechtlichen Verpflichtungsgeschäfts die des dinglichen Erfüllungsgeschäfts grundsätzlich nicht berührt. Dieser fundamentale konzeptionelle Unterschied der beiden Rechtsordnungen zieht sich durch das gesamte Recht. Der Unterschied ist jedoch weitgehend theoretischer Natur. Er liegt in den Lösungswegen und nur selten in den Lösungen selbst.

Abtretung — Assignment
→ Untermiete

Abwasser — Sewage

Abzugssteuern — Withholding Tax

Under German tax law (§ 43 EStG), taxes are withheld on most kinds of investment income (Einkünfte aus Kapitalvermögen) of German and foreign taxpayers.

The Zinsabschlagsteuer (Interest Withholding Tax) imposes a withholding tax of 30% on most interest income, except for bank or bond interest paid to foreigners (see below). This tax was re-introduced with effect as of January 1, 1993 and has driven large amounts of private German capital to countries like Luxembourg, Austria and Switzerland.

The Kapitalertragsteuer levies a 25% withholding tax on dividends and on profit distributions to („typical") silent partners.

§ 50a EStG subjects various types of income paid to nonresident taxpayers to additional withholding taxes. Applicable tax treaties reduce or eliminate most of these withholding taxes.

Similar to „portfolio" interest from U.S. sources, most German-source interest paid to nonresidents is exempt from withholding tax. The exemption does not apply to mortgage interest, or to over-the-counter coupon clipping (Tafelgeschäft), § 49(1) No. 5 c) aa) and cc) EStG. Moreover, all or almost all German income tax treaties eliminate German withholding tax on all types of interest income, including mortgage interest. Exceptions exist under some treaties for certain types of hybrid debt, for example in Art 10(4) of the U.S.-German Income Tax Treaty.

Abzugssteuern / Withholding Tax

Taxes are also withheld on wages (Lohnsteuer) under § 38 EStG.

Pursuant to § 49(1) No. 6 EStG, rental income from German real property owned by nonresidents is subject to net taxation and to the regular tax return and tax assessment procedure (→ Steuererklärung). Non-residents cannot opt to subject their real property income to the flat (withholding) tax regime. Under § 49(1) No. 8 EStG, short-term (2-year holding period) capital gains (→ Spekulationsgewinne) of nonresident aliens derived from the sale of German real property are subject to German tax. Foreign corporate entities are subject to German tax on all gains, long-term and short-term, from German property (→ Veräußerungsgewinn).

In den USA gibt es keine allgemeine Kapitalertrags- oder Zinsabschlagsteuer für US-Steuerinländer. Es gibt jedoch die 31%ige „back up" withholding tax nach Sec. 3406 IRC, die von der Zahlstelle, meist Banken, auf Dividenden und Zinsen einbehalten wird, wenn der Steuerpflichtige seine Sozialversicherungsnummer nicht nachweist oder auf derartige Einkünfte bereits Steuern hinterzogen hat. Steuerausländer, die (in der Regel) keine social security Nummer haben, unterliegen der back up withholding tax nicht, wenn sie nachweisen (auf Form W-9), daß sie in einem DBA Land ansässig sind und das betreffende Abkommen die Quellensteuer eliminiert oder reduziert.

U.S. Steuerausländer haben nach Sec. 871(d) und 882(d) IRC die Option, U.S. Immobilieneinkünfte anstatt auf Nettobasis der Besteuerung auf Bruttobasis zu unterwerfen, d. h. Mieteinnahmen einer 30%igen Abzugssteuer zu unterwerfen, ohne daß Schuldzinsen oder Afa abgezogen werden können. Es wird praktisch immer für die Nettobesteuerung optiert, da sie in fast allen Fällen günstiger ist.

Wie Deutschland verzichten auch die USA auf die Erhebung von Quellensteuer auf fast alle Arten von an Steuerausländer gezahlten Zinsen, z. B. auf Zinsen aus Bankkonten, oder Zinsen aus Anleihen, die auf einen ausländischen Inhaber lauten oder die im Ausland plaziert wurden („foreign targeted"). Diese Quellensteuerbefreiung für „portfolio interest" gilt nach Sections 871(h) und 881(c) IRC nicht für Zinsen, die an eine ausländische Bank oder an einen 10%igen ausländischen Gesellschafter des Zinsschuldners gezahlt werden. Jedoch sind auch letztere Zinsen regelmäßig von Quellensteuer befreit, sofern ein Doppelbesteuerungsabkommen mit dem ausländischen Staat besteht, da fast alle amerikanischen DBA den Quellensteuersatz für Zinsen auf 0% reduzieren, z. B. Art. 11 des deutsch-amerikanischen DBA.

Alleinauftrag / Exclusive Agency

Ansonsten sichern sich die USA die Besteuerung der Einkünfte ausländischer Investoren durch verschiedene quellensteuerartige Abzüge, die es in dieser Art in Deutschland nicht gibt. Quellensteuern werden dabei nicht nur auf Einkünfte aus Kapitalvermögen und andere periodisch fliessende Einkünfte erhoben, sondern beispielsweise auch auf folgende Erträge:

a) U.S. Betriebsstättengewinne ausländischer Kapitalgesellschaften, die nicht reinvestiert werden, unterliegen nach Sec. 884 IRC über die gewöhnliche Betriebsstättenbesteuerung hinaus einer zusätzlichen 30%igen Quellensteuer, der „branch profits tax" (→ Quellensteuer für Betriebsstättengewinne). Sie wird durch Art. 10(9) des deutsch-amerikanischen DBA auf 5% reduziert.

b) Nach den „FIRPTA" Regeln (FIRPTA = Foreign Investment in Real Property Tax Act) der Sec. 897 und 1445 IRC behält der Käufer eines U.S. Real Property Interests (d. h. einer U.S. Immobilie oder einer → Immobilienholding) 10% des an den ausländischen Verkäufer zu zahlenden Kaufpreises ein und führt ihn an die Steuerbehörde ab. Diese Abzugsteuer hat keine Abgeltungswirkung, sondern gilt als Steuervorauszahlung durch den Ausländer.

c) U.S. Personengesellschaften sind nach Sec. 1446 IRC verpflichtet, Steuern auf Gewinnanteile der Gesellschaft abzuführen, die Steuerausländern zurechenbar sind. Auch diese Steuer hat keine Abgeltungswirkung, sondern stellt eine anrechenbare Einkommensteuervorauszahlung dar.

AfA (→ Absetzungen für Abnutzung)

Akzessorietät (→ Hypothek)

Alleinauftrag   Exclusive Agency

Under German law, if a broker (→ Makler) is retained under an exclusive agency, the principal is prohibited from hiring another broker. However, the principal himself may continue to market and sell the property unless the Alleinauftrag expressly prohibits this.

In den USA gilt eine ähnliche Regel wie in Deutschland. Die dem Alleinauftrag entsprechende exclusive agency bedeutet nicht, daß der → Makler automatisch auch ein exclusive right to sell hat, sofern der Alleinauftrag dies nicht ausdrücklich vorsieht.

Allgemeine Geschäftsbedingungen / General Terms and Conditions

Der Alleinauftrag ist auch für die Vermietung gewerblicher Flächen üblich. Leasing agents bestehen wegen des beträchtlichen Marketingaufwands oft auf Exklusivität von einem Jahr oder mehr bei der Suche nach Erstmietern eines Büroobjekts. Der leasing agent teilt dann häufig seine Provision mit dem vom Mieter beauftragten Makler.

Allgemeine   **General Terms**
Geschäftsbedingungen   **and Conditions**

Allgemeine Geschäftsbedingungen are subject to the provisions of the AGB Act. The AGB Act assumes that the party using general terms and conditions clauses in its agreements has stronger footing and that the other party deserves protection. Under § 9 AGB Act, allgemeine Geschäftsbedingungen may not contain clauses which are surprising or which, in deviation from statutorily established principles, are materially disadvantageous to the other party. Certain contractual provisions are deemed per se invalid under the AGB Act. Contractual ambiguities are generally interpreted in favour of the party not using AGB.

The AGB Act applies not only to clauses which are expressly termed „Allgemeine Geschäftsbedingungen", or to mass agreements, but to almost all standard agreements which are applied without any meaningful variations or negotiations in more than a few cases. Thus a lease agreement may be subject to the AGB Act even if it is used only against a handful of tenants.

In den USA ist die Verwendung von Allgemeinen Geschäftsbedingungen, auf die in Standardverträgen verwiesen wird, unüblich. Es gibt, soweit ersichtlich, auch keine landesrechtlichen Bestimmungen, die denen des deutschen AGB Gesetzes entsprechen. Auch in den USA findet die Vertragsfreiheit jedoch ihre Grenzen in sittenwidrigen oder knebelnden Vereinbarungen.

Altenteil (→ Reallasten)

Altlasten   **Contamination**

Soil contamination has become a major issue in real estate transactions in recent years, particularly in Eastern Germany where the communist economy had produced contamination on an unprecedented scale. It was standard agreement in sales by the privatization agency (Treuhandanstalt), that the agency excluded warranties for contamination but assumed part of the clean up costs. Also, the privatization agency usually gave buyers a rescission right if costs exceeded 50% of the pur-

chase price. In some major transactions, the agency has totally asumed all clean up costs.

Generally, however, sellers are rarely prepared to give warranties. Buyers will have to resort to due diligence before the purchase.

There seems to be no case law holding mortgage lenders liable for environmental damage or clean up costs. Thus, banks are not typically concerned about this aspect, other than to the extent it affects the value of the property.

Beim Grundstückskauf in den USA bestehen Käufer zunehmend auf umfassende Environmental Reports, in denen gutachterlich die Altlastenfreiheit des Grundstücks bestätigt wird. Auch Kreditgeber fordern diese Bestätigung, weniger weil sie um die Werthaltigkeit der Hypothek besorgt sind, als um ihre eigene Haftung. Banken werden für die Beseitigung von Altlasten an beliehenen Grundstücken zunehmend selbst in die Haftung genommen.

Anderkonto **Escrow Account**

Aneignung **Appropriation**

Anfechtungsgesetz **Fraudulent Conveyances Voidance Act**
(→ Konkursanfechtung)

Angehörige **~ Related Taxpayers**

Under German tax law, shares or other business interests held by family members (Angehörige) are generally not attributed to each other for purposes of determining certain percentage thresholds. The law postulates that married people should not be penalized. For example, sellers of corporations sometimes arrange that the shares will timely be distributed to family members so that no one holds more than 25%, availing tax free capital gains on the sale to everybody. Of course, many business arrangements between family members are subject to particular armslength scrutiny.

In den USA werden nicht nur verbundene oder anderweitig voneinander abhängige Unternehmen als related taxpayers behandelt, sondern regelmäßig auch Familienangehörige. So würde die künstliche Aufteilung von Gesellschaftsbeteiligungen zum Zweck der Unterschreitung bestimmter Prozentsätze in den USA beispielsweise nichts nützen.

Ankaufsrecht / Purchase Option

Ankaufsrecht   Purchase Option

A purchase option itself is not a recordable estate under German law. However, the BGH has held that such an option can be secured through a priority notice; BGH JR 1974, 513 (→ Vormerkung).

In den USA kann ein Ankaufsrecht im → Grundbuch eingetragen werden. Es wird häufig von Entwicklern gebraucht, die eine Reihe aneinandergrenzender Grundstücke für eine größere Entwicklung zusammenbringen müssen. Durch die purchase option bleibt das finanzielle Risiko des Entwicklers begrenzt.

Anlageberater (-Vermittler)   Investment Adviser

Persons who in their regular course of business sell, or solicit interest in, investment company shares or any publicly traded shares, require a business permit (Gewerbezulassung) pursuant to § 34c GewO (Business License Act). The license requirements are not dissimilar from those for real estate brokers. Since 1998, investment advisers and brokers are also subject to admission and control by the federal banking authority (BAK) in Berlin and the securities trading authority in Frankfurt.

In den USA besteht für Anlageberater oder -vermittler, die mehr als 15 Kunden haben, nach dem Investment Advisers Act die Registrierungspflicht bei der Börsenaufsichtsbehörde in Washington (Securities Exchange Commission).

Anlaufkosten   Start-up Expenditures

In Germany, business start-up cost may be capitalized for financial accounting purposes and written off over four years. For tax purposes, such expenses are immediately deductible.

In den USA müssen Anlaufkosten aktiviert werden. Der Steuerzahler kann jedoch die Option ausüben, diese über nicht weniger als 60 Monate zu amortisieren. Bestimmte Aufwendungen für die Erweiterung eines existierenden Betriebes können jedoch sofort abzugsfähige Betriebsausgaben darstellen.

Anrechnungsmethode   Tax Credit Method

German tax law applies a similar credit method for foreign taxes, including an indirect credit for taxes paid by foreign 10% owned subsidiaries of German parent corporations, as the U.S.

Anstellung und Kündigung / Employee Hiring and Lay Offs

However, most German income tax treaties exempt certain income derived in the other treaty country from German tax (Freistellungsmethode). Typically, such exempt foreign income is from real estate or from permanent establishments (Betriebsstätten) located in the other country, or from participation dividends paid by subsidiaries in that country. An example is Art. 23 of the U.S.-German Income Tax Treaty. A tax credit exists for most other types of foreign-source income, such as dividend and other investment income. Income which is exempt from German tax pursuant to a treaty will, however, be added back in Germany to all other income for purposes of determining the tax rate which would be applicable to the taxpayer's world wide income (Progressionsvorbehalt).

In den USA gibt es ähnliche Anrechnungsvorschriften für ausländische Steuern wie in Deutschland, inklusive der indirekten Anrechnung von ausländischen Tochtergesellschaften gezahlter Einkommensteuern.

Jedoch kennen die USA in ihren Doppelbesteuerungsabkommen nicht die Freistellungsmethode, sondern ausschließlich die Anrechnungsmethode. Diese entspricht wiederum weitgehend der des deutschen § 34c EStG.

Anschluß- und Benutzungszwang ~ Mandatory Public Service

Municipalities in Germany usually prescribe through applicable ordinances (Satzung) the usage by property owners of municipal water and sewer systems (Kanalisation), street cleaning, garbage removal and other municipal services. In rare cases, property owners must also pay for other municipal establishments, such as slaughter houses, graveyards, etc. The usage may only be prescribed if an overriding public interest exists (dringendes öffentliches Bedürfnis). Generally, fiscal purposes alone are not sufficient grounds for imposing mandatory usage unless the municipal service can not practically function without broad-based usage.

In den USA sind Müllabfuhr und andere Versorgungsleistungen häufig frei, d. h. sie werden durch die allgemeinen Steuereinnahmen der Gemeinde (in erster Linie Grundsteuer) finanziert. Wasserversorgung und Abwassersysteme werden dagegen meist durch separate Gebühren finanziert. De facto besteht zumindest in größeren Gemeinden oder Städten Anschluß- und Benutzungszwang.

Anstellung und Kündigung   Employee Hiring and Lay Offs

Rigid workers' protection laws are often blamed for the high unemployment rate and the growth of outsourcing and manpower („Leiharbeit") or part-timer ar-

rangements in Germany. The Workers Termination Act ("Kündigungsschutzgesetz") applies to any business with more than 10 employees. It provides that the workers' council ("Betriebsrat") must be heard and may reject any dismissal. Dismissals must be "socially justified", i. e. they must be for cause, such as the severe neglect by the employee of his duties, or for compelling business reasons. In the latter case, due regard must be taken of the length of the employment which also determines the notice requirement (time period), as well as the age and support obligations of the employee. Employees may challenge their termination before the workers' council and the labor court ("Arbeitsgericht"). In the absence of substantial violations by the employee, the employer will usually be required to offer a separation payment of anywhere between 3 and 12 months compensation.

Special rules apply to the dismissal of pregnant or handicapped workers, as well as members of the workers' council. "Mass terminations" require timely notice to the workers' council and the Federal Employment Agency ("Arbeitsamt").

Wer noch glaubt, die USA seien das Land des unbeschränkten „hiring and firing" hat weit gefehlt. Die Prozeßflut des Landes gilt nicht nur für Produkthaftungs- und andere Schadensfälle. Prozesse wegen „discrimination" bei Einstellung oder Entlassung beschäftigen die Gerichte unterdessen mehr als alle anderen Klagen.

Bei der Einstellung dürfen Minderheiten nicht diskriminiert werden. In manchen Staaten gibt es sogar Quotensysteme („affirmative action plans"). In einem Plebiszit in Kalifornien von 1997 hat die Mehrheit der Wähler für die Abschaffung des Quotensystems gestimmt. Das daraufhin angerufene kalifornische Verwaltungsgericht hielt dieses auf demokratischem Weg erzielte Abstimmungsergebnis für verfassungswidrig.

Bei Kündigung ist die Klage durch den Entlassenen unterdessen immer häufiger Routine, zumindest wenn er einer der als Minderheiten geltenden Gruppen angehört (Frauen, Schwarze, Lateinamerikaner, Mitarbeiter über 40, usw.), „Minderheiten", die zusammengenommen natürlich die große Mehrheit der Bevölkerung darstellen. Es ist meist ratsam, eine Abfindung von mehreren Monaten, oder auch einem Jahreslohn anzubieten, anstatt sich auf langwierige und in der Schadenshöhe nicht bezifferbare Prozesse einzulassen (→ Zivilprozeß).

Anwälte Lawyers

Germany has about 80,000 registered lawyers, of whom about 50,000 have an active practice. Lawyers are admitted to practice before a certain district court. How-

Anwälte / Lawyers

ever, they can in effect practice everywhere in the country, or theoretically the EC. There are about 30 major commercial law firms with over 50 practitioners each, ten firms with over 100 lawyers each. Most lawyers in these firms are quite conversant in English. Firms are now allowed to have offices nationwide. They may also be affiliated with accounting firms („Wirtschaftsprüfern").

Contingency fees („Erfolgshonorare") are not allowed. Fees are based on a statutory percentage-based minimum schedule („Gebührenordnung"). However, most major firms charge on a time-basis, which may be lower than value-based fees in large transactions.

Patent attorneys have no formal legal training, but a degree in the chemical, engineering or other sciences. They are only admitted to practice intellectual property law.

Notaries are lawyers who primarily or exclusively perform notarial services which are of an entirely different nature than what notaries do in the U.S. (→ Notar).

Ungefähr eine Million Anwälte praktizieren in den USA. Dazu kommen Anwälte in der Industrie und der Verwaltung. Die USA haben weit mehr Anwälte, absolut und pro Kopf der Bevölkerung, als jedes andere Land der Erde. Anwälte spielen im Wirtschaftsleben eine wichtigere Rolle als in Deutschland. So ist der Chefsyndikus der meisten Unternehmen Vorstandsmitglied. Bei vielen Verhandlungen sitzen Anwälte von vornherein gestaltend mit am Tisch.

Nach Abschluß der Universität (law school) und der einzelstaatlichen Zulassungsprüfung („bar exam") dürfen sie im betreffenden Einzelstaat praktizieren. In anderen Einzelstaaten dürfen sie normalerweise nur auftreten, wenn sie auch dort das bar exam abgelegt haben. Die Spezialisierung ist noch größer als in Deutschland. Dennoch gibt es keinen rechtlichen Unterschied zwischen Wirtschafts-, Prozeß- oder auch Patentanwälten.

Es gibt mindestens 200 Großkanzleien, von denen jede mehr als 200 Anwälte hat, davon typischerweise ein Drittel Partner, zwei Drittel angestellte Anwälte (associates). Viele dieser Großkanzleien haben Niederlassungen in mehreren Großstädten der USA. Anwälte und Wirtschaftsprüfer (CPAs) dürfen sich nicht zusammenschließen.

Wirtschaftsanwälte und große Kanzleien rechnen fast ausschließlich auf Zeitbasis ab, mit Stundenhonoraren zwischen $ 150 und $ 500. Kanzleien, die sich auf → Zivilprozesse (litigation) spezialisieren, arbeiten auf Wunsch häufig auch auf Erfolgsbasis („contingency fee"). Nach dem Recht der meisten Staaten sind diese auf maximal etwa ein Drittel des

Erlöses begrenzt. Auch dürfen dem Mandanten die tatsächlich entstehenden Spesen (Reisen, Zeugenvernehmungen, Telefon, etc.) nicht vorfinanziert werden. Da der → Zivilprozeß in den USA sehr langwierig und damit teuer werden kann, und im Ergebnis oft noch weniger kalkulierbar als deutsche Gerichtsentscheidungen, empfiehlt es sich häufig, als Kläger, und wenn irgend möglich auch als Beklagter, den eigenen Anwalt weitgehend auf Erfolgsbasis zu honorieren. Letzteres ist meist schwierig zu gestalten.

Anwartschaft / Future Interest (Reversions, Remainders)

The most frequent examples of Anwartschaft under German law are the right of the remainder man (Nacherbe) and the right of the purchaser to acquire title to property financed by the seller under a deed-of-trust security interest (Eigentumsvorbehalt). Anwartschaftsrechte may be transferred through sale or inheritance, they may also be encumbered. However, the mere expectation of a future property interest does not constitute a transferable Anwartschaftsrecht. An example for this is the position of the contingent remainder man (Ersatzerbe).

In den USA verbergen sich hinter dem Begriff future interests in aller Regel testamentarische Anordnungen oder Schenkungen, z. B. die Nacherbeneinsetzung (vested remainder), die Ersatzerbeneinsetzung (contingent remainder) oder der Heimfallanspruch des Schenkers bzw. der Erbengemeinschaft (reversion oder possibility of reverter genannt). Nach herrschender Meinung und dem Recht der meisten Einzelstaaten sind nicht nur die zur Anwartschaft erstarkten Rechte (vested interests) übertragbar, vererblich und eintragungsfähig, sondern auch bedingte Anwartschaftsrechte (contingent interests).

Anzahlung / Downpayment

The purchaser of German real property (→ Grundstückskauf) is generally not required to make a downpayment. The reason for this is that execution of the purchase agreement and closing (→ Auflassung) often take place in the same notarial meeting (→ Notar; → Notarielle Beurkundung), or are only a few days apart. The purchaser performs most of his due diligence before signing the agreement. The recording of new title generally takes place several weeks or more after the closing. It is usual to have the purchaser secure the priority of his right (→ Rang) by recording a priority notice (→ Vormerkung). At the time of its recording, the purchase price usually becomes payable or disbursable to the seller.

Architektenpläne / Architectural Plans

In den USA gibt es kaum einen → Grundstückskauf ohne Anzahlung. Diese verfällt, wenn der Käufer in Verzug gerät. Vom Downpayment zu unterscheiden ist das „earnest money", welches die Ernsthaftigkeit des Käufers bei Eintritt in die Kaufverhandlungen untermauern soll, aber nicht verfällt, wenn der Käufer vom Geschäft Abstand nimmt.

Architekten   Architects and Building Engineers

The remuneration of architects and building engineers in Germany is subject to statutory fees (HOAI), which provide for certain minimum and maximum fees. The maximum fees are mandatory, the minimum fees may be waived in certain exceptional cases.

In den USA bzw. den US-Einzelstaaten gibt es, soweit ersichtlich, keine vergleichbare gesetzliche Honorartabelle. Es gibt jedoch Standardverträge für Architekten, die in der großen Mehrzahl der Fälle verwendet werden.

Architektenbindung   ~ Architectural Clause

A contractual clause binding the purchaser of a property to retain a certain architect for future development is invalid. The invalidity of this clause, if any, does not affect the entire agreement.

In den USA gibt es kein vergleichbares gesetzliches Verbot der Architektenbindung. Es mag jedoch in manchen Staaten entsprechende Gerichtsentscheidungen geben.

Architektenpläne   Architectural Plans

In Germany, the architect owns the copyright (Urheberrecht) to his plans. In the absence of appropriate contractual provisions, they can not be changed or used by other architects or the developer without his consent. In Germany as in the U.S. the architect may also acquire a statutory lien (gesetzliches Pfandrecht) on the property (→ Bauhandwerkerhypothek).

In den USA gehört das Urheberrecht (Copyright) an den Architektenplänen dem Auftraggeber, sobald er den Architekten bezahlt hat. Auch in den USA erwirbt der Architekt ein gesetzliches Pfandrecht am Bauwerk für seine Leistung (s. jedoch Unterschiede unter → Bauhandwerkerhypothek).

Arrest / Attachment

Arrest **Attachment**

Aufenthalt **Abode**
(→ Beschränkt Steuerpflichtige)

Aufenthaltsgenehmigung **Residence Permit**

Citizens of any EC country may take residence and employment in Germany as of right. Other foreigners may apply for residence permit („Aufenthaltsgenehmigung") if they carry a valid passport. The permit ranges from short-term visits allowed for specific purposes („Aufenthaltsbewilligung") to permanent visas and work permits („Aufenthaltsberechtigung"). The latter permits have certain requirements, for example a minimum prior residence period of eight years, or five years for certain privileged persons. The „Aufenthaltsbefugnis" is a permit which may be granted for humanitarian or political purposes, or if no other residence and work permit is available. Tourist visas are not required for citizens of most Western countries, including the U.S.

Germany has rather liberal political asylum laws which have been increasingly used or abused by immigrants, particularly from Eastern European countries, and hence have become a major issue of political debate.

Die USA sind traditionell ein Einwanderungsland. Jedoch hat sich auch das Immigrations- und Naturalisationsrecht zu einem Spezialgebiet entwickelt, das einige Kanzleien zu ihrer hauptsächlichen Einnahmequelle gemacht haben. Es gibt eine allgemeine Visapflicht für Touristen. Für längere Aufenthalte gibt es etliche verschiedene Visa. Die dauerhafte Aufenthalts- und Arbeitserlaubnis („green card") wird quotenmäßig vergeben, d. h. für jedes Land werden jährliche Maximalquoten festgelegt. Innerhalb der Quote gibt es verschiedene Prioritäten, z. B. für ausländische Eltern, Kinder oder Ehegatten, für politische Flüchtlinge und Berufstätige, deren U.S.-Arbeitgeber nachweist, daß sie spezielle Kenntnisse haben, die in den USA schwer zu finden sind. Letztere ist die am häufigsten beantragte Priorität.

Auflassung **Closing**

The Auflassung is defined by § 925 BGB as the declaration of consent (Einigungserklärung) of both parties on the transfer of title rendered before a German notary (→ Notar; → Notarielle Bekurkundung) or before another competent authority. Usually, the notary will be requested by the seller to record new title only after the purchase price has been paid in full. The purchaser normally secures his right to obtain title through the recording of a priority notice *(Auflassungsvormerkung;* → *Vormerkung).*

Das Closing in den USA erfolgt formlos. Es werden dabei im wesentlichen Dokumente und Urkunden gegen Zahlung des Kaufpreises ausgetauscht. Die wichtigsten Urkunden sind dabei die Deed und die Title Insurance Policy. Die Deed ist eine vom Verkäufer unterzeichnete Urkunde, in der das Eigentum des Käufers verbrieft wird. Zur Eintragung (recording) der Deed muß die Unterschrift des Verkäufers notariell beglaubigt (acknowledged) sein, typischerweise durch einen notary public. In manchen Staaten genügt auch die Beglaubigung durch Zeugen (witness). Der beim amerikanischen Closing immer anwesende title insurer, eine private Versicherungsgesellschaft, versichert dem Käufer gegen Einmalprämie das dauernde und unbelastete Eigentum am Grundstück. In manchen Closings übernimmt der title insurer darüber hinaus, ähnlich wie der deutsche Notar, die Aufgabe, für die möglichst zeitgleiche Überweisung des Kaufpreises und die Eintragung der Deed Sorge zu tragen.

Zum Zeitraum zwischen Abschluß und Vollzug des Vertrages s. → Vollzug(szeitpunkt) – Time of the Essence.

Aufsichtsrat   Board of Directors

German corporations, other than certain small corporations (small GmbHs), have a supervisory board of directors. Members of the management board (Vorstand; Geschäftsführung) may not at the same time be on the supervisory board.

Larger companies are subject to the workers' co-determination laws (Mitbestimmung). 50% of the members of the supervisory board of such companies are elected by the employees, 33% of the members in companies with more than 500 and less than 2000 workers.

In den USA ist es nicht verboten, und im Gegenteil üblich, daß der Vorstandsvorsitzende (President oder Chief Excecutive Officer) eines Unternehmens gleichzeitig Aufsichtsratsvorsitzender (Chairman) ist.

In den USA gibt es keine Mitbestimmung.

Ausländische Immobilieninvestoren / Foreign Real Estate Investors

Ausländische Immobilieninvestoren / Foreign Real Estate Investors

The acquisition of German real property by foreigners does not require any approval by Federal Government agencies. However, Art. 86 and 88 of the Introductory Act to the Civil Code (EGBGB) permit individual states to subject real property purchases by non-EEC persons to state approval. Only a few states still have such approval requirements. They apply only to purchases by foreign institutions and only in certain limited cases. The states are Bayern, Schleswig-Holstein, Nordrhein-Westfalen, Saarland and Berlin.

All sales of German farm or forest lands are subject to Governmental approval, whether the sales are to German or foreign purchasers (→ Grundstücksverkehrsgesetz).

Auch in den USA ist der Kauf von Immobilien durch US-Ausländer genehmigungsfrei. Jedoch ist der Kauf landwirtschaftlicher Flächen durch US-Ausländer in einer Reihe von Einzelstaaten verboten oder genehmigungspflichtig. Im übrigen unterliegen Immobilien und Landinvestitionen durch Ausländer ab einer gewissen Größenordnung ($ 1 Million oder 200 acres) der Meldepflicht beim US-Handelsministerium. Diese dient ausschließlich statistischen Zwecken.

Viele der größeren ausländischen Investoren in U.S. Immobilien sind Mitglieder eines in Washington ansässigen Verbandes, der Association of Foreign Real Estate Investors („AFIRE"). Zu den Aufgaben des Verbandes gehört es, ausländerfeindliche Bestimmungen in Gesetzesvorlagen zu erkennen und entsprechend auf Regierungsstellen einzuwirken.

Ausnahmegenehmigung / Special Exception Special Use

German → Bebauungspläne, like American zoning ordinances, may provide that certain projects can obtain building permit even if they are inconsistent with the zoning ordinance, provided overriding public interests are not affected. The Ausnahmegenehmigung must be distinguished from the Befreiung (→ Dispens), which resembles the American variance. The Befreiung is not provided for in the Bebauungsplan and may only be granted in cases of hardship.

Wie deutsche Bebauungspläne können auch amerikanische zoning ordinances vorsehen, daß gewisse Projekte in Abweichung vom Bebauungsplan genehmigungsfähig sind, wenn öffentliche Interessen nicht entge-

Bankgeheimnis / Bank Secrecy

genstehen. Von der Special Exception zu unterscheiden ist die Variance, die der deutschen Befreiung entspricht und nur in Härtfällen erteilt wird (→ Dispens).

Außenbereich   Outlying Areas

Außensteuergesetz   Subpart F Taxation

The Außensteuergesetz in Germany is vagely similar to the „Subpart F" tax regime of the U.S. Internal Revenue Code. Originally, in 1972, it was fashioned somewhat similar to the Kennedy legislation of Subpart F. However, retained earnings of an investment character of foreign tax-haven companies are attributed to 10% or greater German shareholders, even if Germans in the aggregate own 50% or less of the stock.

Das amerikanische Steuergesetzbuch enthält in „Subpart F" in etwa vergleichbare Vorschriften zur Besteuerung ausländischer Zwischengesellschaften bzw. deren amerikanischer Gesellschafter wie das deutsche Außensteuergesetz.

Bankgeheimnis   Bank Secrecy

Under the Bank Secrecy Ruling („Bankenerlaß") which has now been incorporated into Sec. 30a Abgabenordnung, fiscal authorities in Germany may not request banks to release account information on a random or routine basis. Unless a tax-avoidance investigation has already been formally initiated against a taxpayer, banks may only be asked to release information if similar requests against the taxpayer have not yielded anything.

Despite these seemingly stringent rules, fiscal authorities have handled bank secrecy somewhat lax. This was most clearly evidenced in the recent mass investigations against several large banks because of money transfers into Luxembourg accounts, orchestrated in order to avoid the new interest withholding tax regime. The investigations occurred under the pretense that the banks themselves committed felonies by aiding and abetting tax avoiders.

In den USA gibt es kein steuerliches Bankgeheimnis im deutschen Sinn. Im Gegenteil sind Banken sogar verpflichtet, laufende Kontrollmitteilungen über Zins- oder Dividendenzahlungen auf vorgedruckten Formularen abzugeben, mit Angabe der Sozialversicherungsnummer des Zahlungsempfängers. Da U.S. Steuerausländer keine social security number benötigen, und Bankzinsen und die meisten anderen Zinszah-

Bauaufsicht (→ Baubehörde)

lungen an sie ohnehin von U.S. Quellensteuer befreit sind (→ Abzugssteuern), gilt die Mitteilungspflicht nicht. Jedoch verlangt die Bank vom Steuerausländer ein entsprechendes Freistellungsformular. Dieses müßte auf Ersuchen des amerikanischen Fiskus herausgegeben werden. Theoretisch wäre es daher möglich, daß die deutsche Finanzverwaltung ihre amerikanischen Kollegen im Rahmen des DBA-Amtshilfeartikels ersucht, bei amerikanischen Banken nach deutschen Kontoinhabern zu fahnden.

Bauaufsicht (→ Baubehörde)

Baubehörde (Bauaufsichtsbehörde) — Building Authority

In Germany, individual states have jurisdiction over regional planning (Raumordnungsrecht, Landesplanung). Counties and communities are in charge of local development plans (Bauleitplanung). Both regional and local planning are subject to federal acts, in particular the federal Building Act (Baugesetzbuch) and the Building Use Ordinance (Baunutzungsverordnung).

The Baubehörde, generally the county or municipal government, reviews building applications and issues permits if the application is consistent with the local development plans (Flächennutzungsplan, → Bebauungsplan). The building authority generally also controls building code matters regarding construction quality and safety.

In den USA liegen sowohl das Raumordnungs- und Planungsrecht als auch das Baugenehmigungsverfahren und die baupolizeiliche Überwachung in der Hand von Bezirks- und Gemeindebehörden.

Baubeschränkungen — Building (Zoning) Restrictions

Baudarlehen — Construction Loan
(→ Kreditgeberhaftung)

Baudenkmal (→ Denkmal)

Baugenehmigung — Building Permit

Building permits in Germany are granted by local or regional authorities (Bauaufsichtsbehörde). The permit procedure distinguishes between three areas:
(1) areas within the local zoning ordinance (→ Bebauungsplan), § 30 BauGB;

Baugenehmigung / Building Permit

(2) built-up areas outside the zoning ordinance (Innenbereich), § 34 BauGB;
(3) undeveloped land outside the built-up areas and the zoning ordinance (Außenbereich), § 35 BauGB.

Under § 30 BauGB, a builder is entitled to a building permit as of right if his land is within the zoning ordinance, if it does not conflict with the ordinance's provisions and if public service (→ Erschließung) has been secured. Building permits in the Innenbereich will be granted under § 34 BauGB if the structure's character and architecture conform to the existing neighbourhood and the provision of public service is secured. In the Außenbereich, building permits are only granted in exceptional cases, if, among other, public service is provided, there are no public interest concerns, the architecture of the building conforms to the area or the project is privileged, such as an agricultural or forestry project, § 35 BauGB.

Under § 21 BauGB, a developer will generally be entitled to a building permit, if, within three years before the application, he obtained subdivision approval for the underlying land under § 19 BauGB.

A building permit which is inconsistent with the zoning ordinance (→ Ausnahmegenehmigung) may be granted if the ordinance specifically provides for the exception. In contrast, a variance (Befreiung, → Dispens) will only be granted in cases of hardship.

Adjoining property owners must be heard before the granting of a permit only if the building authority considers a variance. However, the authority will inform neighbours and solicit their comments in most other cases as well. Neighbours may file a complaint (Anfechtungsklage) under § 42 VwGO with the administrative courts (Verwaltungsgerichte) to strike down a building permit. They must be able to show the violation of public law provisions whose very purpose is the protection of neighbours. The developer may move the court under § 80a VwGO to permit construction despite the complaint. The neighbor may counter by requesting a Baustopp (construction halt). If the developer prevails in the action he normally has no recourse against the complaining neighbor for losses incurred as a result of the project delay.

In addition to the administrative action, neighbours may file civil actions against the developer.

In den USA werden Baugenehmigungen auf gemeindlicher Ebene erteilt. Im allgemeinen kann man sagen, daß Baugenehmigungen in den USA leichter und schneller erhältlich sind als in Deutschland. Dabei gibt es jedoch regionale und lokale Unterschiede. Am liberalsten sind einige der Südstaaten. Aufwendiger ist das Verfahren in Staaten wie Kalifornien,

Baugrundrisiko / Building Ground Risks

New York und New Jersey. Generell sind die Behörden jedoch „pro business" ausgerichtet, da sie auch an wachsendem Grundsteueraufkommen interessiert sind.

Baugrundrisiko / Building Ground Risks

Generally, the developer alone carries the risk of the plan's technical feasibility on the underlying soil, and of potential contamination. Sometimes, developer and contractor will agree to share the risk.

Auch in den USA liegt das Baugrundrisiko üblicherweise beim Entwickler, es sei denn, der Bauunternehmer hat es vertraglich übernommen („turnkey contract").

Bauhandwerkerhypothek / Mechanic's Lien

In Germany, contractors, subcontractors, architects, engineers and others who contribute to the construction of a building, do not automatically acquire a statutory lien (gesetzliches Pfandrecht) on the property. Rather, they obtain the right to claim and record such a lien, § 648 BGB. This right may be secured through the recording of a priority notice (→ Vormerkung). The right to record a Mechanic's Lien arises at the time the work or a certain identifiable part of it (Bauabschnitt) has been completed.

The parties may contractually exclude mechanic's liens to alleviate future bank financing. On the other hand, mechanic's liens in Germany are of minor concern to bank lenders. Since prior recorded mortgages take full priority (→ Rang) over subsequent liens even for the unfunded portion of the prior mortgage loan, Bauhandwerkerhypotheken often turn out to be worthless when bank lenders foreclose against developers.

Im Gegensatz zur deutschen Handwerkerhypothek geht das amerikanische Mechanic's Lien in den meisten Staaten Bankhypotheken im → Rang meist vor. Eine der wenigen Ausnahmen von dieser Regel scheint im Staat Washington zu gelten. In den meisten Staaten entsteht das Mechanic's Lien in voller Höhe bereits mit dem Beginn der betreffenden Bauleistung und nicht erst mit deren Vollendung, in einigen Staaten sogar schon bei Abschluß des betreffenden Werkvertrages. Einige Staaten verlangen, daß der Unternehmer bzw. Handwerker sein Pfandrecht durch Registrierung beansprucht und es innerhalb von ein bis zwei Jahren nach Beendigung seiner Tätigkeit im Klagewege verfolgt.

Baurecht / Zoning Law; Building Law

Bankhypotheken können einem Mechanic's Lien im Rang nur vorgehen, wenn sie eingetragen sind, bevor das Lien durch Arbeitsbeginn entsteht. In einigen Staaten gilt der Vorrang der rechtzeitig eingetragenen Hypothek jedoch nur, soweit die Hypothek vor Entstehung des Mechanic's Lien auch valutiert wurde. Banken schützen sich in ihren Kreditverträgen vor einem ranghöheren Mechanic's Lien häufig dadurch, daß Bauunternehmer und Handwerker direkt von der Bank bezahlt werden oder daß der Kredit automatisch in Verzug gerät, wenn der Bauherr die Handwerker nicht rechtzeitig bezahlt.

Bauherr **Developer**

Bauleitpläne **Development Plans**
→ Flächennutzungsplan (Master Plan)
→ Bebauungsplan (Zoning Ordinance)

Bauordnung **Building Code**

Building Code regulations are a matter of State and local law in Germany, as in the U.S. It can generally be said, that they are more extensive and burdensome in Germany than in the U.S. Careful planning is required before construction begins. One of Germany's largest office towers was built in Frankfurt by American developers and architects. Since the applicable building code required a certain minimum of day light for each work place the building lost a significant portion of its interior space, possibly because of a planning oversight.

Baupolizeiliche Vorschriften in den USA sind Gemeindesache. Im allgemeinen kann man feststellen, daß sie weniger detailliert und einschneidend sind als in Deutschland.

Bauordnungsbehörde (→ Baubehörde)

Baurecht **Zoning Law; Building Law**

In Germany, zoning and building laws are federal laws. The three most important statutes are the Building Act (Baugesetzbuch), the Urban Renewal Act (Städtebauförderungsgesetz) and the Building Use Ordinance (Baunutzungsverordnung). The German states (Länder) have some jurisdiction over regional planning and over substantive and procedural issues of building permits. Counties and municipalities are entitled under the Baugesetzbuch to develop master plans for land use (Flächennutzungsplan) and local zoning ordinances (→ Bebauungsplan).

Bausparkassen / ~ Savings and Loan Banks

In den USA ist das gesamte Baurecht nicht Bundesangelegenheit, sondern Sache der Gemeinden und Bezirke, inklusive Raumordnung, Planungsrecht und baupolizeiliche Genehmigung.

Bausparkassen ~ Savings and Loan Banks
~ Building and Loan Associations

Bausparkassen are lending institutions which may be organized under private or public law. They accept savings deposits for the primary purpose of financing residential properties. Since 1991 Bausparkassen have been authorized to provide limited financing also for commercial properties which are developed in conjunction with residential units.

Die Building and Loan Associations oder Mutual Savings Banks sind im Gegensatz zu den deutschen Bausparkassen genossenschaftlich organisiert. Den Bausparkassen entsprechen insofern eher die amerikanischen Savings and Loan Banks. Diese sind in den 80er Jahren dadurch in Verruf gekommen, daß Hunderte von ihnen infolge fallender Immobilienpreise in Konkurs gerieten, mit Wertberichtigungen, die auf mindestens $ 500 Milliarden geschätzt werden. Ein wichtiger Grund für diese Katastrophe war die durch den Bundesgesetzgeber veranlasste weitgehende Liberalisierung der Zins- und Anlagepolitik dieser früher konservativ arbeitenden Banken, die einen ungerechtfertigten Bauboom durch ungehemmten Kreditzufluß anheizte.

Die U.S. Regierung errichtete Ende der 80er Jahre die Resolution Trust Corporation (RTC), um die Aktiva der insolventen S&L Banken zu verwerten. Immobilien konnten einige Jahre lang zu historisch günstigen Preisen eingekauft werden. Es entstand die wahrscheinlich größte Immobilienkrise seit der Depression der 30er Jahre.

Bausperre (→ Veränderungssperre)

Bauträger Developer

Like the term Developer, the term Bauträger refers not only to the principal (Bauherr), but also to the builder who may act under his own name but builds on behalf of another person. A professional developer who is engaged in the trade or business of developing land (gewerbsmäßiger Bauträger) requires a business permit (Gewerbeerlaubnis) pursuant to § 34c GewO. Generally, it is not difficult to obtain the permit.

Bebauungsplan / ~ Zoning Ordinance

Wie in Deutschland wird unter dem Begriff des Developers in den USA nicht nur der Bauherr verstanden, der für eigene Rechnung baut, sondern auch der, der im eigenen Namen und manchmal auf eigenen Grundstück auf Bestellung eines anderen den Bau durchführt. Das Erfordernis einer entsprechenden Gewerbeerlaubnis gibt es in den USA nicht.

Bauwich **Building Distance**

Bauzeitzinsen **Construction Period Interest**

Under German tax law, a developer may expense construction period interest incurred by him. The purchaser of property may not expense it even if the seller (developer) separately bills the interest.

In den USA müssen Bauzeitzinsen für steuerliche Zwecke grundsätzlich aktiviert werden, Sec. 263 IRC.

Bebauungsplan **~ Zoning Ordinance**

Similar to the U.S., the German Bebauungsplan distinguishes between different zones. Generally, there are residential, mixed-use, commercial and industrial areas. German communities usually apply the principle of cumulative zoning, i. e. residential properties will be permitted in commercial or industrial zones, but not vice versa.

Property owners who are affected by the local zoning ordinance may generally challenge the ordinance before the administrative courts (Normenkontrollverfahren), § 47 VwGO. Owners may also claim damages under §§ 40 et. seq. BauGB if the ordinance changes a prior permitted use causing the devaluation of the affected property or the discontinuance and write-off of partially finished construction. A claim for compensation may also exist if a property is designated as a landmark.

In den USA wird in den zoning ordinances generell zwischen Wohn-, Misch-, Gewerbe- und Industriegebieten unterschieden. Dabei gilt – wie in Deutschland – der Grundsatz des cumulative zoning, d. h. Wohnungen sind in Gewerbe- oder Industriegebieten erlaubt, aber nicht umgekehrt. In amerikanischen Gemeinden gibt es heute einen gewissen Trend zum non-exclusive zoning, d. h. es werden immer häufiger Mischgebiete ausgewiesen.

Auch in den USA können sich beschwerte Grundstückseigentümer gegen Beschränkungen der Nutzung oder Bebaubarkeit wehren, z. B.

Befreiung (→ Dispens)

indem sie eine Verletzung von Grundrechten geltend machen. Die betreffenden Klagen haben selten Aussicht auf Erfolg, wenn die Planungsbehörden zwingende („compelling") Gründe für die Beschränkungen vorweisen können.

Befreiung (→ Dispens)

Belastungen   **Encumbrances**

Beleihung des Mietrechts   **Leasehold Mortgage**

German property law (Sachenrecht) only allows a limited number of property interests. They are defined in the Civil Code (BGB) and certain other acts, such as the Condominium Act (WEG) or the Statutory Ground Lease Act (Erbbau-RVO). Interests other than those statutorily defined may not be recorded in the deed registry.

Pursuant to § 567 BGB, a lease agreement with a term of more than 30 years may be terminated by either party after 30 years, upon the applicable statutory notice period. This term limit manifests the German law principle that leasehold interests are not permanent or recordable property interests. However, certain leases or usage rights are recordable estates in land, such as the Statutory Ground Lease (→ Erbbaurecht) and the statutory long-term leasehold estate of § 31 WEG (→ Dauerwohnrecht and Dauernutzungsrecht).

In den USA können nicht nur das Eigentum, Erbbau- oder Dauerwohnrecht eingetragen oder beliehen werden, sondern die meisten schuldrechtlichen Vereinbarungen von einer gewissen Zeitdauer. So können Mietrechte (leasehold estates) in einigen Einzelstaaten eingetragen und beliehen werden, sofern der Mietvertrag die Beleihung nicht ausdrücklich verbietet. Dabei gibt es einen technisch nicht unbedeutenden Unterschied in verschiedenen Staaten: In Staaten, in denen Hypotheken als Sicherungseigentum angesehen werden (sog. title states), bedeutet die leasehold mortgage, daß der Hypothekengläubiger dem Vermieter für die Mietzahlung haftet. Er gilt gewissermaßen als der neue Mieter. Der Inhaber der leasehold mortgage kann seine Haftung dadurch verhindern, daß der letzte Tag der Mietperiode von der Hypothekenhaftung ausgenommen wird. Dadurch wird der Hypothekengläubiger in diesen „title states" fiktiv zum Untermieter (subtenant), und nicht zum Abtretungsempfänger des Mietvertrages (assignment) (→ Untermiete).

Mitunter verlangt der Gläubiger einer leasehold mortgage, daß der

Beschränkt Steuerpflichtige / Non-resident Aliens

Grundstückseigentümer (Vermieter) im Rang zurücktritt, als läge die mortgage nicht nur auf dem leasehold, sondern auf dem Eigentum. Der Eigentümer wird dem nur zustimmen, wenn der Mietvertrag für ihn besonders günstig ist und er damit ein erhöhtes Interesse hat, dem Mieter die Finanzierung zu erleichtern.

Berechtigtes Interesse ~ **Plausible Interest**

Practically every German residential unit is subject to statutory tenant protection and rent control (→ Mieterschutz). The landlord can not easily terminate residential leases. Under § 564b BGB, he must show a plausible interest (berechtigtes Interesse) to reject a tenant's request for lease term renewal. The necessity of owner-occupancy (→ Eigenbedarf) is the most frequently used and litigated ground for termination (→ Kündigungsschutz).

In den USA gibt es eine dem deutschen Mieterschutz entsprechende Gesetzgebung nur noch als Ausnahme und in wenigen Großstädten (→ Mieterschutz).

Bereitstellungsprovision **Commitment Fee**
Stand-by Fee

Beschlagnahme **Sequestration**
Attachment
Seizing

Beschränkt persönliche Dienstbarkeit **Easement in Gross**

Beschränkt Steuerpflichtige **Non-resident Aliens**

A person is tax-resident (unbeschränkt steuerpflichtig) in Germany if the person has taken domicile (Wohnsitz) or usual abode (gewöhnlicher Aufenthalt) in Germany. Domicile is the place where a person owns or rents a home, manifestly with the intent to stay for a long time. Usual abode is any stay manifestly not of a transient nature, in any case a substantially uninterrupted stay of more than six months, unless solely as a visitor, tourist or medical patient.

Corporations are considered tax-resident if they have either their place of executive management (Geschäftsleitung) or their legal domicile (Sitz) in Germany.

Unlike the U.S., Germany does not tax its non-resident nationals on a worldwide basis, but as regular non-residents.

Besitz / Possession

Germany has expatriation rules (Wegzugsbesteuerung) both for income and estate tax purposes („erweitert beschränkte Steuerpflicht") which are different, and in many ways less stringent than the new expatriation rules enacted in the U.S.

In den USA wird ein Ausländer unbeschränkt steuerpflichtig, wenn er ein permanentes Aufenthaltsvisum hat (z. B. die „green card"), oder den gewöhnlichen Aufenthalt („substantial presence"). Letzterer ist gegeben, wenn sich der Ausländer im Steuerjahr mehr als 182 Tage, in einem oder mehreren Besuchen, in den USA aufhält. Die genannte Tagesgrenze wird über drei Jahre kumulativ gerechnet, d. h. zu den Tagen des betreffenden Jahres werden $1/3$ der in den USA verbrachten Tage des Vorjahres, und $1/6$ der Tage des Vor-Vorjahres hinzugezählt. So kumuliert sich ein Drei-Jahres-Aufenthalt von jeweils 120 Tagen pro Jahr auf 180 Tage im dritten Jahr, obwohl im Beispielsfall der U.S. Aufenthalt im dritten Jahr nur 120 Tage betrug. Liegt der U.S. Aufenthalt in einem Jahr jedoch bei weniger als 183 Tagen, kann der Ausländer auf einem Standardformular („Closer Connection Statement") nachweisen, daß er zu einem ausländischen Wohnsitz eine „engere Beziehung" hat.

Unter wohl sämtlichen neueren DBAs (z. B. Art. 4 des deutsch-amerikanischen) gilt im übrigen die salomonische „tie breaker" Regel. Danach soll es keinen steuerlichen Doppelwohnsitz mehr geben. Können sich die Vertragsstaaten nicht darüber einigen, wo der Steuerzahler seinen Lebensmittelpunkt hat und damit unbeschränkt steuerpflichtig ist, gehen beide Staaten (theoretisch) leer aus, d. h. der Steuerzahler gilt als in keinem der Staaten ansässig.

Ausländische Kapitalgesellschaften werden grundsätzlich nicht dadurch unbeschränkt steuerpflichtig, daß sie ihre Geschäftsleitung in den USA haben. Dies könnte allenfalls eine U.S. Betriebsstätte begründen, oder bestimmte Einkünfte, z. B. aus U.S. Kapitalvermögen und Handelsgewinnen, der vollen U.S. Steuer unterwerfen. Im übrigen gelten Ausschüttungen ausländischer Gesellschaften, deren Einkünfte zum Großteil aus U.S. Quellen stammen, als „U.S.-source" Dividenden, die dem U.S. Quellensteuerabzug unterliegen. Dieser indirekten Quellensteuer stehen jedoch die meisten DBAs entgegen, so auch Art. 10(7) des deutsch-amerikanischen.

Besitz **Possession**

Besitzaufgabe **Abandon**

Betriebsübergang / Sale of Business; Bulk Sale

Besitzstörung **Trespass**

German federal, state or local law restricts a land or forest owner's ability to exclude the public from access. For example, most forest lands or waterfront properties must be open for hikers.

In den meisten Staaten der USA kann der Grundeigentümer auch Waldflächen und Strände dem Zugang der Öffentlichkeit entziehen. In den Südstaaten hat man schon Schilder an Privatbesitzen gefunden, die ungefähr so weit gehen wie: „No hiking, no fishing, no hunting, no nothing!"

Bestandteil (→ wesentlicher Bestandteil)

Betriebsgewöhnliche Nutzungsdauer **Useful Life**

Under § 7 EStG, the useful life of buildings is between 25 and 50 years, depending on the class and construction date of the property (→ Absetzungen für Abnutzung).

In den USA beträgt die betriebsgewöhnliche Nutzungsdauer für Wohnimmobilien 31 Jahre, für gewerbliche Immobilien 39 Jahre.

Betriebsübergang **Sale of Business**
~ Bulk Sale
(→ Vermögensübernahme)

The acquirer of a business will generally be deemed to also have assumed all liabilities of the business. However, pursuant to Sec. 25 HGB, he may exclude the assumption if the parties so agree and register and publish the respective clause in the Commercial Register (Handelsregister).

If a business or part of a business is sold or otherwise transferred, the new owner inherits all existing labor and union contracts, pursuant to Sec. 613a BGB. He cannot avoid the assumption of such contracts. Lay-offs are subject to stringent work force protections laws (Kündigungsschutz) in Germany.

Auch in den USA tritt der Übernehmer eines Betriebes gewöhnlich in bestehende Arbeits- und Gewerkschaftsverträge ein. Dies geschieht entweder, weil es sich um eine → Vermögensübernahme handelt oder weil der Betrieb mit denselben Produkten, Mitarbeitern, Fertigungsstätten und Namen fortgeführt wird („continuity of enterprise") oder weil der

Betriebsvermögensvergleich / Accrual Basis Accounting

Übernehmer mit eigenen Aktien bezahlt hat („de facto merger"). Jedoch gibt es in den USA keine dem deutschen Kündigungsschutzgesetz vergleichbare gesetzliche Vorschriften. (Siehe auch → Vermögensübernahme).

Betriebsvermögensvergleich   **Accrual Basis Accounting**
                                                             Balance Sheet Accounting

Bewegliches Vermögen   **Personal Property**
                                                                          Chattel

Bewertung (steuerlich)   **Assessment**

Bezugsrechte   **Preemptive Rights**

Corporations in Germany, including publicly traded Aktiengesellschaften, generally must first offer newly issued stock to existing shareholders under German statutory law. This presents one of the legal hurdles for German corporations in registering their shares, or ADRs in the U.S. as each new issue would entitle also U.S. shareholders to exercise their preemptive rights, requiring re-registrations in the U.S. In 1994, Sec. 186 AktG was liberalized allowing corporations (Aktiengesellschaften) to exclude the statutory preemptive rights if the new issue does not exceed 10% of total outstanding common stock, and if the shares are offered for cash and at an issue price not substantially below market price.

Falls nicht ausdrücklich in den Gesellschaftsstatuten (corporate charter) festgelegt, wie bei kleineren Gesellschaften meist der Fall, können börsennotierte amerikanische Gesellschaften Anteile ohne Bezugsrecht der Altaktionäre im Markt anbieten. Ein gesetzliches Bezugsrecht gibt es nicht.

BGB-Gesellschaft   **~ General Partnership**
(see also → Offene Handelsgesellschaft)

Bodenschätze   **Minerals**

The Federal Minerals Act (Bundesberggesetz) provides that practically all precious minerals in Germany are excluded from the landowner's estate. They are public property (bergfreie Bodenschätze) and may only be explored and recovered with governmental license. The license is a recordable estate (Bergwerkseigentum).

Buchungszwang / ~ Mandatory Recording

In den USA gehören sämtliche Bodenschätze dem Grundstückseigentümer bzw. anderen vertraglich oder zivilrechtlich berechtigten Personen und nicht der öffentlichen Hand. Insofern muß man beim Kauf größerer Flächen darauf achten, daß Schürfrechte nicht bereits anderweitig veräußert wurden.

Bodenverschmutzung **Soil Contamination**

Briefhypothek (→ **Verkehrshypothek**)

Bruchteil **Fractional Interest**

Bruchteilsgemeinschaft **~ Tenancy in Common**
(see also → Teilung – Partition)

Buchersitzung **Adverse Possession**
Easement by Prescription

Adverse possession of real property or easements by prescription under German law require that the possessor or user has been recorded in the deed registry (→ Grundbuch) as the owner of title or of the easement and that he has held or used the property for at least 30 years under claim of right (Eigenbesitz), § 900 BGB. After such period, the original owner looses all interests in the property as well as his right to request correction of the deed registry (→ Grundbuchberichtigung).

In den USA ist die Ersitzung ohne Eintragung möglich. Es genügt, daß das Grundstück oder die Dienstbarkeit ununterbrochen und nach außen erkennbar in unmittelbarem Eigenbesitz gehalten wird („actual, hostile, notorious, exclusive, continuous, under claim of right"). Die für die Ersitzung in den USA benötigte Zeitfrist beträgt in vielen Staaten nur 10 Jahre. Die Eintragung des neuen Eigentümers kann nach wirksamer Ersitzung erfolgen, beispielsweise durch eine Feststellungsklage (action for quiet title).

Buchungszwang ~ Mandatory Recording

As a matter of principle, all property ownership in Germany must be recorded in the deed registry („Grundbuch"). Property owned by the government or governmental agencies is exempt from the recording requirement, § 3(2) and (3) GBO.

Theoretisch gibt es in den USA keinerlei Buchungszwang, da die Eintragung keinen konstitutiven, sondern nur deklaratorischen Charakter

Buchwert / Basis

hat. Dennoch wird wohl jeder Erwerber oder Hypothekengläubiger seinen Grundeigentumsbrief (deed) im deed registry eintragen lassen. Im Gegensatz zum deutschen Grundbuch ist in den USA auch die öffentliche Hand als Grundstückseigentümer regelmäßig eingetragen. Noch Mitte des 19. Jahrhunderts gehörte mehr als 90% des gesamten US-Grundvermögens der öffentlichen Hand (Bund und Einzelstaaten) und wurde danach durch „land patents" an private Eigentümer übertragen.

Buchwert **Basis**

Bürgschaft **Surety, Guaranty**

Suretyships which mainly promote the interests of the surety („Schuldmitübernahme") are valid without writing. Also, merchants („Kaufleute") may in some cases be bound by oral promises. Guaranties („Bürgschaft"), including bank letters of credit, must be in writing. They usually do not require notice or demand on the main debtor. The agreements normally state that the „Bürge" is directly liable („selbstschuldnerisch"). Guaranties, including bank LCs, are narrowly interpreted and strictly dependent on a specific debt. This principle of strict „Akzessorietät" sometimes helps banks to escape liability under an LC.

Im Recht vieler U.S.-Einzelstaaten benötigen Bürgschaften ausnahmsweise keiner Schriftform, wenn der Bürge in erster Linie ein eigenes Interesse am Zustandekommen des Hauptgeschäftes verfolgt. Dies ist insoweit ähnlich der deutschen Schuldmitübernahme. Auch in den USA sind Bürgschaften akzessorisch, jedoch weniger streng als in Deutschland, sofern das Bürgschaftsversprechen nicht entsprechend spezifisch ist. Zweideutigkeiten werden zu Ungunsten des Bürgen ausgelegt, zumindest sofern er weitgehend standardisierte Vertragstexte benutzt.

Bundesstraßen **~ Interstate Highways**

Bundeswaldgesetz **~ Federal Forestry Act**

The Federal Forestry Act (Bundeswaldgesetz) contains numerous rules and limitations requiring forest owners to preserve forests and to maintain them for the enjoyment and recreation of the population and for the preservation of the environment and waterways. Timber cutting (Rodung) and reforestation (Aufforstung) are subject to strict governmental approval and tight supervision.

Dauerwohnrecht / ~ Long-term Leasehold Estate

Forest roads must be kept open for the public. Certain wooded areas may be publicly designated as recreational or environmentally protected forest lands.

Tight Government regulation and depressed timber prices from increased competition by Scandinavian and Eastern European companies have made the forestry business in Germany marginally profitable, at best. Some forest owners argue that Government regulation has made them nothing more than fiduciary holders of forest lands for the benefit of the public.

Soweit ersichtlich gibt es in den Einzelstaaten der USA keine ähnlich einschneidenden Beschränkungen für Waldbesitzer. Im Gegenteil herrschen in den meisten Einzelstaaten recht liberale Vorschriften. Da beim Walderwerb in den USA für stehendes Holz häufig mehr gezahlt wird als für den Grund und Boden, ist der Kahlschlag durch große Holz- und Papiergesellschaften ohne entsprechende Wiederaufforstungspflichten in manchen Gegenden zu einem Umweltproblem geworden.

Dachfonds   Fund of Funds

Under German law, mutual funds which invest more than 5% of their assets in other funds (fund-of-funds; „Dachfonds") may not be sold to the public. The respective legislation was a reaction to the IOS debacle of the early 70ties. However, under EC Directive 85/611 (the „OGAW" directive), the public offering of funds-of-funds is permissible in all EC member states if the lower funds are closed-end. It is expected that, through legislative action, the fund-of funds prohibition will be abolished in 1998.

Soweit ersichtlich, gibt es in den USA kein generelles Verbot der öffentlichen Plazierung von Dachfonds.

Damnum (→ Geldbeschaffungskosten)   Points

Dauerwohnrecht   ~ Long-term Leasehold Estate

Generally, leaseholds are not considered recordable or transferable estates in Germany. There are a few statutory exceptions to this rule, such as the Statutory Ground Lease (→ Erbbaurecht). Another is the long-term leasehold on residential property (Dauerwohnrecht), or on commercial property (Dauernutzungsrecht), set forth in § 31 of the Condominium Act (→ Wohnungseigentumsgesetz; WEG). Another recordable leasehold estate is the residential leasehold (Wohnungsrecht) set forth in § 1093 BGB. The Wohnungsrecht is considered an easement in gross (→ Grunddienstbarkeit) which can be recorded but is not transferable by assignment or inheritance.

Denkmal / Landmark; Historical Monument

Im amerikanischen Recht gibt es nicht die grundsätzliche Unterscheidung zwischen obligatorischen und dinglichen Rechten. Obligatorische Rechte von einer gewissen Zeitdauer sind häufig eintragungsfähig, so auch längerfristige Mietverträge in manchen Einzelstaaten.

Denkmal	**Landmark** **Historical Monument**
Dereliktion	**Abandon**
Dienstbarkeit (→ Grunddienstbarkeit; → beschränkt persönliche Dienstbarkeit)	**Easement**
Disagio (→ Geldbeschaffungskosten)	**Discount** **Points**
Dispens	**Variance**

Even if a German zoning ordinance (→ Bebauungsplan) does not provide for an exception in a given case (→ Ausnahmegenehmigung), the building authority may grant a variance (Befreiung, Dispens) in cases of unintended hardship.

Auch in den USA gibt es die Möglichkeit der Befreiung von den Vorschriften des → Bebauungsplans. Über variances wird in amerikanischen Gemeinden typischerweise von einem eigens dafür eingerichteten Board of Adjustments oder Board of Appeals entschieden.

Dividendenbesteuerung   Dividend Taxation

The double taxation of corporate earnings at the corporate and shareholder level has been abolished in 1977, at least for German shareholders. Also, under the EC „Parent-Subsidiary" Directive, inter-European dividends from 10%-owned subsidiaries are exempt from withholding tax at source, and must entitle the parent to an indirect tax credit for income taxes paid by the subsidiary, or under German law, a tax exemption.

Retained earnings in Germany („Verwendbares Eigenkapital") are subject to a different income tax rate (45%) than distributed earnings (30%). All domestic shareholders, corporate or individual, are entitled to an indirect credit („Steuergutschrift") for the 30% German corporate income tax on dividends. A lowering of the above rates is part of the 1997 tax reform debate in Bonn.

Durchgriffshaftung / ~ Piercing the Corporate Veil

Because of this indirect credit mechanism, corporations must make sure that dividends are actually burdened with the 30% tax. This requires the maintenance of different categories of retained earnings, i. e. earnings which have been fully or partially taxed in Germany, or untaxed earnings. The latter are usually derived from branch or real estate profits in foreign tax-treaty countries. Since 1994, the dividend distribution of such foreign earnings no longer triggers the 30% corporate tax, making Germany a potential domicile for international holding companies.

Dividends are also subject to a 25% withholding tax („Kapitalertragsteuer") which is credited at the shareholder level. If paid to foreigners, such withholding rate is reduced to 15% (5% for foreign parent companies) under most tax treaties, including the U.S. treaty.

There exists no tax consolidation as in the U.S., but a related concept (→ Organschaft).

In den USA gilt der Grundsatz der Doppelbesteuerung von Dividenden, auf Gesellschafts- und Gesellschafterebene. Dies gilt sogar für Liquidationsausschüttungen. Jedoch haben U.S.-Muttergesellschaften bestimmte Schachtelprivilegien für inneramerikanische Dividenden. 70% solcher Dividenden, 80% bei Besitz von mindestens 20% der Tochter, sind steuerfrei. Bei Anteilsbesitz von mindestens 80% können sogar konsolidierte Steuererklärungen abgegeben werden.

Es gilt außerdem die indirekte Steuergutschrift für 10%ige ausländische Töchter.

Dividenden an U.S.-Steuerzahler, im Gegensatz zu solchen an Steuerausländer, unterliegen keiner Kapitalertragsteuer, es sei denn, es besteht der Verdacht der Steuerhinterziehung beim Empfänger (back-up withholding).

Durchgriffshaftung   ~ Piercing the Corporate Veil

In Germany, there have been extremely few cases where board members or owners have been held liable for corporate debts, particularly in cases where the sole shareholder completely dominates the daily business. Thin capitalization or interlocking directorships are generally no cause for liability.

Under the Corporation Act (Aktiengesetz) and general corporate case law developed under the subject „faktischer Konzern" (de facto consolidation), if one corporation manages and controls the business of another related corporation to the

Eigenbedarf (→ Kündigungsschutz für Wohnraum)

exclusion of such corporation's management, the controlling corporation will be liable for the debts and losses of the other corporation.

In den USA ist die Durchgriffshaftung ein wesentlich häufigeres und erfolgreicheres Angriffsmittel als in Deutschland. Sie kommt nicht nur dann zur Anwendung, wenn mehrere Gesellschaften unter einheitlicher Leitung praktisch wie ein Unternehmen geführt werden. Durchgriff wird z. B. auch gewährt, wenn schon bei Gründung oder auf Grund der Geschäftsentwicklung eine deutliche Unterkapitalisierung vorliegt, oder wenn die gesellschaftsrechtlichen Mindestformalitäten nicht beachtet werden (periodische Aufsichtsratssitzungen, Protokollbücher, usw). Bei Haftungsprozeßen wegen unerlaubter Handlung (z. B. Produkthaftung) halten sich die Klägeranwälte ohnehin kaum mehr an körperschaftliche Schranken, da man in den USA praktisch ohne Kostenrisiko Klage erheben kann.

Eigenbedarf (→ Kündigungsschutz für Wohnraum)

Eigene Aktien   **Treasury Stock**

Pursuant to Sec. 71 AktG, German Aktiengesellschaften (large corporations) may not buy-back their own shares without shareholder approval unless the buy-back is intended to avoid a severe and immediately theatening damage to the company, or to issue the shares to employees, or to new shareholders in a corporate reorganization. In no case may treasury shares exceed 10% of stated capital.

A defensive (anti-takeover) buy back would probably not be permissible. However, German corporations have many other takeover barriers available, including the long tenancies of Directors (Aufsichtsrat), multiple voting rights of certain stockholders or the limitation of individual voting rights to a certain percentage of total votes, the myriad cross-holdings prevalent particularly in the insurance and banking industry, and the traditional support of the major banks who, among other, often control large blocks of voting rights through proxy (Depotstimmrecht). In addition, unlike U.S. banks, German banks may own corporate stock and are often among the largest shareholders.

In den USA ist der unlimitierte Rückkauf eigener Aktien im allgemeinen auch ohne Beschluß der Hauptversammlung erlaubt. Er wird häufig als frühe Verteidigung gegen vermeintliche Übernahmeangebote eingesetzt. Dabei verlieren eigene Aktien auch in den USA ihr Stimm- und Gewinnrecht. Jedoch treibt der Rückkauf den Kurs nach oben. Das Aktienrecht der meisten Einzelstaaten räumt den Managern im Rahmen

Eigentümergrundschuld (-Hypothek) / ~ Owner-is-Lender

der sehr dehnbaren „business judgement rule" erheblichen Spielraum beim Einsatz aller möglichen Anti-Übernahmestrategien ein, die teilweise ganz offensichtlich nur noch den Interessen des Management dienen können.

Eigentum	**Ownership** **Title** **Fee Simple**
Eigentümergemeinschaft	**Home Owners' Association**
Eigentümergrundschuld (-Hypothek)	**~ Owner-is-Lender** **Mortgage**

Under § 1196 BGB, a mortgage in the form of the Eigentümergrundschuld (owner mortgage) may be recorded with the property owner as the named mortgagee. Such an owner mortgage can be created ab initio to alleviate subsequent bank financing because the owner must only assign his mortgage to the lender to obtain financing. Moreover, the owner mortgage secures the existing priority (→ Rang) over subsequently recorded mortgages.

The owner mortgage in the form of the Eigentümergrundschuld arises automatically upon amortization or cancellation of a third-party mortgage, §§ 1143, 1163, 1168, 1170, 1177 and 1183 BGB. The owner subrogates to the satisfied mortgagee. Unless junior lien holders have agreed to subordinate their liens (→ Rangvorbehalt), they have a right to request release and discharge (→ Löschung) of a senior Eigentümergrundschuld if it was not originally recorded but resulted from such subrogation.

In den USA gibt es die Eigentümergrundschuld bzw. Hypothek nicht. Nach vollständiger Tilgung wird üblicherweise die Löschung (release, discharge and satisfaction) beantragt. Selbst wenn die Löschung nicht eingetragen wird, erlischt das amerikanische Grundpfandrecht automatisch mit Tilgung. Den Rangvorbehalt kann sich der Eigentümer bzw. der ranghöhere Gläubiger nur durch vertragliche Zustimmung nachrangiger Gläubiger sichern (subordination).

Ausnahmsweise gibt es auch in den USA die Eigentümerhypothek, und zwar für den Fall, daß der Hypothekengläubiger durch Vertrag das Grundstück erwirbt. Der neue Eigentümer kann verhindern, daß nachrangige Gläubiger durch die Fusion von Eigentum und Hypothek („merger of interests") ohne Berechtigung aufrücken.

Eigentumsaufgabe / Abandon

Eigentumsaufgabe   Abandon

It is legally possible (§ 928 Civil Code), but almost unheard of in Germany that an owner would abandon his property because it and its neighborhood are too run down to continue operating it profitably. Property is scarce and will almost always find a profitable use or, at the least, a buyer.

In den USA ist die Aufgabe von Hauseigentum in völlig heruntergekommenen Gegenden nichts Ungewöhnliches. Die Kombination von hohen Grundsteuern und dem Zerfall bestimmter Stadtteile machen die weitere Bewirtschaftung im Extremfall wenig sinnvoll.

Eigentumsübergang   Passing of Title

Title to German real property passes only upon recording (Eintragung). The recording has more than just declaratory effect. It constitutes the very act of, and is a condition to, the passing of title, § 873 BGB.

In den USA geht das Eigentum durch Übergabe der Deed, gewissermaßen eines Grundstücksbriefs, über. Die später folgende Eintragung (recording) hat ausschließlich deklaratorische Beweiswirkung.

Einheitswert   ~ Assessed Value

Up until 1996, Einheitswerte were determined for several tax purposes, including the Net Worth Tax (→ Vermögensteuer), real property tax (→ Grundsteuer), and estate and gift taxes (→ Erbschaft- und Schenkungsteuer). § 18 of the General Tax Assessment Act (Bewertungsgesetz) distinguishes the following four property types: Agriculture and forestry, real property (excluding minerals, → Bodenschätze), trade or business property and miscellaneous property.

Real property in the old states (former West Germany) were assessed at their fair market values of 1964 plus 40%. In the five new states of former East Germany, the market values of 1935 governed, plus certain different premiums. While the Bewertungsgesetz principally required that unimproved properties be assessed at their fair market value and improved properties at their replacement value or on a yield basis, actually assessed Einheitswerte remained far below real market values, on average by 60–80%.

In 1995, the German Supreme Court (Bundesverfassungsgericht) had to decide whether the low assessment of real property constitutes unfair discrimination among taxpayers because most other assets, including stocks and bonds, are as-

Einkommensteuer / Income Tax

sessed at full fair market value for tax purposes. The Supreme Court decided that the federal legislature had to take action to eliminate the disparity, at least to the extent it is not warranted by overriding social or economic goals.

By legislative amendment effective as of Jan. 1, 1996, Einheitswerte have been abolished for purposes of estate and gift taxes (not for real property tax) and replaced by values based on capitalized net income. Since yields of German properties have traditionally been lower than interest rates, such assessed values will likely remain about 40% below actual market values.

Due to the anticipated increase of gift and estate taxes, 1995 witnessed an escalating number of property transfers by parents to the next generation.

The Net Worth Tax (Vermögensteuer) has not been formally abolished, but cannot be assessed because it was struck down in its present form by the Federal Constitutional Court. Thus, Einheitswerte remain applicable only for German real property tax.

In den USA orientiert sich das real property assessment an den tatsächlichen Verkehrswerten, wobei in den meisten Staaten und Gemeinden ein einheitlicher prozentualer Abschlag von 30% bis 50% vom Verkehrswert üblich ist. In den USA gilt das assessment nur für Zwecke der → Grundsteuer, da es eine allgemeine Vermögensteuer in den USA nicht gibt, und da Erbschaft- und Schenkungsteuern auf den echten Verkehrswerten von Grundstücken (nach Abzug darauf liegender Schulden) basieren. Ein neues „assessment" wird alle 3–5 Jahre oder nach einem erfolgten Grundstücksverkaufs vorgenommen, manchmal auch nach einer Beleihung.

Da die Grundsteuer eine der wichtigsten Einnahmequellen der Gemeinden ist, kommt es manchmal zu erheblichen Steigerungen der assessed values. Umgekehrt führte die Immobilienkrise der 90er Jahre teilweise zu Grundsteuersenkungen von bis zu 50%. Im allgemeinen kann sich der Grundstückseigentümer gegen die Wertfeststellung durch Beschwerde und Klage wehren (tax certiorari).

Einkommensteuer   Income Tax

All income taxes in Germany are governed by Federal law. They are levied on income of individuals (Einkommensteuer) and corporations (Körperschaftsteuer). Income from trade or business (→ Gewerbebetrieb) is subject to an additional federal tax based on business income (→ Gewerbeertragsteuer).

Einlagensicherung / Deposit Insurance

The maximum individual income tax rate is 53% percent with a preferential maximum rate of 47% for trade or business income.

In den USA werden Einkommen- und Körperschaftsteuern sowohl auf Bundes- als auch auf Landes- und Gemeindeebene erhoben (federal, state and local income taxes). Es gibt keine Gewerbesteuer.

Der Höchststeuersatz der Bundeseinkommensteuer liegt bei 39,6%. Die Sätze in den US-Einzelstaaten liegen zwischen 0% und 12%, im Durchschnitt etwa bei 7%. State und local income taxes sind von der Bemessungsgrundlage der Bundeseinkommensteuer abzugsfähig.

Einlagensicherung   Deposit Insurance

Deposit insurance („Einlagensicherung") is sponsored and funded by the member banks of the Federal Banking Association. It insures deposits up to a maximum of one-third the banks equity capital per deposit. Separate deposit insurance funds exist for savings banks (Sparkassen) and for mutual banks (Genossenschaftsbanken, Volksbanken, Raiffeisenbanken). Germany has had less than a handful of bank failures, and the insurance funds have never been severely tested.

Im Anschluß an den Bankensturz von 1931 führte die Roosevelt-Regierung eine staatlich garantierte Einlagensicherung ein, sowohl für Geschäftsbanken (FDIC) als auch für Sparkassen (FSLIC). Unterdessen ist jedes einzelne Konto bei jeder Bank bis zu $100 000 versichert. Indem man Konten bei verschiedenen Banken unterhält, kann man die Versicherung daher entsprechend erhöhen. Dies führte in den achtziger Jahren zu besonderem Mißbrauch, als die schon schwachen Sparkassen (Savings and Loans) ständig höhere Zinsen boten und sich Geldvermittler etablierten, die Konten von jeweils $100 000 im ganzen Land verteilten. Mißbrauch wurde auch dadurch betrieben, daß Familien etliche verschiedene Konten in ein und derselben Bank unterhielten, z. B. Einzelkonten, Gemeinschaftskonten, Treuhandkonten, etc.

Einnahmen-Ausgaben-Überschußrechnung   Cash Basis

In Germany, the cash method of accounting is never available to corporations, or to any business unless sales and capital of the business are minimal (§ 141 Abgabenordnung).

In den USA können auch Kapitalgesellschaften, deren Jahresumsatz weniger als $5 Millionen beträgt, für die Besteuerung nach dem Zufluß-

Enteignung / Condemnation; Eminent Domain; Expropriation

Abfluß-Prinzip optieren. Sofern der Geschäftsbetrieb jedoch in der Herstellung, Anschaffung und dem Verkauf von Gütern besteht, bzw. ein Inventar geführt wird, besteht für sämtliche Steuerzahler die steuerliche Bilanzierungspflicht.

Einstellung der Zwangsversteigerung ~ **Right of Redemption**
→ Ablösungsrecht

Eintragung   **Recording**

Elektrizität (→ Umlagen)   **Electricity**

Enteignung   **Condemnation**
                 Eminent Domain
                 Expropriation

Both under U.S. and German law, a distinction is made between public acts which amount to an expropriation requiring reasonable compensation (enteignender or enteignungsgleicher Eingriff), and mere land use controls which are reasonable restrictions and serve overriding public interests. The notion of Art. 14 of the German Constitution (Grundgesetz) is that title confers on the holder not only rights but also social responsibilities (→ Sozialbindung des Eigentums).

Examples for an overriding public interest are the preservation of historic areas, landmarks, wetlands, navigable waters, beaches and the environment in general (→ Umweltschutz). Environmental and other restrictions, particularly for land and forest owners (→ Bundeswaldgesetz), have steadily expanded in Germany on the grounds of the Sozialbindung mandated by Art. 14 Grundgesetz. It is fair to say that the uninhibited use and enjoyment of private lands in Germany has become significantly more restrained than that of land in the United States. This may partly rest on the scarcity of land in a densely populated industrial country like Germany, and to a lesser degree on political traditions.

Auch in den USA unterscheidet man zwischen Eingriffen, die im Rahmen der Sozialpflichtigkeit des Eigentums erlaubt sind (z. B. Gründe des Natur- oder Landschaftsschutzes), und solchen, die enteignungsgleich oder enteignend und daher entschädigungspflichtig sind. Während der Grundsatz der sozialen Bindung des Eigentums in Deutschland politisch zunehmend ausgedehnt zu werden scheint, zeichnet sich in den USA ein gegenläufiger Trend ab. Mehr als 30 Einzelstaaten haben bereits Gesetze erlassen, denen zufolge Grundeigentümer Entschädigung für besonders beeinträchtigende → Umweltschutzbestimmungen verlangen können.

Erbbaurecht / ~ Statutory Ground Lease

Erbbaurecht ~ Statutory Ground Lease

The Erbbaurecht is the right to erect structures on or under a certain land lot. It is governed by a federal act, the ErbbauRVO. It is a property interest which generally reverts to the land owner after 30 to 99 years. The Erbbaurecht is transferable through sale or succession. However, the land owner and the ground lessee often agree that the transfer of the Erbbaurecht or the mortgage financing of improvements thereon is subject to the land owner's approval. Such clauses generally make the Erbbaurecht an inadequate basis for most commercial development projects.

The law regarding Erbbaurecht has been modernized in 1994. In the foreclosure sale of a ground lease, the senior bank mortgage will not destroy the property owner's junior right of collecting ground rent. Also, ground rents can not only be indexed to a general CPI index, but to the appreciation of specific properties.

Unter dem typischen amerikanischen ground lease versteht man in den meisten Staaten einen langfristigen Mietvertrag. Häufig erhält der Mieter eine zusätzliche Kaufoption für das Land. Insofern hat der amerikanische ground lease oft den Charakter der Kaufpreisfinanzierung durch den Verkäufer.

Erbrecht (Erbstatut) Inheritance Law

German conflict-of-law rules provide that the law of the country of which the decedent is a national governs the inheritance of the decedent's worldwide assets. However, under Art. 25 EGBGB, German inheritance law may apply to the passing of German real property if the last will of a foreign decedent expressly requires the application of German law.

Soweit ersichtlich gilt in den meisten Einzelstaaten der USA, daß für unbewegliches Vermögen grundsätzlich das Erbrecht des Belegenheitsstaats gilt und nicht das der Staatsangehörigkeit des Erblassers.

Erbschaftsteuer Estate Tax

Estate and gift tax principles in Germany and the United States differ in several important respects:

In Germany, heirs or donees are the primary taxpayers, § 20 ErbStG. The estate or the donor are subsidiary taxpayers.

The tax rate schedule applies to each individual share of the estate and devise, not to the entire estate, resulting in a lower applicable tax rate, § 10 ErbStG.

Erbschaftsteuer / Estate Tax

The top marginal tax rates apply only to transfers exceeding DM 50 Million (~ $ 28 Million). Transfers to spouses and offsprings, or all transfers of business assets („Betriebsvermögen"), including 25% interests in corporations, are subject to a maximum rate of 30%. A 40% maximum rate applies to siblings and certain other relatives, 50% for all other heirs or donees.

Because of the splitting of the estate and the overall lower tax rate schedule, the estate tax burden in Germany is comparatively lower than in the United States. The margin has, however, narrowed somewhat for real estate after the 1996 abolishment of low assessed values (Einheitswerte) and the application of fair market values as the basis of the German estate tax.

Die Erbschafts- und Schenkungsbesteuerung in den USA unterscheidet sich in vielfacher Hinsicht von der deutschen. Zu den wichtigeren Unterschieden gehören folgende:

In den USA ist primärer Steuerschuldner nicht der Vermächtnisnehmer bzw. Beschenkte, sondern der Nachlaß selbst, Sec. 2001 IRC, bzw. der Schenker, Sec. 2501(a) IRC.

Es gelten schon immer Verkehrswerte als Bemessungsgrundlage, Sec. 2031 IRC, nicht Einheitswerte. Es gibt die beschränkte Möglichkeit, landwirtschaftliche oder Betriebsgrundstücke mit dem Teilwert zu versteuern, jedoch darf der Nachlaß dadurch um nicht mehr als $ 750,000 verkürzt werden, Sec. 2032A IRC.

In den USA gilt die Tabelle nicht für das einzelne Vermächtnis, sondern für den gesamten Nachlaß, mit der Folge der höheren Progression, Sec. 2033 IRC.

In den USA wird nicht zwischen verschiedenen Klassen von Erben unterschieden. Der Höchststeuersatz von 55% gilt bereits bei einem Nachlaß (Verkehrswert) von $ 3 Millionen, Sec. 2001(c) IRC.

Die US Erbschaftsteuer ist in der Regel deutlich höher als die deutsche, insbesondere wegen der höheren Sätze und der anwendbaren Progression auf den Gesamtnachlaß. Vor U.S. Erbschaftsteuer schützt hohe Fremdfinanzierung, oder die Zwischenschaltung einer amerikanischen oder deutschen Kapitalgesellschaft. Letzteres bringt den Nachteil der Doppelbesteuerung laufender Einkünfte mit sich. Dies kann unter Umständen unterlaufen werden, indem eine GmbH & Co KG bewußt so ausgestaltet wird, daß sie nach U.S. Steuerrecht wie eine corporation besteuert wird. Es gibt andere Modelle, mit denen die Gefahr der hohen U.S. Erbschaftsteuer recht elegant reduziert oder eliminiert werden kann, beispielsweise durch Schenkung plus Darlehen oder durch ein bindendes Verkaufsangebot des Erblassers.

Erdbebenversicherung / Earthquake Insurance

Earthquakes occur too rarely in Germany to be of any concern to property owners or insurers.

In den USA ist das Thema der Erdbebenversicherung besonders in Kalifornien relevant. Für gewerbliche Objekte ist diese Versicherung zu akzeptablen Kosten schwer zu beschaffen. Für private Hausbesitzer hat der kalifornische Gesetzgeber Abhilfe geschaffen. Versicherer müssen Hauseigentümern die Erdbebenversicherung zu vernünftigen Prämiensätzen anbieten.

Erfüllungsanspruch / Specific Performance

Generally, in a German real property purchase, either party can request specific performance of the other party, i. e. the buyer can request the transfer of the property, the seller may request the payment of the purchase price. The seller sometimes requires the purchaser to secure the payment of the purchase price by delivering a „power of sale" certificate (→ vollstreckbare Urkunde under § 794 ZPO) authorizing the seller to immediately foreclose against all assets of the purchaser upon his default. Of course, instead of specific performance either party may ask for damages if the other party defaults.

In den USA hat der Verkäufer beim typischen → Grundstückskauf keinen Anspruch auf Erfüllung durch den Käufer. Er behält bei Verzug des Käufers lediglich die geleistete Anzahlung als → Vertragsstrafe (liquidated damages) ein. Der Käufer hingegen hat regelmäßig den Erfüllungsanspruch, d. h. auf Übertragung des Grundstücks.

Erfüllungsbürgschaft / Completion Bond / Performance Bond / Builder Bond

General performance bonds will be required of a German contractor only in special cases. Normally, the only security will either be a deferred payment of approximately 5% of the contract value which the developer may retain until the expiration of any warranty periods, or a bond for the same amount. Such bonds are usually provided by banks.

In den USA arbeitet der Bauunternehmer (general contractor) in den meisten Fällen wie ein deutscher Generalübernehmer, d. h. er vergibt fast alle Gewerke an Subunternehmer. Da diese häufig nicht finanzstark sind, wird vom Auftraggeber ein Performance Bond verlangt, der von speziellen Versicherungsgesellschaften (bonding companies) für den jeweiligen Subunternehmer oder auch durch den Generalunternehmer in Höhe des jeweiligen Auftragswerts herausgelegt wird.

Erhaltungsaufwendungen	**Renovation Expenditures** **Rehabilitation Expenditures** **Maintenance; Repairs**

Expenditures for the maintenance, repair or renovation of rental properties, such as roof and window repairs, are deductible expenses (Erhaltungsaufwendungen) in Germany. In the case of residential property, the taxpayer may elect to deduct these expenditures straight line over not less than two, and not more than five years, § 82b EStDV. Expenditures incurred in the modernization or substitution of existing parts or fixtures of a building are also deductible Erhaltungsaufwendungen. They are distinguished from non-deductible construction costs (Herstellungsaufwand), i. e. from expenditures which add new structural components or fixtures. Specific rules apply since 1994 with respect to expenditures incurred within three years of acquisition of a property (anschaffungsnaher Erhaltungsaufwand). Such expenditures are only deductible to the extent they do not exceed 15% of the building's acquisition cost, No. 157 Para. 5 Einkommensteuerrichtlinien (Income Tax Regulations).

Im Gegensatz zum deutschen Steuerrecht werden in den USA praktisch sämtliche Erhaltungsaufwendungen aktiviert, es sei denn, es handelt sich um reine Reparaturen. Keine Reparatur liegt vor, wenn die betreffende Aufwendung zu einer erheblichen Aufwertung des Objekts oder Verlängerung seiner Nutzungsdauer führt, Reg § 1 162–4. Rehabilitation expenditures an Gebäuden, die vor 1936 errichtet wurden, berechtigen in bestimmten Fällen zu einer Einkommensteuer-Gutschrift in Höhe von 10% der Aufwendungen, Sec. 47 IRC. Bei historischen Gebäuden gibt es eine Steuer-Gutschrift bis zu 20%.

Erhaltungssatzung	**~ Preservation Ordinance**
Erschließung	**~ Provision of Public Service**

Erschließungsaufwand / ~ Public Service Development

Under the Building Act (Baugesetzbuch), property owners are not entitled, as of right, to the delivery of public services to their property. However, such a right may exist in certain cases, for example if a building permit has been granted within the area covered by the local zoning ordinance, or if the municipality already levies public service fees on the respective property.

In den USA muß der Entwickler die sogenannten „utilities" (Strom, Gas, Wasser, Straße) häufig selbst an ein zu entwickelndes Grundstück heranbringen. Soweit möglich, versucht er dabei, diese Kosten mit anderen anliegenden Parteien zu teilen. Bei einer Siedlungserschließung versucht der Entwickler, die Straßen nach deren Erstellung an die örtliche Gemeinde zu übertragen, um die zukünftigen Instandhaltungskosten einzusparen. Dies gelingt häufig, da die Gemeinde durch die Entwicklung in den Genuß höherer Grundsteuereinnahmen kommt. Die Regelungen und Gebräuche sind jedoch örtlich sehr unterschiedlich.

Erschließungsaufwand ~ Public Service Development and Connection Cost

Under §§ 127 et. seq. BauGB, municipalities may charge owners for 90% of the initial public service development and connection cost to their properties (beitragsfähiger Erschließungsaufwand).

If the local authority sub-contracts the provision of public services with a private developer, it remains liable for at least 10% of the development cost which it must reimburse to the developer (Erschließungsträger), § 129 BauGB. The developer may, through private agreements, pass his cost on to purchasers of the various lots. The local authority looses the right to charge landowners for its share of the development or connection fee. The statute makes the municipality bear 10% of the development cost in either alternative, presumably because it will eventually benefit from the increased tax base.

Once the developer has transferred title to the public service installations, such as roads and parks, to the community, the community may charge property owners for the continuing maintenance (Benutzungsbeiträge). Fees charged by the community must be commensurate with the services provided (Äquivalenzprinzip).

In den USA ist es auch in diesem Punkt schwierig zu generalisieren, da die Gebräuche von Ort zu Ort verschieden sind. Im allgemeinen erheben Gemeinden eine einmalige Anschlußgebühr (hook-up fee). Nur ausnahmsweise wird sich die Gemeinde durch Vertrag mit einem Bauträger verpflichten, auf Dauer einen Teil der Kosten zu tragen.

Ferienwohnung / Vacation Home

Ersitzung (→ Buchersitzung)

Eskalationen (→ Steigerungen)   **Escalations**

Fälligkeitsklausel   **Acceleration Clause**

For consumer loans, acceleration clauses will be valid only if the borrower is in default partly or wholly with two subsequent installments amounting to at least 10% of the total loan and if he is given a two-weeks grace period.

Similarly, leases may be terminated if the tenant is in default with a substantial part of the rent for two subsequent periods or for an amount exceeding two months' rent. Termination by the landlord will be invalid if the tenant pays up before receiving the notice of termination. For residential leases, arrears will be deemed substantial only if exceeding one month's rent. The tenant can cure the default and invalidate the termination by fully paying all arrears even up to one month after the landlord has filed the eviction notice with the court.

Das Recht einiger US-Einzelstaaten schützt den Schuldner oder Mieter, indem es die Fälligstellung einer Summe gegen den säumigen Schuldner einem gewissen Verfahren unterwirft. Z. B. kann in den meisten Staaten der Schuldner oder Mieter auch nach Fälligstellung der Gesamtsumme den überfälligen Betrag schuldbefreiend zahlen und dadurch die Fortführung des Vertragsverhältnisses erlangen.

Ferienwohnung   **Vacation Home**

In Germany as in the U.S., the owner of a vacation home which is rented to third parties only for part of the year may deduct his expenses (taxes, maintenance, etc.) only in the same ratio which exists between the owner-occupied part and the rental part of the year. Vacancy time counts as owner-occupancy (Eigennutzung) if the home is ready for use by the owner. Vacancy periods will, however, count as rental periods, if they are relatively short or if the owner has retained a property manager or travel organization as leasing agent. Details are provided in German Treasury Department Release, BMF Schreiben vom 4. 5. 94 (Az. IV B3-S 2253).

Wie in Deutschland können auch in den USA Aufwendungen für das zeitweise vermietete, zeitweise eigengenutzte Ferienhaus nur in dem Verhältnis abgezogen werden, das dem Zeitraum der Vermietung im Vergleich zum Zeitraum der Eigennutzung entspricht, Sec 280A IRC. In den USA ist dabei streitig, ob es für die Abzugsfähigkeit der Aufwendungen (insbesondere Schuldzinsen und Grundsteuern) auf das Verhältnis der

Fertighäuser / Manufactured –; Modular –; Prefabricated Homes

Vermietungszeit zum gesamten Jahr inklusive oder exklusive Leerstandszeiten ankommt. Außerdem gilt in den USA folgendes: Benutzt der Eigentümer das Haus weniger als 15 Tage im Jahr und weniger als 10% der gesamten Vermietungszeit, können die Aufwendungen vollständig abgezogen werden. Vermietet er umgekehrt die Ferienwohnung für weniger als 15 Tage im Jahr, gilt sie insgesamt als eigengenutzt. Er kann in diesem Fall nichts absetzen, muß aber auch die Mieteinnahmen nicht versteuern.

Fertighäuser   Manufactured Homes
Modular Homes
Prefabricated Homes

Germany does not have, and probably would not allow, homes which would be equivalent to mobile or trailer homes in the U.S. Also, while there exists an active modular home market, homeowners in Germany prefer the more expensive and solid construction of brick and cement structures. Since disposable income in East Germany remains below the level of West Germany, and since building code authorities have become a little more sensitive to the market, some developers have recently tried to introduce U.S. style prefabricated homes to the market, apparently with mixed results so far.

In den USA setzt sich der Trend zu Fertighäusern fort. Es gibt unterdessen 9 Millionen Fertighäuser. Jährlich kommen mehr als 300,000 dazu. Jedes dritte neue Haus ist ein Fertighaus. Am unteren Ende sind dabei die trailer homes, die es seit den dreißiger Jahren gibt. Manche gemeindlichen Bebauungspläne verbieten trailer parks ausdrücklich, zum Schutz angrenzender Hauseigentümer. Die Bauqualität von trailer homes ist auf Grund bundesbehördlicher Verordnungen der HUD von 1976 besser geworden. Die Verordnungen wurden in Folge der verheerenden Schäden, die Hurrikan „Andrew" 1992 anrichtete, nochmals verschärft.

Modular Homes sind teurer gebaut als mobile oder trailer homes. Sie werden lokalen Richtlinien angepaßt, und nicht denen der HUD. Modular Homes sind bei Auslieferung typischerweise 90% fertiggestellt.

Fertigstellungsgarantie (→ Erfüllungsbürgschaft)

Festzins   Fixed Rate Interest

In the early nineties, a new Section 609a was added to the German Civil Code. It provides commercial borrowers with a pre-payment option once a fixed rate loan converts to variable rate, or if variable rate interest adjustments occur less frequently

Fonds / Fund; Mutual Fund

than at least once a year. All variable rate loans may be pre-paid upon three months notice.

Section 609a also gives takers of fixed rate consumer loans a three-month notice pre-payment option, beginning six months after the loan has been funded. The provisions of Section 609a are mandatory. Only foreign lenders may in certain circumstances exclude these provisions by subjecting the loan agreement to foreign law.

In den USA scheint es Regeln, die denen des § 609 BGB entsprechen, weder auf Bundes- noch auf Landesebene zu geben. Zwischen Kaufleuten besteht weitgehende Vertragsfreiheit, mit Ausnahme der einzelstaatlichen Wuchergrenzen. Jedoch sind Hypothekendarlehen für selbstgenutzte Wohnungen und Häuser in aller Regel durch den Schuldner jederzeit kündbar.

Firmenwert **Goodwill**
Going Concern Value

As in the U.S., goodwill may only be capitalized in Germany if acquired through the purchase of another business. However, goodwill is depreciable in Germany over 15 years. Goodwill of an acquired professional firm, such as a law or consulting firm, whose continuation depends largely on the services of the sellers, may be amortized over 3 to 5 years.

Auch in den USA sind grundsätzlich nur derivative immaterielle Wirtschaftsgüter aktivierungsfähig, z. B. nur der erworbene Firmenwert. Nach neuerem Steuerrecht ist auch der reine Firmenwert (goodwill; going concern value) über 15 Jahre amortisierbar, so wie es andere immaterielle Wirtschaftsgüter (intangibles) sind. Gewisse immaterielle Wirtschaftsgüter, z. B. Computersoftware, werden jedoch nach ihrer betriebsgewöhnlichen Nutzungsdauer abgeschrieben.

Flächennutzungsplan **Master Plan**
City Plan

Flurstück **Lot**
Parcel

Fonds **Fund**
Mutual Fund

(Offener Fonds – Open-End Fund;
Geschlossener Fonds – Closed-End Fund)

Forderungserlaß / Discharge of Indebtedness

Forderungserlaß   Discharge of Indebtedness

The discharge of debt is tax free to an insolvent debtor under certain circumstances, § 3 No. 66 EStG. This exemption may, however, be abolished after 1998. The discharge may also give rise to a deduction for the creditor.

If, however, corporate debt is discharged by a shareholder, a „hidden" capital contribution (verdeckte Einlage) is generally assumed, which the shareholder, of course, may not deduct. The fair-market value of such debt discharge is a tax-free capital contribution to the corporation even if it is not insolvent and even if the corresponding liability previously represented a tax expense for the corporation. However, the tax-free portion of the discharge may be small if the discharged debt was largely worthless. Also, the discharging shareholder may be deemed to receive taxable income, for example if the discharged debt arose from prior services of the shareholder.

In summary, the tax-benefit logic of the German cancellation of debt (COD) rules in the context of shareholder-corporation are not dissimilar from those of the U.S.

Auch in den USA stellt der Forderungserlaß ausnahmsweise kein steuerliches Einkommen beim Schuldner dar, wenn dieser in Konkurs oder zahlungsunfähig ist, Sec. 108(a)(1) IRC. 1994 wurden auf das langjährige Betreiben der durch fallende Preise unter Druck geratenen Immobilienbranche Sec. 108(a)(1)(D) in den IRC aufgenommen. Danach werden notleidende Bauträger auch ohne Insolvenz von der Einkünftefiktion befreit, die beim Forderungsverzicht in Folge einer Zwangsvollstreckung entsteht. Die Steuervergünstigung der Sec. 108(a)(1) bewirkt immer nur einen Steueraufschub, da der Schuldner den Betrag des steuerfreien Forderungserlasses von den Anschaffungskosten seiner Immobilien abziehen muß. Hat er nicht mehr ausreichend Buchwert in seinem gesamten Immobilienvermögen, kommt er um die Besteuerung der erlassenen Forderung nicht herum.

Der Forderungsverzicht durch den Aktionär bereichert seine Kapitalgesellschaft steuerlich nur, wenn die Entstehung der Forderung bei der Gesellschaft erfolgswirksam war, beispielsweise bei Rückstellungen für Leistungen des Gesellschafters.

Freianteile   ~ Stock Dividend

Principally, stock dividends should be taxable in Germany. However, since 1983, Sec. 1 of the Capital Increase Tax Act (KapErhStG) makes the issuance of new stock after the conversion of retained earnings into stated capital tax free to shareholders. Of course, upon liquidation or redemption, the shareholders will be deemed to receive a dividend for the new stock because converted retained earnings remain earnings and profits (verwendbares Eigenkapital) for tax purposes.

In den USA sind Freianteile, sofern sie nicht wahlweise neben Bardividenden, oder in ungleichen Verhältnissen ausgegeben werden, grundsätzlich steuerfrei beim Empfänger.

Fusionskontrolle   Merger Control

Under the Securities Exchange Act („Wertpapierhandelsgesetz"), a filing is required in Germany once the holdings of an acquirer exceed the threshold of 25% of a public company's traded stock.

Also, under EC merger control guidelines, the acquisition of 25% of the share capital or voting rights of another corporation requires a pre-merger filing with the antitrust department of the EC Commission if acquirer and target together have 10,000 employees, or combined sales of DM 500 Million, or a combined market share of 20%. The Commission generally takes a liberal view and has blocked less than a handful of mergers in its history. Mergers and acquisitions below these thresholds are in some cases still subject to filings and antitrust clearance by the German „Bundeskartellamt" in Berlin which traditionally has been stricter than the EC.

Der Erwerb von börsennotierten Aktien wird auch in den USA ab einer Beteiligung von 5% bei der Wertpapieraufsichtsbehörde in Washington (SEC) anzeigepflichtig (das sogenannte „13-D filing").

Kartellrechtlich ist der Kauf von 15% oder $ 15 Millionen des Aktienkapitals einer anderen Gesellschaft, auch nicht-börsennotierter, bei der Kartellbehörde (Federal Trade Commission) und dem Justizministerium (Department of Justice) anzeigepflichtig. Das gleiche gilt für joint ventures, sofern eine der Parteien einen Umsatz von mindestens $ 100 Mio, die andere einen von mindestens $ 10 Mio hat, und das Gemeinschaftsunternehmen eine Bilanzsumme von wenigstens $ 10 Mio haben wird. Falls die Behörden nicht innerhalb 30 Tagen nach Anzeige reagieren, gilt die Transaktion als genehmigt.

Die Behörden verwenden eine bestimmte Formel (den „Herfindahl-Hirshman"-Index), um die kartellrechtliche Bedenklichkeit eines Vorhabens abzuschätzen. So würde ein Zusammengehen im allgemeinen verboten, wenn eine der Parteien einen Marktanteil von 35% im rele-

Garagenablösung / ~ Public Parking Cost

vanten Produktbereich hat und damit bereits Marktführer ist, die andere Partei einen Anteil von mindestens 1%.

Garagenablösung ~ Public Parking Cost

If a project is likely to cause increased vehicle traffic, a building permit will only be granted if the developer contractually agrees to provide sufficient parking ground on his or on adjacent properties. If there is a lack of space in the immediate vicinity, the building authority may require the developer, in accordance with the Building Act and any applicable state building and parking laws, to reimburse the municipality for the cost of construction and maintenance of public parking facilities.

In den USA muß der Entwickler im Normalfall dafür Sorge tragen, daß ausreichend Parkraum vorhanden ist. Bei Einkaufszentren ist dies regelmäßig ein besonders wichtiger Punkt. Die Anforderungen der lokalen Behörden sind jedoch sehr unterschiedlich. Wegen der generell günstigeren Bodenpreise ist die Parkflächenplanung in den USA meist ein geringeres Problem als in Deutschland.

Gas (→ Umlagen) Gas

Gebäudeabstand Building Distance

Gebäudebrand Fire
→ Abbruchkosten – Demolition
→ Sachversicherung – Property Insurance

Gebrauchsabnahmeschein Certificate of Occupancy

Not all German states require the routine inspection of completed buildings or the issuance of a Certificate of Occupancy. Developers generally do not have a right to request the issuance of such a certificate either.

In den meisten Gemeinden der USA ist es üblich, daß ein Gebäude erst dann bezugs- oder benutzungsfertig ist, wenn die zuständige Behörde das Gebäude inspiziert und ein offizielles certificate of occupancy erteilt hat. Wenn für ein fertiggestelltes Gebäude kein Gebrauchsabnahmeschein vorliegt, ist es im übrigen nahezu unmöglich, eine Langfristfinanzierung zu erhalten. Bei großen Bürogebäuden wird häufig der Gebrauchsabnahmeschein bei Fertigstellung verschiedener Etagen abschnittsweise ausgestellt.

Gefahrstoffe   Hazardous Waste

Gefahrübergang (Preisgefahr)   Risk of Loss

Purchase agreements generally provide that the risk of loss passes on the date of closing. Absent such a contractual clause, risk of loss passes to the purchaser of property at the earlier of the date of recording of the title or the passing of possession of the property pursuant to § 446 BGB (Gefahrübergang).

In der amerikanischen Praxis wird der Gefahrübergang meist vertraglich geregelt. Mangels vertraglicher Bestimmung geht nach dem Recht der meisten Einzelstaaten die Gefahr bei Auflassung auf den Käufer über oder, falls früher, mit dem Besitzwechsel. Es gibt jedoch Staaten, in denen der Käufer mangels vertraglicher Regelung bereits mit Vertragsschluß die Gefahr übernimmt.

Geldbeschaffungskosten   Finance Costs

Loan origination fees and similar financing costs are generally deductible expenses in Germany. For cash basis taxpayers, the same it true of loan points (Disagio or Damnum) if they are retained by the lender at the original funding and if the points are not excessively high.

In den USA müssen sämtliche Geldbeschaffungskosten aktiviert werden. Auch ein Disagio (points) kann nur über die Laufzeit des Darlehens steuerlich amortisiert werden, Sec. 461(g) IRC.

Gemeindliches Vorkaufsrecht ~ Municipal Right of First Refusal

Under § 24 of the Building Act (Baugesetzbuch), municipalities have a general right of first refusal for all properties which are designated for public purposes in an existing zoning ordinance or which lie in a land reallocation or urban renewal area. Also, pursuant to § 25 Baugesetzbuch, municipalities may and often do include in their Charter a special preemptive right relating to all undeveloped properties within the zoning ordinance, or to properties which are considered for urban renewal. The municipality must exercise its preemptive right within two months after notice by the parties of a property sale. The deed registry office (Grundbuchamt) may record new title only upon certification by the municipality that a preemptive right does not exist or that it has been waived.

In den USA gibt es in den meisten Einzelstaaten, soweit ersichtlich, keine dem deutschen Recht vergleichbare Ermächtigung für ein allge-

Gemeinflächen / Common Areas; Common Elements

meines oder besonderes Vorkaufsrecht der Gemeinden. Es gibt jedoch für bestimmte Grundstücke ein Vorkaufsrecht der Bundesregierung, welches von der „General Services Administration" (GSA) jedoch nur in Ausnahmefällen ausgeübt wird.

Gemeinflächen	**Common Areas**
	Common Elements
Generalmietvertrag (Vermietungsgarantie)	**Master Lease**
Geringstes Gebot	**~ Minimum Bid**

In a German foreclosure auction, bids must as a minimum cover the claims of all creditors senior to the foreclosing creditor, the cost of the foreclosure, and accrued taxes and other public encumbrances for up to two years, § 44 ZVG (Foreclosure Sales Act). The court will determine the minimum bid (Geringstes Gebot) before the auction begins. Each bid will be assumed to include the assumption of senior claims which the court determined to be covered by the minimum bid. Lower bids bid will not be accepted since the judicial sale (Zuschlag) will extinguish all claims pursuant to § 91 ZVG. A junior creditor should not get a bargain deal at the expense of senior creditors.

In the USA gibt es das Prinzip des „geringsten Gebots" nicht. Vorrangige Gläubiger müssen durch Abgabe entsprechender Gebote selbst sicherstellen, daß ihre Forderungen aus dem Versteigerungserlös zurückgezahlt werden können.

Gesamthandseigentum	**Joint Tenancy**
(see also → Teilung – Partition)	
Gesamthypothek	**Blanket Mortgage**
Gesamtschuldnerisch	**Joint and Several Liability**
Geschäftsführer	**Officer**
(→ Aufsichtsrat)	
Geschäftswert (→ Firmenwert)	
Geschlossener Fonds	**Closed End Fund**

Gesellschafterfremdfinanzierung / Shareholder Loans

Geschoßflächenzahl ~ **Height Density Floor to Area Ratio (FAR)**

Gesellschafterfremdfinanzierung **Shareholder Loans** ~ **Earnings Stripping**

Sec. 8a KStG has introduced an earnings stripping rule. If a foreign or other tax-exempt shareholder, directly or indirectly owning 25% or more of the shares of a German corporation, lends money to the corporation, interest on the loan is not deductible to the extent the loan-to-equity ratio, allocable to the lending shareholder, exceeds certain „safe haven" thresholds. Different thresholds apply: If the interest is dependent on the sales or profits of the corporation, a loan-to-allocable equity ratio of only 1–2 will be allowed. If the interest is not so dependent, a ratio of 3–1 is allowed, or greater if such ratio is still at arm's length or if the subsidiary is in the financing or banking business.

Unlike in the U.S., loans by partners to their partnership are generally not treated as loans for tax purposes. Interest on such loans is not deductible by the partnership, but represents part of the profits allocable to the lending partner („Sondervergütungen").

In den USA limitiert Sec. 163(j) IRC die Fremdfinanzierung amerikanischer Kapitalgesellschaften durch Darlehen ausländischer Gesellschafter. Sofern das Verhältnis Fremd- zu Eigenkapital höher als 60–40 ist, und der Netto-Zinsaufwand (Schuldzinsen minus Zinseinkünfte) mehr als die Hälfte des Betriebsergebnisses verzehrt, wird der Abzug nicht erlaubt, und kann bis zu drei Jahren vorgetragen werden.

Darüber hinaus gelten die allgemeinen auch für U.S. Steuerzahler geltenden debt-equity Grundsätze zur Abgrenzung von Eigen- und Fremdkapital. Die Finanzbehörde entscheidet nach einer umfangreichen Kriterienliste, ob Fremdkapital nicht eigenkapitalersetzend ist. Zu den Kriterien gehört die Branchenüblichkeit (Höhe) der Fremdfinanzierung, die Fälligkeit, der Rang, die Gewinnabhängigkeit von Zinsen, und weiteres.

Bei der Fremdfinanzierung direkter U.S. Investitionen ausländischer Investoren (in Form der Personengesellschaft oder des Alleininvestors) sind darüber hinaus die Richtlinien unter Sec. 861 IRC zu beachten. Danach wird in den USA grundsätzlich nur die Verschuldung anerkannt, die dem durchschnittlichen Verschuldungsgrad des Investors weltweit entspricht. Da letzterer meist ungern eine Weltbilanz abgibt, enthalten die Richtlinien eine Ausnahme für bestimmte Fremdfinanzierungen. Sofern das

Gesetzliche Pfandrechte / Statutory Liens

Fremdkapital für den ursprünglichen Erwerb des U.S. Vermögens, z. B. Grundbesitz, aufgenommen wird, und nicht als Betriebsmittelkredit, und sofern keine persönliche Haftung sondern reine Objekthaftung („non-recourse") besteht, sind die Zinsen grundsätzlich abzugsfähig.

Zinsen oder ähnliche Vergütungen, die von amerikanischen Personengesellschaften an Gesellschafter gezahlt werden, sind im Gegensatz zum deutschen Steuerrecht nicht Sondervergütungen, sondern werden wie abzugsfähige Zinsen behandelt. Unter dem früher geltenden Doppelbesteuerungsabkommen ergaben sich durch die Konstruktion „deutscher Gesellschafter empfängt Zinsen von seiner amerikanischen Partnership" weiße (d. h. völlig unbesteuerte) Einkünfte.

Gesetzliche Pfandrechte **Statutory Liens**
(→ Bauhandwerkerhypothek)

Gewährleistung **Warranty**
→ „Wie besichtigt"
→ Zugesicherte Eigenschaften

Gewerbebetrieb **~ Trade or Business**

Gain from the sale of an asset held outside of an individual taxpayer's trade or business (Privatvermögen) is not taxable in Germany if the asset has been held for a certain minimum holding period (→ Spekulationsfrist). Assets will, however, be considered trade or business assets (Betriebsvermögen) if they are not held with a view to medium- or long-term investment and appreciation. The distinction between passive portfolio management (Vermögensverwaltung) and active trade or business is an important issue for individual taxpayers as they want to preserve the tax exemption of their long-term capital gains (→ Veräußerungsgewinn).

The primary factor in classifying an activity is not the size of the securities or real property portfolio, but its turnover and the nature of the activity. If the activity involves a „participation in general commerce" a Gewerbebetrieb will be assumed. Even a one-time sale to a controlled corporate entity may be considered gewerblich, if the purpose is to step-up the basis and resell the property to third parties.

If the owner of real property primarily aims at the production of rental income, he will generally be deemed to be a passive investor. If his portfolio strategy is geared to short-term appreciation and profit realization through sales, a trade or business may be assumed.

Gewerbeerlaubnis / ~ Business License

Under a 1986 decision of the BFH (BStBl II 88, 244), up to three property sales within any five-year period have generally been held to be within the private investment activity parameters. A greater number of sales will generally indicate that the taxpayer is in the business of dealing in real estate. For purposes of this three strike rule, sales of German and foreign real property assets will be combined. Sales of properties by partnerships will be counted against the partners, at least against those partners holding more than 10% of the partnership interests. By contrast, property sales by a corporate entity will not taint the real estate activities of a shareholder, not even of the sole shareholder.

Private entrepreneurs often lease assets, including real property to their own business entity. One reason can be to exclude the assets from general liabilities of the business. The main goal, however, usually is to hold such assets as capital assets (Privatvermögen) and, thus, to avoid trade or business tax (Gewerbesteuer) and gains tax on any future sale of the asset. Such arrangements are disregarded by the tax authority as an artificial business split-up („Betriebsaufspaltung") if the owners of the leased asset and of the business are substantially the same and if the assets are specifically required for the operation of the business. This may include a built-to-suit office building.

In den USA gibt es im Gegensatz zum deutschen Steuerrecht keine grundsätzliche Unterscheidung zwischen verschiedenen Einkunftsarten. Dennoch haben sich zunehmend Differenzierungen zwischen aktiven und passiven Einkünften, oder solchen aus Gewerbebetrieb und Kapitalvermögen, an verschiedenen Stellen des amerikanischen Steuergesetzbuches etabliert. Diese Unterscheidungen bestehen in erster Linie, um die Ausgleichsfähigkeit passiver Verluste zu beschränken, z. B. „passive activity losses" nach Sec. 469 IRC (→ Negatives Kapitalkonto). Für die Besteuerung von → Veräußerungsgewinnen spielt die Unterscheidung zwischen Vermögensverwaltung und Gewerbebetrieb eine untergeordnete Rolle, da alle Veräußerungsgewinne in den USA steuerpflichtig sind, und erst neuerdings wieder ein etwas günstigerer Steuersatz für longterm capital gains natürlicher Personen (20%) gilt. Im übrigen gibt es in den USA keine Gewerbesteuer.

Gewerbeerlaubnis   ~ Business License

In Germany, any person or entity planning a commercial activity requires a business license („Gewerbeerlaubnis") which usually is granted as a matter of course. Commercial activities include not only production, but most services, such as brokers, agents, professional real estate developers and similar businesses. Excluded

Gewerbegebiet / Commercial Zone

from the license requirement are wholesale and retail, agriculture, the professions and non-commercial rental activities. The license will be granted if the applicant is generally qualified and his business satisfies all regulatory minimum standards. It may be withdrawn if a person is irresponsible. Quota restrictions ("Bedürfnisprüfung") are generally not allowed.

In addition to the personal business license, many projects require multiple permits from different local, state or federal agencies governing environmental control (→ Umweltschutz), noise emissions and zoning (→ Baurecht; → Bebauungsplan). It can take years to obtain all required permits, particularly for industrial projects. For example, permits under the Genetic Engineering Act ("Gentechnikgesetz"), which was enacted under a European directive, are so difficult to obtain that many pharmaceutical companies have relocated such projects to foreign countries, including to the U.S. The regulatory framework is a subject of increasing public concern. With the "Green Party" having gained representation in the Federal parliament and most state legislators, it is hard to see why environmental regulations should yield to economic considerations in the future.

Eine allgemeine Gewerbeerlaubnis-Pflicht scheint es in den meisten Einzelstaaten der USA nicht zu geben.

Gewerbegebiet — **Commercial Zone**

Gewerbeobjekt — **Commercial Property**

Gewerbepark — **Industrial Park**

Gewerbesteuer — **~ Trade and Business Tax**

Income from trade or business (Gewerbebetrieb) is subject to an additional federal tax based on business income (Gewerbesteuer). A trade or business is defined as a continuous and profit-oriented activity through which the taxpayer participates in the general commerce (→ Gewerbebetrieb; → Einkommensteuer).

While the Gewerbesteuergesetz is federal law, it is levied by local authorities at different local rates (Hebesätze).

The Gewerbesteuer is deductible from individual or corporate income. The average Gewerbesteuer burden in the Federal Republic represents approximately 15% of trade or business income.

Income from real property derived by individual taxpayers generally represents "rental income" (Einkünfte aus → Vermietung und Verpachtung), one of the

Gewerkschaften / Unions

seven income categories defined in the Income Tax Act. Rental income of an individual taxpayer, or of a corporate entity that has solely holding functions, will generally not be subject to the Gewerbesteuer; (→ Einkommensteuer). If, however, the nature of the real estate activity assumes the characteristics of a commercial business, the income will be viewed as trade or business income, with two adverse consequences: All capital gains (→ Veräußerungsgewinn) will become taxable. All income may become exposed to Gewerbesteuer.

In den USA gibt es weder auf Bundesebene noch, soweit ersichtlich, auf Landes- oder Gemeindeebene eine der deutschen Gewerbesteuer vergleichbare Steuer.

Gewerblicher Grundstückshändler　　　　　　Property Dealer

In Germany, long-term capital gains (→ Veräußerungsgewinn) of individual taxpayers from the sale of non-trade-or-business assets are tax free. Capital gains of property dealers are taxable (→ Gewerbebetrieb).

The tax exemption of capital gains seems to erode steadily. Fiscal authorities increasingly consider property sales a trade or business activity (3-strike rule → Gewerbebetrieb). Also, the holding period required for real estate will be extended from two years to five years, possibly ten years.

In den USA unterliegen alle → Veräußerungsgewinne (capital gains) der Einkommensteuer, wobei für long-term capital gains natürlicher Personen ein begünstigter Steuersatz von 20% Anwendung findet, Sec. 1(h) IRC (→ Veräußerungsgewinn). Veräußerungsgewinne aus dem Inventar eines property dealers werden nicht als capital gains besteuert, sondern als gewöhnliches Einkommen (ordinary income). Ob gewerblicher Grundstückshandel vorliegt, wird nach ähnlichen Kriterien wie in Deutschland entschieden, z. B. Häufigkeit von Verkaufstransaktionen und Art des Betriebs.

Gewerkschaften　　　　　　Unions

In Germany, union contracts (Tarifverträge) are usually concluded regionally or superregionally for an entire industry (steel, or automobile, or banking, etc). All employees in the particular industry are beneficiaries of the contract. Tarifverträge may not expressly exclude non-union members from the benefits. However, they only become entitled to those benefits after the contract has been declared „generally applicable" („allgemeinverbindlich") by the Federal Secretary of Labor (Bundesminister für Arbeit und Sozialordnung).

Gewinnerzielungsabsicht / ~ Profit Motivation

Because of the varying recessionary pressures of different companies, particularly in East Germany, a slight trend towards individual union contracts may be discernible.

In den USA gibt es Flächentarifverträge praktisch nicht, sondern Einzeltarifverträge zwischen Unternehmen und deren betriebsspezifischer Gewerkschaft. In einigen Gebieten Amerikas gibt es im übrigen zahlreiche völlig gewerkschaftsfreie Betriebe. Dies ist auch einer der Gründe für die starke Industrieansiedlung in Staaten wie North und South Carolina.

Gewinnerzielungsabsicht ~ Profit Motivation

German tax authorities apply the somewhat subjective criterion of a taxpayer's profit motivation as a yardstick to allow or disallow tax losses. If the tax authority, after examination of the structure and financing of an investment and considering all relevant factors, concludes that the sole or primary objective of the taxpayer is tax avoidance, and if the likelihood of an economic profit is remote, the losses may be disallowed. If total rental and other taxable income over the life of a partnership exceed total expenses (interest, depreciation, etc.), a profit motivation will be assumed to have existed.

Tax shelter companies (Verlustzuweisungsgesellschaften) are presumed to have no profit motivation. A Verlustzuweisungsgesellschaft is defined as a company with limited partners whose equity contributions are largely financed through tax losses.

The profit motivation requirement does not exist under U.S. tax law, except in the context of hobby losses, such as a weekend farming activity. Since all capital gains are taxable in the U.S., taxpayers cannot permanently avoid tax. Tax shelters in the U.S. can only defer tax because depreciation will be fully recaptured at the time of sale or liquidation. In other words, a U.S. taxpayer would not knowingly accept a true economic loss only to gain the benefit of tax deferral. By contrast, in Germany, individuals can sell properties free of any gains tax.

Under BdF-Schreiben, BStBl. I, 434, the presumption of lacking profit motivation does not apply in the case of real estate partnerships whose income is of the „trade or business" type (gewerblich), because their capital gains are not tax free.

Im amerikanischen Steuergesetzbuch gibt es zwar zahlreiche Vorschriften, in denen die Abzugsfähigkeit bestimmter Verluste verneint wird, wenn ein Steuervorteil (tax avoidance) das vorrangige Ziel des Steuerzahlers ist. Jedoch gibt es keinen allgemeinen Grundsatz, demzufolge die

Finanzbehörde bei fehlendem Nachweis einer kommerziellen Gewinnmöglichkeit den → Verlustausgleich verbietet. Eine Ausnahme gilt für Liebhaberei („hobby losses"), beispielsweise für Wochenend-Farmer. Eine etwa fehlende Gewinnmöglichkeit bei Verlustzuweisungsgesellschaften hindert den Verlustabzug in den USA deshalb nicht, weil es mit wenigen Ausnahmen (→ Übertragung stiller Reserven; → Tausch) keine steuerfreien → Veräußerungsgewinne gibt, auch nicht im Privatvermögen. Das bedeutet, daß bei der Liquidation eines abgeschriebenen Investments meist ein steuerlicher Buchgewinn entsteht. Es ist daher für amerikanische Steuerzahler in fast allen Fällen wirtschaftlich unsinnig, für das ausschließliche Ziel der Steuerstundung einen endgültigen Kapitalverlust in Kauf zu nehmen.

Gewinnvorab — Preferred Return

The German Gewinnvorab is the equivalent of the preferred return, both for civil law and tax purposes.

Der amerikanische preferred return entspricht weitgehend dem deutschen Gewinnvorab, sowohl gesellschaftsrechtlich als auch steuerlich. Er ist zu unterscheiden vom „guaranteed payment". Die Zahlung des letzteren wird in der betreffenden Abrechnungsperiode geschuldet, auch wenn nicht genügend Liquidität vorhanden ist.

Gewohnheitsrecht — Custom / Usage

Gewöhnlicher Aufenthalt — ~ Usual Abode
(→ Beschränkt Steuerpflichtige)

Gläubigeranfechtung (→ Konkursanfechtung) — Voidance

Gläubigerbenachteiligung — Preferential Transfer / Fraudulent Conveyance

(→ Konkursanfechtung)

Gratisaktien (→ Freianteile)

Grenzmauer — Party Wall

Grundbuch / Rec. of Deeds; County Recorder; Reg. of Deeds

Grundbuch

**Recorder of Deeds
County Recorder
Register of Deeds**

Recording in the German Grundbuch has more than declaratory and evidence purposes. It constitutes the very act, and is an essential condition, of the passing of title (→ Eigentumsübergang) or other property interests, § 873 BGB. However, the most important difference between the German Grundbuch and the American Deed Registry is the following: An entry in the Grundbuch constitutes an irrefutable presumption that the recorded interest validly exists, at least vis a vis a bona fide purchaser (→ Öffentlicher Glaube des Grundbuchs), §§ 892, 893 BGB. A bona fide purchaser (→ Guter Glaube) may rely not only on the nonexistence of unrecorded interests (negative Publizität). He may also rely on the correctness of an existing entry. This is why title insurance in Germany is not necessary and does not exist.

Das amerikanische Grundbuch hat keinen öffentlichen Glauben. Der gutgläubige Erwerb eines in ununterbrochener Kette eingetragenen Rechts kann durch den Nachweis der Unrichtigkeit des Grundbuchs zunichte gemacht werden. Käufer bzw. Hypothekengeber lassen sich daher regelmäßig die Richtigkeit des Grundbuchs durch Abschluß einer Versicherung (title insurance) gegen Einmalprämie versichern. (Zu den Kosten → Öffentlicher Glaube)

Das amerikanische Grundbuch wird nicht von einem Gericht geführt, sondern von der zuständigen Behörde des jeweiligen Landkreises (county clerks' office, county recorder, registrar of deeds). Es hat folgende rechtliche Bedeutung:

a) Wird eine Verfügung nicht eingetragen, so ist ein späterer Käufer oder Hypothekengeber geschützt, sofern er gutgläubig ist, d. h. von der früheren Verfügung tatsächlich nichts wußte (negative Publizität), und auch nicht von einer möglichen Inbesitznahme des Vorerwerbers Kenntnis erlangen konnte (→ Guter Glaube). In manchen Staaten ist darüber hinaus erforderlich, daß der gutgläubige Erwerber sein Recht einträgt, bevor die vorhergegangene anderweitige Verfügung eingetragen wird.

b) Es gilt das Prinzip der fiktiven Kenntnis („constructive notice") der Eintragung gegen jedermann, d. h. niemand kann sich darauf berufen, er habe eine bestehende Eintragung nicht gekannt.

Grunddienstbarkeit / Easement

Grundbuchberichtigung ~ **Correction of Deed Registry**

Under § 894 BGB, a party may request the consent of another party to correct a false entry in the Grundbuch. The right to request correction (Grundbuchberichtigungsanspruch) is a quasi property interest not subject to the statute of limitations, § 898 BGB.

Pursuant to § 22 GBO the German Deed Registry may also be corrected ex parte if the person requesting correction can substantiate the inaccuracy of an entry through public documents (notarized documents or court orders).

Auch in den USA gibt es den Grundbuchberichtigungsanspruch. In manchen Staaten der USA ist das Erfordernis der Grundbuchberichtigung häufiger als man erwartet. Das Verfahren kann langwierig und aufwendig sein, insbesondere, wenn der Nachweis der falsch eingetragenen Voreigentümerschaft erbracht werden muß. Unter Umständen müssen Detektivbüros beschäftigt werden, um Voreigentümer oder deren Rechtsnachfolger zu finden.

Grundbucheinsicht ~ **Deed Registry Review**

A person who requests inspection of the German Grundbuch, must show a plausible interest (berechtigtes Interesse).

Die Einsicht in das amerikanische Grundbuch (register of deeds) steht jedermann zu. Das Vorbringen eines berechtigten Interesses ist im Gegensatz zum deutschen Recht nicht erforderlich.

Grundbucheintragung **Recording**

Grunddienstbarkeit **Easement**

Like U.S. law, German law distinguishes between the easement appurtenant, § 1018 ff BGB, and the easement in gross (beschränkt persönliche Dienstbarkeit), § 1090 ff BGB. The first gives the owner of the dominant tenement (das herrschende Grundstück) certain rights over a neighbouring property (das belastete Grundstück), such as a right of way or a right to enjoin the owner of the servient tenement from certain activities. By contrast, the beschränkt persönliche Dienstbarkeit does not run with the land but is owned by a person, not necessarily the owner of a dominant tenement.

Wie das deutsche Recht kennt das amerikanische Recht die Dienstbar-

Grunderwerbsteuer / Real Property Transfer Tax

keit in ihrer gewöhnlichen Form und der der beschränkt persönlichen Dienstbarkeit (easement in gross). Die gewöhnliche Dienstbarkeit gibt dem Eigentümer eines Grundstücks (dominant tenement) gewisse Nutzungsrechte an belasteten Nachbargrundstücken (servient tenement), häufig z. B. ein Wegerecht (right of way) oder einen Anspruch auf Unterlassung bestimmter Handlungen auf dem Nachbargrundstück. Beim easement in gross muß der Berechtigte nicht notwendigerweise Eigentümer eines benachbarten Grundstücks sein.

Grunderwerbsteuer   Real Property Transfer Tax

The Grunderwerbssteuer is regulated through federal German law. The tax rate was lowered from 7% to 2% of the purchase price in the early 79ties. As of 1997, the rate has been increased to 3.5% of the consideration paid for real property. If the amount of consideration cannot be determined, the tax is applied to the assessed value of the property (→ Einheitswert). Customarily, the purchaser pays the Grunderwerbsteuer. The statute, however, makes both parties jointly and severally liable for the tax.

The taxable event in Germany occurs already at the execution of the purchase agreement, not only at the closing or recording, § 1(1) GrEStG. Similarly, the assignment of a purchase agreement triggers the transfer tax.

Grunderwerbsteuer is due also when all shares of a real property holding corporation are transferred. In such case, the tax basis generally is the value of the underlying real property and not the consideration for the shares. The tax can be, and frequently is, avoided by having the new owner acquire all but a nominal number of shares, § 1(3) GrEStG.

Under new § 1(2a) GrEStG, the transfer, other than through inheritance, of all or most (always when 95% or more) of the shares of a partnership within any five-year period will also trigger property transfer tax to the extent of the partnership's real property assets. No tax is generally due in tax-free reorganizations (→ Umwandlung).

In den USA werden Grunderwerbssteuern von den meisten Einzelstaaten, Bezirken und Gemeinden erhoben. Im Landesdurchschnitt dürften sie bei etwa 2% des Kaufpreises liegen. Einige wenige Staaten kennen keine Grunderwerbsteuer.

In den meisten Einzelstaaten fällt die Steuer erst bei Auflassung und Eintragung an, und nicht schon bei Abschluß oder Abtretung des Kaufvertrages.

Grundschuld / ~ Non-accessory Mortgage

In manchen Einzelstaaten, z. B. New York gibt es auch eine mortgage recording tax, die in Höhe und Art der real property transfer tax entspricht. Um diese Kosten zu umgehen, verzichten Hypothekengläubiger in Ausnahmefällen auf die Eintragung und erhalten vom Schuldner eine vertragliche Zusage, keine anderen Belastungen eintragen zu lassen („negative pledge"; → Verbot der weiteren Belastung). Natürlich stellt der negative pledge nur eine unvollkommene Sicherheit dar.

Grundförderung ~ Depreciation of Taxpayer's Home

Home ownership in Germany is not similarly tax-incentivized as in the U.S. For example, German tax law does not have the general deductibility of the taxpayer's home mortgage interest. Also, German taxpayers could previously deduct 5% p. a. of the cost of their own home, but not more than DM 15,000 p. a. as a special deduction (Sonderausgaben), pursuant to Sec. 10e EstG. This deduction has recently been curtailed to homes built or acquired before 1996.

Das amerikanische Einkommensteuerrecht begünstigt das eigengenutzte Wohnungseigentum durch die Möglichkeit der Abschreibung nicht. Jedoch ist das US-Einkommensteuerrecht im Gegensatz zum deutschen Steuerrecht großzügig bei der Abzugsfähigkeit von Schuldzinsen für das selbstgenutzte Haus- und Wohnungseigentum (→ Hypothekenzinsen für Eigenheim).

Grundschuld ~ Non-accessory Mortgage

A frequently used form of the real property lien in Germany is the Grundschuld, § 1191 BGB. The Grundschuld, unlike the mortgage (→ Hypothek) is not dependent upon the existence of a valid underlying claim. The Grundschuld is an abstract promise by the owner of a property to pay a sum certain „out of the property". The term „out of the property" does not mean that the Grundschuld is non-recourse (→ Objekthaftung) but that the property secures payment of a certain sum irrespective of the existence or validity of any underlying claim.

German bank lenders prefer the Grundschuld over the mortgage because it can be transferred or liquidated irrespective of the underlying claim and irrespective of whether the underlying claim belongs to a third party or whether the claim is subject to defenses by the debtor.

Im amerikanischen Recht gibt es die Grundschuld nicht, sondern nur die Hypothek (mortgage), deren Wirksamkeit vom Bestehen einer Forderung abhängt. Es gibt aber auch in Amerika den verkehrsfähigen Hy-

Grundsteuer / Real Property Tax

pothekenbrief (negotiable mortgage note), der es einem gutgläubigen Erwerber ermöglicht, nicht nur eine einredebehaftete Forderung durchzusetzen, sondern auch die Hypothek gegen den Grundstückseigentümer durchzusetzen, selbst wenn dieser gültige Einreden hat. Nur wenige Einzelstaaten verbieten die Zwangsvollstreckung einer einredebehafteten Forderung gegen das Grundstück und beschränken den Gläubiger auf die persönliche Verfolgung des Schuldners. In jedem Fall ist es ratsam, bei Erwerb der mortgage note das Anerkenntnis des Grundstückseigentümers einzuholen, daß die Hypothekenforderung wirksam und einredefrei besteht.

Grundsteuer **Real Property Tax**

The German Grundsteuergesetz is a federal tax act authorizing municipalities to collect real property tax. The tax is based on the low assessed value (→ Einheitswert). The applicable tax rate depends on the class of property (agricultural, apartments, homes, commercial properties) and varies between 0.26% and 0.6%. Each municipality will apply its own multiplier (Hebesatz) to the real property tax base (Grundsteuermeßbetrag). The multipliers are anywhere between 130% and 400%. Thus the actual tax burden depends both on the property class and the municipality in which the property is situated. The overall tax burden varies between 0.5% and 1.5% of the Einheitswerte, i. e. between 0.1% and 0.5% of fair market values. The Grundsteuer for income producing properties is deductible from income, § 9(1)No. 2 EStG. It is not deductible for the taxpayer's own residence.

In den USA werden real property taxes meist von verschiedenen lokalen Behörden bzw. Körperschaften erhoben, regelmäßig von der Gemeinde und dem School District, manchmal auch von der County oder von öffentlichen Versorgungsbetrieben. Bemessungsgrundlage ist das real property assessment (→ Einheitswert). Die real property tax stellt eine deutlich höhere Belastung als die deutsche Grundsteuer dar, da sie eine wesentliche Einnahmequelle der Gemeinden und Bezirke (Counties) ist. Sie dürfte im Landesdurchschnitt annähernd zehnmal so hoch sein wie deutsche Grundsteuern. Mit der real property tax werden in erster Linie die Schulen, die Polizei, öffentliche Krankenhäuser und örtliche Straßen finanziert. Da hohe Grundstückspreise Mehreinnahmen für den betreffenden School District bedeuten, oder umgekehrt gute Schulen die Grundstückspreise innerhalb des School District nach oben treiben, ist heute überall erkennbar, daß die Besserverdienenden ihre Kinder in bessere öffentliche Schulen schicken können als die ärmeren Bevölkerungs-

Grundstückskauf / Purchase of Property

schichten. Mit diesem Problem befassen sich zunehmend die Verfassungsgerichte der Einzelstaaten.

Auch in den USA haftet neben dem Eigentümer das Grundstück selbst für die Steuer. Unbezahlte real property tax begründet automatisch eine erstrangige Hypothek. Aus diesem Grunde verlangen Hypothekengeber häufig, daß der Kreditnehmer in seinen Schuldendienst auch die Grundsteuer einschließt, die bei dem Hypothekengeber in einem Anderkonto (tax escrow) hinterlegt wird.

Im Gegensatz zum deutschen Steuerrecht ist in den USA auch die für das Eigenheim gezahlte Grundsteuer vom Einkommen abzugsfähig, Sec. 164 IRC.

Grundstücksgrenzen   Boundaries (Bounds; Property Lines)

In Germany, all land is surveyed and registered in cadastral maps by the Cadastral Office (Katasteramt). The exact metes and bounds of a lot cannot be found in the deed registry (→ Grundbuch), but in the books of the Katasteramt.

In den USA obliegt die → Vermessung nicht einer Behörde, sondern öffentlich beglaubigten Landvermessern (surveyors). Der genaue Verlauf der Grundstücksgrenzen ist in der Regel Teil oder Anhang des eingetragenen Grundeigentumsbriefs (deed).

Grundstückskauf   Purchase of Property

In Germany, execution of the purchase agreement and closing (→ Auflassung) usually take place in the same notarial meeting (→ Notar; → Notarielle Beurkundung). The purchase price will generally be paid or disbursed to seller already before the actual closing, i. e. upon the recording of a priority notice (Auflassungsvormerkung; → Vormerkung).

In den USA liegen zwischen Abschluß des Kaufvertrags und Auflassung (Closing) dagegen regelmäßig mehrere Wochen oder gar Monate (Vollzugszeitpunkt). Der Käufer überprüft in diesem Zeitraum, ob → zugesicherte Eigenschaften (representations and warranties) tatsächlich bestehen und keine Sach- oder Rechtsmängel vorliegen. Bei Kaufabschluß zahlt der Käufer regelmäßig einen Teil des Kaufpreises an (downpayment). Die Anzahlung gilt bei schuldhaftem Verzug des Käufers als → Vertragsstrafe (liquidated damages) und verfällt. Darüber hinausgehende Ansprüche hat der Verkäufer in der Regel nicht. Wie hoch die Anzah-

Grundstücksverkehrsgesetz / ~ Sales of Agricultural or Forest Land

lung sein muß, und wie lange der Käufer das Grundstück danach inspizieren kann, hängt in erster Linie von den jeweiligen Marktbedingungen ab. In einem schwachen Immobilienmarkt räumen die Verkäufer Interessenten gegen minimale Anzahlungen (ca. 1%) lange Fristen ein, um das Objekt zu überprüfen und die Finanzierung zu organisieren. In den Boomzeiten der frühen achtziger Jahre waren dagegen Anzahlungen von 10% des Kaufpreises die Regel.

Durch den schwächeren Markt der vergangenen Jahre, und vielleicht auch durch die wichtiger gewordene Überprüfung von Altlasten (die Erstellung von Environmental Reports beträgt oft 2 Monate) wird dem Käufer immer häufiger auch eine unverbindliche Inspektionszeit eingeräumt, innerhalb derer er ohne Angabe von Gründen zurücktreten und seine Anzahlung („earnest money") zurückverlangen kann.

Im Gegensatz zur deutschen Grundbucheintragung, die manchmal erst Wochen nach der Auflassung erfolgt, findet das recording in der Regel innerhalb eines oder weniger Tage nach dem closing statt.

Grundstücksverkehrsgesetz   ~ Sales of Agricultural or Forest Land

Sales of any German agricultural or forest lands to German or foreign buyers require government approval pursuant to § 1 of the Property Transfer Act (Grundstücksverkehrsgesetz). A sale under the Act is also deemed to occur upon the transfer of an undivided interest in such lands, or of a fractional interest, a usufruct (→ Nießbrauch under § 1030 BGB) or of an inheritance share (Erbteil).

Approval may be withheld, or granted under conditions, if the proposed transaction will result in an unsound distribution of lands, or if the purchase price is unreasonable in light of the market value of the property. The overriding goal of the Act is the preservation of agricultural and forest lands.

The conditions under which the approval will usually be granted include the subsequent leasing of the property to an active farmer, the entering into a management agreement with the agricultural or forest authority, or the management by the new owner pursuant to an approved business plan. Another condition may sometimes be that the acquirer surrenders an equivalent piece of farm or forest land.

Soweit ersichtlich gibt es in den USA weder auf Bundes- noch auf Landesebene ein vergleichbares Gesetz zum Schutz landwirtschaftlicher Flächen. Dies ist vielleicht auf die Größe der vorhandenen Gesamtfläche und die mangelnde Sorge um ernährungswirtschaftliche Autarkie zurückzuführen. Es gibt jedoch in einigen Einzelstaaten Beschränkungen beim Erwerb landwirtschaftlicher Flächen durch US-Ausländer (→ ausländische Immobilieninvestoren).

Grundstücksverwaltung — Property Management

It can generally be said that property management in Germany costs slightly less than in the U.S. This may partly be due to a lesser fluctuation of tenants or owners of properties. Property management in Germany will typically cost about 3% of gross rental income.

Also, the concept of asset management in real property has not become appreciated in Germany. This may gradually change with increasing diversity of portfolios and faster turnover in the market place.

Im allgemeinen läßt sich sagen, daß U.S. Immobilien mit etwas höheren Verwaltungsgebühren belastet sind als vergleichbare deutsche Objekte, unter anderem für die Objektverwaltung, die Bauleitung bzw. Überwachung von Innenausbauten, Vermietungskommissionen, Finanzierungskommissionen, und unter Umständen für allgemeine Beratungsdienstleistungen (asset management). Gründe hierfür sind sicherlich der im Vergleich zu Deutschland häufigere Mieterwechsel, das auf Grund relativ liberaler Baugesetze schnellere Entstehen konkurrierender Objekte und der damit verbundene Wettbewerb um Mieter, sowie der annähernd dreimal so häufige Eigentümerwechsel bei amerikanischen Immobilien.

Vom property management in den USA ist das asset management zu unterscheiden. Dieses wird institutionellen Immobilieninvestoren oder anderen Investoren mit relativ umfangreichem U.S. Immobilienbesitz angeboten. Dabei handelt es sich um die Beratung bei Fragen der weiteren Entwicklung und langfristigen strategischen Ausrichtung einzelner Objekte, der Vermietung, Finanzierung und des Verkaufs, sowie der Auswahl oder Überwachung des Objektverwalters (property managers). Der Asset Manager erhält typischerweise zwischen 0,5% und 1,25% p. a. des Kaufpreises oder Verkehrswerts der Immobilien. Mitunter verhandelt er auch eine „Incentive Fee", d. h. eine Beteiligung an der Wertsteigerung des Objekts bzw. Portfolios.

Guter Glaube — Bona Fide; Good Faith

A purchaser or mortgage lender in Germany may rely not only on the non-existence of an unrecorded property interest (negative Publizität), but also on the valid

Hafteinlage (→ Kapitaleinlage)

existence of all recorded interests, § 892 BGB. However, if the acquiror positively knows that an entry is incorrect he cannot claim the protection of § 892 BGB.

Im Gegensatz zum deutschen Grundbuch kann sich der gutgläubige amerikanische Käufer oder Hypothekengläubiger nicht auf die Richtigkeit einer bestehenden Eintragung verlassen. Er kann sich auf die Richtigkeit der deed registry nur insoweit verlassen, als etwaige frühere Verfügungen nicht eingetragen sind (negative Publizität; → Grundbuch). Sein guter Glaube schützt ihn jedoch auch dann nicht, wenn die tatsächlichen Besitzverhältnisse keinen Zweifel aufkommen lassen dürften. Ist beispielsweise ein vorhergegangener Verkauf oder ein Nutzungsrecht nicht eingetragen worden, der Käufer oder Nutzungsberechtigte jedoch erkennbar im Besitz des Grundstücks, so gilt der Grundsatz der fiktiven Kenntnis (constructive notice) des späteren Erwerbers, da dieser sich jederzeit über die tatsächlichen Besitzverhältnisse hätte informieren können.

Hafteinlage (→ Kapitaleinlage)

Haftpflichtversicherung   Liability Insurance

In Germany, liability insurance is available at relatively low cost and without complications. Germany does not suffer from the excesses of liability litigation prevalent in the U.S. Legal costs of defending liability suits are comparatively modest, contingency fees for lawyers are prohibited, the losing party bears the cost of the other party, and there are no punitive or exemplary damages, or excessive awards for pain and suffering.

In den USA ist die Haftpflichtversicherung ein sehr ernst zu nehmendes Thema. Da das Zivilprozeßrecht grundsätzlich nicht verlangt, daß die unterliegende Partei die Kosten trägt, und da Anwälte außerdem auf Erfolgsbasis (Contingency Fee) bezahlt werden können, werden in den USA meist alle verklagt, die auch nur entfernt Mitverursacher eines Schadensfalls sein könnten. Besonders begehrt sind dabei naturgemäß reiche oder gut versicherte Parteien („deep pockets"). So werden Eigentümer von Gewerbeimmobilien fast regelmäßig mit verklagt, wenn Unfälle in den vermieteten Flächen entstehen. Bei Einkaufszentren sind dies die sogenannten „slip and fall" Fälle, bei Bürogebäuden das Einklemmen in Aufzugstüren und ähnliches. Die Beratung durch Spezialisten ist beim Abschluß der Haftpflichtversicherung wegen der zunehmenden Komplexität empfehlenswert.

Handelsgesetzbuch / Uniform Commercial Code

Haftungsgegenstände   **~ Mortgage attaches to...**
(für Hypothek)

Under §§ 1120, 1123, 1126 and 1127 BGB, a mortgage automatically attaches to fixtures (Bestandteile; → Wesentliche Bestandteile), appurtenant chattels (→ Zubehör), fructus (Erzeugnisse), emblements (Früchte), insurance claims and claims for rentals. Rentals are exempt from the mortgage liability only if they have been overdue for more than a year and have not previously been sequestered, § 1123(2) BGB.

Mortgages or other liens do not attach to „after-acquired property", unless the debtor already has a future interest (Anwartschaft) in the property. The parties would have to conclude and record a separate mortgage agreement for each newly acquired property.

Im Gegensatz zur deutschen Hypothek erstreckt sich die amerikanische Hypothekenhaftung im allgemeinen nur auf das unbewegliche Vermögen und Bestandteile (fixtures). Sie erstreckt sich auf Miet- und Pachtzinsforderungen nur, soweit dies ausdrücklich durch Sicherungsabtretung (assignment) vereinbart ist. Zubehör (chattels) oder Erzeugnisse (fructus; emblements) können nicht durch Hypothek belegt werden. Letzteres wird üblicherweise durch Registrierung nach dem Modell-Handelsgesetzbuch (U. C. C. Filing) abgesichert (perfecting).

Es ist möglich, durch Vertrag eine Hypothek oder ein Pfandrecht allgemein auf Gegenstände zu erstrecken, die der Schuldner erst später durch Kauf oder anderweitig erwirbt („after-acquired" clause). Vorrang der Sicherheit an den neuen Gegenständen gegenüber Dritten entsteht jedoch nur, wenn das zusätzliche Pfandrecht auch „perfected" wird, d. h. bei Grundpfandrechten durch Eintragung (recording), bei anderen Pfandrechten durch Anmeldung beim Handelsregister (U. C. C. filing) oder durch Inbesitznahme.

Handelsgesetzbuch   **Uniform Commercial Code**

Commercial law, like civil law, is federal law in Germany. It is separately codified in the Commercial Code (Handelsgesetzbuch).

In den USA ist das Handelsrecht, wie das Zivil- und Gesellschaftsrecht, Landesrecht. Es ist in den Einzelstaaten zunehmend kodifiziert, wobei meist nur geringe Abweichungen vom Uniform Commercial Code, einem Modellgesetz, bestehen.

Handelsvertreter / Sales Agent

Handelsvertreter | Sales Agent

Pursuant to Sec. 98b HGB (Commercial Code), a sales agent in Germany may request compensation after termination of his agency for customers acquired by him („Ausgleichsanspruch"). He may be entitled to commissions of up to one-year's average prior commissions (three years for insurance agents). There are several exceptions to this rule, such as termination by the agent, or by the principal for cause, or sale of the agency. According to some cases, not only agents but also distributors or dealers, (Vertragshändler) may be entitled to such post-contract compensation.

Das U.S. Recht kennt den gesetzlichen Ausgleichsanspruch des Handelsvertreters nicht. Jedoch ist die Kündigung durch den Unternehmer im prozeßfreudigen und für Kläger weitgehend risikolosen Amerika (→ Zivilprozeß) nicht unriskant. Insofern sind möglichst klare Verträge mit Handelsvertretern oder Vertriebspartnern ratsam.

Hausfriedensbruch | Trespass

Heizung (→ Umlagen) | Heating

Höchstbetragshypothek | ~ Maximum Amount Mortgage

The German Höchstbetragshypothek under § 1190 BGB secures a certain recorded maximum debt amount. The maximum includes principal and accrued interest. Similar to the more customary security mortgage (Sicherungshypothek), the validity and enforceability of the Höchstbetragshypothek depends on the size and validity of the underlying claim. Bank lenders prefer the → Grundschuld over these forms of mortgages as the Grundschuld can be enforced or transferred independent of any underlying claim.

Auch in den USA gibt es Hypotheken, bei denen ein Höchstbetrag festgelegt ist, und deren Umfang von der jeweiligen Valutierung (future advances) des Darlehens, z. B. eines Kontokorrent, abhängt. Im Gegensatz zum deutschen Recht ist die amerikanische mortgage nach dem Recht vieler Einzelstaaten trotz rechtzeitiger Eintragung jedoch nur insoweit ranghöher, als auch ihre Valutierung vor der Valutierung und Eintragung späterer Grundpfandrechte erfolgt.

Ausnahmsweise erwirbt und behält die amerikanische Hypothek ihre Rangstelle in voller nomineller Höhe, wenn der Gläubiger vertraglich unwiderruflich verpflichtet ist, das Darlehen in voller Höhe zu valutieren (obligatory advances). Valutiert der Gläubiger freiwillig weiter, gehen zwischenzeitlich entstandene Grundpfandrechte im Rang vor, zumindest wenn er von dem späteren Grundpfandrecht aktuelle Kenntnis erworben hat.

Einige Staaten haben die Unterscheidung zwischen obligatory und optional advances gesetzlich aufgehoben. Sie geben der zuerst eingetragenen Höchstbetragshypothek Vorrang, auch soweit sie freiwillig valutiert wird.

Höhere Gewalt   **Acts of God**
                                                    Force Majeure

Hotelpacht   **Hotel Management**
(Hotelbetreibervertrag)   **Agreement**

In the prevailing arrangement, hotel management companies („Hotelpächter"; „Hotelbetreiber") enter into long-term (20 years plus) leases and pay flat or indexed rentals, plus a small override. Thus, they keep the lions share of the downside and upside potential during the lease term.

Üblicherweise gehen Hotelbetreiber in den USA kein großes finanzielles Risiko ein. Sie zahlen in aller Regel keine wesentlichen Festpachten, sondern verwalten Hotels als bezahlte Manager, die durch Umsatz- oder Gewinnbonus erfolgsbeteiligt sind.

Hybride Gesellschaftsformen   **Hybrid Entities**

The German KGaA is a corporation which is managed by a personally liable partner. It is taxed as a corporation. However, all profit and bonus payments to the managing partner are deductible and directly attributed to him, except for commercial trade tax purposes (→ Gewerbesteuer) and except to the extent they represent dividends on such partner's capital contribution. The managing partner's capital is treated as a business asset („Betriebsvermögen"). This has advantages for estate and gift tax purposes (lower assessment), but the disadvantage that the managing partner's share, unlike regular corporate shares, cannot be sold tax free (→ Veräußerungsgewinn).

The KGaA has been chosen by a number of large and medium-sized companies who want to combine the tax advantages of the partnership with access to the public securities markets and continuing management control by the founding family, i. e. avoidance of some of the elaborate provisions of the Stock Corporation Act („Aktiengesetz"). Under new case law, not only individuals, but also corporations or

Hybride Gesellschaftsformen / Hybrid Entities

partnerships may become managing partners of a KGaA. This could make the KGaA even more attractive for family-owned companies which consider going public.

Another German specialty is the silent partnership („stille Gesellschaft"). It allows investors to participate in a business without being registered as co-owners. The „atypical" silent partner participates both in current profits and goodwill and is treated, for tax purposes, as a limited partner of a corporate or partnership business. The „typical" silent partner does not own any of the goodwill. His investment really is hybrid debt, similar to a participating loan. Under some tax treaties, the typical silent partnership can be a smart structure since payments to the partner may be deductible in one country, but dividends in the other.

German law has also introduced the „Partnerschaftsgesellschaft", which is similar to the LLP in the U.S.

Eine in den meisten Einzelstaaten der USA unterdessen eingeführte Alternative zur limited partnership (KG) ist die limited liability company (LLC). Sie kombiniert die volle Haftungsbeschränkung auch für geschäftsführende Komplementäre („managing members") mit der transparenten Besteuerung der partnership. Es fehlt gegenwärtig immer noch eine klare Stellungnahme der deutschen Finanzverwaltung, ob die LLC in Deutschland als U.S.-corporation oder -partnership angesehen wird. Angesichts dieser steuerlichen Unsicherheit kann man die LLC in manchen Fällen noch nicht empfehlen.

Nach den 1996 veröffentlichten „check-the box" Richtlinien können nunmehr amerikanische und ausländische Gesellschaften frei entscheiden, ob sie in den USA als Kapital- oder Personengesellschaft besteuert werden wollen. Gesellschaften, die eindeutig Kapitalgesellschaften sind, z. B. U.S.-corporations, deutsche AGs oder GmbHs oder französische S. A. s, haben dieses Wahlrecht nicht. Personengesellschaften, aber wohl auch die KGaA, haben das Wahlrecht. Die Verordnung, anscheinend das Werk einiger junger von zuviel Erfahrung unbelasteter Steuerjuristen des Bundesfinanzministeriums, wirft ungezählte Fragen. Die Lücken und Qualifikationskonflikte, die sich dadurch bei grenzüberschreitenden Steuerfragen auftun könnten, werden den Steueranwälten noch einige Arbeit bescheren.

Einige Einzelstaaten haben auch die limited liability partnership eingeführt, die es Freiberuflern ermöglicht, wie bei der deutschen Partnerschaftsgesellschaft ihre Haftung auf solche für eigene Handlungen, insbesondere Kunstfehler, zu beschränken.

Hypothek / Mortgage

Hypothek   **Mortgage**

The customary form of mortgage in Germany is the negotiable mortgage (→ Verkehrshypothek, Briefhypothek) which provides a certain protection to a bona fide purchaser (→ Guter Glaube) from having the mortgage invalidated by defenses which may exist against the underlying claim, § 1138 BGB. This does not mean that the purchaser of the negotiable mortgage note may rely upon the existence of the claim. Rather, the holder in due course (gutgläubiger Käufer) of the mortgage note may foreclose against the property even if the debtor of the underlying claim (Forderung) has valid defenses. The mortgagor has no defense against the foreclosing bona fide mortgagee, § 1147 BGB. But the law creates a presumption for the existence of the mortgage claim which the owner of the property must disprove.

German law also has the Sicherungshypothek of § 1184 BGB. It is largely the equivalent of the American mortgage because its creation, transferral and validity depend on the existence of a valid underlying claim (principle of the accessory mortgage; Akzessorietät). A bona fide purchaser cannot acquire a Sicherungshypothek which is recorded, but which lacks a valid underlying claim, § 1185 BGB.

Die amerikanische Hypothek ähnelt dem Grundsatz nach der deutschen Sicherungshypothek. D. h. unter anderem, daß auch in den USA der Grundsatz der Akzessorietät gilt: Entstehung, Übertragung und Bestand der Hypothek hängt vom Bestehen einer zugrundeliegenden Forderung ab. Die Brief- bzw. → Verkehrshypothek, bei der ein gutgläubiger Erwerber sich auf die Eintragung verlassen kann, gibt es unterdessen jedoch auch in den meisten Einzelstaaten der USA. Dies bedeutet nicht, daß sich der Erwerber, wie in Deutschland, auf die Richtigkeit des → Grundbuchs verlassen kann. → Öffentlichen Glauben hat das amerikanische Grundbuch nicht. Es bedeutet nur, daß der gutgläubige Käufer (holder in due course) eines verkehrsfähigen (negotiable) Hypothekenbriefs (mortgage note) die Zwangsvollstreckung gegen das Grundstück betreiben kann, auch wenn der Schuldner Einreden gegen die zugrundeliegende Forderung hat.

Die deutsche Grundschuld, bei der die zugrundeliegende Forderung und das Sicherungsrecht theoretisch getrennt voneinander übertragen werden können, gibt es in Amerika dagegen nicht.

In einigen Einzelstaaten wird die Hypothek üblicherweise in der Form der Deed of Trust gegeben, einer Art von Sicherungsübereignung. Im Gegensatz zur gewöhnlichen Hypothek ist die Deed of Trust meist mit

Hypothekenbank / ~ Mortgage Bank

einer vollstreckbaren Urkunde gekoppelt (power of sale). Ansonsten ist sie im wesentlichen der Hypothek gleich.

Hypothekenbank   ~ Mortgage Bank

German banking law distinguishes between commercial banks and mortgage banks. The latter are established under the Mortgage Banking Act (Hypothekenbankgesetz). Unlike mortgage bankers in the U.S., German Hypothekenbanken are long-term lenders. They are authorized to refinance their loan portfolio consisting of mortgages and municipal loans (Kommunaldarlehen) through the issuance of mortgage-backed securities (→ Pfandbrief) and municipal bonds (→ Kommunalobligationen). It is important to note that the bonds are backed not only by the mortgage and loan pool, but also by the capital of the issuing bank itself.

Mortgage banks require a significantly smaller statutory equity capital than commercial banks because of the conservative lending limits the Mortgage Banking Act imposes. For example, a mortgage loan may not exceed a loan-to-value ratio of 60%.

Only about 25 mortgage banks have been chartered in Germany. Almost all of them are subsidiaries of, or controlled by, the major German commercial banks. The statutory loan-to-value lending limit is sometimes bypassed by the parent banks which can provide additional financing, junior or unsecured, to the same project.

In den USA gibt es keine Hypothekenbanken im deutschen Sinne. Auch die deutsche Form des Pfandbriefes gibt es in Amerika nicht. Der amerikanische mortgage-backed bond wird nicht durch die ausgebende Bank besichert, sondern ausschließlich durch den mortgage pool und bei Wohnimmobilien darüber hinaus häufig durch Garantien eigens dafür errichteter Bundesbehörden bzw. Anstalten. Mit dem Beginn der Immobilienkrise der frühen 90er Jahren entwickelten sich „Commercial Mortgage Backed Securities" (CMBS) zunehmend zu einem begehrten Finanzierungsinstrument, eine zinsgünstige Alternative zur gewöhnlichen Hypothek (→ Pfandbrief).

Unter dem Begriff mortgage banker versteht man in den USA Unternehmen, die meist lokal oder regional Baudarlehen oder Überbrückungskredite geben, im wesentlichen aber als Vermittler für langfristige Hpothekenkredite auftreten.

Immobilienholding / Real Property Holding Corporation

Hypothekenzinsen für Eigenheim   **Home Mortgage Interest**

Principally, home mortgage interest is not deductible from income in Germany.

Im Gegensatz zum deutschen Steuerrecht ermöglicht das amerikanische Einkommensteuerrecht in Sec. 163(h) IRC die volle Abzugsfähigkeit der Hypothekenzinsen für die selbstgenutzte Wohnung bzw. das Eigenheim („qualified residence"), soweit die betreffende Hypothek nicht höher als $ 1 Million ist. Abzugsfähig sind dabei nur die Schuldzinsen, die im Zusammenhang mit der Anschaffung oder baulichen Verbesserung der Hauptwohnung („principal residence") und eines weiteren Eigenheims stehen. Zinsen für eine nach der Anschaffung aufgenommene zusätzliche Hypothek (home equity loan) sind abzugsfähig, soweit der aufgenommene Kapitalbetrag $ 100 000 nicht übersteigt, und die gesamten Belastungen den Verkehrswert der Immobilie(n) nicht übersteigen.

Ideeller Anteil   **Undivided Interest**

Immaterielle Wirtschaftsgüter   **Intangibles**
(→ Firmenwert)

Immissionen   **~ Nuisance**

Immobilienfonds   **Real Estate Investment Fund**
(→ Kapitalanlagegesellschaft)

Immobilienholding   **Real Property Holding Corporation**

Individual taxpayers in Germany hardly ever hold real property through corporate entities. Not because they need to avoid the double taxation of income, which has been abolished through the Corporate Income Tax Reform Act of 1977 (→Körperschaftsteuer). Rather, corporations do not enjoy the privilege of tax-free long term capital gains (→ Veräußerungsgewinn). This may, however, slowly change.

Unlike the U.S. real property holding corporation of FIRPTA Code Section 897, shares in a German Immobilienholding are not considered real property, except for purposes of property transfer tax if 100% of the shares are sold (→ Grunderwerbsteuer). Thus, foreign shareholders can sell shares of German property corporations without paying capital gains tax in Germany. However, if these shareholders hold substantial participations (Wesentliche Beteiligung) they may be subject to

Immobilienrecht / Real Property Law

German gains tax. Arguably, in such case, the U.S.-German Income Tax Treaty will not provide protection from German tax (→ Veräußerungsgewinn).

In den USA werden → Veräußerungsgewinne von Kapitalgesellschaften zu gewöhnlichen Steuersätzen besteuert, während long-term capital gains natürlicher Personen einem reduzierten Steuersatz von 20% unterliegen. Im übrigen gilt in den USA noch immer das Prinzip der Doppelbesteuerung von Gewinnen auf Gesellschafts- und Gesellschafterebene (→ Einkommensteuer).

In den USA gelten Kapitalgesellschaften, deren Vermögen zu mehr als 50% aus amerikanischen Immobilien besteht („U.S. real property holding corporations"), nach Sec. 897(c)(2) als U.S. Immobilien. Ihr Verkauf gilt als steuerpflichtiger Immobilienverkauf. Die betreffende amerikanische Gesetzgebung, die als „FIRPTA" (Foreign Investment in Real Property Tax Act) bekannt ist, geht seit 1985 auch entgegenstehenden DBA Bestimmungen vor.

Auch in den USA gilt die Regel, daß die Veräußerung von Anteilen an nicht-körperschaftlich organisierten Immobiliengesellschaften, z. B. Personengesellschaften, dem Belegenheitsstaat der Immobilien unterliegt, Revenue Ruling 91–32. Dem steht auch nicht Art. 11(3) des deutschamerikanischen Einkommensteuer-DBA's entgegen, s. Ziff. 14 des Protokolls zum DBA.

Immobilienrecht   Real Property Law

Almost all real property law in Germany is federal law, with the exception of certain State and local building code regulations (→ Bauordnung).

Das amerikanische Immobilienrecht ist Landesrecht, wobei die Unterschiede in den einzelstaatlichen Regelungen in der Regel geringfügig sind.

Immobilienpreise   Real Estate Prices

Cap rates of commercial and residential property in Germany have been historically lower than those in the U.S. and many European countries, for several reasons. Because of artificially low assessed values („Einheitswert") real estate was and to some extent still is a favored asset for estate tax planning (→ Erbschaftsteuer). Also, for individual taxpayers, long-term capital gains (→ Veräußerungsgewinn) are tax free. The more important reason may be scarcity and the proven

Insolvenz / Insolvency

long-term appreciation of property. Real estate prices are almost competitive with the performance of the German stock market over long time periods.

Property yields should gradually approach those in other European countries and get closer to those in the U.S. The above tax advantages are being reduced through legislative action. Also, the re-unification and massive privatisations of Government-owned land (Mail and Railway Systems with almost 10,000 acres of inner-city land) suddenly increase supply. Also, many investors shun the residential market because of the sweeping tenant protection and rent stabilization laws.

It seems real estate prices have historically been less volatile than those in the U.S. Among the reasons for this may the lower rate of ownership change, stricter zoning and less excessive lending, the main cause of most boom-bust cycles. Since 1994, however, prices in some German cities, including Berlin and Hamburg, have come down somewhat.

Die Ausgangsrenditen von U.S.-Immobilien bewegen sich historisch, je nach Lage des Objekts und Marktzyklus zwischen 5% und 10% oder mehr. Sie sind damit deutlich höher als es deutsche Renditen in normalen Zeiten sind. Dies liegt in erster Linie an der fast unbegrenzten Vermehrbarkeit von Immobilien und der fehlenden Gewißheit, daß Grundstücke über mehr als eine oder zwei Generationen werthaltig sind.

Immobilienpreise in den USA, auch in den größeren Städten, erscheinen historisch um einiges beweglicher als in Deutschland. Die seit der Great Depression der 30er Jahre wohl größte Immobilienkrise fand in den Jahren 1982 bis 1992 statt. Sie begann in Texas und rollte von dort über das ganze Land. Ein Preisverfall von mehr als 50% war selbst für erstklassige Objekte nicht ungewöhnlich. Der Krise ging, wie meist, ein künstlicher Boom voraus, angefacht durch die bis 1986 geltenden ungewöhnlichen Abschreibungsvorteile des Immobilieninvestments, und schließlich durch exzessive Bankfinanzierung praktisch jeden Bauvorhabens durch die unterdessen mehrheitlich pleite gegangenen Sparkassen (Savings and Loan Banks).

Industriegebiet　　　　　　　　　　　　　　　　**Industrial Zone**

Insolvenz　　　　　　　　　　　　　　　　　　　**Insolvency**
(→ Konkurs; → Vergleich)

Jagdrecht / Hunting Rights

Jagdrecht   Hunting Rights

In Germany, hunting and fishing rights run with the land. The landowner is subject to numerous restrictions under the Federal Hunting Act (Bundesjagdgesetz) and the hunting acts of individual states. For example, land below a certain minimum size (75 hectares, i. e. 185 acres) may not be hunted as a separate hunting ground (Eigenjadgbezirk). Also, the issuance of a hunting license requires a rather difficult written and practical examination. Quotas for individual game exist for each individual hunting district and the legal hunting seasons.

Soweit ersichtlich, gehört in den meisten Einzelstaaten der USA das Jagdrecht der Öffentlichkeit, wobei der Privateigentümer das Bejagen seiner Flächen ausdrücklich verbieten kann (posting). Das Abschußrecht wird durch den Erwerb einer jährlichen Hunting License von der zuständigen Landesbehörde erworben. Diese erhält man ohne eine eigentliche „Jägerprüfung" gegen eine relativ geringe Gebühr und in der Regel gegen Vorlage eines gültigen Führerscheins.

Junk Bonds   Junk Bonds

While the investment public is used to buy unrated paper, it has shown little appetite for fixed income securities other than treasuries („Bundesanleihen"), mortgage bonds (→ Pfandbriefe) or commercial paper of major issuers. Some junk, of course, is always created and held by lenders although, at least by U.S., Japanese, Australian or French standards, Germany's banks have been rather prudent in their property and corporate lending.

Anfang der achtziger Jahre entdeckte der legendäre Wall Street-Bankier Michael Milken, daß Unternehmen erheblichen Fremdfinanzierungsbedarf für Übernahmeschlachten hatten, aber die Qualität ihrer Bilanzen keine weiteren Anleiheausgaben hergaben. Gleichzeitig entdeckte er, daß Anleger, gerade die großen institutionellen Käufer, Interesse an höherverzinslichen Papieren hatten. So wurden junk bonds geboren, die ohne die sonst erforderlichen Gütebezeichnungen der großen „rating agencies" Moodys oder Standard & Poors begeben wurden. Anfänglich sahen die Anleger dabei gut aus, auch wenn bei manchen Anleihen Zinsen in den ersten Jahren nur teilweise in cash bezahlt werden konnten, sondern durch Ausgabe zusätzlichen Papiers an die Anleiheinhaber (payments in kind oder „PIKs" genannt). Die Realität setzte dann in den späten achtziger Jahren ein. Aber auch heute noch werden riskante hochverzinsliche Papiere plaziert, z. B. die nachrangigen Tranchen verbriefter Hypotheken oder Konsumentenkredite (→ Verbriefung).

Kapitalanlagegesellschaft / Investment Company

Juristische Personen ~ **Juridical Entities**

Under German civil law, all natural persons and juridical entities are legal subjects („rechtsfähig"), i. e. they can be owners or debtors of legal rights and interests, they can be registered as such, an sue or be sued in court. In addition, certain unincorporated entities, such as the registered (trade or business) partnership („OHG"), the limited partnership („KG") or the professional limited partnership („Partnerschaftsgesellschaft") are treated as rechtsfähig.

Under one view (the „Sitztheorie"), a foreign entity moving its headquarter to Germany must register with the companies register of the District Court (Handelsregister) in order to preserve its company status and the limited liability, if any, of its owners.

For tax purposes, however, such registration would not be necessary. The tax classification of a foreign entity, either as a corporate or partnership entity, is based on the characteristics of the entity.

In den USA spielt die Frage der juristischen Person keine wesentliche Rolle. So kann sogar eine nicht gewerbetätige general partnership, das Äquivalent der deutschen GbR, unter ihrem Namen (z. B. „Jim and Jack Partners") im Grundbuch oder anderweitig eingetragen werden bzw. Prozesse führen.

Kapitalanlagegesellschaft **Investment Company**
Real Estate Investment Trust
Mutual Fund

German Kapitalanlagegesellschaften may invest in real estate or securities. There are about fifteen publicly owned real estate funds with total assets of approximately DM 80 Billion, exceeding stock mutual funds, and representing about 9% of total mutual fund assets in Germany. As a consequence of the real estate slump of the mid Nineties, investment-grade properties have become scarcer increasing the cash positions of these funds. Principally, only up to 49% of total assets of these funds may be invested in non-real estate assets.

Like the American Regulated Investment Company (RIC) for security investments, or the Real Estate Investment Trust (REIT), the Kapitalanlagegesellschaft (KAG) requires diversification of risk and provides transparent taxation, i. e. profits are taxed only once. Also, capital gains (distributed and undistributed) retain their character in the hands of shareholders. It seems this is where the similarities end. The following are the most important differences between the German KAG and the American REIT.

Kapitalanlagegesellschaft / Investment Company

(a) Conceptually, the Kapitalanlagegesellschaft is not a company like the American REIT or RIC, or the Luxembourg SIVAV. Is is a fiduciary holding a separate asset pool (Sondervermögen) on behalf of ist investors, similar to the English unit trust or the Luxembourg fond commun de placement.

(b) Income of the Kapitalanlagegesellschaft is directly attributed to shareholders whether it is distributed or not.

(c) The legal investment rules applicable to Kapitalanlagegesellschaften are more liberal than those for German insurance companies. For example, the charter may provide that up to 20% of the assets may be invested in real property outside of Europe. This provides German insurance companies with an opportunity to increase their international (i. e. non-European) diversification by investing through Kapitalanlagegesellschaften.

(d) Since 1990, the Mutual Fund Act (KAGG) has availed the tax benefits of the Kapitalanlagegesellschaft also to „special funds" (Spezialfonds). Spezialfonds are entities whose shares are registered in the name of not more than ten institutional shareholders and whose shares are subject to transfer restrictions (vinkuliert). Spezialfonds presently manage about DM 400 Billion and continue to grow at a annual rate of 20% because of the accounting and tax benefits they afford their shareholders. The main tax benefit is that capital gains recognized but not distributed by the Spezialfonds remain untaxed until distributed.

(e) Principally, foreign shareholders are subject to German withholding tax on dividends paid by German entities. It seems, however, that income of a German real property KAG may be distributed to foreign shareholders without any German tax. Neither the 30% corporate tax nor the 25% dividend withholding tax appears applicable to such distributions to foreign shareholders. The German Treasury Department could decide to impose the regular withholding tax on such dividends through regulation (Rechtsverordnung). Under the tax treaty, such withholding would then be subject to the reduced rate of 15%.

(f) Under German law, mutual funds which invest more than 5% of their assets in other funds (fund-of-funds; „Dachfonds") may not be sold to the public. The respective legislation was a reaction to the IOS debacle of the early Seventies. Funds of funds will likely be permitted in 1998.

Germany also has more than twenty publicly listed real property corporations (Aktiengesellschaften) organized as regular corporations. Often, these companies are spin-offs of industrial corporations. Few of them have deep markets. Unlike in the U.S., holding real estate through corporate entities is reasonably tax efficient for

Kapitalanlagegesellschaft / Investment Company

German shareholders because the double taxation of dividends has been abolished in 1977 through a credit system. However, by contrast to individual shareholders, capital gains of corporation are subject to tax. Nevertheless, publicly traded real estate corporations may increasingly become competitors of the mutal funds (KAG).

Die amerikanische Regulated Investment Company (RIC) für Wertpapiere nach Sec. 851 IRC, bzw. der Real Estate Investment Trust (REIT) für Immobilien nach Sec. 856 IRC, verkörpern das der deutschen Kapitalanlagegesellschaft ähnelnde Prinzip der transparenten Besteuerung und der risikogemischten Anlage. Es gibt mehr als 200 REITs in den USA mit einem Gesamtimmobilienvermögen von über $ 150 Milliarden. Folgende Merkmale des REIT sind für einen deutschen Investor erwähnenswert:

a) Der REIT muß mindestens 95% seiner Einkünfte aus Vermietung und Verpachtung ausschütten, um nicht das Privileg der transparenten Besteuerung insgesamt zu verlieren. Veräußerungsgewinne (capital gains) dürfen dagegen thesauriert und auf Ebene des REIT versteuert werden, Sec. 857 IRC, wobei amerikanische Anteilsinhaber eine Gutschrift für die gezahlte Steuer erhalten.

b) Das deutsch-amerikanische Doppelbesteuerungsabkommen (DBA) reduziert die Quellensteuer für REIT-Dividenden auf 15%, jedoch nur, soweit sie an eine natürliche deutsche Person gezahlt werden, die weniger als 10% der REIT-Anteile besitzt, Art. 10(2)b) des DBA. Andere deutsche Anteilseigner, insbesondere institutionelle Investoren unterliegen der ungemilderten 30%igen US-Quellensteuer. Die REIT Industrie verstärkt derzeit ihre Bemühungen in Washington, die reduzierte 15%ige Quellensteuer in den neueren DBAs (z. B. Luxemburg) auf sämtliche ausländischen REIT Anteilsinhaber zu erstrecken.

c) Ausschüttungen von Veräußerungsgewinnen (capital gains dividends) unterliegen nach den Regeln des Foreign Investment in Real Property Tax Act (FIRPTA) einer 35%igen US-Quellensteuer. Nach den vom Treasury Department veröffentlichten Auslegungsrichtlinien zum deutsch-amerikanischen DBA gehen die FIRPTA-Regeln der Sec. 897(h) auch in diesem Punkt entgegenstehenden Bestimmungen der DBA vor.

Seit 1996 unterliegen nach Sec. 1445(e)(3) IRC auch Ausschüttungen von nicht-verwendbarem Eigenkapital eines REITs an Steuerausländer, also Rückzahlungen von Kapital, einer 10%igen Quellensteuer. Der Gesetzgeber schießt hier über das Ziel hinaus. Denn der Steuerausländer sollte logischerweise zur Erstattung dieser Abzugsteuer nicht nur berechtigt sein, wenn er nachweist, daß die Kapitalrückzahlung seine Anschaffungskosten (basis) nicht übersteigt, sondern auch, wenn die Mehrheit der REIT Anteile in amerikanischen Händen liegen („domestically controlled REIT"). In letzterem Fall, der die Regel ist, ist die Veräußerung der REIT Anteile durch Steuerausländer nämlich von U.S. capital gains tax befreit.

d) US-Steuerausländer, die ihre REIT-Anteile verkaufen, unterliegen nicht der capital-gains Besteuerung in den USA, sofern die Mehrheit der REIT-Anteile amerikanischen Investoren gehört („domestically controlled" REIT), oder sofern die Anteile regelmäßig an einer Börse gehandelt werden und der Verkäufer weniger als 5% des Kapitals hält.

e) Deutsche Gesellschafter amerikanischer REITs unterliegen im übrigen der Hinzurechnungsbesteuerung der §§ 17ff des Auslandsinvestmentgesetzes (AuslInvestG). In der Regel optieren amerikanische REITs mit deutschen Gesellschaftern für die Besteuerung unter § 18 Auslandsinvestment-Gesetz durch Benennung eines deutschen tax representative. Die Hinzurechnungsbesteuerung des AuslInvestG ist in erster Linie relevant für thesaurierte capital gains der amerikanischen REIT.

f) Da auch REIT-Aktien von dem allgemeinen Boom der amerikanischen Börse während der vergangenen drei Jahre erfaßt wurden, wurden zunehmend geschlossene Fonds in REITs eingebracht. Der Preis für die attraktive Börsenbewertung und die höhere Fungibilität des Investments ist die Aufdeckung der in den eingebrachten Immobilien liegenden stillen Reserven. Aus diesem Grund wurden in den vergangenen Jahren einige neue REITs als „umbrella partnership REITs" (UPREIT) gegründet. Bei dieser Konstruktion wird eine Limited Partnership gegründet, deren Komplementärin ein REIT ist. Die Einbringenden haben die Wahl, entweder REIT-Anteile oder Kommanditanteile zu erwerben. Letztere sind in aller Regel später in REIT-Anteile wandelbar. Wählt der Investor Kommanditanteile, muß er stille Reserven bei Einbringung grundsätzlich nicht aufdecken, sondern erst bei späterer Umwandlung in REIT-Anteile.

g) REITs haben auch Vorteile bei der Beschaffung von Fremdkapital. Während die Finanzierung von Einzelobjekten eine zeitaufwendige

Kapitaleinlage / Capital Contribution; Capital at Risk

Untersuchung der Werthaltigkeit des Objekts durch das finanzierende Institut erfordert, besitzen REITs häufig bereits die laufende Bewertung einer Wertpapier Rating Agency und deren spezialisierter Analysten. Dies ermöglicht die relativ schnelle Beschaffung von Firmenkredit, auch unbesicherten Kreditlinien, und das meist zu günstigeren Sätzen als die traditionelle Objektfinanzierung.

Kapitaleinlage **Capital Contribution Capital at Risk**

Similar to U.S. tax law, German tax law allows losses only to the extent the taxpayer has capital at risk, either because of contributed capital, additionally subscribed capital or guarantees (→ negatives Kapitalkonto). A disallowed partnership loss may be carried forward against future partnership profits allocable to the respective partner. If a partnership loss exceeds the partners basis he may be able to claim the loss by making an additional capital contribution before the end of the loss year, BFH-IV R 106/94.

§ 15a EStG further provides that a partner may deduct losses only up to the amount of actually paid-in capital, if his additional subscription − even though legally binding − is unlikely to be called in light of the business of the partnership, or if other parties, such as the promoters of the company or a general contractor of a real estate development, contractually indemnify the investor.

Tax losses may also be disallowed if, considering the nature of the partnership's business, it is economically unlikely that additional partner capital will be required to cover losses. The latter criterion is rather subjective and, in addition, appears to be in a certain conflict with another loss deductibility requirement, that of profit motivation (→ Gewinnerzielungsabsicht). German tax law seems to require that the taxpayer enter the business with a view to generating profits not losses, but simultaneously with a realistic assumption that all of his subscribed capital will be required to cover losses, a possibly fine line in some circumstances.

In den USA wie in Deutschland gilt der Grundsatz, daß Verluste nur abzugsfähig sind, soweit der Investor durch bereits geleistete Einlagen sowie darüber hinaus gehende Bürgschaften persönlich im Kapitalrisiko ist (→ negatives Kapitalkonto), Sec. 465 IRC. Ähnlich wie in Deutschland gilt ein Investor nicht als „at risk", sofern er durch vertragliche Abmachungen direkt oder indirekt von persönlicher Haftung freigestellt ist.

Eine wichtige und regelmäßig genutzte Ausnahme von der at-risk rule gilt nach Sec. 465 (b) (6) IRC für amerikanische Immobiliengesellschaf-

Kapitalertragsteuer (→ Abzugsteuern) / Withholding Tax

ten, deren Kommanditisten non-recourse Hypotheken anteilig ihren Kapitalkonten zuschlagen können (→ negatives Kapitalkonto).

Im Gegensatz zum deutschen Steuerrecht wird in den USA die steuerliche Hafteinlage nicht in Frage gestellt, nur weil aus wirtschaftlichen Gründen mit einer Inanspruchnahme des Investors nicht zu rechnen ist. Es kommt einzig auf die rechtliche Möglichkeit der Haftung an.

Kapitalertragsteuer (→ Abzugsteuern) **Withholding Tax**

Kauf bricht nicht Miete **~ Leases Survive Property Sale**

Similar to U.S. law, a sale of real property does not terminate, or entitle the purchaser to terminate, existing leases, § 571 BGB. However, different rules exist in Germany for foreclosure sales. Under §§ 57 et. seq. ZVG (Foreclosure Sales Act), a purchaser may terminate all existing leases by giving proper statutory notice. By contrast to U.S. law, this applies even to leases which already existed before the foreclosing lien creditor recorded his lien. Tenants are, however, protected against early termination to the extent they have prepaid rent or improved the property in lieu of paying rent.

Auch in den USA gilt der Grundsatz, daß Kauf nicht Miete bricht. Unterschiede zum deutschen Recht bestehen jedoch bei der Zwangsversteigerung von vermieteten Immobilien. Mietverträge, die erst nach Eintragung der Hypothek abgeschlossen worden sind, stehen im → Rang hinter dieser und können daher in der Zwangsvollstreckung abgeschnitten werden, sofern sich der Mieter nicht – wie häufig – im Mietvertrag durch eine „non-disturbance"-Klausel gegen die automatische Auflösung des Mietvertrages geschützt hat. Umgekehrt hat der nachrangige Mieter grundsätzlich ein Kündigungsrecht gegen den Hypothekengläubiger, sobald dieser wegen Verzugs des Hypothekenschulders die Verwaltung des Objekts übernimmt. Gegen dieses Kündigungsrecht schützen sich Hypothekengläubiger, indem sie sich von vornherein auch die Mietforderungen sicherungshalber abtreten lassen (assignment of leases and rents) oder indem sie Antrag auf Einsetzung eines Zwangsverwalters (receiver) stellen.

Im Gegensatz zum deutschen Recht werden vor Eintragung des zwangsvollstreckten Grundpfandrechts bestehende Mietverträge dagegen grundsätzlich nicht berührt. Sie bleiben bestehen.

In einigen Staaten, z. B. in New York, New Jersey und Florida, hat der

Kommanditgesellschaft / Limited Partnership

Käufer des zwangsversteigerten Grundstücks das Recht, nachrangige Mietverträge bestehen zu lassen. In anderen Staaten dagegen werden die nachrangigen Mietverträge automatisch aufgelöst, sofern der betreffende Mietvertrag nicht ausdrücklich etwas anderes bestimmt.

Klimatisierung (→ Umlagen)   Air Conditioning

Kommanditgesellschaft   Limited Partnership

The German Kommanditgesellschaft is largely similar to the U.S. limited partnership. Among the noteworthy differences is the fact that a German limited partner (Kommanditist) may participate in the management of the partnership without becoming exposed to personal liability for partnership debts.

A frequently used form of the Kommanditgesellschaft is the GmbH & Co. KG where a corporation is the sole general partner of the partnership. If a corporation is the sole general and managing partner, all income of the partnership is deemed to be trade or business income (gewerbliche Einkünfte), even if the nature of the business is a passive investment activity, § 15(3) EStG. This statutory fiction of trade or business income through form rather than substance („gewerblich geprägt") means, among other, that individual partners of the typical GmbH & Co. KG loose the privilege of tax-free long-term capital gains (→ Veräußerungsgewinn).

German law has also introduced the Partnerschaftsgesellschaft, a general partnership which, similar to the Limited Liability Partnership in the U.S., is available for lawyers, consultants and other professionals. The advantages of the Partnerschaftsgesellschaft are that the company can act in its own name and that the liability of individual partners may be restricted to their own acts (for example for malpractice).

German entities are classified for tax purposes according to their civil-law form. Unlike U.S. tax law, a German partnership generally cannot be viewed as a corporation for tax purposes, vice versa. However, foreign entities are classified according to their characteristics (→ Juristische Personen).

Die amerikanische Limited Partnership entspricht weitgehend der deutschen Kommanditgesellschaft. Auch in den USA ist die GmbH & Co. KG eine weitverbreitete Form der KG. Im Gegensatz zur deutschen KG verliert ein amerikanischer limited partner automatisch die Haftungsbeschränkung, wenn er sich aktiv an der Führung der Geschäfte beteiligt.

Die Steuerrichtlinien unter Sec. 7701 IRC lassen die Umqualifizierung der KG in eine Corporation zu, wenn die KG mindestens drei der fol-

Kommanditgesellschaft / Limited Partnership

genden körperschaftlichen Kriterien aufweist: Volle Haftungsbeschränkung, freie Übertragbarkeit der Anteile, Zentralisierung des Managements, und unbegrenzte Lebensdauer der Gesellschaft (welche die Personengesellschaft z. B. bei Tod, Geschäftsunfähigkeit oder Rücktritt des Komplementärs üblicherweise nicht hat). Die Umqualifizierung ist wegen des Wegfalls von möglichen Verlustzuweisungen und der Doppelbesteuerung von Gewinnen in der Regel nachteilig. Es ist meist nicht schwer, die aufgezeigten körperschaftlichen Kriterien durch entsprechende Klauseln im Gesellschaftsvertrag zu umgehen. Bei Einhaltung gewisser Eigenkapitalquoten kann man sich die Qualifizierung als Personengesellschaft auch durch → verbindliche Auskunft (letter ruling) bestätigen lassen.

Neue Richtlinien („check-the-box Regulations"), die im Mai 1996 verkündet wurden, stellen es Steuerzahlern ohnehin weitgehend frei, die steuerliche Klassifikation für verschiedene Gesellschaftsformen zu wählen. Inländische und ausländische Gesellschaften können sich wahlweise für die Besteuerung als Personengesellschaft oder Kapitalgesellschaft zu entscheiden. Amerikanische oder ausländische Kapitalgesellschaften in der Form der corporation oder AG haben nicht die Wahl. Sie bleiben nach den Richtlinien immer als Kapitalgesellschaften steuerpflichtig. Jedoch könnte beispielsweise eine deutsche GmbH für die Besteuerung in den USA als partnership optieren, oder umgekehrt eine KG für die Besteuerung als corporation. Die Richtlinien werfen eine Reihe von Ungereimtheiten und Fragen auf. Insofern muß man die endgültige Fassung vorerst abwarten. Jedoch sind sie als „temporary regulations" bereits anwendbar.

Deutsche Investoren haben vereinzelt versucht, eine deutsche oder amerikanische GmbH & Co so zu gestalten, daß sie in den USA als corporation besteuert wird. Da die deutsche Finanzverwaltung bei der formalen Betrachtungsweise der Personengesellschaft bleibt, hat die Umqualifierung auf amerikanischer Seite keine Doppelbesteuerung der Gewinne zur Folge. Die Ausschüttungen der corporation würden in Deutschland als Gewinnverteilungen einer Personengesellschaft angesehen, deren Gewinne nach dem DBA von deutscher Besteuerung freigestellt sind. Der Vorteil dieser Konstruktion ist der Schutz, den die corporation vor den hohen U.S. Erbschaftsteuern bietet.

Als attraktive Alternative zur Limited Partnership hat sich zunehmend die Limited Liability Company (LLC) entwickelt. Die LLC hat den Vorzug der transparenten Besteuerung von Personengesellschaften bei gleichzei-

Komplementär / General Partner

tiger Haftungsbeschränkung für alle Gesellschafter (members), auch für die geschäftsführenden. Es bleibt allerdings abzuwarten, ob die deutsche Finanzverwaltung die amerikanische LLC als Kapital- oder Personengesellschaft einstuft.

In einigen Staaten gibt es auch die Limited Liability Partnership, eine der deutschen Partnerschaftsgesellschaft vergleichbare general partnership (BGB Gesellschaft), die es Anwaltskanzleien, Beratungsfirmen und ähnlichen Freiberuflern ermöglicht, die persönliche Haftung der Partner auf ihre eigenen Handlungen (z. B. Kunstfehler) zu beschränken.

Kommunalobligationen Municipal Bonds
(→ Hypothekenbanken)

Municipal bonds in Germany are mostly issued by mortgage banks (Hypothekenbanken) whose own credit backs the repayment of bonds. Interest on bonds issued by German states, counties or municipalities is not exempt from income tax.

Anleihen von Einzelstaaten, Gemeinden und anderen Gebietskörperschaften sind in den USA üblicherweise nicht durch das Kapital der ausgebenden Bank besichert, so wie es etwa bei deutschen Hypothekenbanken der Fall ist. Zinsen für derartige Anleihen sind jedoch von Einkommensteuer befreit, und zwar von der des betreffenden Einzelstaates und auch der Bundeseinkommensteuer (federal income tax), Sec. 103 IRC.

Dieses Steuerprivileg verleihen die Gemeinden und Bezirke an Industrieunternehmen zum Zwecke der Ansiedlung. Dabei geben sie exempt facility bonds (früher: industrial revenue bonds genannt) im Namen und für Rechnung des angesiedelten Industrieunternehmens aus. Schuldner dieser steuerbefreiten Anleihen ist nicht die ausgebende Gebietskörperschaft, sondern ausschließlich das betreffende Industrieunternehmen. Als Sicherheit für die Anleihen dienen häufig Hypotheken auf dem Anlagevermögen des Unternehmens sowie Bankbürgschaften. Da diese zinsbegünstigte Form der Unternehmensfinanzierung zu wuchern begann, hat das amerikanische Steuergesetzbuch zahlreiche Beschränkungen auferlegt, u. a. hinsichtlich der Art der begünstigten Industrieinvestition und auch des Volumens, welches für ein bestimmtes Projekt und für eine Gebietskörperschaft insgesamt aufgelegt werden kann, Sec. 141 IRC.

Komplementär General Partner

Konkurs / Bankruptcy

### Konkurs	Bankruptcy

While U.S. bankruptcy law appears to put the protection of debtors over that of creditors in several respects, German Konkursrecht is mostly concerned with the preservation and orderly distribution of the debtors assets. A few prominent examples of this are the following:

1) Under § 102 and § 207 Konkursordnung, a corporate debtor must file for bankrupcty protection as soon as insolvency (Zahlungsunfähigkeit) or negative equity (Überschuldung) occur. Non-filing may expose officers and other legal representatives of the debtor to personal liability.

2) There exists no cram-down of secured creditors in Germany.

3) Unless a German debtors' reorganization plan („Vergleichsvorschlag") secures a certain coverage (35%) of outstanding liabilities and is accepted by the unsecured creditors, the debtor may be forced into liquidation.

4) In a bankruptcy liquidation, by contrast to U.S. law, the debtor will not be relieved of his liabilities.

5) In a bankruptcy of the tenant, not only the bankruptcy trustee, but also the landlord has the option to continue or reject the lease, § 19 Konkursordnung. Moreover, if the trustee rejects the lease the landlord's claim for damages is not limited to a certain portion of the remaining rent or lease term, but extends to the entire remaining term of the lease.

Some of these features have been viewed increasingly critically and a completely new Insolvency Act (Insolvenzordnung) will enter into force in 1999. It will provide debtors greater protection and will bring German insolvency law a little closer to U.S. bankruptcy law principles.

The new law will force debtors to seek bankruptcy protection at an earlier stage than prior law by including the criteria of „threatening insolvency" („drohende Zahlungsunfähigkeit") to the existing criteria of insolvency or negative equity. The new law contains provisions resembling the Chapter 11 proceeding in certain respects. Thus, the bankruptcy trustee, with the participation of the creditors committee, or the debtor may submit a reorganziation plan („Insolvenzplan") for the liquidation, transfer or continuation of the business. Also, with the approval of creditors, the debtor may continue managing his business under the scrutiny of the bankruptcy trustee. The new law will afford greater protection to debtors and to unsecured or junior creditors, at the expense of first-lien or priority creditors. Priority claims will be abolished, such as certain compensation and wage claims, and claims for taxes or other public dues. Also, lien creditors can no longer charge the cost of selling the collateral, including sales taxes, back to the debtors estate. Such

Konkursanfechtung / Voidance

cost, which can amount to 24% of the collateral's value, will go against the proceeds from the sale of the collateral. However, the law will continue to give a secured creditor 100% of his claim if the proceeds from the sale of his collateral, after cost and taxes, suffices. There will be no cram-down option, as it exists under U.S. bankruptcy law.

Im amerikanischen Konkursrecht dürfte der Schutz des Gemeinschuldners und sein wirtschaftliches Fortbestehen einen höheren Rang einnehmen als die Interessen der Gläubiger. Einige der wichtigsten Beispiele hierfür sind folgende:

1) Das Konkursgericht hat relativ weitgehende Rechte, selbst besicherte Forderungen zu beschneiden („cram-down"; → Absonderung), um dem Vergleichsvorschlag des Gemeinschuldners („Reorganization Plan") eine Überlebenschance zu geben.

2) Selbst bei Ablehnung des Reorganization Plans und dem anschließenden Liquidationskonkurs wird der Schuldner von sämtlichen Verbindlichkeiten befreit, sofern er sich nicht eines Konkursvergehens schuldig gemacht hat.

3) Es besteht keine Pflicht des Gemeinschuldners, bei Eintreten der Zahlungsunfähigkeit oder Überschuldung Konkursantrag zu stellen.

4) Auch das Einkommensteuerrecht gibt dem von Forderungen befreiten Gemeinschuldner attraktive Wahlrechte, so auch neuerdings insolventen Immobilieneigentümern, Einkommensteuern aufzuschieben (→ Forderungsverzicht).

5) Insolvente Mieter werden im U.S. Konkursrecht ebenfalls vorteilhaft behandelt. Sie haben die Option, bestehende Mietverträge aufzukündigen oder zu bestätigen. Kündigt der Mieter, ist die Maximalforderung des Vermieters nach § 502(b)(6) des Bankruptcy Code auf 15% der Restlaufzeit des Mietvertrages begrenzt, jedoch nicht weniger als ein Jahr und nicht mehr als drei Jahre der Restlaufzeit. Große Einzelhandelsunternehmen, die in den frühen Neunziger Jahren zunehmend in Liquiditätsschwierigkeiten gerieten, hatten so die Gelegenheit, sich durch Kündigung teurer Mietverträge bei gleichzeitiger Bestätigung der vorteilhaften Verträge zu sanieren.

Konkursanfechtung   Voidance

The German Bankruptcy Code (Konkursordnung) sets forth three grounds for voiding acts of the debtor: (a) fraudulent conveyances (Absichtsanfechtung or

Konkursbeschlag / Automatic (Bankruptcy) Stay

Schiebungsanfechtung) where both the debtor and the transferee have an intent to defraud creditors; (b) gifts by the debtor (Schenkungsanfechtung) where property is transferred by gift within one year before the bankruptcy filing (within two years before filing if the gift is to a spouse); (c) preferential transfers where (i) a creditor receives what he is owed at a time when he already knows of the debtor's insolvency or the bankruptcy filing (congruent satisfaction; kongruente Deckung), or (ii) where the creditor obtains property or collateral to which he is contractually not entitled (incongruent satisfaction; inkongruente Deckung). Under the Fraudulent Conveyances Voidance Act (→ Anfechtungsgesetz), voidance is available to creditors without bankruptcy proceeding in cases of fraudulent conveyances and gifts.

Die amerikanische Konkursanfechtung ist, wie das gesamte Insolvenzrecht (→ Konkurs), vorwiegend bundesrechtlich geregelt (Bankruptcy Code). Die meisten Einzelstaaten haben darüber hinaus weitgehend gleichlautende Anfechtungsgesetze für gläubigerschädigende Vermögensübertragungen erlassen, oft nach dem Muster des Uniform Fraudulent Transfer Act. Auch im Bankruptcy Code gibt es die Absichtsanfechtung (attempt to hinder, delay or defraud creditors) sowie die Anfechtung einer Schenkung oder gemischten Schenkung, die innerhalb eines Jahres vor Vergleichs- oder Konkursantrag erfolgte und mitursächlich für die spätere Überschuldung oder Zahlungsunfähigkeit war. Die eigentliche Konkursanfechtung (voidable preferences) gilt für jede Befriedigung von Gläubigerforderungen innerhalb von 90 Tagen vor Vergleichs- bzw. Konkursantrag, bei bestimmten „Insider"-Gläubigern innerhalb eines Jahres davor.

Es gibt bundesgerichtliche Rechtsprechung, derzufolge auch der Zuschlag eines Grundstücks an den die Zwangsversteigerung betreibenden Hypothekengläubiger als preference anfechtbar ist, wenn das Meistgebot dieses Gläubigers unter dem Wert des Grundstücks lag. Diese Urteile gehen in verschiedener Hinsicht über den Zweck der Konkursanfechtung hinaus, insbesondere deshalb, weil das Auktionsverfahren gerade sicherstellt, daß Vermögen nicht unter Wert veräußert wird.

Konkursbeschlag	**Automatic (Bankruptcy) Stay**
Konkursverwalter (→ Vergleichsverwalter)	**Bankruptcy Trustee**

Körperschaftsteuer / Corporate Income Tax

All income taxes in Germany are governed by Federal law. They are levied on income of individuals (Einkommensteuer) and corporations (Körperschaftsteuer). Income from trade or business (→ Gewerbebetrieb) is subject to an additional tax based on business income and capital, including long-term debt (→ Gewerbesteuer).

The Corporate Income Tax Act (KStG) applies different rates to retained and distributed earnings. Retained earnings are taxed at 45%, § 23 KStG, dividends at 30% (Ausschüttungsbelastung), § 27 KStG. Also, since 1977, corporate profits are not subject to double taxation. Under § 36(2) No. 3 EStG, shareholders obtain a tax credit for the (30%) corporate income tax levied at source on their dividends. Foreign shareholders usually cannot use this indirect credit unless they are parent companies holding 20% or more.

Tax rates are presently under intense political debate and are likely to change, possibly in 1998.

In den USA werden Einkommen- und Körperschaftsteuern sowohl auf Bundes- als auch auf Landes- und Gemeindeebene erhoben (federal, state and local income taxes). Es gibt keine Gewerbesteuer.

Der Höchststeuersatz der Bundeseinkommensteuer liegt bei 39,6%, der für Körperschaftsteuer bei 35%. Es gibt weder einen gesonderten Ausschüttungssteuersatz für Kapitalgesellschaften, noch die Anrechnung von Körperschaftsteuer beim Dividendenempfänger, d. h. es gilt die volle Doppelbesteuerung der Gewinne auf Gesellschafts- und Gesellschafterebene. Diese Doppelbesteuerung wird für verbundene Unternehmen ausgeschaltet oder reduziert. 80%ige Tochtergesellschaften können konsolidierte Konzern- Steuererklärungen abgeben (consolidated tax returns), Sec. 1501 ff IRC. Bei niedrigeren Beteiligungen gilt ein 70%iges Schachtelprivileg, ab einer 20%igen Beteiligungshöhe können 80% der Dividenden steuerfrei vereinnahmt werden, Sec. 243(c) IRC.

Die Einkommen- und Körperschaftsteuern in den US-Einzelstaaten liegen zwischen 0% und 12%, im Durchschnitt der Einzelstaaten etwa bei 7%. State und local income taxes sind von der Bemessungsgrundlage der Bundessteuer abzugfähig.

Kreditgeberhaftung / Lender Liability

It does not appear that German case law has ever held lenders liable for construction defects or for soil contamination or other environmental damage.

Kündigungsschutz für Arbeitnehmer (→ Betriebsübergang)

In den USA ist die Haftung des Kreditgebers für Altlasten zunehmend ein Thema, welches das Kreditvergabeverfahren erschwert. Gerichte in Kalifornien und einigen anderen Staaten haben in Einzelfällen Kreditgeber auch haftbar für Schäden gemacht, die durch Baufehler entstanden sind.

Kündigungsschutz für Arbeitnehmer (→ Betriebsübergang)

Kündigungsschutz für Wohnraum ~ **Tenant Protection Laws**

Under § 564b BGB, a landlord must renew a residential lease unless he can substantiate a plausible interest (→ Berechtigtes Interesse) in the termination. A plausible interest exists if the tenant has materially breached the lease agreement, e. g. by creating significant nuisance to neighbours, by substantially defaulting on rental payments, by improper uses of the property or illegal subleasing. § 564b BGB enumerates certain other causes for termination by the landlord. The most frequently alleged termination cause is the required use of the rental unit by the landlord himself or by his family or other members of the household (Eigenbedarf). Civil actions involving Eigenbedarf of landlords is one of the most frequent types of civil action in Germany.

In den USA gibt es das Prinzip des Kündigungsschutzes für Mieter von Wohnräumen nicht. Ausnahmen bilden einige Großstädte, in denen für bestimmte steuerlich begünstigte Objekte noch → Mieterschutz und → Mietpreisbindung (rent stabilization) gelten.

Landstraßen ~ **State Roads**
State Highways

Landvermessung (→ Vermessung)

Lasten **Encumbrances**

Lebenshaltungs(kosten)index **Consumer Price Index**

Commercial leases in Germany are typically indexed for consumer price inflation. Under § 3 of the Currency Act (Währungsgesetz), most contractual indexing clauses require the approval of the regional federal reserve bank (Landeszentralbank) (→ Mietanpassung; → Wertsicherungsklausel). If the lessor is bound to a lease term of at least 10 years, approval will generally be given.

Leerstand / Vacancy

In den USA sind Mietverträge gewöhnlich nicht an den Consumer Price Index gekoppelt. Vielmehr werden steigende Kosten für Grundsteuern und Unterhaltung an die Mieter weitergegeben. Im Gegensatz zu dem Erfordernis des deutschen § 3 Währungsgesetz unterliegen vertragliche Gleitklauseln, die an den Lebenshaltungskostenindex oder andere Preisentwicklungen gekoppelt sind, in den USA im übrigen keiner behördlichen Genehmigung.

Lebensversicherung / Life Insurance

As under U.S. tax law, life insurance proceeds, including accrued interest, are generally tax free also in Germany, Sec. 20 Para. 1 No. 6 EStG. Moreover, unlike in the U.S., premium payments under most non-single-premium life insurance policies are tax deductible as special deductions (Sonderausgaben) under Sec. 10 Para. 2 EStG even if they are not for keyman or other business-related purposes. Also, German tax law appears more generous than U.S. tax law with respect to using life insurance contracts as collateral for financing. Principally, taxpayers may secure borrowings with life insurance contracts without losing the beneficial tax treatment of life insurance premiums and proceeds, as long as the financed activity is expected to generate taxable income. For example, taxpayers may finance real estate investments or investments in real estate partnership by using life insurance contracts as additional collateral.

Auch in den USA sind Lebensversicherungszahlungen und die darin enthaltenen Sparanteile in der Regel steuerfrei. Jedoch gibt es in den USA keinen Sonderausgabenabzug für Prämienzahlungen. Diese sind nur in bestimmten Fällen abzugsfähig, beispielsweise für die vom Arbeitgeber gezahlte Prämie auf das Leben leitender Angestellter (keyman insurance). Auch ist das U.S. Steuerrecht (Code Section 264) restriktiver als das deutsche Steuerrecht in der Verwendung von Lebensversicherungspolicen als Sicherheit für Finanzierungen.

Leerstand / Vacancy

Headline office vacancy rates in Germany are significantly lower than in the U.S. at the bottom of each country's property market cycle. However, the real rates in Germany are higher than published since almost 50% of office space is owner-occupied.

Die amerikanischen Leerstände für Büroraum waren am Tiefstpunkt des Marktes in den frühen Neunziger Jahren mehr als doppelt so hoch wie

Löschung / Cancellation Deletion

die deutschen Leerstände in der Mitte der Neunziger Jahre. Bei diesem Vergleich ist jedoch nicht berücksichtigt, daß fast die Hälfte der deutschen Bürofläche von den Eigentümern genutzt ist, d. h. die deutschen Leerstände sich damit prozentual den amerikanischen annähern.

Löschung **Cancellation Deletion**

Under § 1179a BGB, a junior lien holder may request the owner of property to release and discharge an owner's mortgage (→ Eigentümergrundschuld) resulting from the repayment of a third-party mortgage. In other words, lien holders who are pari passu or junior to an existing mortgage have a right to climb up in priority (→ Rang) once a senior or pari passu mortgage has been repaid. Generally, the right for release and discharge cannot be recorded as a priority notice (Löschungsvormerkung; → Vormerkung). However, other pari passu or junior holders of certain estates, such as usufructuary rights (→ Nießbrauch) or long-term leasehold (Wohnrecht) may record a priority notice for their right to request release and discharge.

In den USA gibt es die Löschungsvormerkung nicht, da es die Eigentümergrundschuld bzw. Eigentümerhypothek nicht gibt.

Luftraum (-rechte) **~ Air Rights**

As under U.S. law, a German property owner may sell the right to develop space lying above his land provided the local zoning rules permit the height density (Geschoßflächenzahl) over the respective lot. However, air rights can only be granted and recorded as an easement (→ Grunddienstbarkeit). Any structures built under the air right easement will belong to the owner of the underlying property.

Wie in Deutschland kann auch ein US-Grundstückseigentümer das Recht, sein Grundstück zu überbauen, an andere verkaufen, sofern die weitere Bebauung des Luftraums über der betreffenden Parzelle nach dem Bebauungsplan (zoning ordinance) zulässig ist. Im Gegensatz zum deutschen Recht ist das amerikanische air right keine Dienstbarkeit (easement), sondern eine eigene Parzelle, die als solche eingetragen, veräußert oder belastet werden kann, gewissermaßen als „Luftparzelle". Wenn der Eigentümer die im Bebauungsplan zulässige Gebäudehöhe selbst nicht ausnutzt, versucht er mitunter, das verbleibende air right an Grundstücksnachbarn zu verkaufen.

Mantelkauf (Verlustvorträge) / NOL Trafficking

Makler **Broker**

As in the U.S., real estate brokers in Germany require a business license under § 34c GewO. In addition the Brokers' and Developers' Ordinance (Makler- und Bauträger VO; MaBV) contains various provisions relating to consumer protection. These provisions, inter alia, relate to the uniformity of purchase price deposits, to security deposits, to disclosure duties of brokers and developers and other rules furthering greater protection of real estate purchasers or tenants.

Usually, the parties agree that the purchaser of property pays the broker's fee. In some areas of Germany, however, it is customary for the parties to share the fee. In the absence of a contractual clause, the Civil Code (BGB) provides that the brokerage fee shall be paid by the party who retained the broker. Broker agreements do not have to be in writing (→ Schriftform) to be enforceable.

Auch in den USA bedürfen Immobilienmakler der Zulassung durch die zuständige Behörde des betreffenden Einzelstaates. In vielen Einzelstaaten sind Rechtsanwälte auch ohne zusätzliche Maklerprüfung berechtigt, die Zulassung als Immobilienmakler zu beantragen. Meist einigen sich die Parteien vertraglich auf die Verantwortlichkeit für die Maklergebühr. Mangels vertraglicher Vereinbarung schuldet, wie in Deutschland, die Partei die Maklergebühr, die den Makler eingeschaltet hat.

Soweit ersichtlich gibt es in den USA jedoch keine der deutschen Makler- und Bauträger VO vergleichbare Verbraucherschutzregeln. Im übrigen benötigen Maklerverträge in einer Reihe von Einzelstaaten der Schriftform.

Mängel **Defects**
(→ „Wie besichtigt" – „As Is")

Mantelkauf (Verlustvorträge) **NOL Trafficking**

Under German tax laws, loss carry-overs (→ Verlustabzug) will be disallowed after an acquisition of corporate shares if the target company looses its legal or economic identity (rechtliche oder wirtschaftliche Identität) in the course of the acquisition. However, a corporate entity which is merged into another entity by way of a tax-free reorganization, is not deemed to have lost its legal identity. Loss carryovers may be preserved. Pursuant to § 8(4) KStG, economic identity will be deemed lost if more than 75% of the loss corporation's shares change hands and its business is continued with substantially new assets.

Mehrwertsteuer / Value-Added (Sales) Tax

In contrast to the U.S. market with its more stringent rules, NOL trafficking continues to be a lively business in Germany.

In den USA ist die Beschränkung von → Verlustabzügen nach Mantelkauf deutlich restriktiver als in Deutschland, Sec. 382 IRC. Nach einem Gesellschafterwechsel dürfen Verlustvorträge jährlich nur bis zu folgendem Höchstbetrag abgezogen werden: Dem Verkehrswert der Gesellschaft zum Zeitpunkt des Gesellschafterwechsels multipliziert mit dem jeweiligen Zinssatz für steuerbefreite Anleihen (derzeit ca. 5,5%). Ein Gesellschafterwechsel wird bereits angenommen, wenn ein oder mehrere 5%-Gesellschafter ihren Aktienbesitz zusammengenommen um mehr als 50% der ausstehenden Aktien erhöhen.

Die USA beschränken nicht nur den Verlustabzug bei Gesellschafterwechsel, sondern auch den → Verlustausgleich zwischen zwei Gesellschaften nach dem Erwerb und der steuerlichen Konsolidierung einer neuen Gesellschaft, wenn die Bilanz einer der beteiligten Gesellschaften zum Zeitpunkt des Erwerbs nicht-realisierte Gewinne enthielt (built-in gains) und die andere Gesellschaft Verlustvorträge hat, Sec. 384 IRC. Der Verlustausgleich alter Verluste gegen derartige built-in gains ist für fünf Jahre nach dem Erwerb ausgeschlossen. Beispiel: Gesellschaft A mit Verlustvorträgen erwirbt Gesellschaft B, deren Bilanz stille Reserven (built-in gains) hat. Gesellschaft A kann in ihrer Konsolidierungssteuerbilanz fünf Jahr lang ihren Verlustvortrag nicht mit bei Gesellschaft B zur Auflösung kommenden stillen Reserven ausgleichen.

Mehrwertsteuer   **Value-Added (Sales) Tax**

The German value-added sales tax (Umsatzsteuer, generally called Mehrwertsteuer) in effect only taxes the margin made by the seller of goods or services over his cost of goods by allowing a credit for sales taxes which were levied on his prior purchase of the goods or services. This principle applies in all E. U. countries.

The tax rate presently is 16% (as of April 1, 1998), which puts Germany at the lower end of the scale in Europe. Certain goods, including food and newspapers, are taxed at 7%. No Mehrwertsteuer is due on transfers which are subject to real property transfer tax (→ Grunderwerbsteuer). Similarly, rental payments are exempt from the tax.

A landlord may waive the latter exemption and volunteer to add the VAT to his rental bills. Since commercial tenants, other than most financial institutions or professionals, are generally themselves subject to collecting and paying Mehrwertsteuer

Mietanpassung (Umlagen) / Escalations

on their sales, they may benefit from the tax credit (Vorsteuerabzug) they can claim for Mehrwertsteuer collected by the landlord. Also, by charging Mehrwertsteuer the landlord will himself be able to use the tax credit for Mehrwertsteuer paid on goods or services delivered to him.

In den USA gibt es keine bundesgesetzliche Umsatzsteuer. Die sales tax wird ausschließlich auf Landes- und Gemeindeebene erhoben. Im Gegensatz zur deutschen (bzw. europäischen) Umsatzsteuer basiert die amerikanische sales tax nicht auf dem Mehrwert der gehandelten Ware oder Leistung, d. h. es gibt keinen Vorsteuerabzug. Sie wird theoretisch auf jeder Handelsstufe erhoben und trifft damit den Verbraucher, wenn mehrere Handelsstufen durchlaufen werden. Jedoch sind generell nur „retail"-Umsätze, also Verkäufe an Endverbraucher, umsatzsteuerpflichtig. Händler und andere Gewerbetreibende in vielen Einzelstaaten können beim Einkauf gegen Nachweis vom Verkäufer Umsatzsteuerbefreiung beantragen. Im Landesdurchschnitt dürfte die amerikanische sales tax bei 6% liegen.

Soweit ersichtlich sind in allen oder den meisten Einzelstaaten der USA Umsätze aus Vermietung und Verpachtung oder aus Immobilienverkäufen wie in Deutschland von sales tax befreit.

Meistgebot **Highest Bid**

Mietanpassung (Umlagen) **Escalations**

Long-term commercial leases are often CPI-indexed in Germany. In addition, landlords charge (Umlagen) tenants for property taxes and operating cost („Betriebs- und Nebenkosten"), usually not just for the increase over a base year, but for the entire cost. Individual metering of electricity, water or gas is more prevalent in Germany than in the U.S. Thus, even multi-tenant buildings are sometimes rented on a net lease basis.

For residential leases, the law strictly defines operating cost which may be charged to tenants, and excludes many items, such as maintenance, administrative or security cost.

In den USA sind zumindest Bürogebäude nur selten mit separaten Strom-, Wasser und Gaszählern für jeden einzelnen Mieter ausgestattet. Deshalb gibt es den sogenannten „triple net lease", bei dem der Mieter direkt sämtliche Betriebs- und Nebenkosten zahlt, meist nur für Ein-Mieter Gebäude. Im Gegensatz zu Deutschland werden auf die Mieter

Miete / Lease; Rental

in der Regel nur die Kostensteigerungen (Grundsteuer, Erhaltung, Energieversorgung, Verwaltung, etc.) über die Kosten des Basisjahrs (d. h. zu Beginn der Mietperiode) umgelegt. Mit anderen Worten sind die Basisjahr-Kosten in der Grundmiete (base rent) enthalten. Auch ist die Inflationsindexierung selbst bei langfristigen Mietverträgen ungebräuchlich.

Miete	**Lease** **Rental**
Mieterschutz	**Rent Stabilization** ~ **Tenant Protection**

Mietpreisbindung

After the Second World War, most residential rental properties were extensively regulated under the managed housing economy (Wohnungszwangswirtschaft). The Wohnungszwangswirtschaft was later replaced by various tenant protection laws included in the Civil Code (BGB) and the Residential Lease Termination Act (Wohnraumkündigungsgesetz) which provides for restricted rent increases.

Im Gegensatz zum deutschen Recht gibt es rent control-Bestimmungen nur noch in wenigen US-Großstädten, und dort nur für bestimmte Objekte (→ Mieterschutz; → Kündigungsschutz).

Mietrecht	**Landlord and Tenant Law**
Mietsteigerungen	**Escalations**
Mischgebiet	**Mixed-Use Zone**
Mitarbeiter-Optionen	**Incentive Stock Options**

Incentive stock options are still rarely used in Germany, among other reasons, because shareholders have statutory stock rights and would have to agree, through resolution or amendment of the charter, to issue stock options to employees. U.S. companies sometimes give senior managers of their German subsidiaries options in parent company stock. For tax purposes, the courts and the tax authorities see no value accruing to an employee who receives stock options at a strike price equal to the share value, if he cannot sell the options and if they expire at the end of his

Negatives Kapitalkonto / Negative Capital Account; At-Risk Rule

employment. The taxable event occurs when the employee exercises the options, not only when, as in the U.S., he later sells the shares at a gain.

In den USA ist die incentive stock option ein überaus verbreitetes Instrument, die leitenden Angestellten von Unternehmen zu motivieren. Wenn man in der Presse über amerikanische Vorstandsbezüge von 10 oder auch 30 Millionen Dollar liest, so liegen diese zu 90% in der Ausübung oder Liquidierung (durch Verkauf an die Gesellschaft) von Mitarbeiter-Optionen. Sofern die gesetzlichen Voraussetzungen erfüllt sind, ist die stock option beim Empfänger weder zum Zeitpunkt der Ausgabe noch der Ausübung steuerbar. Erst wenn der Arbeitgeber die erworbenen Aktien später mit Gewinn verkauft, entstehen steuerpflichtige Einkünfte.

Mitverschulden **Contributory Negligence**

Nachrangig **Subordinated; Junior; Second**
(→ Rang)
(→ Verkäuferhypothek – Wraparound Mortgage)

Negative Ausländische Einkünfte **Foreign Losses**

Similar to U.S. tax laws, German tax law allows a German taxpayer to deduct foreign losses from German income. Under § 2a EStG losses from a foreign rental activity (→ Vermietung und Verpachtung) and from certain other passive foreign sources are not deductible (→ Verlustausgleich). They may only be deducted from, or carried forward against, income derived from a similar activity in the same foreign country.

Auch US-Steuerzahler können ausländische Verluste mit positivem US-Einkommen ausgleichen. Das in Deutschland geltende Verbot der Abzugsfähigkeit passiver ausländischer Verluste, z. B. solcher aus Vermietung und Verpachtung, gilt in den USA nicht. Sämtliche ausländischen Verluste sind abzugsfähig.

Negatives Kapitalkonto **Negative Capital Account**
 ~ At-Risk Rule

§ 15a EStG provides rules that are substantially similar to the at-risk rules in the United States. Investors, typically limited partners (→ Kommanditgesellschaft), may deduct losses only up to the amount of capital they paid in and/or subscribed

Niederlassungssteuer / Branch Profits Tax

for or guaranteed. An investor is not considered at risk if, considering all circumstances, losses and additional assessment calls are legally possible, but economically unlikely. (→ Kapitaleinlage; → Gewinnerzielungsabsicht.)

Die amerikanische at-risk rule der Sec. 465 IRC entspricht im wesentlichen § 15a EStG. Im Unterschied zu § 15a EStG gilt in den USA gezeichnetes oder verbürgtes Kapital als steuerliche Hafteinlage, solange rechtlich die theoretische Möglichkeit der Inanspruchnahme besteht, auch wenn aus wirtschaftlichen Gründen das Verlustrisiko extrem gering erscheint.

In Sec. 465(b)(6) IRC gibt es im übrigen eine wichtige Ausnahme von der at-risk rule, die insbesondere für Immobilien-Partnerships von Bedeutung ist: Sofern keiner der Gesellschafter, auch nicht der Komplementär, persönlich für eine Hypothekenverbindlichkeit der Gesellschaft haftet (non-recourse liability), erhöht diese die steuerlichen Kapitalkonten aller Gesellschafter anteilig, d. h., die Kommanditisten können Verlustzuweisungen auch in der Höhe der bestehenden non-recourse-Hypotheken geltend machen. Da die reine → Objekthaftung bei Hypotheken in den USA üblich ist, gilt das Verbot des negativen Kapitalkontos für die meisten Immobilien-KGs in den USA de facto nicht.

Das US-Steuerrecht beschränkt die Abzugsfähigkeit von Verlusten im übrigen an verschiedenen anderen Stellen. So dürfen natürliche Personen und corporations mit wenigen Gesellschaftern nach Sec. 469 IRC bestimmte passive Verluste (passive activity losses) nur gegen positive Einkünfte aus ähnlichen passiven Tätigkeiten ausgleichen bzw. vortragen. Das typische Beispiel für eine passive activity ist die Rolle des Kommanditisten.

Nach Sec. 163(d) IRC können natürliche Personen Schuldzinsen, die im Zusammenhang mit Kapitalanlagen stehen (investment interest), nur mit Einkünften aus Kapitalvermögen („net investment income") ausgleichen. (→ Verlustausgleich).

Niederlassungssteuer   **Branch Profits Tax**
→ Quellensteuer für Betriebsstättengewinne

Nießbrauch   **Usufruct**
       Life Estate

Notarielle Beurkundung / ~ Notarial Deed

Notar ~ **Notary**

All transactions relating to title or other real property estates must be validated before a notary under German law. The notary is a qualified lawyer who impartially advises both parties of their rights and sees to it that the desired transaction will be properly recorded. The notary is payed on the basis of a statutory fee schedule.

In some parts of Germany, such as Hessen, Berlin and Lower Saxony, notaries may also practice law. In other parts, notaries are only allowed to exercise their public office of notary.

Den Notar im deutschen Sinne gibt es im amerikanischen Recht nicht. Die Funktion des amerikanischen notary public beschränkt sich ausschließlich darauf, Unterschriften zu beglaubigen. Eine Urkunde, durch die das Eigentum übertragen wird („deed"), oder durch die eine Hypothek oder ein anderes Grundstücksrecht entsteht, bedarf regelmäßig eines Beglaubigungsvermerks durch den notary public, um wirksam eingetragen (recording) werden zu können. In manchen Staaten genügt die Beglaubigung durch Zeugen.

Notary public kann jeder werden, der nicht vorbestraft ist. Häufig sind Büroangestellte in Anwaltskanzleien als notary publics bestellt.

Notarielle Beurkundung ~ **Notarial Deed**

Practically all agreements and transactions in which recordable estates in real property are transferred require to be signed, executed and closed before a notary. The notary will read, in the presence of all parties, the full text of the respective document and will, upon request by a party, advise the party of its rights or obligations. The cost for the notarielle Beurkundung and subsequent recording is approximately 1 % of the consideration for larger properties and greater than 1 % for smaller properties. The parties usually agree that the acquiror bears the cost of the notary and the recording.

A U.S. notary public may not render a valid notarial deed under German law. Certain transactions, including acquisitions of German corporations (GmbHs), can be, and often are, validly executed before notaries of certain other European countries where notary fees can be substantially lower, notably in Switzerland.

To be distinguished from the notarial deed (Beurkundung) is the mere notarization of signatures (Beglaubigung). It is required for certain publicly recorded documents, such as powers of attorney or approvals. In a Beglaubigung, the notary will not read the document to the parties, or instruct them about its legal implications.

Notweg / Easement by Necessity

He will simply confirm the identity of the parties and that the document was signed in his presence. Notarization is much less costly than a notarial deed. It may be done also by a German consulate office abroad or by a U.S. notary public. In the latter case, legalization by the Secretary of State will be required by German authorities.

Kaufverträge, Hypothekenbestellungen und andere Verpflichtungsgeschäfte über Grundstücke oder Grundstücksrechte bedürfen in den USA zwar der → Schriftform („Statute of Frauds"). Sie bedürfen jedoch keiner notariellen Beurkundung. Sie sind ohne öffentliche Beurkundung und auch ohne Unterschriftsbeglaubigung rechtswirksam. Die spätere Eintragung einer Verfügung (recording) benötigt jedoch die Unterschriftsbeglaubigung des Verfügenden durch einen notary public.

Notweg	**Easement by Necessity**
Numerus Clausus im Sachenrecht	**~ Defined Property Interests**

Like U.S. law, German civil law allows complete freedom of contractual agreement, the only limits being public policy and equity. However, in contrast to U. S, law, German law acknowledges only those estates and property interests (dingliche Rechte) as are set forth in the Civil Code and certain other acts. The parties cannot contractually create or record property interests of another kind than those specifically set forth in those acts.

Auch in der amerikanischen Praxis gilt der Grundsatz der Vertrags- bzw. Gestaltungsfreiheit. Auch die wichtigeren dinglichen Rechte sind weitgehend typisiert, beispielsweise Grundeigentum, Dienstbarkeiten, Hypotheken, ground lease und ähnliches. Jedoch ist es im Recht vieler US-Einzelstaaten möglich, beliebige vertragliche Absprachen von längerfristiger zeitlicher Dauer einzutragen und damit zum veräußerbaren und belastbaren dinglichen Recht erstarken zu lassen.

Nutzungswert der selbstgenutzten Wohnung	**~ Fictitious Income from Home Equity**

Under former German income tax law, persons residing in their own homes paid tax on fictitious income derived from the enjoyment and use of their own residence. This unusual income tax concept has been abolished in 1987 for most homes.

In den USA hat es das in Deutschland bis 1987 geltende Prinzip des steuerlichen Nutzungswerts der eigenen Wohnung nie gegeben.

Objekthaftung

Offener Fonds / Open-End Fund

Non-Recourse

The owner of a mortgaged property is generally not personally liable for the mortgage. His sole obligation is to allow foreclosure against his property. In most cases, however, the property owner is also the debtor of the underlying mortgage claim. German mortgage lenders generally do not fully waive personal liability of the borrower.

Im Gegensatz zur deutschen Praxis überwiegt in Amerika die Form des non-recourse-Darlehens bei der Hypothekenfinanzierung langfristig solide vermieteter Objekte. Dem Kreditgeber haftet dabei nur das Objekt. Der Kreditnehmer ist darüber hinaus nicht persönlich haftbar. Nach der Immobilienkrise der Achziger Jahren sind die Banken (vielleicht nur vorübergehend) etwas zurückhaltender mit der non-recourse Finanzierung geworden. Bei Entwicklungsobjekten wird im übrigen häufig eine erweiterte Haftung oder zusätzliche Garantie des Entwicklers verlangt.

Das Recht einiger Einzelstaaten beschränkt die persönliche Haftung des Hypothekenschuldners, wenn der Gläubiger nicht die Forderung durch Zahlungsklage verfolgt, sondern unmittelbar die Zwangsversteigerung betreibt. In manchen dieser Einzelstaaten besteht nur in Ausnahmefällen das Recht auf Ausfallurteil bei Unterdeckung nach erfolgter Zwangsversteigerung („deficiency judgement").

Offene Handelsgesellschaft

General Partnership

Germany has both the general, and the limited partnership (→ Kommanditgesellschaft). They are substantially similar to their U.S. counterparts. If a German general partnership becomes engaged in a commercial trade or business it is called an Offene Handelsgesellschaft and must be registered in the commercial register (Handelsregister).

Die amerikanische general partnership und limited partnership entspricht der deutschen BGB-Gesellschaft, OHG bzw. KG. Eine general partnership bedarf jedoch keiner Eintragung in ein Register, auch wenn sie gewerblich tätig ist.

Offener Fonds

Open-End Fund

(→ Kapitalanlagegesellschaft)
(→ Öffentliche Plazierung)

Öffentliche Plazierung / Public Offering

Öffentliche Plazierung   Public Offering

Any public offering of securities in Germany normally requires publication of a prospectus in accordance with the Securities Sales Prospectus Act (Verkaufsprospektgesetz). If the securities are to be listed on a stock exchange, they need to be admitted by the exchange under the Exchange Act.

The Securities Prospectus Act contains a less explicit, but more generous definition of the term private placement than „Reg D" in the U.S. No regular prospectus must be published or registered if an issue is offered to brokers, dealers or other investment professionals (even if later resold to the public), or to a restricted set of investors, or to employees of the issuer, or if it is offered in minimum subscriptions per investor of DM 80,000.

Units in open-end mutual funds, if they are to be distributed publicly, are subject to the detailed provisions of the Investment Companies Act (Kapitalanlagengesetz). Also, under the Foreign Investment Companies Registration and Tax Act (Auslandsinvestmentgesetz), any foreign investment company, open- or closed end, must register with, and obtain the permission of, the Federal Banking Authority in Berlin before it can publicly offer its securities in Germany. Privately placed foreign mutual funds must appoint a German tax representative who translates and files annual tax reports with German tax authorities. Without the appointment of such tax representative, German investors will be subject to the punitive tax regime of Sec. 19 of the Act.

Both of the above Acts contain no clear distinction between public offerings and private placements. A large number of subscribers, theoretically a few hundred, does not necessarily mean that a public offering has taken place. It is the method of advertising and selling that governs the issue. If shares are offered or advertised to an indiscriminate number of people a public offering will be assumed. If they are targeted to selected investors who are known, directly or indirectly, to the issuer or the selling agents, a private placement will be assumed.

Private placements subject issuers and selling agents to full disclosure and prospectus liability for false or misleading statements. The applicable rules have been developed by extensive case law.

In den USA unterliegt jedes öffentliche Anbieten von Wertpapieren und Beteiligungen den börsen- und wertpapierrechtlichen Bestimmungen, die auf bundesrechtlicher, und meist auch landesrechtlicher Ebene existieren (securities laws). Diese Bestimmungen erfordern grundsätzlich die vorherige Anmeldung (registration) einer Plazierung und umfangreiche Offenlegung aller relevanten Einzelheiten und Risiken.

Öffentlicher Glaube / ~ Deed Registry is presumed correct

Besondere Regeln gelten für Privatplazierungen (private placements). Im Gegensatz zum deutschen Recht gibt es in Regulation D und Rule 144 (bzw. Rule 144 A) spezifische Regeln zur Unterscheidung von Privatplazierung und public offering. Dabei kommt es in erster Linie auf die Anzahl der Investoren, sowie deren finanzielle Mittel und Erfahrung („accredited investors") an. Auch für Privatplazierungen legt das U.S. Wertpapierrecht den Verkäufern weitreichende Offenlegungspflichten auf, die sich im Umfang nur unwesentlich von denen des public offerings unterscheiden.

Das Anbieten von Wohnungseigentum liegt nach den Richtlinien der amerikanischen Börsenaufsichtsbehörde (Securities and Exchange Commission) dann der Registrations- und Prospektpflicht, wenn die condominiums weniger zu Wohn- als zu Anlagezwecken angeboten werden, oder der Käufer zur Teilnahme an einem rental pool aufgefordert wird. Eine Registrierung ist unter Umständen auch nach den Wertpapiergesetzen des betreffenden Einzelstaates erforderlich. Die zuständige Behörde ist in der Regel das Attorney General Office des betreffenden Staates.

Nach dem Interstate Land Sales Full Disclosure Act von 1969 muß der Verkauf von unbebauten Landparzellen bei dem Department of Housing and Urban Development angemeldet werden. Der Verkäufer unterliegt dabei umfangreichen Offenlegungspflichten. Es gibt einige Ausnahmeregelungen. Insbesondere findet das Gesetz keine Anwendung, wenn das Projekt weniger als 100 Parzellen umfaßt.

Öffentlicher Glaube ~ Deed Registry is presumed correct

The German Deed Registry (→ Grundbuch) carries with it the irrebuttable presumption that all recordings are correct. A good-faith acquirer of an estate in real property may rely not only on the absence of non-recorded interests. He also has absolute security that he validly acquired the recorded estate. § 892 BGB. However, if the purchaser positively knows that an entry is incorrect he cannot claim the protection of § 892 BGB. One consequence of the irrebuttable correctness of the deed registry is that title insurance is not required and does not exist in Germany.

In den USA kann sich der gutgläubige Erwerber eines Rechts nur auf das Fehlen der Eintragung etwaiger früherer Verfügungen verlassen. Auf die Richtigkeit einer positiv bestehenden Eintragung dagegen kann sich der gutgläubige Käufer oder Hypothekengeber nicht verlassen (→ Grundbuch). Der Erwerber kann nie sicher sein, ob irgendwann in der Kette

Organschaft / Tax Consolidation

der Übertragungen eines der Verpflichtungsgeschäfte unwirksam war und deshalb ein früherer Eigentümer oder Hypothekengläubiger Ansprüche geltend machen könnte. Aus diesem Grunde schließt praktisch jeder Käufer eines Grundstücks oder jeder amerikanische Hypothekengläubiger eine title insurance ab. Diese Versicherung wird typischerweise durch eine Einmalprämie in Höhe von ca. 0,15% des Kaufpreises bezahlt, bei größeren Objekten auch zu einem niedrigeren Promille-Satz. Bei Verkäufen oder Refinanzierungen, die sich in relativ kurzen Zeitabständen wiederholen, kann man erhebliche Rabatte verhandeln, sofern man den gleichen title insurer benutzt. Es gibt in den USA etwa sieben große, überregional tätige title insurer, die einen Marktanteil von annähernd 90% haben.

Organschaft — Tax Consolidation

Corporations in Germany can only file the equivalent of a consolidated tax return if parent and subsidiary have entered into a control agreement („Beherrschungsvertrag") and a profit distribution agreement („Gewinnabführungsvertrag").

In den USA können Kapitalgesellschaften ab einer Beteiligungshöhe von 80% automatisch konsolidierte Steuererklärungen abgeben. (Siehe auch → Dividendenbesteuerung; → Körperschaftsteuer.)

Partiarisches Darlehen — Participating Loan ~ Equity Kicker

(→ Gesellschafterfremdfinanzierung)

Parzelle (Flurstück) — Lot

Parzellierung — Subdivision

Parzellierungsplan — Plat

Pauschalpreisvertrag — Fixed-Price Contract

In Germany, general contractors (Generalunternehmer) are usually hired on the basis of fixed-price contracts. If the volume of the required work is difficult to assess, a combination of fixed price and „cost plus fee" is sometimes used.

In den USA ist der „cost plus fee" Vertrag eher üblich. Der Generalunternehmer, der üblicherweise alle Gewerke subkontrahiert, erhält dabei ein Gebühr zuzüglich zu den Gesamtkosten des Projekts. Um dem Auftraggeber etwas mehr Kostensicherheit zu geben, gibt es die Variante des „Top Ceiling" Preis, bei dessen Unterschreitung sich Unternehmer und Auftraggeber die Ersparnis teilen, etwa im Verhältnis 25–75. Sofern alle Spezifikationen und Detailzeichnungen bei Auftragsvergabe bereits vorliegen, wird vom Generalunternehmer ausnahmsweise auch ein „Fixed-Price Contract" akzeptiert.

Pensionkassen **Pension Funds**

Pensionskassen generally are insurance companies which are tax exempt and receive contributions from employers. The contributions are subject to a flat wage-withholding tax of 20%.

It was a deliberate policy of the early post World War II government in Germany not to burden businesses with funded pension liabilities. Thus, funded pensions represent a much smaller capital base in Germany than, for example, in the U.S., the U. K. or the Netherlands. German businesses generally create pension liabilities (reserves) on their balance sheets. The reserves are tax deductible only to the extent of their present (cash) value and to the extent the pension promise is in writing and has become fully vested. There is an increasing debate to further funded pension plans through legislation.

A mandatory, industry sponsored, entity (Pensions-Sicherungs-Verein; comparable to the Pension Benefit Guaranty Corporation in the U.S.), insures accrued pensions owed by bankrupt employers.

In den USA werden Pensionsverpflichtungen grundsätzlich in Pensionskassen laufend eingezahlt. Sofern der Plan steuerlich begünstigt (qualified plan) ist, ist nicht nur der Pension Fund körperschaftsteuerbefreit, es sind auch die Arbeitgeberbeiträge lohnsteuerfrei. Für die Steuerfreiheit der Beiträge gelten gewisse Höchstbeträge, je nachdem ob es sich um einen Plan mit festgelegten Leistungen (defined benefit plan) oder einen mit festgelegten Beiträgen (defined contribution plan) handelt. Das (Steuer-)recht der betrieblichen Altersversorgung in den USA ist umfangreich und komplex.

Auch in den USA ist der Ausfall von verdienten Pensionen durch eine dem deutschen Pensions-Sicherungs-Verein ähnliche Anstalt, der Pension Benefit Guaranty Corporation versichert.

Pfandbrief / ~ Mortgage-Backed Security

Pfandbrief ~ Mortgage-Backed Security

In contrast to the mortgage-backed security in the U.S., the German Pfandbrief is backed not only by the mortgage pool, but also by the credit of the issuing mortgage bank (→ Hypothekenbank). The mortgage bank itself is restricted to mortgage and municipal lending.

It appears that securitization, i. e. the public offering of securities which are secured solely by a mortgage or other lien pool and not by the credit of the issuing bank, does not yet exist in Germany. Less than a handfull of such securities may have been sold so far, although no fundamental legal or other barriers seem to exist against securitization. In May 1996, the Federal Banking Authority (Bundesaufsichtsamt für das Kreditwesen) issued detailed proposed guidelines under which commercial German banks may originate and sell U.S. style asset backed securities.

Im Gegensatz zu Deutschland haftet in den USA die begebende Bank, in der Regel eine Investment-Bank nicht für die mortgage-backed security.

In aller Regel steht hinter dem amerikanischen Pfandbrief für Wohnimmobilien jedoch der „full faith and credit" der U.S. Regierung. Er hat sich in den vergangenen 50 Jahren weitgehend zu einer Bundesanleihe entwickelt, da er durch die Bundesregierung bzw. Bundesbehörden und Anstalten garantiert ist. In diesem Markt, dessen Volumen die Billionen Dollar Grenze überschritten hat, sind die Mehrzahl der Pfandbriefe durch die Federal Housing Administration oder die Veterans Administration garantiert, oder werden von der Government National Mortgage Association („Ginnie Mae") oder der Federal National Mortgage Company („Fannie Mae") übernommen und weiter plaziert. Darüber hinaus gibt es auch private Unternehmen, welche die Rückzahlung von Pfandbriefen versichern. Der amerikanische Pfandbrief ist dadurch zu einem extrem liquiden und diversifizierten Instrument geworden.

Für Gewerbeimmobilien hat sich durch die Immobilienkrise der frühen 90er Jahre die „Commercial Mortgage Backed Security" („CMBS") zu einer attraktiven Alternative der gewöhnlichen Bankhypothek entwickelt. CMBSs werden zur Finanzierung großer vermieteter Einzelobjekte oder auch für Pools verschiedener Objekte plaziert. Hintergrund hierfür ist, daß mit der Immobilienrezession Banken und Versicherungen zunehmend unter den Druck der Aufsichtsbehörden gerieten, höhere Rückstellungen für direkte Immobilienrisiken zu bilden. Dagegen werden

Pfandrecht /Security Interest; Lien

CMBS-Anleihen von Rating Agencies bewertet und am Kapitalmarkt in kleiner Stückelung plaziert. Für den Schulder brachten CMBSs den Vorteil frischer Liquidität und anfangs auch günstigerer Zinsen als gewöhnliche Hypotheken. Diese Marge schrumpft jedoch wieder. Außerdem ist die Ausgabe von CMBSs mit höheren Nebenkosten belastet, sowie einer komplexeren Struktur und erhöhtem Verwaltungsaufwand (Abwicklung über Treuhänder, etc.).

Im Vergleich zum Gesamtmarkt der Pfandbriefe für amerikanische Wohnimmobilien ist das Volumen der CMBSs immer noch gering. Während etwa 60% aller residential mortgages als Anleihen öffentlich plaziert werden, stellen CMBSs nur 10% aller gewerblichen Hypotheken dar, bzw. ein Gesamtvolumen von ca. $ 300 Milliarden. CMBSs wurden jedoch erst in den frühen 90er Jahren erfunden. Man darf annehmen, daß das Wachstum bis auf weiteres anhalten wird.

Pfandrecht   **Security Interest**
                   Lien

In Germany, perfection of a security interest in a chattel normally requires possession (Besitz) of the chattel by the lienholder. In certain cases, joint possession (Mitbesitz) or indirect possession (mittelbarer Besitz) may be sufficient. Because of the burdensome possession requirement, security interests are usually granted in the form of a full transfer of title or assignment as collateral obviating the need to transfer possession or to record or publish the transaction.

Similarly, the seller of goods usually retains title (Eigentumsvorbehalt) until full payment. That is why German companies often own less than their balance sheets shows, and why trade creditors fare comparatively well in bankruptcies of their customers.

Das amerikanische Pfandrecht an beweglichen Sachen entsteht – wie in Deutschland -durch Inbesitznahme. Jedoch kann das amerikanische Pfandrecht auch ohne Besitzübergabe an den Pfandgläubiger entstehen, und zwar durch Eintragung bei der zuständigen Behörde (dem Country Clerk oder dem zuständigen Landesministerium) nach dem im betreffenden Staat geltenden Handelsgesetzbuch (das sog. U. C. C. filing). Es gibt jedoch keine besitzlose und stille Sicherungsübereignung oder -abtretung mit Außenwirkung.

Pfändungsschutz ~ Homestead

Similar to U.S. law, German law exempts certain properties of a debtor from attachment and foreclosure by creditors. Examples are parts of the debtor's income from wages or salaries, social security claims as well as personal property which is indispensable in the debtor's household, or in his agricultural or personal service business. German law does not, however, know the homestead exemption for the debtor's residence.

Auch im US-Recht sind gewisse Forderungen und Gegenstände aus sozialen Gründen vor Pfändung und Zwangsvollstreckung geschützt, beispielsweise Teile des Arbeitseinkommens, Ansprüche aus Sozialversicherungsleistungen sowie Gegenstände, die im Haushalt, in der Landwirtschaft oder für die persönliche Arbeitsleistung des Schuldners unentbehrlich sind.

Im Gegensatz zum deutschen Recht gibt es darüber hinaus in vielen US-Einzelstaaten Vorschriften, die das Eigenheim der Familie vor der Zwangsversteigerung schützen. Zweck dieser „homestead" Regeln ist es, die Familie oder auch nur die Ehefrau vor dem Zugriff der Gläubiger des überschuldeten Familienvaters bzw. Ehemanns zu schützen. Dabei ist die homestead exemption meist auf einen relativ geringen Geldbetrag und auf geringe Land- bzw. Wohnfläche beschränkt. In manchen Staaten, z. B. Florida und Texas, kann es jedoch auch einem Multi-Millionär gelingen, seine Privatvilla dem Zugriff der Banken durch die homestead exemption zu entziehen.

Auch ohne homestead Gesetzgebung legt die Rechtsprechung vieler Einzelstaaten dem Hypothekengläubiger bei Zwangsvollstreckungsmaßnahmen Beschränkungen auf. So gilt es unter Umständen als unangemessen (unconscionable), die Zwangsversteigerung gegen einen Hauseigentümer zu betreiben, der, wenn auch mit starker Verspätung, die Zahlung der aufgelaufenen Zins- oder Tilgungszahlungen anbietet.

Privatisierung Privatization

Germany has seriously entered the privatization mode. It began with the establishment of a „Trust Agency" („Treuhandanstalt", as of 1995 renamed „Bundesanstalt für vereinigungsbedingte Sonderaufgaben") in Berlin which offered and sold, between 1990 and 1997, practically all of East Germany's formerly nationalized industrial, agricultural, real estate and other income producing assets. It is well known that the process overall was a failure. Many privatized compa-

Quellensteuer für Betriebsstättengewinne / Branch Profits Tax

nies, after receiving significant subsidies, were returned bankrupt to the Government.

In West Germany, after the privatization of Lufthansa and later Telekom, the pace seems to increase, also in order to dress up for EC currency union. On the block are, among other assets, vast amounts of urban land holdings and more than 200,000 low income rental apartments, owned by the (formerly federal) railway and mail systems.

Außer erheblichen Flächen von Agrar- und Forstbesitz, besonders im Westen des Landes, sind in den USA wesentlich weniger Produktivgüter in öffentlicher Hand als in den meisten Ländern der Welt. Daher gibt es nicht viel zu privatisieren. Eine größere Transaktion war jedoch die Re-Privatisierung von Immobilienbesitz in Höhe mehrerer Milliarden Dollar Anfang der neunziger Jahre. Nachdem der Steuerzahler im Zuge der Pleite fast der gesamten Sparkassenbranche (Savings and Loans) den → Einlagensicherungs-Fonds wieder auffüllen mußte, wurde eine Bundesanstalt („Resolution Trust Corporation") eingerichtet, die das Vermögen, mehrheitlich Immobilien, der insolventen Banken übernahm. Die frühen Käufer dieser re-privatisierten Grundstücke kauften teilweise für weniger als 30% der ursprünglichen Anschaffungskosten, und verdienten im sich erholenden Immobilienmarkt erhebliche Renditen.

Privatplazierung   **Private Placement**
(see → Öffentliche Plazierung – Public Offering)

Quellensteuer für Betriebsstättengewinne   Branch Profits Tax

Germany does not impose any withholding tax on the repayment of profits by a German branch to a foreign corporation. Pursuant to the German-U.S. Income Tax Treaty, Germany would be barred from introducing a branch profits tax as long as German law taxes retained earnings of a German corporation more than 5 percentage points higher than distributed profits. Presently, retained earnings of German corporations are taxed at a corporate income tax rate of 45%, distributed earnings at a reduced rate of 30%.

In den USA werden Gewinne der U.S. Betriebsstätte einer ausländischen Kapitalgesellschaft, die nicht re-investiert werden, so behandelt, als wären sie von einer U.S. Tochtergesellschaft als Dividende an die Muttergesellschaft ausgeschüttet worden, Sec. 884 IRC. Dadurch sollen Betriebsstätten steuerlich möglichst weitgehend wie Tochtergesellschaften behandelt werden. Die USA erheben auf solche Gewinne die für Divi-

Rang / Priority

denden geltende 30%-ige Quellensteuer, bzw. die durch Doppelbesteuerungsabkommen reduzierte Quellensteuer, im Falle deutscher Muttergesellschaften 5%.

Die branch profits tax gilt auch für Einkünfte einer ausländischen Kapitalgesellschaft aus der Vermietung oder Verpachtung amerikanischer Grundstücke, sofern die Gesellschaft für die nach internem U.S. Steuerrecht übliche Netto-Besteuerung optiert. Nach dem DBA ist die Erhebung der branch profits tax grundsätzlich auch für → Veräußerungsgewinne aus U.S. Immobilien erlaubt. Jedoch wird sie nach internen U.S. Steuerrichtlinien (Reg. § 1 884−2T(a)(1)) nicht bei der vollständigen des gesamten U.S. Immobilienbestandes gelten sollte.

Rang **Priority**

The priority of a recorded real property interest is determined by the sequence of the recordings in the German Deed Registry (→ Grundbuch). The priorities of interests which are recorded in different sections of the registry (Abteilungen des Grundbuchs) are determined by their recording dates. If more than one application for the recording of the same interest comes in, the Deed Registry must record according to the time at which the applications arrive, § 17 GBO.

Praktisch alle Einzelstaaten der USA haben recording acts, die unter anderem das Rangverhältnis (→ Rang) eingetragener Rechte regeln. In den meisten Staaten gilt dabei ein ähnliches Prinzip wie in Deutschland: Der zuerst Eingetragene hat Vorrang („race recording" acts). In einigen Staaten gilt jedoch, daß der Vorrang nicht entsteht, wenn der Eintragende positive Kenntnis von einem früher entstandenen, aber noch nicht eingetragenen Recht hatte („race-notice" recording).

Rangvorbehalt **~ Reservation of Priority Rank Subordination**

Under Section 881 of the German Civil Code, the owner of property may reserve a senior position for some future recordable interest whenever he grants a lien or other encumbrance on his property. For future mortgages this result is more conveniently achieved by registering an „owners mortgage" (→ Eigentümergrundschuld) which later can be used directly for obtaining bank financing without any further recording. In practice, therefore, the reserving of rank is rarely used.

Was in Deutschland durch den Rangvorbehalt bewirkt wird, wird in den USA in aller Regel durch eine subordination Klauseln erreicht, durch

Rechtsmangel / Legal Defect

die ein Gläubiger oder anderer Berechtigter den Vorrang bestimmter anderer Rechte vertraglich anerkennt. Ein Rangrücktritt anderer Rechte, beispielsweise von → Ground Leases, wird von Hypothekengebern regelmäßig verlangt.

Ratenzahlung   **Installment Payment**

Similar to U.S. tax law, installment payments in Germany are considered to contain an interest and an amortization element. The effect of this is that long-term capital gains of individual taxpayers, which generally are entirely tax free (→ Veräußerungsgewinn), will be deemed to include imputed interest in the case of an installment sale.

Unlike in the U.S., the installment basis reporting will not have a tax deferral effect. Gains derived from the sale of inventory or similar trade and business assets are taxable in Germany without the possibility of installment basis reporting. Sales of property by individual taxpayers outside of their trade or business (Privatvermögen) are non-taxable altogether, except for imputed interest.

In den USA ist jeder → Veräußerungsgewinn steuerpflichtig. Der Ratenverkauf auf „installment basis" nach Sec. 453 IRC (Zuflußprinzip) hat im US-Steuerrecht daher den Vorteil der Steuerstundung, es sei denn, der Verkäufer optiert gegen die Besteuerung auf installment basis. Die Beleihung von Ratenforderungen gilt steuerlich als Zufluß. Auch in den USA enthalten Ratenzahlungen fiktive Zinsen (imputed interest).

Nach Sec. 453(b)(2) IRC steht Händlern (dealer) die Besteuerung nach der installment-Methode nicht zur Verfügung, von wenigen unbedeutenden Ausnahmen abgesehen.

Räumungsklage   **Dispossess Proceedings**
                                                                                                            Eviction

Reallast   **Personal Servitude**
                                                                                                                      Usufruct

Rechtsfähigkeit   **~ Legal Subject**
(→ Juristische Personen)

Rechtsmangel   **Legal Defect**
Rechtsübung (→ Gewohnheitsrecht)

Rendite / Yield; Cap Rate

Rendite   **Yield**
                                                                                                                  ~ Cap Rate

While yields or cap rates are usually determined in slightly different ways in Germany than in the U.S., it can generally be said that they have been historically much lower than in the U.S., both for commercial and residential properties. There are two main reasons for this: German tax law has favored real estate more than U.S. tax law by applying artificially low assessed values (→ Einheitswert) and by exempting long-term (2-years) capital gains of individual taxpayers from tax. The more important reason probably is that investors in German property know that they are buying a scarce commodity. German real estate prices are almost competitive with the performance of the German stock market if compared over long periods of time.

Apart from a strong cyclical down turn which became apparent in 1993–94, there are other reasons why the German property market may gradually approach yields which are comparable to those of other European countries, such as the U.K., France or Sweden, and closer to yields prevalent in the U.S. The reasons are the changes in assessed values, considerations to rewrite the law regarding tax exempt capital gains and a sudden increase in available land and property (former East-Germany, privatisations of the Federal Mail System, or of the Federal Railways with almost 10,000 acres of inner city lots). It should be noted that the residential market is shunned by some investors because of the prevailing tenant protection and rent stabilization laws in Germany.

Renditen in amerikanischen Immobilien sind historisch und auch gegenwärtig deutlich höher als in Deutschland. Dies liegt einmal daran, daß Immobilieninvestments steuerlich nicht ähnlich begünstigt sind wie in Deutschland. So ist die steuerliche Bemessungsgrundlage, etwa für Erbschaftsteuern, der volle Verkehrswert. Auch sind Veräußerungsgewinne grundsätzlich steuerpflichtig. Der wohl wichtigste Grund für die hohen Renditen ist, daß sich Investoren bewußt sind, ein fast beliebig vermehrbares Wirtschaftsgut zu kaufen. Über lange Zeitläufe kann man mit einer deutlich über der Inflation liegenden Wertsteigerung nicht unbedingt rechnen. Auch verändern sich die guten Lagen und der Mieter- oder Käufergeschmack in den USA schneller als in Deutschland.

Rentenschuld   **~ Mortgage-backed Annuity**

Sacheinlagen / Contributions of Property

Rückerwerb ~ **Repossession**

Under German tax law, if the purchaser of property defaults on the payment obligation or seller mortgage, and title to the property reverts back to the seller, the seller may claim a loss only if the property clearly has less value than his remaining purchase price claim.

Wenn die Verkäuferhypothek nicht bezahlt wird, und das Grundstück an den Verkäufer zurückgeht, kann dieser nach Sec. 1083 IRC niemals einen steuerlichen Verlust wegen Abschreibung der Kaufpreisforderung gelten machen. Ein etwaiger Gewinn bleibt jedoch auf den Betrag des bis dahin geleisteten Kaufpreises beschränkt.

Für die Rücknahme beweglicher Gegenstände gelten in den USA jedoch ähnliche Regeln wie in Deutschland, d. h. ein Verlust wird nur anerkannt, wenn das zurückgenommene Sicherungsgut eindeutig weniger wert ist als die betreffende (Kaufpreis-)forderung.

Sacheinlagen **Contributions of Property**

If a single property or an entire business is transferred to the capital of a partnership, the parties have the option, under applicable tax guidelines („Mitunternehmererlaß") or under the Tax Reorganization Act („UmwStG") to defer gain by continuing book values („Buchwert"), or to recognize gain and step up the properties to fair market value („Teilwert"), or to choose an intermediate value („Zwischenwert"). The same option exists, under the UmwStG, for contributions to privately held corporations if the contributed property is an entire business („Betrieb"), or a separate business unit („Teilbetrieb"), whether owned directly or in partnership form. Real estate which is leased to third parties generally does not constitute a Betrieb or Teilbetrieb.

Under German corporate law, contributions of non-cash to the capital of a corporation are problematic. German law requires minimum statutory capital and par-value shares. Consequently, it also requires that capital is not repaid or diluted. The Stock Corporation Act („Aktiengesetz") strictly limits the issuance of shares for property other than cash. Property contributions by founding shareholders must be specifically authorized in the corporate charter („Satzung") and obtain the fairness approval of an independent appraiser. Subsequent increases of authorized or issued capital against property contributions must be authorized by shareholders resolution and confirmed by appraisal. Contributed property must have a value not substantially below par-value or trading value of the issued shares. Shares may never be issued against services. The Small Corporations Act („GmbH-Gesetz") contains similar but less detailed rules.

Sachmängel / Defects

Another problem for such property contributions is that German shareholders have statutory preemptive rights for new stock (→ Bezugsrechte). These stock rights have to be waived if property is purchased for stock.

In den USA werden bei Sacheinlagen in Personengesellschaften oder im Rahmen von steuerfreien Umwandlungen (reorganizations), ähnlich wie in Deutschland, keine stillen Reserven aufgedeckt. Bei Einlagen in neu gegründete Gesellschaften müssen die Einlegenden unmittelbar danach mindestens 80% aller Aktien der Gesellschaft besitzen.

Das U.S.-Aktienrecht ist wesentlich liberaler in bezug auf Sacheinlagen als das deutsche. Da Bezugsrechte in den meisten größeren Gesellschaften nicht bestehen, und das Aktienrecht außerdem keine dem deutschen Recht vergleichbaren Kapitalerhaltungs- und Gläubigerschutzvorschriften hat, ist der mit eigenen Aktien bezahlte Kauf anderer Unternehmen oder Betriebe in den USA Bestandteil fast aller großer Transaktionen. Wie man in den USA auch sagt: Die Börsennotierung ist eine staatliche Lizenz, sein eigenes Geld zu drucken. Natürlich darf das Management die Aktionäre nicht durch unangemessene Bewertungen bei Sacheinlagen verwässern, oder Gläubigern in der Bilanz überbewertetes Eigenkapital zeigen.

Sachmängel   Defects
(→ „Wie es steht und liegt" – „As Is")

Sachversicherung   Property Insurance
→ Versicherung

Sale – Leaseback   Sale – Leaseback

Whether the sale and leaseback of property, including real property, will be qualified as a true operating lease or merely as a secured loan depends on similar criteria in Germany as in the U.S. The overriding factor in both countries will be which of the parties substantially carries the risk of depreciation or obsolescence, and which of the parties enjoys most of the appreciation. In contrast to U.S. tax laws, German fiscal authorities and the German Supreme Tax Court (BFH) have issued highly specific rules relating to various types of operating or financial leases, including full pay-out leases (Vollamortisationsleasing), partial pay-out leases (Teilamortisationsverträge), real property leasing and the leasing of personal property. Many of these rules have been in existence largely unchanged for more than 15 years. They provide relatively reliable safe-harbour rules.

Schriftform / Writing; Statute of Frauds

In den USA wird der Sale and Leaseback von Betriebsgrundstücken nicht nur aus steuerlichen, sondern häufig aus bilanzoptischen Gründen vorgenommen. Börsennotierte Gesellschaften wollen ihre Bilanzen nicht mit „brick and mortar" belasten. Im übrigen kann man durch den sale leaseback Kapital annähernd in Höhe des Verkehrswerts der Immobilie beschaffen, was durch eine Hypothek meist nicht möglich ist.

Steuerlich gelten ähnliche Regeln wie in Deutschland. Als wirtschaftlicher Eigentümer gilt die Partei, die den Löwenanteil des Verlustrisikos bzw. der Gewinnchancen besitzt.

Sanierungsgebiet — **Redevelopment Area / Urban Renewal Area**

Sanierungsgewinn (→ **Forderungsverzicht**)

Schadensersatz — **Damages**

Scheinbestandteile (→ **Wesentlicher Bestandteil**)

Schenkungsteuer — **Gift Tax**
→ Erbschaftsteuer – Estate Tax

Schiebungsanfechtung (→ **Konkursanfechtung**) — **Voidable Preference / Fraudulent Conveyance**

Schiedsgericht — **Arbitration Tribunal**

Schriftform — **Writing / ~ Statute of Frauds**

Agreements to transfer or encumber real property interests in Germany require notarial reading and acknowledgement deed (→ Notar; → Notarielle Beurkundung) to be valid, § 313 BGB. The law is intended for the protection of seller and buyer. Courts will uphold such agreements despite the lack of notarial acknowledgement only in exceptional cases of severe hardship. However, performance of an otherwise invalid agreement will cure the defect. There is some case law to the effect that notarial action is not required if the agreement is concluded abroad. Transfers of property holding entities require no notarial action, unless the entity was formed mainly to avoid the notarial form requirement. An assignment of a real property

Sicherheiten / Collateral; Security

contract also requires notarial acknowledgement if the assignee is obligated to acquire the property.

Certain other agreements do not require a notarial deed, but must be in writing, such as guaranties („Bürgschaft"), promises of gift („Schenkung") or lease agreements with terms of more than one year (§ 566 BGB). Without a written agreement, such leases will be deemed to have been concluded for an indefinite period but may be terminated one year after their beginning. The termination may, however, be subject to the residential tenant protection laws (→ Mieterschutz; → Mietpreisbindung; → Kündigungsschutz). Broker agreements do not require writing.

In contrast to the laws of many states in the U.S., German law generally requires the signature of all parties to satisfy the statute of frauds, as well as a permanent joining (such as by stapling) of the pages forming the agreement.

Grundstücksveräußerungen oder Belastungen erfordern im amerikanischen Recht keine Beurkundung, sondern einfache Schriftform und Unterschriftsbeglaubigung (notarization).

Mietverträge, deren Laufzeit länger als ein Jahr ist, bedürfen in den meisten Einzelstaaten der USA der Schriftform. Dieses Erfordernis entspricht der Vorschrift des § 566 BGB. Wird das Schriftformerfordernis in den USA nicht eingehalten und zieht der Mieter ein, so entsteht eine „periodic tenancy", bei Wohnraum typischerweise eine „month-to-month tenancy", die von beiden Parteien jeweils zum Monatsende gekündigt werden kann. Maklerverträge bedürfen in manchen Staaten der Schriftform.

Im Unterschied zum deutschen Recht müssen Verträge, deren Wirksamkeit die Schriftform voraussetzt, in vielen Einzelstaaten der USA nur von einer Partei unterschrieben werden, und zwar jeweils von der, gegen die die andere Partei Erfüllung verlangt. In einer steigenden Zahl von Einzelstaaten wird unterdessen jedoch die Unterschrift durch beide Parteien verlangt.

Sicherheiten **Collateral**
 Security

Sicherungseigentum **Deed of Trust**
(→ Hypothek)

Sitz **Domicile**
(→ Beschränkt Steuerpflichtige)

Sofortige Fälligkeit ~ Due-on-Sale Clause

In Germany, as in the U.S., lender and borrower may agree that the mortgage becomes due on the sale of the property, although this is not free from doubt. However, a German mortgage lender may not restrain the property owner from selling or further encumbering the property, § 1136 BGB. Under existing German insolvency law, a first mortgage enjoys better protection than its equivalent in the U.S. The statute, therefore, assumes that the mortgage lender has sufficient security. He does not need additional protection by restraining the owner from further encumbrances.

Outside the context of mortage lending, however, an owner may be contractually bound not to sell a property, § 137 BGB.

Wie in Deutschland kann auch in den USA vereinbart werden, daß die Hypothek bei Veräußerung des Grundstücks sofort fällig wird. Im Gegensatz zum deutschen Recht kann ein Hypothekengläubiger es dem Hypothekenschuldner auch verbieten, das Grundstück weiterzubelasten.

Die Gerichte der Einzelstaaten vertraten über die Zulässigkeit von due-on-sale clauses sehr unterschiedliche Meinungen. Einige hielten diese Klauseln grundsätzlich für wirksam, andere erklärten sie für nichtig als unzulässige Verfügungsverbote (restraint of alienation). Durch Bundesgesetz (Garn-St. Germain Depository Institutions Act von 1982) ist heute klargestellt, daß due-on-sale clauses grundsätzlich wirksam sind. Unwirksam sind sie nur in bestimmten Fällen des belasteten Wohneigentums, z. b. bei dessen weiterer Belastung, oder Übertragung an Familienmitglieder oder Erben, sowie dessen kurzfristiger (3 Jahre) Vermietung.

Sonderabschreibungen ~ Special Depreciation

Under German tax law, certain expenditures may be depreciated under generous special depreciation rates which are cumulative to regular depreciation. One of the most generous tax shelters available to German taxpayers were the special depreciations available to real property development or renovation expenditures in the five re-united Eastern German states. After 1996, the special depreciation rates for Eastern German construction expenditures will be reduced. They will remain particularly attractive for renewal and renovation expenditures. In 1999, most Eastern German special depreciations will likely be phased out.

Im US-Steuerrecht gibt es das Prinzip der Sonderabschreibung nicht.

Sondermüll Hazardous Waste

Sozialbindung d. Eigentums / ~ Social Resp. of Ownership

Sozialbindung   **~ Social Responsibility of Ownership**
des Eigentums

German law, in Article 14 of the Grundgesetz provides constitutional protection of private property. Private property can only be taken or curtailed (→ Enteignung) against fair compensation (angemessene Entschädigung). As in the U.S., certain restrictions of free use and enjoyment of private property may be valid without compensation if the restriction lies within the social responsibility (Sozialbindung) of private ownership. It is fair to say that German law has gradually encroached the principle of private property rights under the pretext of social responsibility to a greater extent than U.S. law. It seems there is an opposite trend in the two countries. For example, environmental causes (→ Umweltschutz) increasingly override private property rights in Germany while many states in the U.S. have enacted legislation entitling property owners to compensation for particularly burdensome environmental laws.

Wie die deutsche Verfassung schützt auch das US-Recht auf Bundes- und Landesebene das private Eigentum und erlaubt die Enteignung nur gegen angemessene Entschädigung (just compensation). Jedoch geht die Sozialbindung des Eigentums in den USA sicherlich nicht soweit wie in Deutschland. Sie beschränkt sich bei Grundvermögen in erster Linie auf Landschafts- und Naturschutz. Auch haben in den vergangenen Jahren viele US-Einzelstaaten Gesetze erlassen, denen zufolge Grundeigentümer im Falle besonders beeinträchtigender → Umweltschutzbestimmungen angemessene Entschädigung verlangen können. Hier zeichnet sich wahrscheinlich ein gegenläufiger Trend zur politischen und rechtlichen Entwicklung in Deutschland ab.

Sozialer Wohnungsbau   **Low Income Housing**

A major part of new housing construction after World War II in Germany was conducted under Government sponsored low income housing projects. These are developed by municipal agencies, cooperatives or affiliates of trade unions. Important subsidies for these projects are tied to rent control and income ceilings for admissible tenants. However, if a tenant's income rises above the applicable threshold he may remain in the apartment and become subject to a compensation levy.

Conversion of low income housing into „free housing", i. e. rent control free housing, is prohibited for periods of 20 years or more after construction. In recent years, low incoming housing projects have been reduced, but they still account for around 15% of all new housing.

Sparkassen / Savings Banks

Das "Low Income Housing" wird in den USA durch eine Bundesbehörde, die "Housing and Urban Development" (HUD) geregelt. Diese Behörde unterstützt den gemeinnützigen Wohnungsbau durch eine Reihe verschiedener Förderprogramme.

Soziales Mietrecht ~ Tenant Protection Laws

German law provides extensive protection for the interests of residential tenants, primarily by limiting rent increases and generally giving tenants the right to permanently renew their leases (Bestandsschutz; → Kündigungsschutz). The renewal rights are primarily described in the "social clauses" of §§ 556a through c BGB. Social needs of the residential tenants must be weighed against the plausible interests (→ Berechtigte Interessen) of the landlord. The plausible interest usually forwarded by landlords is the need for owner-occupancy (→Eigenbedarf). The "Eigenbedarfsklage" is one of the most frequent legal actions prevailing in German courts.

Generally, increases in rent are limited under the Rent Level Act (Miethöhegesetz) and the Wohnungsbindungsgesetz. Depending on the kind of property, subsidized housing (Sozialwohnungen) or other residential properties, increases of rent are limited either to the cost basis (Kostenmiete) or to market rents for comparable property (Vergleichsmiete).

In den USA gibt es den Schutz des Wohnungsmieters vor Kündigung oder Mieterhöhung nur noch vereinzelt (→ Mieterschutz). Vermieter von Wohnraum, die Finanzierung durch die FHA (Federal Housing Administration) erhalten oder Befreiung von → Grundsteuern genießen, stehen jedoch unter dem Gebot der Gleichbehandlung (non-discrimination) von Mietern aus verschiedenen Einkommens- oder Bevölkerungsgruppen.

Sparkassen Savings Banks

German Sparkassen generally are non-profit institutions established under public law and owned by municipalities, counties or states. A large part of their refinancing comes from the issuance of mortgage-backed securities (→ Pfandbriefe). Generally, the mortgage lending of Sparkassen is limited to residential properties and, to a lesser degree, small commercial properties. (→ Bausparkassen – Savings and Loan Associations).

Ein Äquivalent für die deutsche Sparkasse scheint es in den USA nicht zu geben. In der Regel sind savings banks privatwirtschaftlich organisiert

Spekulationsfrist / Capital Gains Holding Period

und auf Gewinn ausgerichtet. Sie sind zu unterscheiden von den Savings and Loan Associations (→ Bausparkassen).

Spekulationsfrist — Capital Gains Holding Period

The required holding periods for tax-free capital gains in Germany are two years for real property, six months for other property (→ Spekulationsgeschäft). These periods will likely be extended to five, possibly ten years for property, one year for securities. In contrast to U.S. tax law, the holding period is determined by the dates of execution of the underlying purchase or sale agreements, not the closing dates.

In den USA kommt es für die 18-Monats-Frist des short term capital gains grundsätzlich auf den Zeitpunkt der jeweiligen closings an, und nicht wie in Deutschland auf den Abschluß der jeweiligen Kaufverträge.

Spekulationsgeschäft — Short-term Capital Gain

Under German tax law, gain from the sale of real property held by individual taxpayers as a non-trade or business asset (Privatvermögen) is taxable only if the holding period (→ Spekulationsfrist) was less than two years (soon to be extended to five or ten years). After such holding period, capital gains will be tax free unless a commercial real estate business activity is assumed to exist. The distinction between commercial property dealing and private investment activity is primarily based on the turnover of assets (→ Gewerbebetrieb; → gewerblicher Grundstückshändler).

In den USA ist jeder → Veräußerungsgewinn steuerpflichtig, auch solche im Privatvermögen. Jedoch gilt für long-term capital gains natürlicher Personen (Zeitraum zwischen Anschaffung und Veräußerung mehr als 18 Monate, IRC § 1222) ein Steuersatz von 20% im Gegensatz zu dem gewöhnlichen Spitzensteuersatz von 39,6%. Insofern spielt der Besitzzeitraum auch im US-Steuerrecht eine Rolle.

Spekulationsgewinn — Short-term Capital Gain

Under German law, the amount of short-term capital gain used to be measured as the difference between the sales proceeds and the original cost before depreciation. For property purchased after August 1, 1995, a new recapture rule is in effect, § 23(3) EStG: Gain is the difference between sales proceeds and the depreciated basis of the property, i. e. original cost after depreciation, including increased de-

preciation or special depreciation. Since special depreciation (→ Sonderabschreibungen) can be extremely high, a sale within the short-term holding period may result in a significant tax liability.

In den USA ist jeder Veräußerungsgewinn steuerpflichtig. Jedoch sind long-term capital gains (18 Monate) im Privatvermögen günstiger besteuert. Bei bestimmten Immobilien und anderen Wirtschaftsgütern wird ein Teil des Veräußerungsgewinns jedoch als gewöhnliches Einkommen besteuert, soweit damit zurückliegende degressive Abschreibungen ausgeglichen werden („depreciation recapture"). In jedem Fall bemißt sich der Gewinn als Unterschied zwischen Verkaufserlös und Restbuchwert.

Spekulationsverlust / Short-term Capital Loss

Under German tax law, individual taxpayers may offset short-term capital losses against short-term capital gains realized in the same fiscal year. Such losses may not be deducted from other types of income or gains, nor may they be carried back or forward.

In den USA wird der net short term capital loss erst gegen long term capital gains verrechnet. Verbleibt danach immer noch ein Verlust (capital loss), so ist dieser gegen anderes Einkommen abzugs- und vortragsfähig, jedoch nur bis zu $ 1500 jährlich ($ 3000 für Zusammenveranlagte). Ein verbleibender capital loss ist in der Höhe unbegrenzt gegen spätere capital gains vortragsfähig. U.S. Kapitalgesellschaften können capital losses immer nur gegen capital gains ausgleichen und vortragen.

Spezialitätsprinzip / ~ Specification Requirement

Under § 1115 BGB, a mortgage can only be recorded if its nominal principal amount, or a maximum principal amount (Höchstbetrag), as well as the applicable interest rate and any other debt service requirements (Nebenleistungen) are recorded.

Im Recht der meisten US-Einzelstaaten ist die exakte Angabe des Kapitalbetrags und der Zinsen für die wirksame Eintragung der Hypothek theoretisch nicht erforderlich. Jedoch ginge der Hypothekengläubiger bei fehlender Angabe des Kapitalbetrags das Risiko ein, daß spätere Grundpfandrechte im → Rang vorgehen können.

Staatsangehörigkeit / Citizenship, Nationality

Staatsangehörigkeit   Citizenship, Nationality

In Germany, the citizenship of father or mother, rather than the place of birth, determines a person's citizenship. Adoption can also create citizenship. Children born out of wedlock („nichteheliche Kinder") inherit their mother's citizenship.

Citizenship may be acquired („Einbürgerung", „Naturalisation") upon application by any permanent resident who is able to support his/her own livelihood and has a clean record. Priority is given to foreign spouses of Germans, to young applicants, to long-term residents and to persons without foreign citizenship. The granting of citizenship is entirely in the discretion of the Government. Public interest rather than individual concerns will determine the decision. With few exceptions, foreign citizenship must be abandoned before German citizenship can be acquired.

Citizenship is lost if a person permanently resides abroad and acquires foreign citizenship without having obtained prior approval by Germany to retain German citizenship. However, no German can lose citizenship against his will if he was left without any citizenship („staatenlos") thereafter.

Die amerikanische Staatsbürgerschaft wird durch Geburt in Amerika oder die amerikanische Staatsangehörigkeit eines Elternteils erworben, oder auch durch Einbürgerung. Letztere kann nach einem festen Aufenthalt von mindestens fünf Jahren von jeder nicht vorbestraften Person beantragt werden.

Steuer   Tax
(→ Einkommensteuer; → Körperschaftsteuer; → Gewerbesteuer;
→ Mehrwertsteuer; → Erbschaftsteuer)

Almost all taxes are governed by federal law in Germany. However, the tax revenues are divided among the Federal Government, the States and municipalities.

The Federal Government receives all revenues from the insurance, liquor, tobacco and similar other consumption taxes, as well as customs duties, and the „solidarity surtax" (re-unification tax).

Individual and corporate income taxes, VAT tax (Mehrwertsteuer) and part of the trade and business tax (Gewerbesteuer) are divided among Federal and State governments.

The states collect all revenues from the net worth tax (Vermögensteuer; presently abolished), estate and gift tax, property transfer tax, motor vehicle tax, beer tax and gambling tax.

Steuererklärung / Tax Return

Municipalities are entitled to the revenues from the real property tax, local consumption taxes (dogs, beverages, etc.), and part of the trade and business tax.

In den USA gibt es auf Bundesebene (federal tax) im wesentlichen die Einkommensteuern für natürliche Personen und Kapitalgesellschaften, sowie Erbschaft- und Schenkungssteuern.

Auf Länderebene (state taxes) gibt es in den meisten Einzelstaaten die gleichen Steuerarten wie auf Bundesebene, wobei die Bundessteuererklärung mit meist geringen Abweichungen als Grundlage für die Erhebung der Ländersteuer gilt. Darüber hinaus gibt es in fast allen Einzelstaaten Umsatzsteuern (sales tax) und Grunderwerbssteuern.

Größere Städte erheben alle oder die meisten der genannten Steuern ebenfalls auf Gemeindeebene, und darüber hinaus Grundsteuer (Real Property Tax), die eine der wichtigsten Einnahmequellen der Gemeinden und Kreise darstellt.

Steueranrechnung (→ Anrechnungsmethode)	**Tax Credit**
Steuerbefreiung	**Tax Exemption**
Steuerbilanz	**Tax Balance Sheet** **Tax Accounting**

In Germany, with some exceptions, if an accounting entry has been chosen for financial reporting purposes, either optional or mandatory, the same accounting method will apply for tax purposes. Tax returns generally mirror the financial statements („Maßgeblichkeitsgrundsatz").

Häufig sind auch in den USA Ansätze in der Handelsbilanz verbindlich für die Steuerbilanz. Jedoch gibt es in den USA wesentlich mehr Durchbrechungen dieses „Maßgeblichkeitsgrundsatzes" als in Deutschland.

Steuererklärung   **Tax Return**

In Germany, income tax and most other tax liabilities, except for witholding taxes, do not arise on the taxpayer's filing of a return, but with the subsequent tax assessment (Steuerbescheid) by the fiscal authority pursuant to 155 Abgabenordnung. In theory, fiscal authorities doe not accept a tax return on its face, but issue a Steuerbescheid after a summary review of the return.

Non-residents must file tax returns only for certain types of German-source income, including real estate income or business income (Betriebsstätteneinkünfte).

Steuergutschrift / Tax Credit

In den USA gilt das Erklärungsprinzip. Die Steuerschuld wird durch die Steuererklärung (tax return) begründet. An die vermutete Ehrlichkeit des Steuerzahlers und die nur sporadisch durchgeführten Steuerprüfungen (weniger als 3% der Einkommensteuererklärungen erfahren das Schicksal des tax audit) knüpfen sich drakonischere Strafen als bei deutschen Steuervergehen üblich, inklusive erhebliche Zins- und Säumniszuschläge.

Für Steuerausländer ist von besonderer Bedeutung, daß die unentschuldigt verspätete Abgabe (16 Monate nach Jahresende) von Steuererklärungen, z. B. für U.S. Immobilien- oder Betriebsstätteneinkünfte, zur Aberkennung sämtlicher Werbungskosten bzw. Betriebsausgaben führen kann. Im übrigen werden auch ohne Abgabe von Steuererklärungen Afa fingiert, mit der Folge, daß bei späterem Verkauf etwa einer U.S. Immobilie ein entsprechend höherer Veräußerungsgewinn vorliegt (Erlös minus Restbuchwert).

Steuergutschrift / Tax Credit

Stiftung / Foundation Trust

The establishment of a Stiftung requires governmental approval if it is to attain the status of a corporation. Exceptions exist for certain family foundations in some states. German law distinguishes the „Stiftung des Privatrechts", which may either be a family trust (Familienstiftung) or a private foundation (privatrechtlich organisierte, gemeinnützige Stiftung), and the charitable Stiftung, which is established under public law (Stiftung des öffentlichen Rechts). The private Stiftung will qualify as a juridical person (Juristische Person) only through governmental approval.

The private Stiftung is subject to corporate income tax, § 1 (1 No.) No. 4 KStG. Unlike the regular German corporation, the Stiftung does not distinguish between different classes of retained earnings. Also, its earnings are subject to the regular 45% corporate income tax, whether they are retained or distributed.

Non-juridical Stiftungen, i. e. foundations which have not attained the status of corporation, are taxable only to the extent their income is not directly attributable to beneficiaries.

Charitable Stiftungen are exempt from corporate income tax.

German tax law eliminates the double-taxation of income for all categories of foundations. Distributions of a tax-paying foundation are tax free in the hands of

Stiftung / Foundation; Trust

the beneficiaries. Distributions of a tax-exempt foundation are generally taxable to the recipients.

Both the transfer of property to a private Stiftung and its eventual liquidation are subject to estate and gift taxes (→ Erbschaftsteuer). Moreover, the assets of a family foundation (Familienstiftung) are subject to estate taxation recurring every 30 years (Erbersatzsteuer). The Erbersatzsteuer serves a similar purpose as the U.S. generation skipping transfer tax.

In den USA entspricht die (private) foundation der privatrechtlich organisierten gemeinnützigen Stiftung, wobei die foundation einer minimalen Besteuerung unterliegt, insbesondere auf thesaurierte Einkünfte.

Der amerikanische trust entspricht der nicht-gemeinnützigen Stiftung, wobei keinerlei staatliche Genehmigung zur Errichtung oder Rechtsfähigkeit erforderlich ist. Steuerlich gilt ebenfalls das Prinzip der Einmalbesteuerung, jedoch mit anderen Regeln als in Deutschland: Es wird unterschieden zwischen unechten trusts (grantor trusts) und eigentlichen trusts. Beim grantor trust behält sich der Stifter (grantor oder settlor genannt) gewisse Widerrufs-, Kontroll- oder Verwaltungsrechte vor. Er bleibt infolge dessen auf sämtliche Einkünfte des trusts steuerpflichtig, auch soweit diese an Begünstigte verteilt werden. Beim eigentlichen trust entzieht sich das übertragene Vermögen endgültig dem Zugriff des Stifters. Einkünfte dieses trusts sind auf Ebene des trusts steuerpflichtig. Sie sind jedoch nicht beim trust, sondern bei den Begünstigen direkt steuerpflichtig, soweit sie an diese verteilt werden, oder nach der Stiftungsurkunde verteilt werden müssen und zur Verteilung bereitgestellt sind.

Auch in den USA unterliegt die Übertragung von Vermögen auf einen eigentlichen (unwiderruflichen) trust der Schenkung- bzw. → Erbschaftsteuer (gift or estate tax).

Einen ähnlichen Zweck wie die Erbersatzsteuer verfolgt die generation skipping transfer tax. Sie findet Anwendung, wenn Stiftungsvermögen unter Umgehung der Kindergeneration auf Enkel- oder spätere Generationen übergeht, oder direkt auf diese Generationen übertragen wird.

Hinter dem Begriff trust verbirgt sich in den USA im übrigen nicht nur der der deutschen Familienstiftung vergleichbare echte trust, sondern ganz allgemein die Treuhandschaft, d. h. jedes Rechtsverhältnis, bei dem eine Person im eigenen Namen für Rechnung eines anderen handelt.

Stille Reserven / ~ Hidden Reserves

Stille Reserven   **~ Hidden Reserves**
(→ Übertragung stiller Reserven)

Strom (→ **Umlagen**)   **Electricity**

Subunternehmer   **Subcontractor**

Tarifvertrag (→ Gewerkschaften)

Tausch, steuerfreier   **Tax-free Exchange**

German tax law avails three principal methods of exchanging appreciated property without paying tax: Under the „Tauschgutachten" decision of the Supreme Tax Court (BFH), a taxpayer may exchange shares in a business against shares in another business, if the acquired shares have a similar value, a similar character and a similar function („wert-, art- und funktionsgleich"). Also, the Taxation Reorganization Act (Umwandlungssteuergesetz) allows for various forms of tax-free reorganizations, including, since 1995, spin-offs and split-ups. In addition, § 6b and § 6c Income Tax Act (EStG) permit the sale of certain fixed assets of a business without recognizing gain provided the sales proceeds are reinvested within certain time periods in similar assets (→ Übertragung stiller Reserven).

Except for certain real property, which is part of the fixed assets of a business, German tax law does not have the like-kind exchange which is available for U.S. real property. There are certain limited possibilities for tax-free exchanges of real property in the case of boundary-line adjustments for uneconomically shaped agricultural lots and for certain other reallocation measures (Flurbereinigungs- or Umlegungsverfahren).

In den USA gibt es den steuerfreien Tausch (like-kind exchange) auch für Immobilien. Dabei kommt es für die Frage der Gleichartigkeit (like-kind) nicht auf die Belegenheit der Grundstücke an, oder auf die Frage, ob sie bebaut oder unbebaut sind. Jedoch gelten im Ausland belegene Grundstücke nicht als like-kind.

Falls der Verkäufer eines Grundstückes sein Geld in ein bereits ausgewähltes neues Grundstück stecken will, kann er den Käufer seines Grundstücks bitten, das neue Grundstück zu kaufen und danach mit ihm einen Tausch vorzunehmen. Sofern dieses Geschäft innerhalb der gesetzlich vorgeschriebenen Maximalfristen abgewickelt wird, ist es steuerfrei. (s. weiter → Übertragung stiller Reserven.)

Testament / Will

Teilung　　　　　　　　　　　　　　　　　　　　　　　**Partition**
　　　　　　　　　　　　　　　　　　　　　　　　　　　　Division

Under German law, each owner of a property held in joint tenancy or in tenancy-in-common, may request that the property be divided and/or sold. The request may be made at any time or, if the contractual arrangements otherwise require, for cause. The partition and/or sale resembles the regular foreclosure sale with certain statutory specifics applicable to the partition sale (§ 180 et seq. Foreclosure Sales Act; ZVG)

In den USA gelten ähnliche Regeln für das Bruchteilseigentum (tenancy in common) wie in Deutschland. Eine Partei kann vor Gericht die Teilung begehren, aus wichtigem Grund oder einfach nach Ablauf gewisser Fristen. Das Gesamthandseigentum (joint tenancy) unterliegt dagegen nicht direkt der Teilung. Es muß erst durch einseitige Verfügung eines der Miteigentümer, beispielsweise Verpfändung seines ideellen Anteils, zerstört werden, bevor beim Gericht Antrag auf Teilung bzw. Verkauf des Grundstücks gestellt werden kann.

Teilzeit-Wohnrechtegesetz　　　　　　　　　　　~ Time Sharing Act

Selling of time shares has become a lively business thoughout the European community. Under the Teilzeit-Wohnrechtegesetz (TzWrG) which was enacted in Germany in 1996 pursuant to an applicable E. U. Directive, and took effect in 1997, sellers of time shares are under a duty of full disclosure vis-a-vis purchasers. Also, under the Act, purchasers have an automatic 10-day grace period after execution of the written purchase agreement during which they can freely rescind the agreement. Also during such 10-day period, sellers may not ask for a downpayment.

Nach erheblichen Marktmißbräuchen der frühen Achziger Jahre haben viele U.S. Einzelstaaten umfangreiche Regeln zum Verkauf von time shares entwickelt. Diese Regeln unterscheiden sich oft erheblich, sodaß eine sinnvolle Zusammenfassung an dieser Stelle kaum möglich ist.

Testament　　　　　　　　　　　　　　　　　　　　　　　Will

The ordinary German will (ordentliches Testament) must be written and signed by hand, unless it is made by way of a notarial deed. Similar to the conflict-of-law rules applicable in many U.S. states, a will is valid under German law if it conforms with the laws of the country of which the decedent is a national or with

Testamentsvollstrecker / Executor

the laws of the country where the will was made or, with respect to real property, with the laws of the country where the property is located. Spouses and children can not be totally excluded from the inheritance. They are, as a minimum, entitled to take half ("Pflichtteil") of what would be their intestate share ("gesetzlicher Erbteil").

Das amerikanische Testament kann maschinengeschrieben sein. Jedoch benötigt es nach dem Recht vieler Einzelstaaten die zusätzliche Unterschrift von Zeugen, die nicht im Testament begünstigt sein dürfen (disinterested witnesses).

Ebenso wie nach deutschem Recht ist auch nach dem Recht vieler amerikanischer Einzelstaaten ein Testament formgültig, wenn es entweder nach dem Recht des Staates der Staatsangehörigkeit des Erblassers errichtet ist, oder dem des Ortes der Errichtung, oder, soweit es sich auf Immobilien bezieht, dem ihrer Belegenheit. Ein Pflichtteilsrecht zugunsten des überlebenden Ehegatten sieht das Recht einiger U.S.-Bundesstaaten vor; Kinder und Eltern des Erblassers haben indes, soweit ersichtlich, keine Pflichtteilsansprüche.

Testamentsvollstrecker **Executor**

Thesaurierung **Retaining of Earnings**

Germany, since 1977, has abolished the double taxation of corporate profits, on the corporate and the shareholder level. Since there is no tax incentive for the retaining of corporate earnings, there are no penalty taxes on it either.

In den USA gilt die Doppelbesteuerung von Dividenden, auf Gesellschaftsebene und, bei Ausschüttung, auf Gesellschafterebene. Da Veräußerungsgewinne in der Vergangenheit, und auch heute wieder, deutlich niedrigeren Steuersätzen unterliegen, gibt es den Anreiz, Gewinne zu thesaurieren und durch späteren Verkauf zu realisieren. Dies soll durch zwei unterschiedliche Strafsteuern auf die übermäßige Thesaurierung verhindert werden, die „accumulated earnings tax" und die „personal holding company tax".

Tilgung **Amortization**
Redemption

Tilgungsdarlehen **Amortizing Loan**
Sinking Fund Loan

Übernahme der Hypothek / Assumption of Mortgage

Tilgungsfreies Darlehen ~ **Balloon Loan**

Treuhandschaft **Trust**
Fiduciary

see also → Stiftung

Überbau **Encroachment**
Invasion
Intrusion

Under German law, if part or all of a building is built on adjacent land and the encroached neighbor does not immediately object, the owner of the building will keep title to the encroaching part of the building unless the encroachment is due to wilful misconduct or gross negligence („entschuldigter" or „rechtmäßiger" Überbau), § 912 BGB. The invaded neighbour may request payment of an adequate current rental for his land, or request the invader to purchase the respective piece of his lot, § 915 BGB. If the encroachment is due to gross negligence, title to the encroaching part of the building belongs to the owner of the invaded property, who may keep it or request removal of the building part.

In den USA verliert der Überbauende in jedem Fall das Eigentum an dem Gebäude oder Gebäudeteil, welches auf Nachbarland gebaut ist. Nach herrschender Meinung muß der Nachbar, wenn er durch den Bau ungerechtfertigt bereichert ist, den unabsichtlich Überbauenden entschädigen. Alternativ kann der überbaute Nachbar verlangen, daß der betreffende Gebäudeteil abgerissen wird, es sei denn, der Überbau stellt eine sehr geringfügige Beeinträchtigung dar.

Übernahme der Hypothek **Assumption of Mortgage**

Pursuant to § 416 BGB, if mortgaged real estate is sold and the mortgage creditor does not object to the assumption of the mortgage by the purchaser within six months of receiving notice of the proposed sale and assumption, he is deemed to have consented to the release of the old debtor and the assumption of the mortgage by the purchaser. If the creditor timely objects to the assumption, the seller will remain personally liable for the mortgage; in addition, the mortgage continues to attach to the sold property (→ Haftungsgegenstände). If in such case the seller pays off the creditor he subrogates to the mortgage holder position, i. e. the mortgage secures his claim for reimbursement against the purchaser of the property, §§ 415, 329 BGB.

Übertragung stiller Reserven / ~ Tax Deferral of Gain

In den USA gibt es die Zustimmungsfiktion des § 416 BGB nicht, wonach der Hypothekengläubiger rechtzeitig Widerspruch gegen die schuldbefreiende Übernahme der Hypothek durch den Grundstückskäufer einlegen muß. Der Verkäufer muß sich um die Zustimmung des Hypothekengläubigers und um Schuldbefreiung durch Novation des Darlehensvertrages bemühen.

Übertragung stiller Reserven ~ Tax Deferral of Gain

In addition to the principles of tax free exchange or tax free reorganization (→ Umwandlung; → Tausch) applicable under German law, § 6b and § 6c of the German Income Tax Act permit the non-recognition or deferral of gain upon the sale of certain fixed assets of a business, including real property used in a trade or business. Non-recognition applies if similar fixed assets will be repurchased within one year. If the timely reinvestment is not possible, the taxpayer may defer gain recognition by establishing a gain deferral reserve (steuerfreie Rücklage), which must be amortized over four years (six years in the case of newly constructed buildings). The above non-recognition and deferral rules of the Income Tax Act also apply to reinvestment by German businesses abroad, if the Federal Secretary of Commerce (Wirtschaftsminister), in his discretion, deems the reinvestment supportive of the goals of the international division of labour.

Die Möglichkeit der Übertragung stiller Reserven gibt es in den USA nur beim Tausch (like-kind exchange), nicht bei der Veräußerung. Eine Ausnahme galt früher für den Verkauf und die innerhalb einer Zweijahresfrist erfolgte Wiederanschaffung eines neuen Hauptwohnsitzes (principal residence). Seit 1997 gilt für den Verkauf des Hauptwohnsitzes statt dessen ein Steuerfreibetrag von $ 500 000. Es handelt sich dabei nicht um die Übertragung stiller Reserven, sondern einen permanenten Freibetrag, der im übrigen bei jedem weiteren Verkauf, nach Ablauf jeweils einer Zweijahresfrist, neu geltend gemacht werden kann.

Im übrigen ist es häufig möglich, aus einer Veräußerung einen steuerneutralen Tausch zu machen, indem der Käufer im Auftrag des Verkäufers das Reinvestitionsobjekt kauft und dann im Tausch an den Verkäufer überträgt (→ Tausch).

Seit 1997 können auch Anteile an kleineren Gesellschaften steuerfrei veräußert werden, sofern der Erlös wieder in ähnliche „small business stocks" investiert wird.

Umwandlung / Reorganization

Umlagen **Charges**
Allocations
Assessments

Individual metering of electricity, water or gas is much more prevalent in Germany than in the U.S. Thus, even multi-tenant buildings may be partly rented on a net lease basis.

In den USA ist das separate Ablesen von Strom, Wasser oder Gas für den einzelnen Mieter die Ausnahme. Insofern ist die Form des net leases (triple net lease) auf Gebäude beschränkt, die im wesentlichen an einen einzigen Mieter vermietet sind.

Umsatzmiete **Overage Rent**
Percentage Rent

Umsatzsteuer (→ Mehrwertsteuer) **Sales Tax**
Value Added Tax (VAT Tax)

Umwandlung **Reorganization**

The amended Taxation Reorganization Act (Umwandlungssteuergesetz) allows for various forms of tax-free reorganizations, including, since 1995, spin-offs and split-ups.

Unlike in the U.S., the Act also permits a tax-free reorganization through the transfer of corporate assets into a partnership entity or into the business of a sole proprietor. Since German tax law, after 1977, does not subject corporate earnings to double taxation, the tax-free reorganization from corporate to partnerhip or sole proprietorship form is a logical consequence. It follows from this logic, however, that Sec. 13 UmwStG excludes non-resident owners from the benefits of tax-free reorganizations into partnerships or sole proprietorships.

The new Act also permits the continuation of loss carry-overs of the merged (non-surviving) entity.

Das amerikanische Steuergesetzbuch enthält detaillierte Vorschriften zur steuerneutralen Umwandlung von Kapitalgesellschaften, inklusive der dabei möglichen Übertragung von Verlustvorträgen und anderen steuerlichen Eigenschaften. Jedoch gibt es nicht, wie in Deutschland, die steuerfreie Umwandlung durch Übertragung von körperschaftlichem Vermögen auf Personengesellschaften, da das US Steuerrecht vom Grundsatz

Umwandlung von Wohnraum / Conversion

der Doppelbesteuerung von körperschaftlichen Gewinnen ausgeht, und zwar sowohl bei Ausschüttung als auch bei Auflösung der Gesellschaft.

Umwandlung von Wohnraum   Conversion

Germany, because of its extensive rent control laws applicable to virtually all residential properties, should be an ideal playground for the conversion of rental apartments to condominium ownership. Also, the legal framework for conversions is less burdensome than the complex web of conversion laws applicable in cities like New York and Chicago. Nevertheless, the conversion industry in Germany has never reached a level of activity comparable to that of the U.S. One reason for this is that the deductibility of home mortgage interest (→ Hypothekenzinsen), an important incentive for home ownership in the U.S., does not exist in Germany. Also, Germany has rather extensive building code regulations regarding fire and noise protection, day light, accessibility, static engineering, etc. (→ Bauordnung). Most rental properties would require extensive renovations to satisfy building code laws applicable to condominiums.

In den USA fand die letzte große Welle von conversions Ende der 70iger Jahre statt, und zwar hauptsächlich an der „Gold Coast" von Florida sowie in den Städten Chicago und New York, in denen Mieterschutzbestimmungen (rent control und rent stabilization) zu einem besonders auffälligen Mißverhältnis zwischen Mietpreisen und Verkehrswerten geführt hatten. Es entwickelte sich schnell ein umfangreiches Regelwerk zur Zulässigkeit und Durchführung von conversions, inklusive den verschiedenen Arten von conversions (eviction und non-eviction plans), den jeweils benötigten Mehrheiten von Mieterstimmen, dem Verbot von Leerständen (warehousing), dem Schutz älterer Bewohner, der behördlichen Anmeldung und ähnliches. Umgewandelt wurden Mietwohnungen dabei nicht nur in Wohnungseigentum (condominiums), sondern mitunter auch in cooperative Wohnhäuser (→ Wohnungseigentum).

Umweltschutz   Environmental Protection

Environmental protection laws, in particular waste removal, clean air and noise protection, are largely subject to federal legislation which overrides the environmental laws enacted in the individual German states. The legislative authority of the states pertains primarily to the enforcement of federal environmental laws. Many different statutes in Germany are seen as branches of environmental law, such as planning and urban renewal, the preservation of wildlife and certain species, clean air, water, noise, waste, radiation, dangerous industrial activities, the transporta-

Unpfändbarkeit (→ Pfändungsschutz)

tion of chemicals or other dangerous substances, etc. Among the most important acts are the following: (a) the Environmental Impact Review Law (Gesetz über die Umweltverträglichkeitsprüfung) which subjects numerous industrial and other projects to a special approval procedure; (b) the Clean Air Act (Immissionsschutzgesetz) which primarily regulates clean air and noise protection; (c) the Clean Water Act (Wasserhaushaltsgesetz); (d) the Waste Removal Act (Abfallgesetz); (e) the Environmental Liability Act (Umwelthaftungsgesetz) which subjects operators of certain facilities to the rebuttable presumption of guilt for bodily and property damage, up to certain ceilings; (f) the environmental crimes and infractions provisions of the Criminal Code (Sections 324 et. seq. Strafgesetzbuch) which put the wilfull or negligent violation of environmental procedure regulations (Umweltverwaltungsrecht) under severe punishment as a federal crime, including large fines or imprisonment of up to ten years; (g) the Waste Oil Act (Altölgesetz); (h) the Nuclear Act (Atomgesetz;) (i) the Chemical Substances Act (Chemikaliengesetz); and several other related acts.

In den USA ist das Umweltrecht im Gegensatz zu Deutschland vorrangig Ländersache und wird nur in einigen Bereichen durch federal law ergänzt. Bundesrechtlich von besonderer Bedeutung ist dabei der Comprehensive Environmental Response, Compensation and Liability Act von 1980 („CERCLA"). Umgekehrt ist die Umweltschutzverwaltung nicht wie in Deutschland dezentral auf Gemeinde- und Bezirksebene organisiert, sondern zentral durch die jeweilige Environmental Protection Agency des betreffenden Einzelstaates und des Bundes. Im Gegensatz zum deutschen Umweltrecht geht es in den USA meist nicht um absolute Verschmutzungswerte, sondern um die relative Verschlechterung eines Zustandes. So kann ein Projekt im industriell besiedelten Nord-Osten des Landes noch erlaubt sein, während es in Staaten wie Colorado, Kalifornien oder New Mexiko keine Chance auf Genehmigung hätte. Auch in den USA gibt es zunehmend das Erfordernis der Umweltverträglichkeitsprüfung, bevor ein Projekt genehmigt wird. Diese environmental impact studies werden meist auch auf Länderebene gefordert und werden dort mitunter exzessiv auch für harmlos erscheinende Vorhaben verlangt, z. B. Teilungsgenehmigungen für unbebautes Land.

Unbeschränkt Steuerpflichtige　　　　　　　　**Resident Taxpayers**
(→ Beschränkt Steuerpflichtige)

Unpfändbarkeit (→ Pfändungsschutz)

Untermiete / Sublease

Untermiete	Sublease

Pursuant to § 549 BGB, a sublease requires the landlord's approval. The landlord may withhold his approval for cause. Such cause may lie in the person or character of the proposed subtenant. If the landlord withholds his approval to the sublease of commercial space without showing proper cause, the Civil Code (BGB) permits the tenant to terminate the lease upon the statutory notice periods. Commercial lease agreements may, and often do, override this statutory termination right of the tenant.

Different rules apply to residential leases. The tenant has a statutory right to the landlord's approval of a sublease. The approval may only be withheld if the sublease results in an overcrowding of the space or if there is reasonable cause in the person or character of the subtenant. Residential lease agreements may not exclude the statutory rules.

In den USA hat der Mieter grundsätzlich das Recht der Untervermietung (sublease) oder der Abtretung des Mietvertrages (assignment), es sei denn, der Mietvertrag legt ihm Beschränkungen ausdrücklich auf. Typischerweise enthalten amerikanische Mietverträge die Zustimmungsbedürftigkeit für Untermiete oder Abtretung, wobei der Vermieter seine Zustimmung nur aus wichtigem Grund verweigern darf. Der Unterschied zwischen sublease und assignment besteht darin, daß beim assignment der neue Mieter neben seinem Vorgänger dem Vermieter gegenüber direkt haftet. Es spielt keine wesentliche Rolle, ob die Parteien den Vertrag als sublease oder assignment bezeichnen. Ein assignment wird immer dann angenommen, wenn der Untermieter sämtliche Rechte und Pflichten des Obermieters übernimmt. Dies ist typischerweise der Fall, wenn der Untermietvertrag die gleiche Restlaufzeit hat wie der Hauptmietvertrag.

Unternehmensübernahmen	Takeovers

Corporate mergers and acquisitions are a much smaller business in Germany than in the U.S. Ownership of controlling shareholders changes less frequently, partly for cultural reasons. Privately held companies remain in the hands of the founding families often for many generations.

Also, friendly or unfriendly takeovers of public companies are much rarer in Germany than in the U.S. A simple reason for this is that there are almost 20 times as many public companies in the U.S. Also, German corporate law has a different tool set for takeover defense than is available in the U.S. A defensive share buy

Unternehmensübernahmen / Takeovers

back (Kauf eigener Aktien) probably is not permissible. However, corporations use multiple voting rights for friendly stockholders, or the limitation of voting rights to a certain maximum percentage for new stockholders. Other general barriers are the long and non-terminable tenancies of directors („Aufsichtsrat"), the myriad cross-holdings prevalent particularly in the insurance and banking industry, and the power of the major banks who often own stock and, in addition, control large blocks of voting rights through blank proxy („Depotstimmrecht"). Also, companies cannot easily pay for target companies with stock (→ Sacheinlagen). They must first get cash, debt or equity, which usually again requires going through the major commercial banks. Also, remaining minority shareholders of the target company may not be forced to accept cash. They may thus extract pretty large nuisance values to be paid off.

Unternehmenskäufe und Fusionen sind in den USA aus kulturellen, wirtschaftlichen und rechtlichen Gründen wesentlich häufiger als in Deutschland. Da es annähernd zwanzigmal so viele börsennotierte Gesellschaften gibt als in Deutschland, sind Übernahmeangebote, auch sogenannte „unfriendly" takeovers, täglich Gegenstand der Wirtschaftsnachrichten. Kaufende Unternehmen können dabei ohne Begrenzung mit eigenen Aktien zahlen (→ Sacheinlagen). Nach Verschmelzung verbleibende Minderheitsgesellschafter, üblicherweise mit weniger als 10% der Aktien, müssen angemessene (Bar-)→ Abfindungsangebote („freezeout") annehmen und können nicht, wie in Deutschland, Aktien an der übernehmenden Gesellschaft verlangen.

Andererseits gibt das Recht der meisten Einzelstaaten, insbesondere Delaware, der Sitz vieler großer Gesellschaften, dem Management erheblichen Ermessensspielraum („business judgement"), Übernahmen abzuwehren. Dazu gehört der in Deutschland nur beschränkt mögliche Rückkauf eigener Aktien, wodurch der Börsenkurs nach oben getrieben wird, oder die Ausgabe von „poison pills" an bestehende Gesellschafter, die neue Aktionäre durch Ausübung günstiger Optionen auf weitere Aktien stark verwässern können. Aufsichtsräte, die jedes Jahr nur teilweise neu besetzt werden dürfen (staggered boards), großzügige Abfindungen an Vorstandsmitglieder („golden parachutes") und teure „Vorvertragsstrafen" („break up fees") mit „freundlichen" Übernehmern gehören zu diesem Arsenal. Viele dieser Maßnahmen, die im deutschen Aktienrecht erst gar nicht zulässig wären, dienen ganz offensichtlich nur den Interessen des Managements und führen im Ergebnis zu einer Entreicherung ihrer Aktionäre.

Unternehmer (Bauunternehmer) / (General) Contractor

Unternehmer (Bauunternehmer) **(General) Contractor**
(Subunternehmer – Subcontractor)

Variable Zinsen **Floating Rate Interest**
Variable Rate Interest

Veränderungssperre **Development Freeze**
Development Moratorium

Under § 16 BauGB, the local authority may impose a development freeze in order to prevent non-conforming building activities while a zoning ordinance is in the drafting stage. The development freeze may have a duration of two years, with two renewals of one year each. Property owners are entitled to damages if the freeze was unwarranted or if it lasts for more than four years.

An automatic freeze applies in areas designated as renewal areas (Sanierungsgebiet) under §§ 142, 143 BauGB or in areas affected by reallocation measures (Umlegung) under §§ 45 et seq. BauGB.

Auch in den USA gibt es mitunter gemeindliche Veränderungssperren. Sie werden in der Regel verhängt, wenn sich die entwickelten und geplanten Vorhaben überstürzen.

Veräußerungsgewinn **Capital Gain**

Under German tax law, capital gains of natural persons from sales of investment property (Privatvermögen) are tax free if the applicable short-term gains periods (→ Spekulationsfrist) of § 23 EStG have been met (two years for real property, six months for all other property). If the nature of the investment activitiy and the turnover of the assets indicate a commercial trade or business activity, all capital gains become taxable. (For more detail → Gewerbebetrieb; → Gewerblicher Grundstückshändler)

Certain gains of individual taxpayers are subject to the preferential tax rate of Sec. 34 EStG (50% of the otherwise applicable tax rate). Gains (up to DM 30 Million) from the sale of a business or a separable part of a business, or of a substantial interest (more than 25%) in a corporate entity are entitled to such preferential rate.

Non-resident persons are subject to German capital gains tax on sales of real property (not of personal property) if they sell within the applicable short-term holding period (→ Spekulationsfrist), or if the activity amounts to a trade or business even if it is not conducted through a permanent establishment or representative.

Veräußerungsgewinn / Capital Gain

Before 1994, foreign institutional real estate investors were treated as individual investors, i. e. their capital gains from German real property were tax exempt under the same requirements. This principle of disregarding foreign elements and classifications („isolierende Betrachtungsweise") set forth in § 49 EStG, was curtailed through tax reform. Since January 1, 1994, foreign corporate investors are treated as corporate taxpayers. Thus, all their income is considered trade or business income subjecting gains from real property sales to German taxation even in the absence of a permanent establishment in Germany.

In theory, foreign investors may avoid German capital gains tax by acquiring properties through a holding corporation (→ Immobilienholding) and by selling the shares, rather than the property itself. Most tax treaties, including the treaty between the United States and Germany, exempt foreign investors from German capital gains tax on the sale of such shares.

However, if a U.S. investor owns more than 25% of the capital of a German real property holding corporation, the sale of his shares will arguably be subject to German tax. The applicable tax treaty generally exempts from German tax all sales of German corporate shares, even in the case of material participations under § 17 EStG (→ wesentliche Beteiligung). However, the U.S.-German Income Tax Treaty permits each country to treat real property holdings as real property. Thus, the treaty does not bar Germany from applying its regular rules on the sale of corporate shares by shareholders who have a material participation.

Even if the tax treaty protected the U.S. investor from German capital gains tax, the seller would have to discount the sales price because the purchaser would inherit a deferred tax liability. The purchaser of the shares will not be able to liquidate the corporation and offset the resulting dividend with a corresponding write-off of the shares (prohibition of the „ausschüttungsbedingte Teilwertabschreibung", Sec. 50c EStG).

For foreign real estate investors in Germany, one of the more attractive tax structures may be to invest through a „Spezialfonds" under § 1 KAGG. The Spezialfonds is a mutual fund (Kapitalanlagegesellschaft) which has only, and not more than ten, institutional investors none of which are themselves mutual funds.

In den USA ist jeder Veräußerungsgewinn steuerpflichtig, mit Ausnahme gewisser Tauschgeschäfte (→ Tausch – „like kind exchange"). Langfristige Veräußerungsgewinne (Frist von 18 Monaten) natürlicher Personen unterliegen dabei einem begünstigten Steuersatz von 20%, gegenüber dem gewöhnlichen Höchststeuersatz von 39,6%. Dieser Satz ermäßigt sich auf 18% nach einer Haltezeit von 5 Jahren. Soweit im Gewinn früher geltend gemachte AfA stecken, wird er mit 25% besteuert. Veräuße-

Veräußerungsverlust / Capital Loss

rungsgewinne von Kapitalgesellschaften unterliegen dem regulären Körperschaftsteuersatz.

Capital gains können nur bei Veräußerung von „capital assets" erzielt werden. Inventar oder andere Wirtschaftsgüter, die mit der Absicht des späteren Wiederverkaufs angeschafft werden, beispielsweise beim → gewerblichen Grundstückshändler (property dealer), sind keine capital assets.

Auch in den USA unterliegen Steuerausländer mit ihren Veräußerungsgewinnen aus amerikanischen Immobilien der Steuer, und zwar der FIRPTA capital gains tax (FIRPTA – Foreign Investment in Real Property Tax Act). Im Unterschied zum deutschen Recht gilt dies auch für natürliche ausländische Personen, die nicht gewerblich tätig sind. Ferner gelten auch Anteile an amerikanischen Kapitalgesellschaften, deren Vermögen zu mehr als 50% aus U.S. Immobilien besteht, als unbewegliches Vermögen. Der Anteilsverkauf unterliegt daher auch der U.S. capital gains tax. Von capital gains tax befreit ist jedoch der Verkauf durch Steuerausländer von Anteilen an amerikanischen Immobilienfonds in der Form des REIT (Real Estate Investment Trust), sofern sich die Mehrheit der REIT Anteile in amerikanischen Händen befindet oder an einer Börse aktiv gehandelt wird.

Veräußerungsverlust   Capital Loss

As gains from the sale of investment property („Privatvermögen") by individual taxpayers is tax exempt in Germany, losses from such sales are not tax deductible. However, short-term losses of individual taxpayers (→ Spekulationsverluste) within the applicable holding periods (→ Spekulationsfrist) can be used against short-term gains in the same fiscal year.

In den USA können Veräußerungsverluste nur gegen Veräußerungsgewinne ausgeglichen und vorgetragen werden, und bei natürlichen Personen in sehr beschränktem Umfang auch gegen sonstige Einkünfte (ordinary income) (→ Spekulationsverlust). Für Betriebsvermögen natürlicher Personen (trade or business assets) sowie für deren vermietete Immobilien gilt jedoch die vorteilhafte Regelung der Section 1231 des Steuergesetzbuches. Danach unterliegen Veräußerungsgewinne aus dieser Art des Anlage- bzw. Investitionsvermögens dem für natürliche Personen günstigen Steuersatz auf langfristige Veräußerungsgewinne, während Veräußerungsverluste als gewöhnliche Verluste (ordinary losses) gegen sonstiges Einkommen ausgeglichen werden können.

Verbraucherkreditgesetz / ~ Truth in Lending Act; RESPA

Verbindliche Auskunft (Zusage) — Letter Ruling

The Abgabenordnung (Tax Procedure Act) does not entitle German taxpayers to request advance rulings, other than in connection with a field audit, § 204 ff AO, and in certain other situations. However, if the tax authority volunteers a binding letter ruling it will be bound even if the ruling unfairly favors the taxpayer.

Im amerikanischen Steuerrecht gibt es zwar grundsätzlich auch kein Recht auf Erlass einer verbindlichen Auskunft. Jedoch veröffentlicht das Bundesfinanzministerium, auf welchen Gebieten und Themenkreisen es derartige Auskünfte erteilt, und auf welchen nicht („no ruling areas"). Insoweit kann ein Anspruch des Steuerzahlers auf verbindliche Auskunft entstehen.

Verborgene Mängel — Latent Defects
(→ „Wie es liegt und steht")

Verbot der weiteren Belastung — Negative Pledge

Pursuant to § 1136 BGB, a mortgage lender cannot restrain the property owner from further encumbering the property (→ Sofortige Fälligkeit). The reason is that the first mortgage cannot be crammed down or otherwise be affected by an insolvency proceeding of the mortgagor.

In den USA ist es möglich, und auch üblich, daß der Hypothekengläubiger die Eintragung nachrangiger Hypotheken verbietet. Er tut dies, um die Kontrolle darüber zu behalten, ob und wann der Eigentümer in Verzug gerät, wie hoch die Gesamtbelastung sein darf, und unter welchen Umständen ein Zwangsvollstreckungsverfahren eingeleitet werden kann. Im Gegensatz zum deutschen Recht kann nämlich das vorrangige Pfandrecht im amerikanischen Konkursverfahren vom Gericht beschnitten werden (cram down; → Absonderung).

Verbraucherkreditgesetz — ~ Truth in Lending Act
~ RESPA

The German Verbraucherkreditgesetz (Consumer Loan Act) of 1990 applies to practically all consumer loans, irrespective of the form or purpose of the loan. Included are installment sales, real property loans, leasing, overdraft facilities, credit card and any other transactions in which commercial lenders extend credit to individuals for non-business purposes. The Act also applies to business start-up loans under DM 100,000.

Verbriefung / ~ Securitization

The Act subjects the lender to various disclosure duties, particularly with respect to the true cost and effective interest rate of a loan. Borrowers may freely rescind consumer loans within one week after signing. The rescission right does not apply, however, to real property loans.

Der Truth in Lending Act gilt, ähnlich wie das Verbraucherkreditgesetz, für fast alle Verbraucherkredite, auch Realkredite. Das Gesetz legt dem Kreditgeber ähnliche Offenlegungspflichten auf, insbesondere was die effektiven Kosten eines Darlehens angeht. Das Gesetz gilt im allgemeinen jedoch nur für Kleinkredite unter $ 25 000, es sei denn, es handelt sich um Immobilienkredite.

Käufern von Eigenheimen wird durch das Immobilienabschlußgesetz (Real Estate Settlement Procedures Act of 1974, RESPA) zusätzlicher Schutz gewährt. RESPA schützt den Käufer vor überraschenden, ungerechtfertigten oder exzessiven Abschlußgebühren bei Aufnahme einer Hypothek.

Verbriefung   **~ Securitization**

The securitization and public offering of mortgages has existed for over 150 years in several European countries, including France and Germany. In contrast to the mortgage-backed security in the U.S., the German „Pfandbrief" is backed not only by the mortgage pool, but also by the credit of the issuing mortgage bank (→ Hypothekenbank). The Pfandbrief is the primary tool for long-term mortgage financing.

Securitization in the Anglo-Saxon sense of the term, i. e. the offering of securities which are not backed by the issuer's credit, has not entered the German capital market. It seems the only transaction on record was a marginally successful placement by the Commerzbank in 1994. No principal legal barriers exist against securitization. In 1996, the Federal Banking Authority issued guidelines regarding the issuance of U.S.-style asset backed securities by German banks. However, German mortgage banks and Landesbanken are still not ready to lose balance sheet volume for possibly quicker profit and lesser risk. Also, they are not under similar refinancing difficulties as U.S. banks were during the property crisis. The Pfandbrief and commercial paper markets are liquid and relatively cheap financing sources.

Also, the equitization of real estate is lagging. There are less than 30 listed property companies in Germany, most of them small, and often remnants of defunct or split-up industrial conglomerates. However, since the tax benefits of direct own-

Verbriefung / ~ Securitization

ership (tax-free capital gains, tax shelters, low assessed values) are all curtailed or phased out, it is expected that listed property companies may finally arrive with force in Germany as well. Germany has abolished the double taxation of dividends in 1977, obviating the need to create a special vehicle similar to the U.S. REIT. In theory, even capital gains may continue to be tax-free, since the property companies may permanently roll-over portfolio gains tax-free and individual shareholders may sell appreciated shares tax-free.

Die Verbriefung und das öffentliche Anbieten von Eigenheimhypotheken existiert seit mehreren Jahrzehnten in den USA. Privates Hauseigentum ist weitverbreitet, wegen der relativ erschwinglichen Land- und Baupreise, aber auch wegen der Abzugsfähigkeit der privaten Hypothekenzinsen. In einem Land, in dem aus verschiedenen Gründen, so auch der Abzugsfähigkeit privater Hypothekenzinsen, Hauseigentum weit verbreitet ist, stellen home mortgage bonds einen der größten und liquidesten Märkte dar, dessen Größe weit über einer Billion Dollar liegt. Über 60 % aller Eigenheimhypotheken werden mit Garantien verschiedener U.S.-Regierungsbehörden ausgestattet und plaziert, Garantien der Federal Housing Administration, der Veterans Administration, der Government National Mortgage Association („Ginnie Mae") oder der Federal National Mortgage Company („Fannie Mae").

Die Immobilienkrise der späten achtziger Jahre gab Wall Street die Gelegenheit, ein neues Finanzinstrument zu entwickeln, die commercial mortgage backed security (CMBS), die später auch auf andere Gegenstände erweitert wurde, z. B. Kreditkartenforderungen und andere Arten von Verbraucherkrediten, z. B. car loans. Zinsen und Kapitalrückzahlung werden dabei ausschließlich aus den verbrieften Forderungen gespeist, ohne jegliche Bank- oder Regierungsgarantien.

Als gewöhnliche Hypothekenkredite kaum mehr erhältlich waren und Banken ihren Hypothekenstand möglichst schnell reduzieren wollten, bot sich der CMBS als geeignetes Instrument an, um neue Anleger und größere Liquidität in den Markt zu bringen. CMBSs stellen mit fast $ 400 Milliarden etwa 9% des gesamten gewerblichen Hypothekenbestandes dar. Obwohl ihre Ausgabe mit teureren Transaktionskosten verbunden ist als gewöhnliche Hypothekenkredite und ihr Zinsvorteil auch etwas geschrumpft ist, wächst der Markt kräftig weiter.

Die Immobilienkrise gab auch dem REIT (→ Kapitalanlagegesellschaft) die Gelegenheit einer Renaissance. REITs, die Anfang der siebziger Jahre nach einer Pleitewelle praktisch verschwanden, sind heute die aktivsten Käufer von U.S.-Immobilien und haben es innerhalb von nur fünf Jahren auf einen Bestand von fast 5% aller gewerblichen Objekte gebracht. Die Börsenkurse der REITs liegen im Durchschnitt etwa 20% über den Verkehrswerten der Immobilienbestände. Die Befürworter von REITs argumentieren, daß REITs durch ihre Größe (economies of scale), Liquidität und Managementspezialisierung auf Dauer dem direkten Immobilienbesitz überlegen sind. Die Kritiker entgegnen, daß Größe keine Sicherheit sei, wie man am Zusammenbruch vieler der größten Immobilienhäuser sehen könne. Systemimmanent sei außerdem eine gefährliche Wechselwirkung zwischen Aktienkursen und Immobilienpreisen. Da REITs aus steuerlichen Gründen 95% ihrer Gewinne ausschütten müßten, komme Wachstum immer nur aus neuen Aktienemissionen, deren Erlös verwendet werde, den Immobilienbestand zu häufig überzahlten Preisen möglichst schnell zu erweitern. Ein Zinsanstieg, eine schwache Börse oder ein schwächer werdender Immobilienmarkt könne die Spirale schnell umdrehen.

Verdeckte Gewinnausschüttung / Constructive Dividend

The constructive dividend has played a somewhat minor role in German tax law since the corporate income tax reform of 1977 which eliminated the double-taxation of German dividends for German resident shareholders. However, where constructive dividends occur, often inadvertently and without any intent to save taxes, they often still result in a higher tax burden for the corporation (→ Gewerbesteuer).

In den USA sind Gewinne von Kapitalgesellschaften der (doppelten) Besteuerung auf Gesellschafts- und, bei Ausschüttung, Gesellschafterebene ausgesetzt, soweit nicht konsolidierte Steuerbilanzen oder Schachtelprivilegien geltend gemacht werden können (→ Dividendenbesteuerung). Insofern spielen die Themen der verdeckten Einlage, bzw. der überhöhten oder gewinnabhängigen Vergütung an nahestehende Personen eine größere Rolle als im deutschen Steuerrecht.

Verdingungsordnung für Bauleistungen / General Conditions for Contractors

The Verdingungsordnung für Bauleistungen (VOB) are federal regulations setting forth general conditions applicable to the bidding procedure and all contracting agreements in which federal or state governments are principals. The VOB are not mandatory for local governments, but their use is recommended.

The detailed contractual provisions of Part B of the VOB are often referred to in contractor's agreements between private parties. Even if the VOB do not become part of such agreements through reference, the courts have sometimes applied the VOB rules to determine custom and usage in disputes between developer and contractor.

In den USA entwickeln Bundes-, Landes- und Gemeindebehörden ihre eigenen Regeln zur Vergabe von Bauaufträgen (procurement rules). Diese enthalten beispielsweise häufig bestimmte Proporzregeln für Unternehmen, die Minoritäten oder Frauen gehören.

Privatparteien benutzen für Bauaufträge häufig standardisierte Formularverträge, vielfach z. B. die des American Institute of Architects (AIA).

Verfügungsbeschränkung   **Restraint of Alienation**
(→ Sofortige Fälligkeit)

Vergleich   **Chapter 11**

A German debtor who is over-leveraged (überschuldet) or insolvent (zahlungsunfähig) must file for bankruptcy protection, either under a reorganization procedure vaguely similar to Chapter 11 or a liquidation similar to the Chapter 7 proceeding (→ Konkurs). In a Vergleich, the debtor must generally offer the unsecured creditors at least 35% of their claims. He may do so by either offering cash payment, possibly in installments, (Erlaßvergleich) or by offering his assets provided their liquidation is likely to produce a 35% satisfaction. If the required majority of creditors accepts the offer, the debtor will be relieved from all debts. If the debtor's offer is not accepted, the procedure will generally turn into a liquidation bankruptcy (Anschlußkonkurs). In a liquidation, the debtor will not be relieved from any unsatisfied claims unless the bankruptcy court suggests a compulsory settlement (→ Zwangsvergleich) and the non-priority creditors accept the court's proposal.

The new Insolvency Act which will enter into force in 1999 provides relief for debtors in most cases and will bring German insolvency law a little closer to U.S. rules.

Im amerikanischen Insolvenzrecht gibt es sowohl im Chapter 11-Verfahren als auch im Liquidationsverfahren des Chapter 7 regelmäßig den allgemeinen Forderungserlaß, sofern der Gemeinschuldner nicht eines Konkursvergehens schuldig wird. Im amerikanischen Vergleich gibt es keine gesetzliche Mindestquote, die der Gemeinschuldner anbieten muß. Völlig verschieden vom deutschen Insolvenzrecht ist im übrigen die Behandlung besicherter Gläubiger. (→ Absonderung).

Vergleichende Werbung / ~ Comparative Advertising

Vergleichende Werbung ~ Comparative Advertising

Under German law, public advertising which compares products of specifically named, or referred to, competitors is considered illegal unfair competition even if the advertisement is true.

In den USA ist direkte vergleichende Werbung erlaubt und recht üblich. Eine Mißbrauchsgrenze soll unter anderem das Truth in Advertising Gesetz (Wahrheitsgemäße Werbung) einziehen, ein naturgemäß etwas schwammiges Kriterium.

Vergleichsverwalter Bankruptcy Trustee
Composition Procedure Trustee

In the German court composition procedure (→ Vergleich), much like in a U.S. Chapter 11, the debtor remains in possession of his assets and their management. However, the German bankruptcy court will always appoint a trustee whose duties and rights exceed those of an American bankruptcy trustee. The Vergleichsverwalter will continuously review the financial situation of the debtor, review his business decisions and control his personal expenditures.

In den USA beginnt das auf Betreiben des Schuldners eingeleitete Insolvenzverfahren üblicherweise mit einem „Chapter 11 filing", einem dem deutschen Vergleich in ungefähr entsprechenden Verfahren (→ Konkurs). In fast allen Chapter 11-Verfahren führt der Gemeinschuldner die Geschäfte als „debtor in possession" fort. Das Konkursgericht setzt zwar häufig einen unabhängigen Vergleichsverwalter ein, dessen Aufgaben sich jedoch in der Erfassung und Erhaltung des Schuldnervermögens sowie dem Entwurf des Vergleichsvorschlags oder Liquidationsplans erschöpfen. In der Fortführung der täglichen Geschäfte hat der Gemeinschuldner einen größeren Spielraum als ein deutscher Vergleichsschuldner.

Vergleichsvorschlag Reorganisation Plan

Verjährung Statute of Limitations

Verkäuferhypothek Purchase Money Mortgage

A seller of German real property may finance part of the purchase price with a first or subordinated (→ Rangvorbehalt) seller mortgage. German law does not know, however, the wrap-around mortgage.

Verkehrssicherungspflicht / ~ Safe Condition

In den USA ist die Verkäuferfinanzierung ein häufiger Bestandteil von Immobilientransaktionen. Meist rückt der Verkäufer dabei mit seiner Forderung hinter eine höherrangige institutionelle Fremdfinanzierung.

Falls mit dem verkauften Grundstück eine besonders zinsgünstige nichtfällige Hypothek übernommen werden kann, gibt der Verkäufer mitunter eine „wraparound" Hypothek. Sie ist eine nachrangige Hypothek, deren Kapitalbetrag den der höherrangigen Althypothek einschließt. Der wraparound Hypothekengläubiger übernimmt den Schuldendienst für die Althypothek und verdient unter anderem an der Marge zwischen dem günstigen alten Zinssatz und den zu annähernd Marktkonditionen vereinbarten höheren Zinsen der wraparound Hypothek. Der Käufer hat dabei in der Regel immer noch eine etwas günstigere Finanzierung als bei kompletter Neufinanzierung.

Verkehrshypothek   ~ Negotiable Mortgage

While, in principle, the German mortgage is accessory and entirely dependent upon the existence and validity of an underlying claim, the more frequent Verkehrshypothek is negotiable. It requires the issuance to the mortgagee of a negotiable mortgage note (Hypothekenbrief). The holder-in-due-course of the Hypothekenbrief cannot acquire a non-existing claim. However, the owner of the mortgaged property will not have any defence against the foreclosing mortgage holder in-due-course (→ Guter Glaube).

Auch in den USA sind Hypotheken grundsätzlich streng akkzessorisch, d. h. ihre Wirksamkeit hängt vom Bestehen der zugrundliegenden Forderung ab. Jedoch gibt es auch in den USA den verkehrsfähigen (negotiable) Hypothekenbrief (mortgage note), der gutgläubig erworben werden kann, inklusive der Hypothek selbst, auch wenn die ursprüngliche Forderung unwirksam oder mit Einreden behaftet ist.

Verkehrssicherungspflicht   ~ Safe Condition

As in the United States, the landlord and/or the tenant are liable for the safe condition of the property vis-a-vis the public and invitees. Typically, the landlord is responsible for the safety of entrance halls, stairways, outside and other common areas, and, as a matter of principle, also for the sidewalks. Tenants are liable for their premises if they were in safe condition at the commencement of the lease term and if the landlord has no control or duty to maintain individual premises.

In den USA wie in Deutschland hat der Vermieter die Verantwortung

Verkehrswert / Fair Market Value

für die Sicherheit der Hauszugänge, Hof, Treppenhaus und andere gemeinschaftlich genutzte Flächen, grundsätzlich auch des Bürgersteigs. Den Mieter trifft die Verantwortung für die ihm allein zur Verfügung stehenden Räume, sofern diese bei Mietbeginn in sicherem Zustand waren und der Vermieter keine Kontrolle über die Instandhaltung dieser Räume hat. In jedem Fall ist guter Haftpflichtversicherungsschutz nötig, um dem de-facto-Grundsatz „Kein Schaden ohne Ersatz" nicht in voller Höhe ausgeliefert zu sein.

Verkehrswert	**Fair Market Value**
Verlängerungsoption	**Renewal Option**
Verlustabzug	**Net Operating Loss (NOL)**
-vortrag (-rücktrag)	**Carry-Over (Carry-Back)**

Under German tax law, ordinary losses may be carried back two years and carried forward indefinitely. The carry-back is at the election of the taxpayer, but must not exceed DM 10 million. Capital losses of individual taxpayers are subject to special rules (→ Spekulationsverluste). Though less stringent than in the U.S., certain rules curtail NOL trafficking by transferring corporate entities (→ Mantelkauf).

In den USA können Verluste (ordinary losses) drei Jahre zurück- und 15 Jahre vorgetragen werden. Auch in den USA hat der Steuerzahler die Wahl, auf den Rücktrag zu verzichten und unmittelbar den Verlustvortrag geltend zu machen. Für Veräußerungsverluste gelten besondere Regeln (→ Spekulationsverlust; → Veräußerungsverlust). Die steuerlichen Regeln zum → Mantelkauf sind deutlich einschränkender in den USA als in Deutschland.

Verlustausgleich **Loss Deductibility**

Under German tax law, ordinary losses from one activity can be offset against income from other activities. There are a few exceptions to this rule, such as for certain passive foreign-source losses and short-term capital losses (→ Spekulationsverluste).

In den USA können bestimmte passive Verluste („passive activity losses") nicht von Einkünften aus Arbeit oder aus Kapitalvermögen abgezogen werden, sondern nur von gleichartigen Einkünften („passive activity income"). Eine passive activity ist eine gewerbliche Tätigkeit, auf die der

Verlustzuweisungsgesellschaft / Tax Shelter

beteiligte Steuerzahler keinen aktiven Einfluß nimmt (material participation). Der typische Fall hierfür ist die Kommanditistenstellung in einer Verlustzuweisungsgesellschaft. Bei vollständiger Liquidation des betreffenden Betriebes sind jedoch dann noch bestehende passive Verlustvorträge gegen Einkünfte aus aktiven Tätigkeiten oder aus Kapitalvermögen abzugsfähig.

Eine weitere Beschränkung sieht das U.S. Steuerrecht für die Abzugsfähigkeit von Schuldzinsen im Zusammenhang mit Kapitaleinkünften vor („investment interest"). Natürliche Personen können Schuldzinsen für die Finanzierung von Kapitalanlagen nur gegen Zinseinkünfte aus demselben oder späteren Jahren ausgleichen.

Verlustzuweisungsgesellschaft   Tax Shelter

The tax shelter industry in Germany, as opposed to the U.S., is active and alive. Movie, software and other intangible investments can be immediately expensed. Ships, aircraft, East German real property and certain other assets can be depreciated at extremely high rates („Sonderabschreibungen"). These special depreciations have been somewhat curtailed, however. Losses, other than short-term capital losses, are deductible against all other income categories, active or passive. Certain restrictions exist, however:

Similar to U.S. tax law, losses are allowed only to the extent capital is at risk. General partners, because of their theoretically unlimited liability, are considered at risk for their share or partnership debts even to the extent lenders have waived personal recourse against partners. German banks generally require some personal recourse against borrowers, if not jointly then at least severally against partners, and for part of the debt.

Two subjective and somewhat inconsistent rules also curtail tax shelter losses: Losses from activities which have little economic risk of producing definitive losses may be disallowed. On the other hand, taxpayers must have the intent of making profits („Gewinnerzielungsabsicht"), otherwise losses will be disallowed as well. If an activity, at the outset, cannot reasonably be expected to generate total taxable income in excess of total losses, the taxpayer entered it without profit intent. Unlike the hobby loss rule in the U.S. which bars losses from non-profitable fun activities, German tax law seems to consider any permanently unprofitable investment as a hobby, admittedly a somewhat masochistic one. East German real estate, with its 50% first-year depreciation, turns into an expensive hobby for some taxpayers who retroactively are trapped by the tax authorities as lacking profit intent.

Vermessung / Survey

Tax shelter companies, defined as partnerships whose equity is largely financed through tax savings, are generally presumed to have no profit motivation. This presumption does not apply to partnerships whose income is taxed as commercial trade income („gewerblich"), because in such case capital gains are not tax free.

A disallowed partnership loss may be carried forward against future partnership profits allocable to the respective partner. A partner may make a current loss allowable by replenishing his negative capital balance before the end of the loss year.

Verlustzuweisungsgesellschaften waren besonders im Immobiliengeschäft aktiv. Die Steuerreform von 1986 machten weitgehend ein Ende, durch Einführung der „at-risk-rule" (→ Negatives Kapitalkonto) und Verlängerung der Abschreibungszeiten. Im folgenden sind die wesentlichen Beschränkungen:

Bestimmte passive Verluste („passive activity" losses), definiert meist als Kommanditistenverluste einer tax shelter partnership, können nicht gegen andere Einkunftsarten (gewerbliche oder Kapitalvermögen) ausgeglichen werden.

Immobilien werden gradlinig und über längere Perioden (31 Jahre) abgeschrieben.

Es gilt das Verbot des → Negativen Kapitalkontos. Eine wichtige Ausnahme davon besteht weiterhin für die „non-recourse" Hypotheken von Immobilien-KGs. Diese können anteilig den Kapitalkonten der einzelnen Kommanditisten zugeschlagen werden, womit sich die Verlustabzugsfähigkeit erhöht.

Eigentümer von Wochenendfarmen, Jachten und ähnlichen Vergnügungsaktivitäten können Verluste nur abziehen, wenn sie innerhalb jedes Fünfjahreszeitraums mindestens drei Jahre Gewinn ausweisen. Pferdezüchter müssen nur zwei Gewinnjahre in einem Siebenjahreszeitraum produzieren. Andernfalls sind sämtliche Verluste nicht abzugsfähige „hobby losses".

Vermessung **Survey**
(→ Grundstücksgrenzen)

Vermietung und Verpachtung **Rental Income**

Income from Vermietung und Verpachtung is one of the seven income categories established by the EStG for individual taxpayers. By contrast, corporations can

Vermögensteuer / ~ Net Worth Tax

only have income from trade or business (→ *Gewerbebetrieb*) under Sec. 8 KStG.

In den USA wird grundsätzlich nicht zwischen verschiedenen Einkunftsarten unterschieden. Es gibt ausschließlich ordinary income (gewöhnliche Einkünfte) und capital gains (→ *Veräußerungsgewinne*). Dennoch finden sich an vielen Stellen im U.S. Steuerrecht Unterscheidungen zwischen trade or business income (gewerblichen Einkünften), passive activity income (passiven Gewerbeeinkünften), portfolio income (Einkünften aus Kapitalvermögen) oder auch rental income (Vermietung und Verpachtung). Diese Unterscheidungen haben sich allmählich entwickelt und verfolgen verschiedene Zwecke: Zum einen soll damit der → *Verlustausgleich* zwischen bestimmten passiven und aktiven Einkünften beschränkt werden. Eine Rolle spielen diese Unterscheidungen auch bei grenzüberschreitenden Vorgängen, z. B. bei der Hinzurechnungsbesteuerung von Zwischeneinkünften aus Niedrigsteuerländern, oder bei der Frage, ob U.S. Steuerausländer in den USA der Brutto- oder der Nettobesteuerung unterliegen.

Vermögensteuer   ~ Net Worth Tax

The Vermögensteuer was a tax on almost all assets, net of liabilities, of individual or corporate taxpayers, with a tax rate of 1 % for individual taxpayers (0.5% for his business assets and certain securities) and 0.6% for corporate taxpayers. In the case of real property, the Vermögensteuer was based on an assessed value (→ Einheitswert) which is substantially below fair-market value. Mortgaged real property could thus create negative equity. Leveraging property became an attractive net worth, estate and gift tax planning tool for wealthy taxpayers. In 1995, the German Supreme Constitutional Court (BVerfG) mandated the legislator to increase Einheitswerte or replace them with fair market values.

The Net Worth Tax has been struck down by decision of the Supreme Constitutional Court which became effective in 1997. Thus, the tax has not been formally abolished through legislative action which would have been politically difficult to sell to the public, but through court decision.

In den USA gibt es keine allgemeine Vermögensteuer, weder auf Bundesebene noch in den meisten Einzelstaaten. Dafür sind die real property taxes in den meisten Gegenden deutlich höher als die deutschen → *Grundsteuern*.

Vermögensübernahme / Bulk Sale

Vermögensübernahme   Bulk Sale
(Siehe auch → Betriebsübergang)

Under § 419 German Civil Code, the purchaser or other transferee of all or almost all assets of another person will be deemed to have assumed all personal debts, secured and unsecured, of the other person. The parties cannot eliminate such statutory fiction through agreement, nor can the consideration paid to the seller be deducted by the purchaser. The maximum liability of the transferee is limited, however, to the value of the acquired assets. The rules for the Vermögensübernahme apply to all types of assets, not just business assets or inventory.

§ 419 Civil Code, which in many cases prevents the purchase of property from debt-ridden sellers outside of bankruptcy, will be abolished effective in 1999.

The acquirer of a business will generally be deemed to also have assumed all liabilities of the business. However, pursuant to Sec. 25 HGB, he may exclude the assumption if the parties so agree and register and publish the respective clause in the Commercial Register (Handelsregister).

Die meisten Einzelstaaten der USA haben Bulk Sale Acts erlassen, denen zufolge der Übernehmer des gesamten Umlaufvermögens, insbesondere der Vorräte und des Warenbestandes, eines anderen Unternehmens auch die Schulden übernimmt. In aller Regel kann sich der Übernehmer durch rechtzeitige Mitteilung der bevorstehenden Übernahme an sämtliche Gläubiger von der Haftung befreien.

Versicherung   Insurance

Under German law, a mortgage automatically attaches to property insurance claims or proceeds, § 1127 BGB. It is not necessary to expressly include the mortgagee as co-insured in the policy.

Im U.S. Recht fallen Leistungen des Sachversicherers nicht automatisch in die Hypothekenhaftung. Hypothekengeber bestehen deshalb darauf, daß sie in der Sachversicherungspolice des Grundstückseigentümers ausdrücklich als Mitversicherte („co-insured") aufgeführt werden.

Sachversicherungspolicen (Feuer, Wasser, etc.) enthalten üblicherweise die sogenannte „coinsurance" Klausel. Diese besagt, daß der Hauseigentümer bei partiellen Schäden einen Teil des Schadens selbst tragen muß, wenn das Gebäude unterversichert ist. Im allgemeinen reicht es jedoch aus, wenn ein Objekt auf mindestens 80% seines Verkehrswerts bzw. der Wiederherstellungskosten versichert ist. Beispiel: Wenn ein $ 10 Millionen Objekt für nur $ 6 Millionen gegen Feuerschäden versichert ist, und es entsteht ein Brandschaden von $ 5 Millionen, so übernimmt der Versicherer nur $ 3 Millionen.

Versorgungsunternehmen **Utilities**

Vertragsbruch **Breach of Contract**

Vertragsstrafe **Liquidated Damages**

In German real property purchase agreements, both parties customarily have a right to specific performance (→ Erfüllungsanspruch) by the other party, not just damages or liquidated damages.

In den USA ist es üblich, daß bei Verzug des Grundstückskäufers seine → Anzahlung (meist 5–10% des Kaufpreises) an den Verkäufer verfällt, und damit weitergehende Ansprüche des Verkäufers auf Zahlung oder Schadenersatz vertraglich ausgeschlossen sind.

Vollmacht **Power of Attorney**
Authority

Vollstreckbare Urkunde **Power of Sale**

Under § 794 of the German Civil Procedure Code (Zivilprozeßordnung – ZPO), a debtor may execute, before the court or a notary (→ Notar), a document in which he subjects himself and his assets to immediate foreclosure by the creditor upon the debtor's default. Mortgage documents typically contain such a clause.

In den meisten Einzelstaaten der USA ist es wie in Deutschland möglich, daß der Gläubiger die Zwangsversteigerung ohne gerichtliche Klage betreibt, sofern der Schuldner ihm eine solche power of sale eingeräumt hat. Im Gegensatz zur vollstreckbaren Urkunde in Deutschland ist die amerikanische power-of-sale formlos gültig.

Vollzug(szeitpunkt) **Time of the Essence**

In Germany, the closing of a property purchase (→ Auflassung) usually occurs simultaneously with the execution of the purchase agreement. Therefore, German property purchase agreements usually do not contain any time of the essence clause.

Vorbelastung / ~ Nonconforming Use

Im amerikanischen → Grundstückskauf liegen häufig zwei Monate oder mehr zwischen Kaufvertrag und dessen Vollzug durch Auflassung (Closing) und Eintragung (recording). Dieser Zeitraum wird vom Käufer dazu benutzt, die tatsächliche und rechtliche Beschaffenheit des Grundstücks zu überprüfen (due diligence). Der Käufer läßt sich manchmal allerdings Zeit, um seine Finanzierung zu organisieren oder gar, um unmittelbar nach einem gewinnträchtigen Weiterverkauf Ausschau zu halten. Er kann dabei das vertraglich festgelegte Auflassungsdatum mehrfach verschieben, wenn er dafür Gründe dartun kann. Aus diesem Grund bestehen Verkäufer mitunter auf einer vertraglichen „time of the essence"-Klausel. Zahlt der Käufer zum vereinbarten Zeitpunkt nicht, hat der Verkäufer die Wahl, den Vertrag aufzuheben und die Anzahlung als Vertragsstrafe einzubehalten.

Vorbelastung	**~ Nonconforming Use**
Vorfälligkeitsentschädigung	**Prepayment Penalty**
Vorkaufsrecht	**Right of First Refusal** **Right of First Offer** **Preemptive Right**

Under German law, the Vorkaufsrecht exists as an obligatory right under § 504 BGB, or as a recordable estate under § 1094. Of frequent practical importance is the statutory preemptive right owned by municipalities with respect to certain properties (→ gemeindliches Vorkaufsrecht).

Auch in den USA kann ein Vorkaufsrecht grundbuchlich eingetragen werden.

Ein gesetzliches Vorkaufsrecht der Gemeinden gibt es im Recht der U.S. Einzelstaaten, soweit ersichtlich, nicht. Jedoch gibt es für bestimmte Parzellen ausnahmsweise ein Vorkaufsrecht der U.S. Bundesregierung. Dieses wird von der „General Services Administration" (GSA) nur sehr selten genutzt.

Vormerkung	**~ Priority Notice** **~ Lis Pendens**

The German Vormerkung records, and thus secures, a claim for the subsequent recording of an estate, or for the termination or change in priority (Rangän-

Vorzugsaktien / Preferred Stock

derung) of an estate in real property. Any disposal in violation of the recorded priority notice is null and void vis-a-vis the beneficiary of the notice, § 883(2) BGB.

The most frequent form of the prority notice is the notice of title transfer (Auflassungsvormerkung) through which the purchaser of real property secures his title and prevents the subsequent recording of title or of any other competing estate in the name of another party. The recording of an Auflassungsvormerkung is generally one of the conditions for the payment of the purchase price.

According to a decision of the Supreme Civil Court, the Auflassungsvormerkung does not protect the purchaser against subsequent leases of the property concluded by the seller before the new title has been recorded. Thus, the legal principle „purchase does not break lease" (→ Kauf bricht nicht Miete) applies whenever the lessee has taken possession before the transfer of title, even if it occurs after the recording of a Vormerkung by the property purchaser.

While the Vormerkung itself does not amount to an estate in land, the beneficiary may request specific performance of the bankruptcy trustee in an intervening bankruptcy of the property owner.

Die Eintragung einer Auflassungsvormerkung, bzw. des gesamten Kaufvertrages ist im amerikanischen Recht zwar möglich, aber in der Praxis unüblich. Oft verbietet der Verkäufer dem Käufer sogar eine solche Eintragung, um den unmittelbaren Weiterverkauf des Grundstücks nicht zu blockieren, sollte der Käufer mit der Erfüllung in Verzug geraten.

Das amerikanische lis pendens ist eine Eintragung dahingehend, daß über Rechte am Grundstück ein Rechtsstreit anhängig ist.

Vorstand   **Officers**
Management Board

(→ Aufsichtsrat)

Vorzugsaktien   **Preferred Stock**

As often, German corporate law is more detailed and restrictive than U.S. law. Under the Stock Corporation Act (AktG), preferred stock („Vorzugsaktien") may be issued without voting rights. Vice versa, non-voting stock must be given preference rights. If the preferred dividends have not been paid for two successive years, the shares will gain voting rights until the dividends have been paid. The Code limits the issuance of non-voting stock. The nominal value of all non-voting shares must not be greater than the nominal value of all voting stock.

Im Aktienrecht der meisten U.S.-Einzelstaaten besteht weitgehender Gestaltungsspielraum für die Ausgabe verschiedener Aktiengattungen. In der Regel sind Vorzugsaktien sogenannte non-voting cumulative preferred shares. Dies sind stimmrechtslose Aktien mit Gewinnvorabberechtigung und Priorität bei der Liquidation der Gesellschaft. Nicht gezahlte Gewinnvorabs aus früheren Jahren werden kumuliert vorgetragen, theoretisch für mehrere Jahre, ohne daß daraus Stimm- oder andere zusätzliche Rechte für die Inhaber erwachsen.

Warentermingeschäft / Futures Contract

Under German law, private investors who do not have the qualification as stock brokers or similar professionals, may invoke the Civil Code defense of „gambling" („Wetteinrede") against their duty to perform under a futures contract when the market went against them. German commercial banks have sometimes been victimized by this tactic.

For tax purposes, individual taxpayers who are not in the trade or business of trading futures, may pocket gains tax free, much as they can take home gambling winnings free of tax under German law.

In den USA gibt es die „Wetteinrede" des deutschen Zivilrechts nicht. Das Geschäft mit allen Arten von Warenterminkontrakten ist auch wesentlich weiter entwickelt und verbreitet als in Deutschland.

Steuerlich sind in den USA alle Einkünfte steuerbar, auch Gewinne aus Spielkasinos oder aus Warentermingeschäften.

Wegerecht / Right of Way

Wegzugsbesteuerung / Expatriation Rules
(→ Beschränkt Steuerpflichtige)

Werbungskostenpauschale / ~ Lumpsum Expense Deduction / Standard Deduction

German tax law permits the deduction of certain expenses (Werbungskosten) from certain income categories on a lumpsum basis, instead of an itemized basis. An example are expenses in connection with capital investment. Since 1996, a standard expense deduction has also been introduced for rental income from residential property. The annual deduction is DM 42 per square meter. This includes all costs and expenses, except for interest and depreciation. The lumpsum deduction for rental income is allowed to produce a deductible loss, which is not the case for the equivalent lumpsum deduction applicable against capital investment income.

Das US-Steuerrecht kennt die Werbungskostenpauschale nicht. Pauschaliert werden können nur gewisse Sonderausgaben, wie private Schuldzinsen, → Grundsteuern, einzelstaatliche Einkommensteuern, Krankheitskosten und ähnliche Sonderausgaben natürlicher Personen (standard deduction anstelle von itemized deductions).

Wertberichtigung **Write down**
Write off

German lenders have increased their mortgage lending significantly in the late eighties and early nineties. Since 1995, an increasing number of developers, particularly of East German real estate, are getting into financial difficulty, because of overbuilding and/or over-leverage. Most German banks have sufficient equity and hidden reserves to cushion write downs. Also, there are no general banking regulations restricting direct real property ownership by banks. Banks often swap bad mortgage loans against equity in property holdings, sometimes jointly owned with the developer. Unlike in the U.S., neither the German stock market nor regulators seem to put much pressure on financial institutions to liquidate bad property loans. The latter may change, however. The Federal Banking Authority in Berlin (Bundesaufsichtsamt für Banken) is rumored to begin exerting pressure on certain lenders to face up to the problem, either by fully writing off or foreclosing bad loans. It remains to be seen whether „bottom fishers" may be able soon to buy properties at similar discounts from their replacement cost as they could in the early 90ies in the U.S. or the U.K.

In den USA wurden seit Mitte der achtziger Jahre Immobilienkredite in Höhe von mehreren Hundert Milliarden Dollar wertberichtigt. Der ersten Welle fielen hunderte von Savings and Loan Banken zum Opfer, deren Immobilien später von der Resolution Trust Corporation, einer im weitesten Sinne der deutschen Treuhandgesellschaft entsprechenden Organisation, verwertet wurden.

Später folgten die Verkäufe von schlechten Hypothekendarlehen durch Geschäftsbanken, darunter vielen der japanischen Großbanken. Verkaufsdruck erzeugten dabei nicht nur die Aufsichtsbehörden, sondern auch die Wertpapierbörsen, die große Immobilienportfolios als ein sichtbares Zeichen von Bilanzschwäche ansahen.

Wertgutachten **Appraisal**

Wertsicherungsklauseln / Indexing

Wertsicherungsklauseln　　　　　　　　　　　　　　　Indexing

Under § 3 of the Currency Act (Währungsgesetz) index clauses in Germany require the approval of the local federal reserve bank (Landeszentralbank). Certain index clauses are illegal per se, certain others do not require approval. For example, indexing which is not automatic but requires adjustment through negotiations of the parties or determination by independent third parties („Leistungsvorbehalte") does not require approval. The same applies to index clauses which refer to the prices of similar goods or services („Spannungsklauseln"). Cost clauses are also exempt from the approval requirement as long as price adjustments solely reflect the actual and proven cost of the vendor or lessor. 10-year leases may be indexed (→ Lebenshaltungskostenindex).

In den USA gibt es, im Gegensatz zu Deutschland, keine behördliche Genehmigungspflicht für vertragliche Gleit- oder Wertsicherungsklauseln.

Wesentlicher Bestandteil　　　　　　　　　　　　　　　Fixture

The definition of the term „Bestandteil" under § 93 BGB is substantially similar to the definition of the term „fixture" in the United States. Under German law, the previous owner of a fixture may detach and remove the fixture from the real property. He will, however, be charged for any damage caused by the removal, §§ 997 and 946 BGB.

A frequent issue is whether additions made by tenants become part of the property or remain tenant fixtures (Scheinbestandteile). Both in the U.S. and Germany, the original intent of the tenant will determine this issue. However, in Germany the subjective intent of the tenant will decide. If he originally planned to remove the attachment after termination of the lease, the fixture would be considered to be a Scheinbestandteil, even if its removal is physically difficult.

Another difference is the following; The classification of fixture versus chattel under German law is generally independent of the agreement of the parties. For example, a security interest (Eigentumsvorbehalt) in a chattel which becomes a fixture will terminate despite contrary agreements. The secured party must require removal of the fixture in order to regain its security interest.

Definition und Rechtsfolgen des wesentlichen Bestandteils sind in den USA und Deutschland weitgehend gleich. Häufig stellt sich die Frage, ob von Mietern eingefügte Bestandteile nur Scheinbestandteile („tenant fixtures") werden. Hierbei kommt es in beiden Ländern auf die ursprüngliche Absicht des Mieters an. Jedoch ist in den USA nicht der subjektive Wille des Mieters maßgebend, sondern die objektiv erkennbare Absicht, die u. a. aus der Dauerhaftigkeit der Verbindung geschlossen werden kann.

Ein weiterer Unterschied besteht in folgendem: In den USA können Parteien im Innenverhältnis jederzeit regeln, ob eine Sache Bestandteil wird oder nicht, und durch entsprechende Mitteilung der getroffenen Rechtsentscheidung auch Außenwirkung verschaffen.

Wettbewerbsverbote — Non-Compete Clauses

Non-compete agreements („Wettbewerbsverbot", „Konkurrenzverbot") after termination of an employment or agency agreement (→ Handelsvertreter) must be in writing, may not be longer than two years and must give the employee compensation („Karenzentschädigung") during the non-compete term in an amount equal to 50% of his prior yearly earnings.

Auch in den USA müssen Wettbewerbsverbote angemessen sein. Ob sie im Einzelfall gültig sind, hängt unter anderem von ihrer Zeitdauer, ihrer territorialen Geltung und der Verhandlungsposition der Parteien ab. Nachvertragliche Konkurrenzverbote gegenüber Angestellten sind in der Regel nicht anfechtbar, wenn sie kürzer als zwei Jahre dauern, wenn sie auf eine bestimmte Region beschränkt sind, und wenn das Verbot vor dem Hintergrund schutzwürdiger Interessen des Arbeitgebers (Knowhow, Kundenlisten, etc.) ausgesprochen wird. Wettbewerbsverbote gegen Verkäufer von Unternehmen dürfen länger gelten, z. B. fünf Jahre, da Verkäufer meist in einer stärkeren Verhandlungsposition als Angestellte sind, und es geradezu einer der Zwecke vieler Unternehmenskäufe ist, einen Wettbewerber auszuschalten.

„Wie es steht und liegt" — „As Is"

Through the clause „wie besichtigt", the seller of property is relieved from liability for all open or reasonably visible defects. By contrast, the clause „wie es steht und liegt" generally excuses the seller also for hidden defects. The seller is not liable for defects which the purchaser knew or grossly negligently did not know, § 460 BGB. However, the seller will always remain liable for undisclosed hidden defects of which he had knowledge, or for his express representations and warranties (→ Zugesicherte Eigenschaften).

Bei der „as is"-Klausel wird die Haftung des Verkäufers oder auch Vermieters für sämtliche Mängel abbedungen, auch für verborgene, von denen der Verkäufer nichts weiß. Auch in den USA bleibt der Verkäufer oder Vermieter trotz des as-is Haftungsausschluß für verborgene Fehler haftbar, sofern sie wesentlich („material") sind, und er sie arglistig verschwiegen hat.

Wiederherstellungskosten (Wiederbeschaffungskosten) — Replacement Costs

Wiederverkaufswert — Residual Value / Terminal Value

Wohngebiet — Residential Area

The German Building Use Ordinance (Baunutzungsverordnung) distinguishes between pure residential and general residential areas (reine und allgemeine Wohngebiete).

Im allgemeinen unterscheiden die gemeindlichen Bauleitpläne in den USA bei Wohngebieten zwischen Gebieten mit Einfamilien- und Mehrfamilienhäusern und bei letzteren zwischen Flachbauten und Mehrstockgebäuden.

Wohnsitz — Domicile
(→ Beschränkt Steuerpflichtige)

Wohnungseigentum — Condominium

In Germany, condominiums are governed by federal law, specifically through the provisions of the Condominium Act (WEG). In Germany, condominium ownership of apartments is widespread, but probably less prevalent than in the U.S. Reasons for this may be relatively high apartment prices (generally anywhere between DM 3,000 and 12,000 per m^2; ($ 170 or $ 680 per sq.ft.)), the non-deductibility of home mortgage interest and the technical difficulty of converting most rental apartments into ownership units (→Umwandlung von Wohnraum).

In den USA gilt für das Wohnungseigentum Landesrecht. Fast alle U.S. Einzelstaaten haben condominium Gesetze erlassen, wobei die Rechtsform des Wohnungseigentums schon vorher durch common law etabliert war. Das amerikanische condominium entspricht weitgehend dem deutschen Wohnungseigentum. In einigen Bürohäusern in den USA wird auch das Konzept des Stockwerkseigentums verwirklicht.

Wucher / Usury

Vom condominium zu unterscheiden ist das cooperative, eine in wenigen U.S. Großstädten, inbesondere in New York verbreitete Form des Wohnungseigentums. Um die freie Veräußerung von Wohnungen in den eleganteren Häusern besser zu kontrollieren, wird das Eigentum an Grund und Boden einer Kapitalgesellschaft übertragen. Jeder Wohnungseigentümer wird damit zum Mieter seiner Wohnung (proprietary lease). Außerdem erwirbt er Geschäftsanteile an der Besitzgesellschaft. Vermietung und Verkauf der „coop" Wohnung benötigen regelmäßig die Zustimmung des Aufsichtsrats der cooperative corporation, der den Käufer oder Mieter weitgehend nach freiem Ermessen ablehnen kann. Auch die Finanzierung des Kaufs eines coop's ist schwieriger als die eines condominiums, und in manchen Gebäuden nicht oder nur begrenzt gestattet. In den exklusivsten Gebäuden ist die Verwertbarkeit der Wohnungen dadurch so stark gefährdet, daß von einem Kauf abgeraten werden muß, wenn Anlagegesichtspunkte eine Rolle spielen.

Wucher / Usury

German statutory law does not define usury rates („Wucherzinsen") but case law has defined usury as being more than double the prevalent market rates or exceeding such rates by 12 percentage points. These limits are increased by 10% for long-term fixed rate loans extended at times of low interest rates. Under special circumstances, usury will be assumed even for lesser excesses.

Non-commercial lenders are not subject to the same rules. However, commercial borrowers are protected against usury under the same rules as consumers.

The main sanction against usury is the invalidity of the underlying loan agreement.

In den USA sind die gesetzlichen Wucherzinssätze von Staat zu Staat verschieden. Meist gelten auch verschiedene Sätze, je nachdem, ob der Schuldner eine Privatperson oder Gesellschaft ist. In manchen Staaten werden Gesellschaften durch das jeweilige usury law gar nicht geschützt. In anderen Staaten gilt die Zinssatzbeschränkung nicht für Banken und ähnliche institutionelle Kreditgeber. In vielen Staaten wiederum findet das Wuchergesetz keine Anwendung auf Verkäuferhypotheken, oder auf Geschäftsdarlehen.

Die gesetzlichen Sanktionen für Zinswucher variieren erheblich von Staat zu Staat. In manchen Staaten verliert der Wucherer nur den Teil der Zinsforderung, der über dem gesetzlich zulässigen Höchstsatz liegt. In

Zeitmietvertrag / ~ Non-Renewable Lease

anderen Staaten verliert er jeglichen Zinsanspruch. In manchen Staaten verliert der Gläubiger sogar seinen Anspruch auf Kapitalrückzahlung.

Zeitmietvertrag   ~ Non-Renewable Lease

Generally, a German landlord may refuse the renewal of a residential lease only if he can establish plausible interests (→ Berechtigtes Interesse), in particular, if the landlord requires owner-occupancy (→ Eigenbedarf). An exemption exists for qualified term leases (qualifizierter Zeitmietvertrag) under § 564 c II German Civil Code. Such a lease may be terminated by the landlord if the lease had an original term of not more than five years and if the limitation of the term was justified because of a special interest (besonderes Interesse) of the landlord. Such an interest may be the anticipated owner-occupancy, the planned renovation of the premises or the future rental of the premises to employees of the landlord. The landlord must inform the tenant of the future intended use in writing at the beginning of the original lease term.

In den USA sind Mietverträge regelmäßig befristet. Mieter haben kein gesetzliches Verlängerungsrecht, sondern allenfalls eine vertragliche Verlängerungsoption. Ausnahmen gibt es in den wenigen Städten und Mietwohnungs-Objekten, für die noch „rent control" bzw. „rent stabilization" gilt.

Zerobonds   Zerobonds

Interest on any original-discount paper becomes taxable to an individual cash-basis taxpayer only if and when the instrument is paid at maturity or is sold by the holder. In the latter case, the holder picks up the portion of the interest which accrued to the date of sale.

Im U.S. Steuerrecht werden Zinsen aus Zerobonds oder anderen vom Begeber diskontierten Schuldverschreibungen ausnahmslos abgegrenzt versteuert. Aus diesem Grund kaufen amerikanische Privatanleger praktisch nie Zerobonds.

Zinsen   Interest

Zinseszins   Compounded Interest

Zivilprozeß / Civil Procedure

Zivilprozeß **Civil Procedure**

Bringing a civil law suit in Germany is a more costly and risky affair than in the U.S. for several reasons: Plaintiffs have to advance a statutory (percentage based) court fee. Lawyers cannot be retained on a contingency basis. Most important, the prevailing party is entitled to reimbursement of all its legal expenses, including legal fees.

Another important difference is the evidence procedure. There exists no pre-trial discovery, with the limited exception of evidence preservation (Beweissicherung). Most important, the parties generally have no right to subpoena documents from each other. If a party does not possess a document and has no legal right for its delivery, it cannot ask the court for a subpoena (no „fishing expeditions").

Damage awards in Germany are based solely on actual (monetary) damages, and not on any punitive elements. The law does allow for additional pain and suffering compensation (Schmerzensgeld). Such compensation is awarded solely in cases of direct physical or mental invasion. Its amount is based on the severity of the injury and the financial means of the parties. Damage awards in Germany are hardly ever excessive, at least not by American standards.

Das amerikanische Zivilprozeß- und Schadensrecht unterscheidet sich erheblich vom deutschen. Die wichtigsten Unterschiede sind folgende:

Es gibt keine Gerichtskosten. Anwälte dürfen auf Erfolgsbasis honoriert werden (contingency fee). Der unterliegenden Partei werden nur im seltensten Fall die Kosten der anderen Partei auferlegt. In einem Satz: Kläger haben praktisch kein Kostenrisiko.

Der Zivilprozeß kann ungewöhnlich lange verschleppt und damit teuer werden. Es gilt praktisch keinen Unmittelbarkeitsgrundsatz der Beweisaufnahme vor dem erkennenden Gericht. Die „pretrial discovery", ein vor der Hauptverhandlung stattfindendes Zeugen- und Urkundenbeweisverfahren steht weitgehend im Ermessen der Parteien, insbesondere des Klägers. Prozeßökonomie spielt eine untergeordnete Rolle. Die Gegenpartei kann durch „subpoenas", dies sind vom Gericht in aller Regel stattgegebene Ausforschungsanträge, zur Vorlage beinahe jeglicher Beweismittel gezwungen werden.

Schadensersatzurteile in den USA sind oft exzessiv. Dies liegt daran, daß Kläger häufig nicht nur den Vermögensschaden (actual damage) geltend machen, sondern auch Schmerzensgeld (pain and suffering). Dabei steht es im Ermessen des Gerichts, in den Schadensersatz ein Strafelement

Zubehör / Appurtenant Chattels; Personal Property

(punitive damages) einfließen zu lassen. Ist der Beklagte vermögend, z. B. ein Großkonzern, spürt er die Strafe nur, wenn diese entsprechend hoch angesetzt ist. Dadurch kommt es zu Urteilen, die für Ausländer mitunter nicht mehr verständlich sind.

Die Kombination von Erfolgsgebühr und teilweise astronomischen Schadensersatzsummen hat zu einer bedrohlichen Prozeßflut geführt, die seit einigen Jahren zunehmend Gegenstand der öffentlichen und politischen Debatte geworden ist. Auf Ebene einiger Einzelstaaten gibt es erste gesetzgeberische Initiativen zur Beschränkung der Prozeßflut. Die von den Republikanern 1996 vorgeschlagene Reform des Zivilprozeßrechts (tort reform) ist bisher jedoch gescheitert, unter anderem an einem von Präsident Clinton angedrohten Veto.

Zubehör — Appurtenant Chattels; Personal Property

German law distinguishes between four classes of property: Real property, fixtures (→ Wesentliche Bestandteile), → Zubehör and other personal property. Under § 97 BGB, Zubehör is personal property which is located on real estate. It must serve an economically useful purpose related to the real estate and be objectively considered Zubehör, but does not amount to a fixture. Generally, Zubehör runs with the land. For example, unless the agreements expressly provide otherwise, Zubehör is deemed included in a sale of the underlying land. Also, mortgages automatically attach to Zubehör (→ Haftungsgegenstände). Zubehör cannot be separately pledged. The statute wants to preserve the value of the entire property for existing or future real property liens.

In den USA gibt es nicht die vierteilige Unterscheidung in Grundstück, Bestandteile, Zubehör und bewegliches Vermögen, sondern nur die dreiteilige in Grundstück (real property), Bestandteile (fixtures) und bewegliches Vermögen (personal property). Letzteres geht beim → Grundstückskauf im Zweifel nicht über. Es fällt auch nicht in die Hypothekenhaftung. Sicherheiten an beweglichem Vermögen werden durch Verpfändung und entsprechende Eintragung in einem dem Handelsregister vergleichbaren Verzeichnis begründet (das sog. UCC filing; Der Uniform Commercial Code, UCC, ist ein in fast allen Einzelstaaten eingeführtes Modell-Handelsgesetzbuch).

Zugesicherte Eigenschaften / Representations; Warranties

Zugesicherte Eigenschaften **Representations Warranties**

If the agreements are silent on this point, the seller of real property is deemed to sell free and clear of liens or other encumbrances, § 434 BGB. There is an exception for public easements and other non-recordable rights, § 436 BGB. (See also → „Wie es steht und liegt" – „As Is".)

In den USA muß unterschieden werden, welche Art von Eigentumsbrief („Deed") der Verkäufer dem Käufer gibt. Beim „Warranty Deed" versichert der Verkäufer dem Käufer das unbelastete Eigentum und stellt ihn von Ansprüchen und Rechten Dritter frei. Beim „Quitclaim Deed" haftet der Verkäufer dagegen nicht für die Lastenfreiheit des Grundstücks, wobei er nach dem Recht einiger Einzelstaaten zumindest für durch ihn selbst verursachte Lasten haftet. Gleich welche Art von Deed er erhält, wird sich der Käufer jedoch regelmäßig das lastenfreie Eigentum durch Versicherungspolice (title insurance) sichern.

Zuschlag **~ Judicial sale**

Zwangsverwaltung **Receivership**

Zwangsvollstreckung **Foreclosure**

(see important differences at → Absonderung (Adequate Protection); → Bauhandwerkerhypothek (Mechanic's Lien); → Einstellung der Zwangsversteigerung (Right of Redemption); → Geringstes Gebot (Minimum Bid); → Kauf bricht nicht Miete (Leases survive Property Sale); → Objekthaftung (Non-Recourse); → Pfändungsschutz (Homestead); → Vollstreckbare Urkunde (Power of Sale).

(siehe zu wichtigen Unterschieden → Absonderung; → Bauhandwerkerhypothek; → Einstellung der Zwangsversteigerung; → Geringstes Gebot; → Kauf bricht nicht Miete; → Objekthaftung; → Pfändungsschutz; → Vollstreckbare Urkunde)

**Sample Agreements
Formulierungsmuster für Verträge**

German Sample Agreements
(Musterverträge nach deutschem Recht in englischer Übersetzung)

1. Real Property Purchase Agreement:
   Purchase and Sale of an Office Building
   (Grundstückskaufvertrag: Geschäftsgrundstück mit Bürogebäude) 175

2. Office Lease Agreement
   (Gewerberaummietvertrag) 183

U.S. Sample Agreements
(Musterverträge nach dem Recht der USA)

3. Purchase and Sale Agreement
   (Grundstückskaufvertrag) 197

4. Form of Agreement of Lease
   (Gewerblicher Mietvertrag, ausführliche Fassung) 219

   Editor's Note/Anmerkung des Herausgebers 302

5. Form of Agreement of Lease, Basic Version
   (Gewerblicher Mietvertrag, einfache Fassung) 303

1. AGREEMENT FOR THE PURCHASE AND SALE OF AN OFFICE BUILDING

(Grundstückskaufvertrag: Geschäftsgrundstück mit Bürogebäude)
– Translation/Übersetzung –

Negotiated in Frankfurt on Monday, June 22, 1998.

Before me, the notary _____ appeared today the following persons:

_____

_____

_____

The Parties declared before me, and requested to have included in my Protocol, the following Purchase Agreement.

§ 1
Sale of Property

1. Seller hereby sells to Purchaser the property *(„Property")* recorded in the Deed Registry of Frankfurt, Volume 28, page 1229, designated as Parcel No. and located at Street, Frankfurt. The Property comprises 925 m² and is developed.

2. This Agreement comprises the above-described Property, including all statutory fixtures, improvements and appurtenant chattels, and including that certain right-of-way easement over the neighbouring property, recorded in the Deed Registry of Frankfurt in Volume 14, page 1755. The Property is sold as is, in its present state and as inspected by Purchaser. The Property and all improvements, fixtures, appurtenant chattels and rights are hereinafter referred to as *„Property"*.

3. Purchaser hereby agrees to accept the transfer of the Property.

§ 2
Encumbrances

1. The undersigned notary has reviewed the Deed Registry and noticed the following encumbrances on the subject Property:

(a) There are no encumbrances in Section II of the Deed Registry.

(b) Section III of the Deed Registry shows:

> Under Item 3: A negotiable mortgage in the amount of DM 8 million, carrying 6.5% interest, and due and owing to .... Hypothekenbank, Frankfurt. According to information provided by Sellers, out-standing principal and accrued interest under such mortgage, as of June 20, 1998, amounts to DM 5,750,669.

2. The Property is subject to a right-of-way easement, belonging to a parcel of land recorded as lot No. . . . The easement has the following text:

„ . . . ."

§ 3
Purchase Price

1. The purchase price for the Property is DM 12 million (Deutsche Mark twelve million).

2. The purchase price will be paid as follows:

(a) Within seven (7) days after the date of this Agreement, Purchaser shall deposit the purchase price into the escrow account of the undersigned notary. If Purchaser defaults on the payment of the purchase price, the unpaid part of the purchase price shall accrue interest at a rate of 13% p. a.

3. The Parties hereby instruct the undersigned notary to apply the deposited purchase price as follows:

(a) DM 6,249,331 including accrued escrow account interest, shall be paid to Seller as soon as the following requirements have been met:

> (aa) The priority notice *(Vormerkung)* described hereinafter, showing Purchaser as the future title holder, shall have been validly recorded in Section III of the Deed Registry, junior only to the Mortgage recorded as Item 3.

1. Agreement for the Purchase and Sale of an Office Building

(bb) Written confirmation of the holder of the above-described Mortgage stating that outstanding principal, accrued interest and cost under the Mortgage, as of June 15, 1998, amounted to less than DM 5,800,000 and that the Mortgage holder will submit written approval of release and discharge against payment of an amount not in excess of DM 5, 800,000 if paid on or before June 30, 1999.

(cc) Confirmation of the undersigned notary that all documents required for the recording of new title have been submitted to the Deed Registry office, with the possible exception of such documents as are required of Purchaser, and that the Closing and transfer of title has been legally secured.

(b) DM 5,800,000 or such lesser amount as shall be required shall be applied for the repayment and cancellation of the Mortgage recorded in Section III under Item 3. The Parties hereby instruct the undersigned notary to effect the repayment, release and cancellation of the Mortgage as soon as the requirements set forth in subparagraph (a) above have been met. The undersigned notary has authority to undertake any acts required in connection with the above-described cancellation of the Mortgage.

Seller hereby requests cancellation of the Mortgage recorded in Section III, Item 3. Purchaser hereby consents to Seller's request.

If the amount of DM 5,800,000 is not sufficient to amortize and cancel the Mortgage recorded in Section III, Item 3, Seller shall, immediately upon request by the notary, pay the deficiency to the notary. Any excess amounts deposited by Seller shall be returned by the notary to Seller.

§ 4
Preliminary Building Permit

On January 16, 1998, Seller has filed with the Frankfurt Building Authority an application for preliminary permit for the construction of a commercial building. Seller hereby assigns all its rights under the above application to Purchaser.

Upon request by Purchaser, Seller shall provide all consents and declarations required for the issuance of a preliminary or final building permit. Notwithstanding the foregoing sentence, Seller also authorizes

Purchaser to file any required applications and submit any required consents and declarations for the building permits in the name, and on behalf, of Seller. Any costs arising from the building permit application, including application fees, shall be borne by Purchaser.

§ 5
Existing Leases

1. The Property is subject to the leases shown on Exhibit A hereto. Seller hereby represents that (a) the Property is subject to no leases other than those set forth on Exhibit A hereto; (b) no security deposits other than those set forth on Exhibit A have been deposited; (c) rental payments due under the leases are not less than as set forth on Exhibit A hereto; and (d) the leases can be terminated as set forth on Exhibit A hereto, without any liability on the part of the landlord for the repayment of rent, other than the repayment of security deposits.

2. Seller covenants not to enter into any other agreements relating to or in any way affecting the Property. Seller may not modify any existing leases or agreements relating to the Property without the prior consent of Purchaser.

3. Purchaser agrees to assume the existing leases on the day of Closing. Seller agrees to give notice of termination to tenants if requested by Purchaser after the Closing.

4. On the Closing date, Seller shall pay over to Purchaser the security deposits.

5. Seller makes no representations regarding, nor shall he be liable for, the future collectibility of rents.

§ 6
Closing

1. The date of closing and prorating of income and expenses shall be November 8, 1998. On this day, all income, benefits, uses, expenses and encumbrances relating to the Property shall accrue to the Purchaser and shall be prorated at such date.

2. Risk of loss passes to Purchaser on the date of this Agreement. Purchaser shall be entitled to any insurance proceeds relating to the Property, for damages occurring after the date of this Agreement. Seller covenants

1. Agreement for the Purchase and Sale of an Office Building

that it shall maintain the existing insurance on the Property. Seller does not represent that the insurance coverage is adequate.

3. Seller shall be responsible for the continuing maintenance of the Property until the date of closing.

4. The Property shall be deemed transferred, and this Agreement shall be deemed performed, on the date of closing and prorating.

5. Seller shall not be responsible for the maintenance of liability insurance coverage after the date of closing.

§ 7
Files and Records

Upon the request of Purchaser, Seller shall surrender all documents and records, including leases, tax assessments and other documents relating to the Property.

§ 8
Representations and Warranties

1. The Property, including fixtures, is sold „as is". Seller does not make any representations regarding the size or quality of the Property or the underlying soil, nor does Seller guarantee the absence of defects. Seller represents that it has no knowledge of any material defects, including the existence of dry-rot, building code violations or revocable permits.

2. Seller represents and warrants that

(a) Seller is the sole owner of the Property and that Seller has full authority to dispose of the Property;

(b) the Property, on and after the day of the closing, shall be free and clear of any encumbrances which would be recordable in Sections II and III of the Deed Registry;

(c) no fees or other levies for the provision of public services of any kind shall be due and outstanding on the date of closing;

(d) no real property taxes shall be in arrears, due and outstanding on the date of closing.

(e) the Property does not constitute the bulk of the Seller's assets as defined in § 419 Civil Code.

3. Purchaser is aware of the following obligations or defects:

(a) ....

§ 9
Priority Notice, Purchase Money Mortgage and Powers

1. Seller agrees and hereby requests that a Priority Notice (Vormerkung) securing Purchaser's claim for transfer of title be recorded in the Deed Registry. Purchaser hereby consents to the registration of such Priority Notice. Purchaser also agrees and requests that the Priority Notice be deleted as soon as Purchaser has been recorded as owner, provided that no other interests were recorded or applied for in the interim which are not provided for in this Agreement.

2. Should Purchaser decide to obtain third-party mortgage financing for the purchase of the Property, Seller hereby agrees to permit the recording of the desired mortgage before the transfer of title has been completed, provided that (a) the mortgage loan shall be funded into the escrow account of the undersigned notary; (b) the payment of the balance of the Purchase Price shall have been secured; and (c) Purchaser shall have previously made his downpayment set forth in § 3 (2)(a). Seller shall not be personally liable for the mortgage loan or for any cost related thereto.

3. The Parties hereto authorize [certain employees of the notary office] singly and without the conflict-of-interest restrictions of Section 181 Civil Code, to take all actions and make all declarations before the Deed Registry office or otherwise, which are required in connection with this transaction, including the cancellation or registration of liens and the closing described herein. This authority includes the right to appoint other persons as attorneys-in-fact.

§ 10
Right of First Refusal

In case the city of Frankfurt exercises any statutory right of first refusal it may have with respect to the Property, Seller hereby assigns to Purchaser its claims for payment against the city of Frankfurt to the extent

Purchaser has already made payments under this Agreement. Purchaser hereby accepts the assignment.

§ 11
Miscellaneous

1. The invalidity of one or more of the provisions of this Agreement shall not affect the validity of other provisions hereof. Any invalid provision shall be replaced by a provision which reflects the economic purposes of the Agreement and the mutual intent of the Parties.

2. Purchaser shall bear all costs of this Agreement and its execution, including notarial cost, court fees and real property transfer tax.

3. Seller shall bear the cost of deletion from the Deed Registry of encumbrances not assumed by Purchaser.

4. Purchaser shall pay a brokerage commission to the firm of .... Brokers, in the amount of 5% of the Purchase Price set forth in § 3, plus VAT tax. The commission is due and payable on the day of closing. Broker shall have a direct claim against Purchaser unless Purchaser validly rescinds this Agreement.

5. This Agreement is subject to German law. The place of performance shall be Frankfurt. Venue and jurisdiction shall be before the courts of Frankfurt.

THEREAFTER, the Parties jointly declared as follows:

1. We hereby request that the undersigned notary obtain all documents required for the conclusion of this transaction and to conclude this transaction. We authorize the undersigned notary to obtain the real property transfer tax assessment, the municipal waiver of right of first refusal, and the court fee statement.

2. We acknowledge having been instructed by the undersigned notary that

(a) Purchaser will not acquire title to the Property before recording in the Deed Registry has been completed;

(b) Seller and Purchaser are statutorily jointly and severally liable for the real property transfer tax, notary and court fees;

(c) the undersigned notary has inspected the Deed Registry on...,

1998; the Parties hereby waive any request for any additional inspection of the Deed Registry;

(d) a statutory (municipal) right of first refusal may exist.

3. We hereby declare our consent to the unconditional transfer of title.

There shall be only one original of this notarial protocol which shall be held by the undersigned notary. The undersigned notary shall file the protocol with the Deed Registry office only after the full Purchase Price of DM 12 million (Deutsche Mark twelve million) has been paid by Purchaser.

The above original protocol has been recorded, has been read to the Parties in my presence and has been signed by the Parties and by myself, the undersigned notary, as follows:

(Signatures)

_____   _____

_____   _____

2. OFFICE LEASE AGREEMENT

(Gewerberaummietvertrag)
– Translation/Übersetzung –

between

. . . . . ,

hereinafter „Landlord"

and

. . . . . . ,

hereinafter „Tenant",

arranged by . . . . . . Brokers.

§ 1
Leased premises

1. Tenant hereby leases the following premises („Premises") at Landstrasse 46, Frankfurt:

. . . .

2. The Premises are shown on Exhibit 1 hereto. For purposes of this Agreement, the Premises are presumed to comprise 350 m².

3. The Premises will be used as office space for managerial and administrative functions of tenant. Any change of the above use, including an expansion of activities or services, requires the prior written approval of Landlord.

4. Landlord is not restricted from letting other premises to competitors of Tenant.

5. The Premises may only be used in accordance with existing regulatory and zoning provisions, as they may be amended from time to time. Landlord does not make any representations that any required governmental approvals for Tenant's proposed use have been, or will be, obtained or that any obtained approvals will not be withdrawn. Tenant must satisfy any regulatory requirements for the proposed usage at its own cost.

If required approvals cannot be obtained, Tenant shall have no right to rescind this Agreement or to withhold payment of rent.

§ 2
Lease Term

1. The term of this Agreement begins on January 1, 1997 and ends on December 31, 2007. If this Agreement is not terminated by either Party at least six months prior to the expiration of the original lease term, it shall automatically continue for successive one-year periods. Notice of termination must be in writing.

2. If Tenant does not vacate the Premises after the expiration of the lease term, this Agreement shall not be considered extended pursuant to § 568 Civil Code. Any extension of this Agreement must be in writing.

3. Landlord may terminate this Agreement effective immediately for cause, including the following causes:

(a) Tenant defaults in the payment of rent in an aggregate amount of more than one monthly rental;

(b) Tenant's assets are sequestered or otherwise become subject to insolvency proceedings, and such sequestration or proceedings are not withdrawn within four weeks;

(c) Tenant, despite written notice by Landlord, continues to violate any provision of this Agreement or inflicts unreasonable nuisance on other tenants.

4. If Landlord terminates this Agreement for cause, Tenant shall be liable to Landlord for any loss of rental income and any additional rent until the end of the lease term. Notwithstanding the above, Landlord may have additional claims for damages against Tenant.

§ 3
Monthly Rental; Indexing

1. The monthly rental for the Premises shall be DM . . . . .

2. If Landlord has opted to subject rental income to value-added sales tax (VAT tax), Tenant agrees to add to its rental payments such VAT tax to be based on rent, additional rent and other payments due under this Agreement.

2. Office Lease Agreement

3. If the consumer price index established by the Federal Office of Statistics, has changed by more than ten index points since the beginning of the lease term, the rent under this Agreement shall be adjusted accordingly as of the calendar month next succeeding the date when such index threshold has been exceeded.

4. If the consumer price index again changes by more than ten index points from the index level existing as of the last rent adjustment date, rent shall again be adjusted as set forth in sub-paragraph 3 above.

§ 4
Cost Reimbursement – Additional Rent

1. In addition to the base rent, the following cost will be proportionately born by all tenants of the property:

(a) expenses for maintenance, ordinary repairs, operations, cleaning, heating, ventilation and air conditioning, warm water, burners, chimneys and emission control costs;

(b) expenses for maintenance, ordinary repairs, cleaning and operation of the elevators and all other common areas;

(c) fees for public services such as garbage removal, sewage, chimney sweeping and similar services;

(d) real property taxes;

(e) premiums for all property and liability insurance policies;

(f) utilities, including electricity and water;

(g) expenses for cleaning of common areas; (tenants shall be in charge of cleaning their individual windows);

(h) cost for superintendent and other building personnel, including lodging, salaries and bonuses;

(i) other cost of maintenance and operation, including property management fees;

(j) repairs and maintenance in all common areas, except for roof or structural repairs.

In addition to the above cost, Landlord may charge to Tenant all increases in the above costs as well as new fees or other levies related to the operation of the Property.

German Sample Agreements

2. (a) Expenses immediately related to the leased premises, such as cleaning, electricity, gas and similar utilities must be paid by Tenant directly to the providers of such services or utilities.

(b) Tenant shall obtain customary insurance protection, including liability insurance, occurring into the leased premises. Tenant agrees to submit such insurance policies to Landlord upon Landlord's request.

2. Additional rent shall be allocated to tenants in proportion to the size of the premises individually leased by them. For purposes of calculating the fraction of individual premises in relation to total leasable area, only 50% of the basement area shall be added to determine such total leasable area. If individual metering of energy or other utilities is possible and reasonable, the proportional allocation of such cost shall be replaced by individual metering. Landlord may, in its discretion, switch from one method to the other. If possible and reasonable, cost for window glass insurance shall be allocated to tenants in proportion to their individual aggregate window size.

3. If Tenant uses only part of the leased premises, he/she shall continue to be liable for additional rent relating to its entire premises.

4. Tenant shall pay estimated additional rent in the amount of DM...... each month. Landlord will submit to Tenant, at or after year-end, a statement showing actual additional rent for the year. Upon a change of tenancy during the calendar year, Tenant shall not be entitled to such interim statement of additional rent. Rather, Landlord shall be entitled to charge Tenant additional rent on the basis of a best efforts estimate. Any difference between the estimate and the actual additional rent statement at year-end shall be compensated at year-end.

Landlord may, at its discretion, change the statement from a calendar year to a fiscal year.

5. Landlord may adjust the estimated additional rent on the basis of a best efforts estimate. In any case, Landlord may request payment of estimated additional rent equal to the average monthly additional rent payable for the preceding year.

6. Statements for additional rent and other items, including charges to the debit account of Tenant are deemed accepted by Tenant, unless Tenant, within four (4) weeks after receipt of such statement or charges, objects to the charges in writing. Tenant shall be entitled to review Landlord's records within such four-week period.

2. Office Lease Agreement

7. If Tenant's occupancy results in a significant increase of waste, such as packaging or other material requiring additional garbage removal equipment, such as containers, Landlord may request that Tenant pay for such additional equipment.

8. Tenant must obtain prior written approval of Landlord for any refurbishments of Tenant's premises which would increase the risk of fire or similar damage. Tenant shall also be liable for additional fire insurance cost relating to such refurbishments.

§ 5
Payment of Rent and Additional Rent

1. Tenant shall pay rent and additional rent monthly in advance no later than on the third business day of each month. Tenant shall make rent payments into Landlord's account at ..... bank, account number ....., until otherwise instructed by Landlord.

2. Payments of rent are deemed received at the time the payment is irrevocably credited to the account of Landlord. Landlord may charge interest on any overdue rental payment at a rate equal to the discount rate determined by the German Federal Reserve Bank (Bundesbank) plus 4%. Landlord may also charge Tenant a fee of DM 3 for each written default notice. In addition to the above, Landlord may request damages upon Tenant's default if Landlord can substantiate such damages.

3. Tenant may not withhold rental payments or offset against such payments claims he may have against Landlord unless such arise out of this Lease Agreement and have been accepted by Landlord or determined by court in a final judgement.

4. Payments of excess additional rent or other payments shall be made within four (4) weeks after Tenant has received Landlord's statements of such additional rent or other payment.

5. If Tenant makes payments of amounts in arrear, Landlord may, at its discretion, apply such payments first to accrued additional rent and interest, and thereafter to accrued rent.

§ 6
Occupancy

1. Tenant accepts Premises with tenant improvements completed by Landlord in an „as is" condition. Tenant accepts Premises without tenant improvements as they are described in the construction plan and the floor plates, both of which are attached hereto as Exhibit 2. Landlord shall remain responsible for completing improvements, at Landlord's cost, to the extent they are set forth as Landlord improvements on these Exhibits. If Landlord does not discharge such duty to improve the Premises in a timely fashion, Tenant may withhold the payment of rent and additional rent provided the non-performance by Landlord materially affects the intended use of the Premises. Tenant may not, however, rescind this Agreement or request damages.

The delay of the completion of any improvements outside of the leased premises shall not entitle Tenant to any reduction of rent or to rescission or to damages, unless the delay makes Tenant's Premises entirely unusable.

2. Any improvements within the leased premises which are not described on Exhibit 2 as Landlord's improvements shall be made by Tenant at Tenant's cost. Tenant shall take due regard of technical and logistical requirements. In order to preserve the homogenous character of the building, Tenant shall obtain prior written approval for any improvements which deviate from those set forth in this Agreement and the Exhibits thereto.

3. Tenant, in making improvements to its premises, may not create a nuisance for other tenants or a hindrance to the completion of the construction of the building.

4. Landlord shall deliver the Premises for occupancy or further improvement by Tenant on . . . . Landlord shall be entitled to delivery of the Premises only after full payment of rent and additional rent for the first month and after payment of the security deposit described in § 15 hereinafter.

5. If Tenant does not occupy the Premises within fourteen (14) days after the commencement of the lease term (§ 2.1) without showing reasonable cause, or if Tenant has failed to pay rent, additional rent or the security deposit within such fourteen (14) day period, Landlord may, at its discretion, terminate this Agreement and rent the Premises to another party.

2. Office Lease Agreement

Notwithstanding the conclusion of such new lease agreement with a third party, Landlord may claim damages against Tenant pursuant to § 2.4.

6. Unless Tenant gives written notice to Landlord of any specific defects in improvements which have or will have been made by Landlord, within fourteen (14) days after commencement of the lease term, Landlord's improvements shall be deemed accepted by Tenant.

7. Landlord reserves the right to change construction plans and improvements to the Premises provided such changes have no or only an immaterial effect on the utility of the Premises.

§ 7
Tenant Improvements and Maintenance

1. Improvements or changes to the Premises, other than those set forth on Exhibit 3 hereto, require the prior written approval of Landlord. Upon approval by Landlord, Tenant shall be responsible for obtaining any governmental permits for the proposed changes and to make the improvements and changes at its own cost.

2. Tenant agrees to maintain the Premises in good condition at all times and to make any required repairs or renovations. Such maintenance shall include cosmetic improvements to the Premises, such as repainting, cleaning, wallpapering, which must be performed in periodic intervals, not less than every five (5) years, as well as maintenance of ducts, lines, and similar equipment for electricity, water, heating, air conditioning, sanitary equipment, sun protection equipment, windows, doors, etc. Tenant shall be responsible for the unclogging of pipes up to the point where the pipes meet the main pipes. Tenant shall also be responsible for pest control of the leased Premises.

3. Tenant shall be liable to Landlord for any damage caused by Tenant, Tenant's employees or invitees, with or without negligence of Tenant, Tenant's employees or invitees, to sewage and other pipes, toilets, heating and ventilation systems. If the person causing the damage cannot be determined and if no insurance coverage exists for the damage, Landlord shall be entitled to charge the repair cost as additional rent to all tenants. Landlord may also, at its discretion, include damage to any tenants or to the property's superintendent in such additional rent. Tenant shall be liable to Landlord for any damage to windows or other glass, to the extent such damage is not covered through insurance.

Tenant shall give immediate notice to Landlord of any damage and shall be liable for any additional damage caused by a delayed notice.

4. Tenant shall cause any maintenance or repair work to be performed in a state-of-the-art manner. If Tenant does not perform, or causes to be performed, such maintenance and repairs, after written notice by Landlord, Landlord may order the work to be done at Tenant's cost. If there is an immediate risk of damage, or if Landlord cannot locate and notify Tenant, Landlord may order the work to be done without prior written notice to Tenant.

5. Tenant may not move heavy machinery or safes into the Premises unless it has obtained information about the maximum load allowed in the Premises and unless he/she has obtained prior written approval of Landlord. Tenant shall be liable for any damages.

6. Tenant may not inflict any nuisance through noise, odors or other emissions affecting other tenants. Tenant may not store any equipment or other matters on the lease premises without the written consent of Landlord. Tenant shall be liable for any damages resulting from the violation of these provisions.

§ 8
Improvements and Maintenance by Landlord

1. Landlord may make improvements, repairs or construction changes without approval of Tenant if such improvements or changes are required to keep the property in good repair, or to eliminate risk of damage or to remove damage. Any improvements, repairs or changes which are not necessary but reasonable will require the consent of Tenant which may only be withheld for reasonable cause. Tenant must keep the Premises accessible for such improvements, repairs or changes.

2. Landlord, at its discretion, may change the source of energy and burning materials for the warm water supply and for central heating.

3. Tenant shall not be entitled to reduce or withhold rent or to request damages if Landlord properly performs the work described in sub-sections 1 and 2 above. If, however, Tenant's use of the Premises is materially affected as a consequence of such work, rent shall be reasonably reduced during the work. The rent reduction shall be commensurate to the reduced utility of the Premises to Tenant.

2. Office Lease Agreement

4. Landlord shall be responsible for making structural or roof repairs at its own cost. Landlord shall not be responsible for any other repairs or maintenance according to Section 536 and Section 546 Civil Code.

Landlord shall not be liable for damage caused by water, humidity, fire, smoke or similar damage, unless the damage was caused through reckless disregard of maintenance duties by Landlord and Landlord has not removed the defect despite the express request of Tenant. Landlord shall not be liable for actions of other tenants or of management or other personnel which Landlord employs to perform certain services, provided that Landlord has not acted with gross negligence in selecting and controlling these persons. Landlord shall not be liable for damages under Section 538 Civil Code.

4. Repair, maintenance and renovation work other than structural and roof repairs, particularly work in common areas, will be done by Landlord and charged as additional rent to all tenants in accordance with § 4.2.

§ 9
Heating, Ventilation, Electricity and Other Utilities

1. Heating and, if available, airconditioning and other similar jointly used equipment will be in operation as reasonably required by the bulk of all tenants.

If the provision of heating, ventilation or airconditioning is partially or totally interrupted due to bottlenecks in local energy supply or because of technical defects of any kind, tenants shall not be entitled to reduce or withhold rent or to request damages.

2. Tenant may use the existing lines and pipes for electricity, gas and water in accordance with, and commensurate to, the relative size of its premises in the Property. Tenant may not cause an overload of such lines or pipes through excessive use. If Tenant has increased requirements for such services, tenant may, at its own cost, increase the capacity of such lines or pipes upon prior written approval of Landlord and only if such increase in capacity is technically feasible.

3. Tenant may use water only for its own requirements. If Tenant uses water for commercial purposes, it must install separate metering at its own cost and bear the cost of the additional water and sewage system supply.

4. Tenant shall immediately turn off supply pipes if Tenant detects defects. If Tenant cannot turn off such supply pipes or if any resulting nuisance or damage impacts other tenants, Tenant shall immediately notify Landlord of the defect.

Landlord shall not be liable for any changes in energy supply, including any changes in voltage. Landlord shall notify tenants of any such changes.

Tenant shall have no right to reduce or withhold rent or to request damages, if energy, water or sewage system supply is interrupted through no fault of Landlord, or as a consequence of flooding or other calamities.

§ 10
Identity of Tenant; Subleasing

1. If there is any change in the person, the shareholders or the legal entity of Tenant, or if there are other changes which are recordable in the trade register or which affect Tenant's license to do business or other matters which are relevant to this Agreement, Tenant shall immediately notify Landlord of such changes. If, as a consequence of such changes, the credit rating of Tenant is negatively affected, Landlord shall be entitled to terminate this Agreement upon six weeks prior notice to the end of the calendar quarter unless Tenant delivers additional collateral as requested by Landlord.

2. Any subleasing or assignment of this Lease by Tenant requires the prior written approval of Landlord. Section 549(1), second sentence, Civil Code shall not apply. Tenant hereby assigns its rights against any subtenant to Landlord as collateral for Landlord's rights against Tenant.

3. If Tenant subleases the Premises without approval of Landlord, Landlord may request that Tenant terminates the sublease agreement not later than by the end of the then current month. If the sublease is not so terminated, Landlord may terminate this Lease Agreement effective immediately.

4. In the case of an approved sublease, Tenant shall be liable for all actions or omissions of subtenant.

2. Office Lease Agreement

§ 11
Accessibility of Lease Premises

1. Landlord or Landlord's representatives or invitees may enter the leased Premises at normal business hours for purposes of inspection, re-tenanting or the sale of the Property, provided Landlord has previously arranged the date and time of the visit with Tenant. In the case of emergencies, Landlord and its representatives may enter the leased Premises at any time, day and night. During the last remaining six months of the lease term, Landlord or its representatives or invitees may enter the leased Premises at any time during regular business hours.

2. Tenant must keep the leased Premises accessible to Landlord during Tenant's absence. Tenant must notify Landlord or the Property's superintendent of any long-term absence, such as firm holidays.

§ 12
Signage, Vending Machines, Awnings

1. Tenant is entitled to affix a company sign at a designated place in the building lobby and on Tenant's floor. Style and size of the signage shall be determined by Landlord.

2. Tenant may not, without written approval of Landlord and without the required governmental permits, affix any signage or install any vending or other machines outside of the building or on its roof. Tenant shall be responsible for all costs and fees arising from any such installations.

3. Tenant must ensure that any signage, awnings or similar equipment are installed in a safe condition so that damage to persons and Property will be avoided. Upon termination of this lease or upon revocation of required approvals, Tenant must restore the Property at its own cost.

4. Shop windows must be kept clean and in a state of decoration commensurate with the appearance of the building.

§ 13
End of Lease Term

1. At the end of the lease term, Tenant shall deliver the leased Premises in clean and repaired condition, after required repainting, renovations, cleaning and necessary repairs.

2. Tenant shall remove any fixtures or installations and shall restore the leased Premises to their original condition, unless Landlord approves otherwise. Landlord shall have no obligation to compensate Tenant for any improvements made to the Premises. Landlord may request that improvements, fixtures and installations remain in the Premises. In such case, Landlord shall compensate Tenant for the fair-market value of such improvements and installations, taking due regard of technical obsolescence and wear and tear. Tenant and Landlord shall make their efforts to timely agree on the removal or non-removal of improvements and installation.

§ 14
Several Tenants

1. If more than one person or entity enters into this Lease Agreement as Tenant, the persons and entities shall be jointly and severally liable under this Agreement.

2. Notice by Landlord to any one of the persons or entities shall be deemed notice to all persons or entities. Actions or notices by any one of the persons or entities shall be deemed to be notices by all persons or entities.

3. Extensions of the lease term, or early terminations thereof, and claims for damages by or against Landlord, shall apply against or for all persons or entities that have entered into this Lease Agreement.

§ 15
Security Deposit

Upon execution of this Agreement, Tenant shall deposit into a non-interest bearing account an amount equal to three months rental. Alternatively, Tenant may submit an irrevocable bank Letter of Credit in the same amount. If Landlord, during the term of this lease, makes a drawing against the security deposit, Tenant shall immediately restore the security deposit or other collateral to its original amount. The security deposit shall be returned by Landlord or the bank Letter of Credit shall be released by Landlord, upon termination of this lease and upon the determination that Landlord has no further claims against Tenant.

§ 16
Miscellaneous

1. Landlord may, from time to time, promulgate and/or amend house rules regulating the use of the Property, its common areas and the leased Premises. Any such house rules will become part of this Agreement.

2. This Agreement shall override any prior written or oral agreements. Any additional arrangements, clauses, promises or amendments must be in writing.

3. This Agreement shall be subject to the jurisdiction of the courts of Frankfurt.

4. The invalidity of any provision of this Agreement shall not affect the validity of the other provisions. The parties shall attempt to replace the invalid provision by a valid provision which most closely represents the original intent and purposes of the parties.

Frankfurt, _____

_____   _____

Landlord   Tenant

3. Purchase and Sale Agreement

(Grundstückskaufvertrag)

between

_____ , SELLER

AND

_____ , BUYER

FOR

_____

NEW YORK, NEW YORK

TABLE OF CONTENTS

Section	Page
BACKGROUND.	203
TERMS AND CONDITIONS	204
1. Sale and Purchase	204
2. Purchase Price	204
3. Covenants, Representations and Warranties of Seller	204
(a) Authority	204
(b) No Condemnation.	204
(c) Contracts	205
(d) Compliance	205
(e) Litigation	206
(f) FIRPTA	206
(g) Hazardous Substances	206
(h) Special Assessments.	207
(i) Taxes	207
(j) No Further Agreements	207
(k) Definition of Knowledge	207
4. Conditions Precedent to Buyer's Obligations	207
(a) Accuracy of Representations.	207
(b) Performance	207
(c) Documents and Deliveries	207
(d) Materials Provided by Seller; Inspection Period; Access; Purchase „As Is".	208
(e) Condition of Property	210
(f) Title	210
(g) Authority to Convey; Noncontravention	211
5. Failure of Conditions	211
6. Closing; Deliveries	211
7. Apportionments; Taxes; Expenses	213
(a) Apportionments	213
(b) Expenses	213
8. Damage or Destruction; Condemnation; Insurance	213
9. Defaults	214
10. Further Assurances	214
11. Possession	214
12. Notices	214

13. Brokers 215
14. Miscellaneous 216
    (a) Assignability 216
    (b) Governing Law; Parties in Interest 216
    (c) Headings 216
    (d) Counterparts 216
    (e) Exhibits 216
    (f) Survival 216
    (g) Entire Agreement; Amendments 216
    (h) Confidentiality 216
    (i) Time of the Essence 217

EXHIBITS

Exhibit A – Description of the Land
Exhibit B – Contracts
Exhibit C – Disclosures
Exhibit D – Bargain and Sale Deed with Covenants
Exhibit E – Bill of Sale
Exhibit F – Assignment of Contracts

3. PURCHASE AND SALE AGREEMENT

THIS PURCHASE AND SALE AGREEMENT (hereinafter called the *„Agreement"*) is made as of the _____ day of _____, 1997, by and between _____ (hereinafter called the *„Seller"*), and _____ (hereinafter called the *„Buyer"*).

BACKGROUND

I. Seller is the owner of the following real and personal property (hereinafter collectively called the *„Property"*):

A. All that certain real property, commonly known as _____, New York, New York as more particularly described in *Exhibit A* attached hereto, together with all easements, rights and privileges appurtenant thereto (hereinafter called the *„Land"*);

B. The building situated on the Land, being known as _____, New York, New York, containing approximately _____ square feet, together with all improvements appurtenant thereto (hereinafter called the *„Buildings";* the Buildings and such improvements being hereinafter collectively called the *„Improvements";* and the Land and the Improvements being hereinafter collectively called the *„Real Property"*);

C. All intangible property used or useful in connection with the foregoing, including, without limitation, all contract rights, guarantees, licenses, permits and warranties (hereinafter called the *„Intangibles"* and the Real Property, Personalty and intangibles are hereinafter collectively called the *„Property"*).

II. Seller is prepared to sell, transfer and convey the Property to Buyer, and Buyer is prepared to purchase and accept the same from Seller, all for the purchase price and on the other terms and conditions hereinafter set forth.

U.S. Sample Agreements

TERMS AND CONDITIONS

In consideration of the mutual covenants and agreements herein contained, and intending to be legally bound hereby, the parties hereto agree:

1. ***Sale and Purchase.*** Seller hereby agrees to sell, transfer and convey the Property to Buyer, and Buyer hereby agrees to purchase and accept the Property from Seller, in each case for the purchase price and on and subject to the other terms and conditions set forth in this Agreement.

2. ***Purchase Price.*** The purchase price for the Property (hereinafter called the *„Purchase Price"*) shall be _____ Million and no/100 Dollars ($_____) which, subject to the terms and conditions hereinafter set forth, shall be paid to Seller by Buyer, subject to adjustments and apportionments as set forth herein, at the Closing (as hereinafter defined) by wire transfer of immediately available federal funds, in accordance with written instructions for the disbursement thereof provided by Seller to the order or account of Seller or such other person or persons as Seller shall designate in writing. Upon execution of this Agreement, Purchaser shall deliver to Seller's attorney an earnest money deposit (the *„Earnest Money")* in an amount equal to $_____ which shall be held in escrow pending the closing of title. The Earnest Money shall be deposited by Seller's attorney in an interest-bearing account and any accrued interest shall be divided equally between Seller and Buyer at the Closing.

3. ***Covenants, Representations and Warranties of Seller.*** Seller covenants, represents and warrants to Buyer as follows. At the Closing, Seller shall update the following representations and warranties (and the exhibits referred to therein) to reflect any corrections or additional information determined to be necessary as a result of Buyer's due diligence investigation.

(a) ***Authority.*** Seller is a _____ corporation, and has all requisite power and authority to enter into this Agreement and to perform its obligations hereunder. The execution and delivery of this Agreement and the consummation of the transactions contemplated hereby do not contravene the organizational documents of Seller or any material contract, indenture or agreement to which Seller is a party.

(b) ***No Condemnation.*** To the best of Seller's actual knowledge, there is no pending or contemplated condemnation, eminent domain or similar proceeding with respect to all or any portion of the Real Property.

3. Purchase and Sale Agreement

(c) ***Contracts.*** There are no construction, management, leasing, service, equipment, supply, maintenance or concession agreements entered into by and currently binding Seller with respect to the Real Property other than those set forth in ***Exhibit B*** hereto (hereinafter collectively called the *"Contracts"*). Seller shall deliver a copy of each Contract to Buyer within five (5) business days after execution of this Agreement by Seller and Buyer. Except as to Contracts that (a) Buyer notifies Seller in writing to terminate and (b) that Seller can terminate without liability to Seller, all Contracts, if and to the extent assignable, shall be assigned by Seller and assumed by Buyer as part of the Closing (the *"Assigned Contracts"*). Buyer shall notify Seller, no later than fifteen (15) days prior to the Closing, of the Contracts which are to be terminated.

So long as this Agreement shall remain in full force and effect, Seller shall not enter into any new contracts with respect to the Building (except contracts that may be terminated upon no more than thirty (30) days notice without premium or penalty) or modify, amend or supplement any existing contracts in any material respect, without the prior written consent of Buyer.

(d) ***Compliance.*** To the best of Seller's actual knowledge and except as may be disclosed on ***Exhibit C,*** all notes or notices of violations of law or governmental ordinances, orders or requirements which were issued prior to the date of this Agreement by any governmental department, agency or bureau having jurisdiction as to conditions affecting the Property prior to the Closing pursuant to the Administrative Code of the City of New York have been removed or complied with by Seller. If such removal or compliance has not been completed prior to Closing, Seller shall pay to Buyer at the Closing the reasonably estimated unpaid amount to effect or complete such removal or compliance, and Buyer shall be required to accept title to the Property subject thereto. All such notes or notices of violations noted or issued on or after the Closing shall be the sole responsibility of Buyer.

If the reasonably estimated aggregate cost to remove or comply with any violations or liens which Seller is required to remove or comply with pursuant to the provisions of this Section 3.4 shall exceed the Maximum Amount specified in ***Exhibit C*** (or if none is so specified, the Maximum Amount shall be one-half of one percent of the Purchase Price, Seller shall have the right to cancel this Agreement, in which event the sole liability of Seller shall be as set forth in Section 5, unless Buyer elects to accept title to the Property subject to all such violations, or liens, in which event Buyer shall be entitled to a credit of an amount equal to the Maximum Amount against the monies payable at the Closing.

If required, Seller, upon written request by Buyer, shall promptly furnish to Buyer written authorization to make any necessary searches for the purposes of determining whether notes or notices of violations have been noted or issued with respect to the Property or liens have attached thereto.

(e) **Litigation.** To the best of Seller's actual knowledge, there is no action, suit or proceeding pending or threatened against or affecting the Property, or arising out of Seller's ownership, management or operation of the Real Property.

(f) **FIRPTA.** Seller is not a „foreign person" as defined in Section 1445(f)(3) of the Internal Revenue Code.

(g) **Hazardous Substances.** To the best of Seller's actual knowledge, based solely on that certain [Environmental Report] dated _____ (the **„Environmental Report")** and except as disclosed in the Environmental Report, neither the Land nor the Improvements contains any substance known to be hazardous, including without limitation, hazardous waste, asbestos, methane gas, urea formaldehyde insulation or other toxic or hazardous substance other than the asbestos of which Buyer is aware. To the best of Seller's actual knowledge, based solely on the Environmental Report and except as disclosed in the Environmental Report, the Improvements do not contain any hazardous building materials. For the purposes of this Agreement, the term „hazardous substance or waste" shall mean petroleum, including crude oil, polychlorinated biphenyls and any substance identified in CERCLA, RCRA, SARA or any other federal, state or other governmental legislation or ordinance applicable to the Real Property identified by its terms as pertaining to the disposal of hazardous substances or wastes. The term „hazardous substance or waste" shall, in addition, only refer to those substances or waste which are present on the Real Property in amounts or in a condition which constitutes a violation of any such legislation or ordinance. To the best of Seller's actual knowledge, based solely on the Environmental Report, there are no storage tanks located on the Real Property either above or below ground and to the best of Seller's actual knowledge, based solely on the Environmental Report, the Real Property has never been used as a landfill or a dump for garbage or refuse.

3. Purchase and Sale Agreement

Buyer and Seller hereby acknowledge that the foregoing representations are based solely on the Environmental Report and that Seller has not made any further independent investigation regarding environmental matters with respect to the Real Property.

(h) *Special Assessments.* To the best of Seller's actual knowledge, there is no pending or proposed special assessment affecting or which may affect the Property or any part thereof.

(i) *Taxes.* To the best of Seller's actual knowledge, all ad valorem and similar taxes assessed against the Property have been paid through fiscal year 1996.

(j) *No Further Agreements.* So long as this Agreement remains in full force and effect, Seller will not sell, assign, rent, lease, convey (absolutely or as security), grant a security interest in, or otherwise voluntarily encumber or dispose of the Property, any part thereof or any interest or estate therein, or negotiate for the purpose of any of the foregoing.

(k) *Definition of Knowledge.* For purposes of this Section 3 „to the best of Seller's knowledge" or „to the best of Seller's actual knowledge" shall mean the actual knowledge of _____ without independent investigation or inquiry.

4. *Conditions Precedent to Buyer's Obligations.* All of Buyer's obligations hereunder are expressly conditioned on the satisfaction at or before the Closing (as hereinafter defined), or at or before such earlier time as may be expressly stated below, of each of the following conditions (any one or more of which may be waived in writing in whole or in part by Buyer, at Buyer's option):

(a) *Accuracy of Representations.* All of the covenants, representations and warranties of Seller contained in this Agreement shall have been true and correct in all material respects when made, and shall be true and correct in all material respects on the date of the Closing with the same effect as if made on and as of such date.

(b) *Performance.* Seller shall have performed, observed and complied with all material covenants, agreements and conditions required by this Agreement to be performed, observed and complied with on its part prior to or as of the Closing hereunder.

(c) *Documents and Deliveries.* All instruments and documents required on Seller's part to effectuate this Agreement and the transactions contemplated hereby shall be delivered to Buyer and shall be in form and substance consistent with the requirements herein.

(d) ***Materials Provided by Seller; Inspection Period; Access; Purchase ,,As Is".***

(i) Seller will provide Buyer with copies of the material and information described below (the ***,,Materials"***), to the extent within Seller's possession or control, promptly following execution and delivery of this Agreement by Seller and Buyer:

(1) The Contracts;

(2) Tax bills for calendar years ____ – ____ and evidence of payment of real estate taxes for the period ending June 30, 199___;

(3) As-built construction drawings for the Improvements if available;

(4) Existing title policy insuring Seller's interest as owner;

(5) Existing surveys of the Real Property if available;

(6) Certificates of Occupancy for the Building shells and all occupied space.

Buyer acknowledges that the Materials provided to Buyer are for informational purposes only and shall not be construed as a representation or warranty on the part of Seller or any other party regarding the Property. The Materials are confidential and access shall be limited to personnel of the Buyer who have a need to review the Materials in order to make a decision concerning Buyer's purchase of the Property and to Buyer's attorneys, representatives, agents, and other consultants engaged to assist Buyer in its evaluation of the Property, and Buyer agrees not to disclose any information contained in the Material to any other person or entity, unless otherwise required by legal process. The Materials, upon the written request of Seller, shall be returned to Seller if this Agreement shall be terminated for any reason, together with a copy of any surveys, test results, inspection reports and similar matters related to the Property and obtained by Buyer during the Inspection Period.

(ii) During the Inspection Period (as hereinafter defined), Buyer, its representatives, agents and other consultants shall be entitled to enter upon the Property, upon reasonable prior notice to Seller, to perform inspections and tests of the Property, including surveys, test borings, environmental studies, examinations and tests of all structural and mechanical systems within the Improvements. During such Inspection

3. Purchase and Sale Agreement

Period, Buyer shall furnish to Seller proof of insurance covering any risks associated with the foregoing activities. Notwithstanding the foregoing, Buyer shall not be permitted to interfere unreasonably with Seller's operations at the Property. If Buyer wishes to engage in any intensive testing which will disturb or be intrusive with respect to any portion of the Property, Buyer shall obtain Seller's prior written consent thereto, which consent shall not be unreasonably withheld or delayed. Without limiting the generality of the foregoing, Seller's written approval shall be required prior to any testing or sampling of surface or subsurface soils, surface water, groundwater or any materials in or about the Improvements in connection with Buyer's environmental due diligence. Buyer shall repair any damage to the Property caused by any such tests or investigations, and indemnify, defend and hold Seller harmless from any and all liabilities, claims, costs and expenses resulting from Buyer's activities on the Property or the activities of Buyer's agents, employees or contractors. The foregoing indemnification shall survive the Closing or the termination of this Agreement.

(iii) The term *„Inspection Period"*, as used herein, shall mean the period, if any, commencing on the day following the date of execution of this Agreement by Buyer and Seller and ending at 11:59 p. m. on the business day that is thirty (30) business days after the date of execution of this Agreement. Buyer may terminate this Agreement and receive return of the Earnest Money for any reason or for no reason, by giving written notice of such election to Seller on any day prior to and including the final day of the Inspection Period, in which event, except as expressly set forth herein, neither party shall have any further liability or obligation to the other hereunder. If Buyer fails to give such written notice, the condition provided for in this Section 4.4.3 shall be deemed waived and no longer applicable.

(iv) Buyer acknowledges and agrees that Buyer is acquiring the Property in its vacant and broom-cleaned „AS IS" condition, WITH ALL FAULTS, IF ANY, AND WITHOUT ANY WARRANTY, EXPRESS OR IMPLIED. Other than as expressly set forth herein, neither Seller nor any agents, representatives, or employees of Seller have made any representations or warranties, direct or indirect, oral or written, express or implied, to Buyer or any agents, representatives, or employees of Buyer with respect to the condition of the Property, its fitness for any particular purpose, or its compliance with any laws, and Buyer is not aware of and does not rely upon any such representation to Buyer or any other party. Buyer acknowledges that the Inspection Period will have afforded Buyer the opportunity to make such inspections (or cause such inspections to be made by consultants) as it desires to make for the Property, and all factors relevant to its use, including, without limitation, the interior, exterior, and structure of all Improvements, and the condition of soils and subsurfaces. Buyer has not been induced by and has not relied upon any representations, warranties or statements, whether stated or implied, made by Seller or any agent, employee or other representative of Seller or by any broker or any other person representing or purporting to represent Seller, which are not expressly set forth in this Agreement, whether or not any such representations, warranties or statements were made in writing or orally. Buyer shall rely exclusively upon the inspections and examination made, or caused to be made, by Buyer during the Inspection Period as to the condition of the Property and all such factors.

(e) *Condition of Property.* The Property shall be delivered to Buyer at the Closing in vacant and broom-cleaned condition but otherwise in the same condition as it is on the date of this Agreement, reasonable wear and tear excepted.

(f) *Title.* Buyer shall obtain and provide to Seller a complete updated title report or commitment with respect to the Property, with copies of all instruments listed as exceptions to title. Buyer may object to any record title matters disclosed in the title report other than the Permitted Exceptions (as defined below), or to any survey matters disclosed in any survey obtained by Buyer. Buyer shall, within a reasonable time after the date of full execution of this Agreement (considering the length of the Inspection Period), notify Seller in writing, specifying the objectionable matters. Seller may elect (but shall have no obligation whatsoever except as hereafter provided) to cure any such matters prior to the Closing. As promptly as practicable after receiving Buyer's notice, Seller shall notify Buyer whether Seller intends to effectuate such cure. All title matters as to which Buyer has not given Seller notice of objection in the time and manner stated in this Section 4.6 shall be deemed to have been accepted by Buyer.

(i) Notwithstanding the foregoing provisions of this paragraph, Seller shall cause to be removed or discharged any mortgage liens or security titles or interests encumbering all or any portion of the Property caused or incurred by Seller, including without limitation, any other mortgages, deeds of trusts or similar security instruments, any lien assessed against the Property for failure to pay taxes when due, any me-

3. Purchase and Sale Agreement

chanics', materialmen's or similar liens securing claims for unpaid sums due from Seller.

(ii) Buyer acknowledges and agrees that title to the Real Property shall be conveyed subject only to: (i) taxes for the then-current tax period which are not due and payable at the date of the Closing; (ii) easements for utilities serving the Property and (iii) any survey exceptions which would be disclosed by a current survey of the Property. The matters referred to in the preceding clauses (i), (ii) and (iii) above are hereinafter collectively called the *,,Permitted Exceptions"*.

(g) *Authority to Convey; Noncontravention.* Buyer shall be satisfied that Seller has all requisite power and authority to enter into this Agreement and to perform its obligations hereunder and that the consummation of the transactions contemplated hereunder do not contravene such organizational documents.

5. *Failure of Conditions.* In the event that any of the conditions set forth in Section 4 of this Agreement has not been satisfied or waived by Buyer, or in the event that Seller shall not be able to convey title to the Property on the date of the Closing in accordance with the provisions of this Agreement, then Buyer shall have the option, exercisable by written notice to Seller at or prior to the Closing, of (i) accepting at the Closing such title as Seller is able to convey and/or waiving any unsatisfied condition precedent, with no deduction from or adjustment of the Purchase Price, or (ii) terminating this Agreement. If Buyer elects to terminate this Agreement in accordance with clause (ii), all obligations, liabilities and rights of the parties under this Agreement, other than Buyer's indemnification obligations under Section 4.4.2, shall terminate.

6. *Closing; Deliveries.*

(a) The closing under this Agreement (the *,,Closing"*) shall take place commencing at 10:00 a. m. on _____, 199___, unless otherwise agreed to in writing by both Seller and Buyer.

(b) At the Closing, Seller shall deliver to Buyer the following:

(i) Bargain and Sale Deed with Covenants to the Real Property, duly executed and acknowledged by Seller and in proper form for recording, conveying fee simple title to the Real Property to Buyer, subject only to the Permitted Exceptions and such title matters as are accepted by Buyer pursuant to Section 4.6 of this Agreement attached hereto as *Exhibit D.*

(ii) A bill of sale for the Personalty and Intangibles, duly executed and acknowledged by Seller, which shall provide for the acceptance thereof by Buyer and which shall include an assignment to Buyer of all warranties which may have arisen during the period of Seller's ownership of the Property, to the extent assignable attached hereto as ***Exhibit E***.

(iii) An assignment assigning to Buyer the Assigned Contracts, which shall provide for an assumption thereof by Buyer attached hereto as ***Exhibit F***.

(iv) Originals or copies of as-built architectural and engineering drawings, utility layout plans, topographical plans and the like in Seller's possession.

(v) A certification and affidavit as required by the Foreign Investors Real Property Tax Act, as amended.

(vi) Any reasonable and customary certificates, affidavits, instruments or other documents as shall be required by the title insurance company insuring Buyer's interest in the Property as a condition to the issuance of an owner's policy of title insurance in accordance with Section 4.6 hereof.

(vii) All other instruments and documents reasonably required to effectuate this Agreement and the transactions contemplated thereby.

(viii) Transfer Tax Authorization form as required by the City and State of New York.

(c) At the Closing, Buyer shall deliver to Seller the following:

(i) In accordance with Seller's instructions, a transfer of immediately available federal funds in the amount of the Purchase Price required under Section 2.1 of this Agreement.

(ii) The acceptance of the bill of sale referred to in Section 6.2.2 of this Agreement, and the assumption of the Assigned Contracts referred to in Section 6.2.4 of this Agreement, duly executed by Buyer.

(d) The acceptance of a deed by Buyer shall be deemed to be a full performance and discharge of every agreement and obligation to be performed by Seller hereunder, excepting only such obligations and agreements which are expressly stated in this Agreement to survive the Closing.

3. Purchase and Sale Agreement

7. *Apportionments; Taxes; Expenses.*

(a) *Apportionments.* Buyer and Seller agree that there shall be apportionments made as of the Closing Date with respect to real estate taxes, assessments or other municipal charges affecting the Property or with respect to operating expenses and/or common area maintenance charges. All apportionments shall be based on information available at Closing, adjustments to the apportionments shall be made upon demand of either party based on the newly available information.

(b) *Expenses.* Each party will pay all its own expenses incurred in connection with this Agreement and the transactions contemplated hereby, including, without limitation (i) all costs and expenses stated herein to be borne by a party, and (ii) all of their respective accounting, legal and appraisal fees. Buyer, in addition to its other expenses, shall pay at the Closing: (i) all recording charges incident to the recording of the deed for the Real Property, and (ii) all premiums for Buyer's title insurance policy. Seller, in addition to its other expenses, shall pay at the Closing, to the extent applicable, all real property transfer tax imposed by the State of New York and the City of New York by certified check or official bank checks if requested by the taxing authority.

8. *Damage or Destruction; Condemnation; Insurance.*

(a) If at any time prior to the date of the Closing the Property is destroyed or damaged as a result of fire or any other casualty whatsoever to such extent that the cost of repair and restoration exceeds One Hundred Thousand and No/100 Dollars ($100,000.00) or if all or any material portion of the Property is condemned or taken by, or subjected to a bona fide threat of, eminent domain proceedings by any public authority, then, at Buyer's option, this Agreement shall terminate and except as expressly set forth herein, neither party shall have any further liability or obligation to the other hereunder.

(b) If there is any damage, destruction, condemnation or taking that does not entitle Buyer to terminate this Agreement pursuant to Section 8.1 of this Agreement, or if Buyer is entitled to terminate this Agreement but elects not to terminate this Agreement as provided in Section 8.1 of this Agreement, then (i) in the case of damage or destruction, Seller shall assign to Buyer at the Closing all rights to any insurance proceeds paid or payable under the applicable insurance policies, but not exceeding the amount of the Purchase Price, and Buyer shall receive a credit against the purchase price equal to the amount of Seller's deductible under its insurance coverage, and (ii) in the case of a condemnation or taking, all proceeds paid or payable to Seller, but not exceeding the amount of the Purchase Price, shall belong to Buyer and shall be paid over and assigned to Buyer at the Closing.

9. *Defaults.*

(a) In the event Buyer defaults or fails to perform any of its obligations under this Agreement, Seller shall have the right to receive from Buyer as liquidated damages (and not as a penalty) an amount equal to $625,000.00, which shall be Seller's sole remedy for such default. Buyer and Seller acknowledge and agree that damages to Seller resulting from Buyer's breach would be difficult, if not impossible, to ascertain with any accuracy, and that the liquidated damages amount set forth in this Section 9.1 represents both parties" efforts to approximate such potential damages. Upon such payment, this Agreement shall terminate and the parties shall be relieved of all further obligations and liabilities hereunder, except as otherwise expressly set forth herein.

(b) In the event Seller defaults or fails to perform any of its obligations under this Agreement which are not cured before Closing, then Buyer will be entitled either to terminate this Agreement or to proceed by an action for specific performance of Seller's obligations under this Agreement. If specific performance is not available solely because of Seller's voluntary and knowing act, Buyer shall have the right to terminate this Agreement by giving written notice to Seller, whereupon Buyer shall have the right to exercise all of its remedies available at law or in equity on account of such default of Seller.

10. *Further Assurances.* Seller and Buyer each agree to execute, acknowledge and deliver, prior to, at or subsequent to the Closing, such other instruments, documents and other materials as the other may reasonably request and as shall necessary in order to effect the consummation of the transaction contemplated hereby.

11. *Possession.* Possession of the Property shall be surrendered to Buyer at the Closing.

12. *Notices.* All notices and other communications provided for herein shall be in writing and shall be sent to the address set forth below (or such other address as the party may hereafter designate by notice to the other parties as required hereby) for the party for whom such notice or communication is intended:

3. Purchase and Sale Agreement

If to Seller: _____

_____
_____
_____

With a copy to: _____

_____
_____
_____

If to Buyer: _____

_____
_____
_____

With a copy to: _____

_____
_____
_____

Any such notice or communication shall be sufficient if sent by registered or certified mail, return receipt requested, postage prepaid; by hand delivery; by overnight courier service; or by facsimile, with an original by regular mail. Any such notice or communication shall be effective when received by the addressee or, if sent by registered or certified mail, upon rejection of delivery, as the case may be.

13. *Brokers.* Seller and Buyer each represents to the other that neither has dealt with any broker or agent in connection with this transaction other than _____, representing Seller *(,,Seller's Broker")* and _____ *(,,Buyer's Broker"),* representing Buyer. Seller shall be solely responsible for the commission payable to Seller's Broker and hereby indemnifies and holds harmless the Buyer for any amounts claimed by Seller's Broker. Buyer shall be solely responsible for the commission payable to Buyer's Broker and hereby indemnifies and hold harmless the Seller for any amounts claimed by Buyer's Broker. Each party hereby indemnifies and holds harmless the other party from all loss, cost and expense (including reasonable attorneys' fees) arising out of a breach of its representation or undertaking set forth in this Section 13. The provisions of this Section 13 shall survive the Closing or the termination of this Agreement.

14. *Miscellaneous.*

(a) *Assignability.* Buyer may not assign or transfer all or any portion of its obligations under this Agreement to any other individual, entity or other person without the consent thereto of Seller.

(b) *Governing Law; Parties in Interest.* This Agreement shall be governed by the law of the state in which the Real Property is located, and shall bind and inure to the benefit of the parties hereto and their respective heirs, executors, administrators, successors, assigns and personal representatives.

(c) *Headings.* The headings preceding the text of the paragraphs and subparagraphs hereof are inserted solely for convenience of reference and shall not constitute a part of this Agreement, nor shall they affect its meaning, construction or effect.

(d) *Counterparts.* This Agreement may be executed simultaneously in counterparts, each of which shall be deemed an original, but all of which together shall constitute one and the same instrument.

(e) *Exhibits.* All Exhibits which are referred to herein and which are attached hereto or bound separately and initialed by the parties are expressly made and constitute a part of this Agreement.

(f) *Survival.* Each of the warranties, representations and covenants of Seller and Buyer which expressly states that it is to survive the Closing, shall survive for a period of only one (1) year after the Closing and delivery of the deed and other closing documents by Seller and Buyer.

(g) *Entire Agreement; Amendments.* This Agreement and the Exhibits hereto set forth all of the promises, covenants, agreements, conditions and undertakings between the parties hereto with respect to the subject matter hereof, and supersede all prior and contemporaneous agreements and undertakings, inducements or conditions, express or implied, oral or written, except as contained herein. This Agreement may not be changed orally but only by an agreement in writing, duly executed by or on behalf of the party or parties against whom enforcement of any waiver, change, modification, consent or discharge is sought.

(h) *Confidentiality.* This Agreement and all of the terms and provisions hereof are confidential and shall be made known by the parties hereto only to their respective attorneys and other consultants and contractors engaged to assist in the consummation of the transaction contemplated by this Agreement, and shall not be disclosed to any other person or entity without the mutual agreement of the parties.

3. Purchase and Sale Agreement

(i) ***Time of the Essence.*** Time is of the essence of this Agreement, and of each covenant, agreement and condition hereof which provides for notice to be given or action taken on a specific date or within a specified period of time.

IN WITNESS WHEREOF, Buyer has caused this Agreement to be executed and delivered under seal by its duly authorized officer or representative as of the date shown below.

BUYER:

By:_____   Date of Execution:_____,
199__
   Name:
   Title:

SELLER:

By:_____   Date of Execution:_____,
199__
   Name:
   Title:

EXHIBIT A
Description of the Land

EXHIBIT B
Contracts

EXHIBIT C
Disclosures
None
Maximum Amount:

. . .

EXHIBIT D
Form of Bargain and Sale Deed

EXHIBIT E
Form of Bill of Sale

EXHIBIT F
Form of Assignment of Contract

4. FORM OF AGREEMENT OF LEASE

(Gewerblicher Mietvertrag, ausführliche Fassung)

Between

_____

Landlord

AND

_____

Tenant

Premises:

_____ **floor at**

_____

New York, New York

Dated: _____, 199__

TABLE OF CONTENTS

ARTICLE I
DEFINITIONS 225

ARTICLE II
DEMISE, PREMISES, TERM, RENT 226

ARTICLE III
USE AND OCCUPANCY 228

ARTICLE IV
CONDITION OF THE PREMISES 229

ARTICLE V
ALTERATIONS AND INSTALLATIONS 230

ARTICLE VI
FLOOR LOAD 234

ARTICLE VII
REPAIRS 235

ARTICLE VIII
WINDOW CLEANING 236

ARTICLE IX
REQUIREMENTS OF LAW 237

ARTICLE X
SUBORDINATION 239

ARTICLE XI
RULES AND REGULATIONS 241

ARTICLE XII
INSURANCE 242

ARTICLE XIII
DESTRUCTION OF THE PREMISES;
   PROPERTY LOSS OR DAMAGE.................... 245

ARTICLE XIV
EMINENT DOMAIN 248

ARTICLE XV
ASSIGNMENT AND SUBLETTING 250

ARTICLE XVI
ACCESS TO PREMISES 261

ARTICLE XVII
LANDLORD'S LIABILITY 264

ARTICLE XVIII
CONDITIONS OF LIMITATION 264

ARTICLE XIX
RE-ENTRY BY LANDLORD; REMEDIES 267

ARTICLE XX
CURING TENANT'S DEFAULTS 270

ARTICLE XXI
NO REPRESENTATIONS BY LANDLORD;
   LANDLORD'S APPROVAL 271

ARTICLE XXII
END OF TERM 272

ARTICLE XXIII
QUIET ENJOYMENT 273

ARTICLE XXIV
NO WAIVER 273

ARTICLE XXV
WAIVER OF TRIAL BY JURY......................... 275

4. Form of Agreement of Lease

ARTICLE XXVI
INABILITY TO PERFORM 275

ARTICLE XXVII
BILLS AND NOTICES 276

ARTICLE XXVIII
ESCALATION 276

ARTICLE XXIX
SERVICES 285

ARTICLE XXX
STATUS OF TENANT 293

ARTICLE XXXI
VAULT SPACE 294

ARTICLE XXXII
SECURITY DEPOSIT 294

ARTICLE XXXIII
CAPTIONS 296

ARTICLE XXXIV
ADDITIONAL DEFINITIONS 296

ARTICLE XXXV
PARTIES BOUND 297

ARTICLE XXXVI
BROKER 297

ARTICLE XXXVII
INDEMNITY 298

ARTICLE XXXVIII
ADJACENT EXCAVATION-SHORING 299

ARTICLE XXXIX
MISCELLANEOUS................................... 299

4. Form of Agreement of Lease

AGREEMENT OF LEASE,

made as of this ____ day of _____, 199__, between _____, a _____, having an office _____, New York, New York _____ (hereinafter *,,Landlord"*) and _____, having an office at _____, New York, New York _____ (hereinafter *,,Tenant"*).

WITNESSETH:

Landlord and Tenant hereby covenant and agree as follows:

ARTICLE I

DEFINITIONS

SECTION A For the purposes of this Lease, the following terms shall have the following definitions:

,,Additional Rent" shall mean all sums other than Rent payable by Tenant to Landlord under this Lease.

,,Base Expense Year" shall mean the calendar year 199__.

,,Base Tax Year" shall mean the calendar year 199__ Tax Year (as defined in Section 28.01 hereof).

,,Broker" shall mean _____.

,,Building" shall mean the building located at and known as _____, in the Borough of Manhattan, City, County and State of New York.

,,Commencement Date" shall mean _____, 199__.

,,Expiration Date" shall mean _____, 200__.

,,Initial Amount" shall mean $_____.

,,Interest Rate" shall mean (iii) the lesser of two percent (2%) per annum above the then current prime rate charged by Citibank, N. A. or its successor, or (iv) the maximum rate permitted by applicable law.

,,Permitted Uses" shall mean executive and general offices and for no other purpose.

„Premises" shall mean and consist of the entire _____ floor of the Building, known as Suite ____, as more particularly shown on *Exhibit 1* annexed hereto and made a part hereof, together with all fixtures and equipment which at the commencement, or during the Term, of this Lease are thereto attached (except items not deemed to be included therein and removable by Tenant as provided in Article 5 hereof).

„Real Property" shall mean the Building, together with the plot of land upon which it stands.

„Rent" shall mean (v) $_____ per annum for the period commencing on the Commencement Date and ending on the day immediately preceding the fourth (4th) anniversary of the Commencement Date, both dates inclusive; (vi) $_____ for the period commencing on the _____ anniversary of the Commencement Date and ending on the day immediately preceding the _____ anniversary of the Commencement Date, both dates inclusive; and (vii) $_____ per annum for the period commencing on the _____ anniversary of the Commencement Date and ending on the Expiration Date, both dates inclusive.

„Rent Commencement Date" shall mean the Commencement Date.

„Tenant's Proportionate Share" shall mean _____%.

„Security Deposit" shall mean $_____.

ARTICLE II

DEMISE, PREMISES, TERM, RENT

SECTION A Landlord hereby leases to Tenant, and Tenant hereby hires from Landlord, the Premises in the Building, for the term hereinafter stated, for the rents herein reserved and upon and subject to the terms of this Lease.

SECTION B The Premises are leased for a term (the *„Term"*) which shall commence on the Commencement Date and shall expire on the Expiration Date unless the Term shall sooner terminate pursuant to any of the terms of this Lease or pursuant to law.

SECTION C Tenant expressly waives any right to rescind this Lease under Section 223-a of the New York Real Property Law or any successor statute of similar import then in force and further waives the

4. Form of Agreement of Lease

right to recover any damages which may result from Landlord's failure to deliver possession of the Premises to Tenant on the Commencement Date. If Landlord shall be unable to give possession of the Premises on the Commencement Date, and provided that Tenant is not responsible for such inability to give such possession, the Rent and Additional Rent reserved and covenanted to be paid herein shall not commence until possession of the Premises is given to, or the Premises are available for occupancy by, Tenant, and no such failure by Landlord to give possession of the Premises to Tenant on such date shall in any wise affect the validity of this lease or the obligations of Tenant hereunder or give rise to any claim for damages by Tenant or claim for rescission of this Lease, nor shall the same be construed in any wise to extend the Term. If Landlord shall permit Tenant to enter into possession of the Premises or to occupy premises other than the Premises prior to the Commencement Date, Tenant covenants and agrees that such occupancy shall be deemed to be under all the terms, covenants, conditions and provisions of this Lease, including the covenant to pay Rent and Additional Rent.

SECTION E Tenant shall pay to Landlord, without notice or demand, in lawful money of the United States of America, by check subject to collection and drawn on a bank or trust company which is a member of the New York Clearinghouse Association, at the office of Landlord or at such other place as Landlord may designate, (a) Rent, in equal monthly installments, in advance on the first day of each calendar month during the Term from and after the Rent Commencement Date, and (a) Additional Rent, at the times and in the manner set forth in this Lease. If Tenant shall fail to pay any installment of Rent or any payment of Additional Rent within ten (10) days after such installment or payment shall have become due, Tenant shall pay interest thereon to Landlord at the Interest Rate, from the date when such installment or payment shall have become due, to and including the date of payment thereof, and such interest shall be deemed to constitute Additional Rent.

There shall be no abatement of, deduction from or counterclaim or set-off against Rent or Additional Rent, except as otherwise specifically provided in this Lease.

Notwithstanding anything set forth in Section 2.04A hereof to the contrary, Tenant shall pay the Initial Amount on account of Rent upon the execution of this Lease, which shall be credited on a per diem basis toward the payment of the installment of Rent first due and payable hereunder. If the Rent Commencement Date shall occur on a date other than the first day of a calendar month, Rent for the month in which the Rent Commencement Date occurs shall be pro-rated on a per diem basis and Tenant shall pay to Landlord, on the Rent Commencement Date, an amount equal to the same proportion of the monthly installment of Rent payable for the month in which the Rent Commencement Date occurs, as the number of days from and including said Rent Commencement Date bears to the total number of days in said calendar month. Such payment, together with the sum paid by Tenant upon the execution of this Lease, shall constitute payment of Rent for the period from the Rent Commencement date to and including the last day of the next succeeding calendar month. In the event that, on the Rent Commencement Date or at any time thereafter, Tenant shall default in the payment of rent to Landlord pursuant to another lease of space in the Building with Landlord or with Landlord's predecessor-in-interest, Landlord may, at Landlord's option and without notice to Tenant, add the amount of such arrearages to any monthly installment of Rent payable hereunder, and the same shall be payable by Tenant to Landlord, as Additional Rent on demand.

ARTICLE III

USE AND OCCUPANCY

SECTION A   Tenant shall use and occupy the Premises for the Permitted Uses and for no other purpose. Tenant shall not use or occupy or suffer or permit the use or occupancy of any part of the Premises in any manner which in Landlord's reasonable judgment would adversely affect (a) the proper and economical rendition of any service required to be furnished to any tenant in the Building, (b) the use or enjoyment of any part of the Building by any other tenant, or (c) the appearance, character or reputation of the Building as a first-class office building with retail stores. The foregoing statement as to the nature of the business to be conducted by Tenant in the Premises shall not constitute a representation or guaranty by Landlord that such business may be conducted in the Premises or is lawful or permissible under any certificate of occupancy issued for the Premises or the Building, or is otherwise permitted by law. Upon Tenant's request, Landlord shall provide to Tenant the final certificate of occupancy for the Building. Landlord hereby represents that the Certificate issued for the Building permits the use of the Premises as offices.

SECTION B   Tenant shall not use the Premises or any part thereof,

4. Form of Agreement of Lease

or permit the Premises or any part thereof to be used, (a) for the business of photographic, multilith or multigraph reproductions or offset printing, (b) for a banking, trust company, depository, guarantee or safe deposit business, (c) as a savings bank, a savings and loan association, or as a loan company, (d) for the sale of travelers checks, money orders, drafts, foreign exchange or letters of credit or for the receipt of money for transmission, (e) as a „retail" stock broker's or dealer's office which shall be open to the general public (except pursuant to prior appointment), (f) as a restaurant or bar or for the sale of confectionary, soda, beverages, sandwiches, ice cream or baked goods or for the preparation, dispensing or consumption of food or beverages in any manner whatsoever (except as otherwise expressly provided to the contrary herein), (g) as a news or cigar stand, (h) as an employment agency, labor union office, physician's or dentist's office, dance or music studio or school (except for the training of employees of Tenant), (i) as a barber shop or beauty salon, or (j) for the direct sale, at retail or otherwise, of any goods or products. Nothing in this Section 3.02 shall preclude Tenant from using any part of the Premises for photographic multilith or multigraph reproductions in connection with, either directly or indirectly, its own business and/or activities.

SECTION C Tenant shall not use or occupy the Premises in violation of the certificate of occupancy issued for the Premises or of the Building. In the event that any department of the City of State of New York shall contend and/or declare by notice, violation, order or in any other manner whatsoever, at any time or from time to time, from and after the date hereof, that the Premises are used for a purpose which is a violation of any such certificate of occupancy, Tenant shall, upon five (5) days'written notice from Landlord, immediately discontinue such use of the Premises. Failure by Tenant to discontinue such use after such notice shall be a default by Tenant and Landlord shall have the right to exercise any and all rights, privileges and remedies given to Landlord by and pursuant to the provisions of Articles XVIII and XIX hereof.

ARTICLE IV

CONDITION OF THE PREMISES

SECTION A Tenant has examined the Premises and agrees to accept possession of the Premises in the condition which shall exist on the Commencement Date „as is" and vacant, and further agrees that, except as otherwise expressly set forth in Section 29.03 hereof, Landlord shall have no obligation to perform any work, supply any materials, incur any expenses or make any installations, in order to prepare the Premises for Tenant's occupancy, except that Landlord shall [describe Landlord's preparatory work] and disburse to Tenant Landlord's Contribution (as hereafter defined) subject to and in accordance with Section 5.06 of this Lease. The taking of possession of the Premises by Tenant shall be conclusive evidence as against Tenant, that, at the time such possession was so taken, the Premises and the Building were in good and satisfactory condition.

SECTION B Notwithstanding anything to the contrary contained in Section 4.01, to the extent any asbestos exists in the Premises, Landlord will remove same in accordance with applicable law, at Landlord's sole cost and expense *("Landlord's Asbestos Removal"),* and Landlord shall do so in a manner that is coordinated with the Alterations made in connection with Tenant's initial occupancy of the Premises *("Tenant's Initial Alterations").* Landlord and Tenant agree to cooperate so that Landlord's Asbestos Removal shall not unreasonably interfere with the progress of Tenant's Initial Alterations and so that Tenant's Initial Alterations shall not unreasonably interfere with the completion of Landlord's Asbestos Removal.

If Tenant's Initial Alterations cause a modification of any existing Asbestos Containing Material (the *"ACM"*), Landlord shall not be responsible for restoring the pre-existing condition of the Premises after any ACM work.

ARTICLE V

ALTERATIONS AND INSTALLATIONS

SECTION A Tenant shall not make or perform or permit the making or performance of, any alterations, installations, improvements, additions or other physical changes in or to the Premises (hereinafter collectively called *"Alterations"*) without Landlord's prior written consent in each instance. Landlord shall not unreasonably withhold its consent to any Alterations proposed to be made by Tenant to adopt the Premises for those business purposes permitted by Article III hereof which are nonstructural and do not affect the Building's mechanical systems or services; *provided, however,* that such Alterations are performed only by contractors

4. Form of Agreement of Lease

or mechanics approved in writing by Landlord, do not affect any part of the Building other than the Premises, do not adversely affect any service required to be furnished by Landlord to Tenant or to any other tenant or occupant of the Building, and do not reduce the value or utility of the Building.

SECTION B All Alterations shall be done at Tenant's sole cost and expense and at such times and in such manner as Landlord may from time to time designate. Prior to making any Alterations Tenant shall, submit to Landlord, for Landlord's written approval, detailed plans and specifications (including layout, architectural, mechanical and structural drawings) for each proposed Alteration, at Tenant's sole cost and expense, obtain all permits, approvals and certificates required by any governmental or quasi-governmental bodies (and Landlord shall cooperate with Tenant, at Tenant's sole cost and expense, to obtain same), and furnish to Landlord duplicate original policies of worker's compensation (covering all persons to be employed by Tenant, and Tenant's contractors and subcontractors in connection with such Alteration) and comprehensive public liability (including property damage coverage, completed operations/ product liability) insurance in such form, with such companies for such periods and in such amounts as Landlord may reasonably require, naming Landlord, Landlord's employees and agents, and any mortgagees or lessors having an interest in the Real Property, as additional insureds. Landlord shall indicate to Tenant its approval or disapproval of Tenant's plans and specifications within twenty-one (21) business days of Tenant's submission thereof, and in the case of disapproval, Landlord shall indicate the specific reasons therefor. Landlord shall evaluate any subsequent submission of Tenant's revised plans and specifications within ten (10) business days of Tenant's submission thereof. Tenant shall promptly reimburse Landlord, as Additional Rent and upon demand, for any and all out-of-pocket costs and expenses actually incurred by Landlord in connection with Landlord's review of Tenant's plans and specifications for any such Alteration, which expenses may include the cost of retaining plumbing, electrical, HVAC, mechanical, architectural and building and fire code consultants. Landlord's approval of any plans or specifications shall not relieve Tenant of responsibility for the legal sufficiency and technical competence thereof. Upon completion of such Alteration, Tenant, at Tenant's sole cost and expense, shall obtain certificates of final approval of such Alteration required by any governmental or quasi-governmental bodies and shall furnish Landlord with copies thereof together with copies of final "as built" plans. All Alterations shall be made and performed in accordance with the Rules and Regulations (as defined in Article XI hereof), in effect from time to time, all materials and equipment to be incorporated in the Premises as a result of all Alterations shall be new and first quality, and no such materials or equipment shall be subject to any lien, encumbrance, chattel mortgage or title retention or security agreement. With respect to any Alterations costing more than $ 10,000.00, Tenant shall pay to Landlord, as Additional Rent, promptly upon being billed therefor, a sum equal to ten percent (10%) of the cost of all Alterations, other than Tenant's Initial Alterations, on account of Landlord's indirect costs, field supervision and coordination.

SECTION C All personal property, furniture, furnishings, equipment and movable fixtures and partitions supplied by or installed by or on behalf of Tenant at Tenant's sole cost and expense *("Tenant's Property")* and all Alterations in and to the Premises which may be made by or on behalf of Tenant, at Tenant's sole cost and expense *("Tenant's Work")*, prior to and during the Term, or a renewal thereof, shall remain the Property of Tenant and Tenant may, upon the Expiration Date or earlier termination of the Term or any renewal thereof, remove Tenant's Property or Tenant's Work from the Premises; *provided, however,* that Tenant shall repair and restore in good and workmanlike manner to Building standard original condition (reasonable wear and tear excepted) any damage to the Premises and the Building caused by such removal. Any of such fixtures, installations or Alterations not so removed by Tenant at or prior to the Expiration Date or earlier termination of the Term, shall become the property of Landlord and shall remain upon and be surrendered with the Premises as part thereof at the end of the Term. The covenants and agreements set forth in this Section 5.03 shall survive the expiration or earlier termination of this Lease.

SECTION D Tenant shall, at its expense, discharge any mechanic's lien filed against the Premises, the Building or the Real Property, for work claimed to have been done for, or materials claimed to have been furnished to, Tenant, within ten (10) days thereafter, by payment or filing the bond required by law. Tenant shall not, at any time prior to or during the Term, directly or indirectly employ, or permit the employment of, any contractor, mechanic or laborer in the Premises, whether in connection with any Alteration or otherwise, if, in Landlord's sole discretion, such employment will or may interfere or cause any conflict with other contractors mechanics or laborers engaged in the construction, mainte-

4. Form of Agreement of Lease

nance or operation of the Building by Landlord, Tenant or others. In the event of any such interference or conflict, Tenant, upon demand of Landlord, shall cause all contractors, mechanics or laborers causing such interference or conflict, to leave the Building immediately.

SECTION E Tenant shall not move any safe, heavy machinery, heavy equipment, freight, bulky matter or fixtures into or out of the Building without Landlord's prior consent and payment to Landlord of Landlord's costs in connection therewith, as Additional Rent upon demand. If such safe, machinery, equipment, freight, bulky matter or fixtures requires special handling, Tenant agrees to employ only persons holding a Master Rigger's License to do said work, and that all work in connection therewith shall comply with the Administrative Code of the City of New York and all other laws and regulations applicable thereto, and shall be done during such hours as Landlord may designate. Notwithstanding said consent of Landlord, Tenant shall indemnify Landlord for, and hold Landlord harmless and free from, damages sustained by persons or property and for any damages or monies paid out by Landlord in settlement of any claims or judgments, as well as for all expenses and attorneys' fees incurred in connection therewith and all costs incurred in repairing any damage to the Building or appurtenances. The agreements set forth in this Section 5.05 shall survive the expiration or earlier termination of this Lease.

SECTION F Landlord hereby agrees to contribute toward the actual cost of Tenant's Initial Alterations to the Premises *(,, **Tenant's Initial Alterations**")* a sum which shall in no event exceed the sum of $_____ *(,,**Landlord's Contribution**").* Provided the Lease shall be in full force and effect and Tenant shall not be in default thereunder, Landlord and Tenant shall make progress payments to the contractor performing Tenant's Initial Alterations on a monthly basis for the work performed to date and/or for materials delivered to the job site during the previous month, less a retainer of not less than ten (10%), which progress payments shall be paid upon completion of the work (or actual delivery of the materials) described in the contractor's or materialman's invoice. Each of Landlord's progress payments shall be limited to that fraction *(,,**Landlord's Pro Rata Share**")* of the total amount of such payment, the numerator of which shall be the amount of Landlord's Contribution, and the denominator of which shall be the total contract (or estimated) price for the performance of all of Tenant's Initial Alterations shown on all plans and specifications approved by Landlord, except for Landlord's initial progress payment, the amount of which may exceed Landlord's Pro Rata Share but shall in no event be greater than $20,000. Such progress payments shall each be made within thirty (30) days next following requisitions therefor by such contractor, which requisitions shall set forth the names of each subcontractor to whom payment is due by such contractor, and the amount thereof, and, with the exception of the first such requisition, shall be accompanied by copies of partial waivers of lien from all contractors, subcontractors and materialman covering all work and materials which were the subject of previous progress payments by Landlord and Tenant and a written certification from Tenant's architect that the work for which the requisition is being made has been completed substantially in accordance with the plans and specifications approved by Landlord. If Tenant does not pay the contractor as required by this Paragraph, Landlord shall have the right, but shall not be obligated, to promptly pay to the contractor all sums so due from Tenant, and Landlord thereafter shall have all remedies available to Landlord at law or in equity for collection of all sums so paid by Landlord and due to Landlord from Tenant. In addition, Tenant agrees that the same shall be collectable as Additional Rent pursuant to the Lease and, in default of payment thereof, Landlord shall (in addition to all other remedies) have the same rights as in the event of default of payment of Rent under the Lease.

ARTICLE VI

FLOOR LOAD

SECTION A Tenant shall not place a load upon any floor of the Premises that exceeds the floor load per square foot which such floor was designed to carry or which is allowed by law. Landlord reserves the right to prescribe the weight and position of all sages, business machines, heavy equipment and installations which Tenant wishes to place in the Premises. Business machines and mechanical equipment in the Premises shall be placed and maintained by Tenant, at Tenant's sole cost and expense, and in such manner as shall be sufficient, in Landlord's sole judgment, to absorb and prevent vibration, noise, annoyance or inconvenience to Landlord and other tenants.

4. Form of Agreement of Lease

ARTICLE VII

REPAIRS

SECTION A Tenant shall take good care of the Premises. Tenant shall, at its sole cost and expense, promptly make all non-structural repairs to the Premises as and when needed to preserve them in good working order and condition, reasonable wear and tear and damage for which Tenant is not responsible under the terms of this Lease excepted. Tenant shall, at its sole cost and expense, promptly repair or replace scratched, damaged or broken doors, signs and glass (including, but not limited to, exterior windows) in and about the Premises and shall be responsible for all repairs and maintenance of all wall and floor coverings in the Premises. Tenant shall pay Landlord for all replacements to the lamps, tubes, ballasts and starters in the lighting fixtures installed in the Premises, at Landlord's then established rates, as Additional Rent upon rendition of invoices and bills therefor. Notwithstanding the foregoing, all damage or injury to the Premises or to any other part of the Building, or its fixtures, equipment and appurtenances, whether requiring structural or non-structural repairs, caused by or resulting from carelessness, omission, neglect or improper conduct of, or Alterations made by, Tenant, Tenant's servants, employees, invitees or licensees, shall be repaired promptly by Tenant, at Tenant's sole cost and expense, to the satisfaction of Landlord. Tenant shall also repair all damage to the Building and the Premises caused by the moving of Tenant's fixtures, furniture or equipment. If Tenant fails, after ten (10) days' notice, to proceed with due diligence to make repairs required to be made by Tenant, the same may be made by Landlord, at Tenant's sole cost and expense, and the expenses thereof incurred by Landlord shall be paid by Tenant to Landlord, as Additional Rent upon rendition of bills and invoices therefor. Tenant shall give Landlord prompt notice of any defective condition in any plumbing, electrical, air-cooling or heating system located in, servicing or passing through, the Premises, which defects are known or should reasonably be known to Tenant. Except as provided in Article XIII hereof, there shall be no allowance to Tenant for a diminution of rental value and no liability on the part of Landlord by reason of inconvenience, annoyance or injury to business arising from Landlord, Tenant or others making, or failing to make, any repairs, alterations, additions or improvements in or to any portion of the Building or the Premises, or in or to fixture, appurtenances, or equipment thereof. If the Premises shall be or shall become infested with vermin, Tenant shall, at Tenant's sole cost and expense, cause the same to be exterminated, at any time and from time to time, to the satisfaction of Landlord, and shall employ such exterminators and such exterminating company or companies as shall be approved by Landlord. Landlord represents that, to the best of its knowledge and belief, the Premises are not invested with vermin. The water and wash closets, electric closets, mechanical rooms, fire stairs and other plumbing fixtures shall not be used for any purposes other than those for which they were designed or constructed, and no sweepings, rubbish, rags, acids or other substances shall be deposited therein.

SECTION B Any repairs made or performed by or on behalf of Tenant or any person claiming through or under Tenant pursuant to this Article VII, shall be of quality or class at least equal to the original work or construction and shall be made in conformity with, and subject to, the provisions of Article V hereof.

ARTICLE VIII

WINDOW CLEANING

SECTION A. Tenant shall not (a) require, permit, suffer or allow the cleaning of any window in the Premises from the outside (within the meaning of Section 202 of the New York Labor Law or any successor statute thereto) unless the equipment and safety devices required by Section 202 of the New York Labor Law or any successor statute thereto, are provided and used, or (a) permit, suffer or allow the cleaning of the outside of any window from within the Premises except by persons employed by Landlord. Tenant hereby indemnifies Landlord against liability as a result of Tenant's (i) requiring, permitting, suffering or allowing any window in the Premises to be cleaned from the outside in violation of any requirement of Section 202 of the New York Labor Law or any successor statute thereto, or (ii) permitting, suffering or allowing the outside of any window to be cleaned from within the Premises other than by persons employed by Landlord. The covenants and agreements set forth in this Section 8.01 shall survive the expiration or earlier termination of this Lease.

4. Form of Agreement of Lease

ARTICLE IX

REQUIREMENTS OF LAW

SECTION A. Tenant shall, at its sole cost and expense, comply with all laws, orders and regulations of federal, state, county and municipal authorities and with all directions of all public officers, pursuant to law, and all rules, orders, regulations and requirements of the New York Board of Fire Underwriters or any other similar body which shall impose any violation, order or duty upon Landlord or Tenant with respect to the Premises. Notwithstanding the foregoing, Tenant's obligations under the preceding sentence shall impose no obligation on Tenant to make any alterations to the Premises, whether structural or otherwise, unless such obligation under the preceding sentence shall arise as a result of the use or occupation thereof by Tenant for any purpose not authorized by the provisions of Article III hereof, or the conduct by Tenant of its business in the Premises in a manner different from the ordinary and proper conduct of such business and if Tenant shall have knowledge thereof, Tenant shall give Landlord prompt written notice of any such lack of compliance with any of the foregoing.

SECTION B. Tenant shall not do or permit to be done any act or thing upon the Premises which will invalidate or be in conflict with any insurance policies covering the Building and fixtures and property therein and shall not do, or permit anything to be done in or upon the Premises, or bring or keep anything therein, except as now or hereafter permitted by the New York City Fire Department, New York Board of Fire Underwriters, New York Fire Insurance Rating Organization or other authority having jurisdiction and then only in such quantity and manner of storage as not to increase the rate for fire insurance applicable to the Building, or use the Premises in a manner which shall increase the rate of fire insurance on the Building or on property located therein, over that in similar type buildings or in effect prior to this Lease. If by reason of Tenant's failure to comply with the provisions of this Article IX, the fire insurance rate shall, from and after the date of this Lease, be higher than it otherwise would be, Tenant shall reimburse Landlord for that part of all fire insurance premiums thereafter paid by Landlord which shall have been charged because of such failure by Tenant, and shall make such reimbursement, as Additional Rent, upon the first day of the month following such outlay by Landlord. In any action or proceeding wherein Landlord and Tenant are parties, a schedule or „make up" of rates for the

Building or the Premises issued by the New York Fire Insurance rating Organization, or other body fixing such fire insurance rates, shall be conclusive evidence of the facts therein stated and of the several items and charges in the fire insurance rates then applicable to the Premises.

SECTION C. If there now is or shall be installed in the Building a „sprinkler system," and such system or any of its appliances shall be damaged or injured or not in proper working order by reason of any act or omission of Tenant, Tenant's agents, servants, employees, licensees, contractors or visitors, Tenant shall forthwith restore the same to good working condition at its sole cost and expense. If the New York Board of Fire Underwriters or the New York Fire Insurance Rating Organization or any bureau, department or official of the state or city government, shall require or recommend that any changes, modifications, alterations or additional sprinkler heads or other equipment be made or supplied by reason of Tenant's business, or the location of the partitions, trade fixtures, or other contents of the Premises, Tenant shall, at Tenant's sole cost and expense, promptly make and supply such changes, modifications, alterations, additional sprinkler heads or other equipment.

SECTION D. Any work or installations made or performed by or on behalf of Tenant or any person claiming through or under Tenant pursuant to this Article IX shall be made in conformity with, and subject to, Article V hereof.

SECTION E. In the event the Rent or Additional Rent or any part thereof to be paid by Tenant to Landlord under any provision of this Lease, shall during the Term, become uncollectible, be reduced or be required to be refunded by Landlord due to action of any governmental body, agency or instrumentality having jurisdiction thereof; or, as the result of the promulgation of any land rule, regulation or order issued by any body having jurisdiction thereof; or by order of any organization or entity formed pursuant to law, whether such organization or entity by public or private, then in that event, Landlord may, at this option, terminate this Lease by giving Tenant a thirty (30) day written notice of termination and this Lease will terminate and end on the date set forth in that notice, as if that date were the date originally fixed in this Lease as the Expiration Date. Landlord shall not cancel this Lease, however, notwithstanding any imposition of any „rent control" law, as affects commercial real estate properties including the Premises, if Landlord may under such a law legally bill and Tenant may legally consent to pay the rent and additional rent reserved, and Tenant does so waive the im-

4. Form of Agreement of Lease

position of such law and pays the Rent and Additional Rent reserved herein.

ARTICLE X.

SUBORDINATION

SECTION A. This Lease is subject and subordinate to each and every ground, overriding or underlying lease of the Real Property or the Building heretofore or hereafter made by Landlord (collectively the *„Superior Leases"*) and to each and ever trust indenture and mortgage whether such trust indenture or mortgage shall cover other lands or buildings or leases (collectively the *„Mortgages"*) which may now or hereafter affect all or any part of the Real Property, the Building or any such Superior Lease and the leasehold interest created thereby, and to all renewals, extensions, supplements, modifications, consolidations, and replacements thereof or thereto, substitutions therefore, and advances made thereunder. This Section shall be self-operative and no further instruments of subordination shall be required. In confirmation of such subordination, however, Tenant shall execute promptly any certificate that Landlord, the lessor under any such Superior Lease or the holder of any such Mortgage may request and Tenant hereby irrevocably constitutes and appoints Landlord as Tenant's attorney-in-fact, coupled with an interest, to execute any such certificate(s) for and on behalf of Tenant if Tenant shall fail to do so within five (5) days after request from Landlord. The lessor of a Superior Lease or its successor in interest at the time referred to is sometimes hereinafter called a „lessor", and the holder of a Mortgage or its successor in interest at the time referred to is sometimes hereinafter called a „holder". The holder of any Mortgage may elect that this Lease shall have priority over its Mortgage, and upon notification of the Tenant by such party, this Lease shall be deemed to have prior over such Mortgage, regardless of the date of this Lease.

SECTION B. Except as expressly provided herein, Tenant shall not do, or permit to be done, or omit to do anything that Tenant is obligated to do under the terms of this Lease, so as to cause Landlord to be in default under any Superior Lease or Mortgage. If, in connection with any financing of the Real Property, or any part thereof or interest therein, any lending institution shall request reasonable modifications of this Lease that do not materially increase the obligations or materially and adversely affect the rights of Tenant under this Lease, Tenant covenants to promptly consent to such modifications.

SECTION C. In the event of any act or omission of Landlord which would give Tenant the right, immediately or after lapse of a period of time, to cancel or terminate this Lease, or to claim a partial or total eviction, Tenant shall not exercise such right (a) until it has given written notice of such act or omission to each holder and lessor whose name and address shall previously have been furnished to Tenant in writing, and (a) unless such act or omission shall be one which is not capable of being remedied within a reasonable period of time, until a reasonable period for remedying such act or omission shall have elapsed following the giving of such notice and following the time when such holder or lessor shall have become entitled under such Mortgage or Superior Lease to remedy the same (which reasonable period shall in no event be less than the period to which Landlord would be entitled under this Lease or otherwise, after similar notice to effect such remedy); *provided, however,* that such holder or lessor shall, with due diligence, give Tenant written notice of intention to, and commence and continue to, remedy such act or omission.

SECTION D. If the lessor or holder or any person shall succeed to the rights of Landlord under this Lease, whether through possession or foreclosure action or delivery of a new lease or deed, then at the request of such party so succeeding to Landlord's rights (herein sometime referred to as *„successor landlord"*) and upon successor landlord's written agreement to accept Tenant's attornment, Tenant shall be deemed to have attorned to and recognized such successor landlord as Tenant's landlord under this Lease. The foregoing provision shall be self-operative upon demand, and no further instrument shall be required to give effect to said provisions; *provided, however,* that Tenant shall promptly execute and delivery any instrument that such successor landlord may reasonably request to evidence such attornment. Upon such attornment this Lease shall continue in full force and effect as, or as if it were, a direct lease between the successor landlord and Tenant upon all of the terms, conditions and covenants as are set forth in this Lease and shall be applicable after such attornment except that the successor landlord shall not:

(a) be liable for any previous act or omission of Landlord under this Lease;

(b) be subject to any offset, not expressly provided for in this Lease

4. Form of Agreement of Lease

and asserted with reasonable promptness, which shall have theretofore accrued to Tenant against Landlord;

(c) be bound by any previous modification of this Lease, not expressly provided for in this Lease, or by any previous prepayment of more than one month's Rent or Additional Rent, unless such modification or prepayment shall have been expressly approved in writing by the lessor or holder;

(d) be obligated to perform any alteration of the Premises;

(e) be obligated to repair the Premises or the Building or any part thereof, in the event of total or substantial total damage beyond such repair as can reasonably be accomplished from the net proceeds of insurance actually made available to successor landlord; or

(f) be obligated to repair the Premises or the Building or any part thereof, in the event of partial condemnation beyond such repair as can reasonably be accomplished from the net proceeds of any award actually made available to successor landlord, as consequential damages allocable to the part of the Premises or the Building not taken.

ARTICLE XI
RULES AND REGULATIONS

SECTION A. Tenant and Tenant's servants, employees, agents, visitors, and licensees shall observe faithfully and comply strictly with the Rules and Regulations annexed hereto and made a part hereof as Schedule A (the *,,Rules and Regulations"*), and such changes therein (whether by modification, addition or elimination) as Landlord or Landlord's agents may, at any time and from time to time, adopt on such notice to be given as Landlord may elect; *provided, however,* that in case of any conflict or inconsistency between the provisions of this Lease and any of the Rules and Regulations as originally promulgated or as changed, the provisions of this Lease shall control. In case Tenant disputes the reasonableness of any change in a Rule or Regulation hereafter made or adopted by Landlord or Landlord's agents, the parties hereto agree to submit the question of the reasonableness of such Rule or Regulation for decision to the Chairman of the Board of Directors of the Management Division of The Real Estate Board of New York, Inc., or to such impartial person or persons as said Chairman may designate, whose determination shall be final and conclusive upon the parties hereto. During the pendency of any such arbitration, Tenant shall comply with such Rule or Regulation. Tenant's right to dispute the reasonableness of any change in a Rule or Regulation shall be deemed waived unless the same shall be asserted by service of a notice in writing upon Landlord within ten (10) days after receipt by Tenant of written notice of the adoption of any such change in a Rule or Regulation.

SECTION B. No sign, advertisement, object, notice or lettering shall be exhibited, inscribed, painted or affixed by Tenant, in or on the windows or doors, or on any part of the outside of the Premises or the Building, or at any point inside the Premises where the same might be visible outside of the Premises, without the prior written consent of Landlord in each instance. Signs and lettering on doors shall conform to Building standard and shall be inscribed, painted, or affixed for Tenant by Landlord at the expense of Tenant. Landlord may remove same without any liability and may charge the expense incurred by such removal to Tenant.

SECTION C. Nothing contained in this Lease shall be construed to impose upon Landlord any duty or obligation to enforce the Rules and Regulations or terms, covenants or conditions in any other lease, against any other tenant and Landlord shall not be liable to Tenant for violation of the same by any other tenant, its servants, employees, agents, visitors, contractors or licensees. Landlord agrees that it shall not enforce the Rules and Regulations in a manner which discriminates against Tenant or any one claiming through or under Tenant.

ARTICLE XII

INSURANCE

SECTION A. Tenant shall obtain and keep in full force and effect during the Term:

(a) a policy of comprehensive general public liability and property damage insurance with a board form contractual liability endorsement, protecting Tenant, Landlord, Landlord's employees and agents, and any mortgagees or lessors having an interest in the Real Property, as insureds, against claims for personal injury, death and/or property damage occurring in or about the Premises or the Building, and under which the insurer agrees to indemnify and hold Landlord harmless

4. Form of Agreement of Lease

from and against, among other things, all cost, expense and/or liability arising out of or based upon any and all claims, accidents, injuries and damages mentioned in Article XXXVII hereof. Such policy shall contain a provision that no act or omission of Tenant shall affect or limit the obligation of the insurance company to pay the amount of any loss sustained. The minimum limits of liability shall be a combined single limit with respect to each occurrence in an amount of not less than $ 3,000,000 for injury (or death) and damage to property (or in any increased amount reasonably required by Landlord); and

(b) insurance against loss or damage by fire, and such other risks and hazards (including burglary, theft, breakage of glass within the Premises and, if the Premises are located at or below grade, broad form flood insurance) as are insurable under then available standard forms of „all risk" insurance policies, to Tenant's Property and Tenant's Work for the full replacement cost value thereof (including an „agreed amount" endorsement), protecting Tenant, Landlord, Landlord's employees and agents, and any mortgagees or lessors having an interest in the Real Property; and

(c) business interruption insurance in an amount sufficient to prevent Landlord and Tenant from becoming co-insurers.

SECTION B. Prior to the time such insurance is first required to be carried by Tenant and thereafter, at lease thirty (30) days prior to the expiration of any such policies, Tenant agrees to deliver to Landlord evidence of payment for the policies together with certificates evidencing such insurance, which certificates evidencing contractual liability coverage shall have printed thereon Article 37 hereof in its entirety. All such certificates shall contain endorsements that (a) such insurance may not be modified or canceled or allowed to lapse except upon thirty (30) days' written notice to Landlord by certified mail, return receipt requested, containing the policy number and the names of the insured and the certificate holder, and (a) Tenant shall be solely responsible for payment of all premiums under such policies and Landlord shall have no obligation for the payment thereof notwithstanding that Landlord is or may be named as an insured. Tenant's failure to provide and keep in force the aforementioned insurance shall be regarded as a material default hereunder, entitling Landlord to exercise any or all of the remedies as provided in this Lease in the event of Tenant's default. All insurance required to be carried by Tenant pursuant to the terms of this Lease shall be effected under valid and enforceable policies issued by reputable and independent insurers permitted to do business in the State of New York, and rate in Best's Insurance Guide, or any successor thereto (or if there be none, an organization having a national reputation) as having a general policyholder rating of „A" and a financial rating of at least „13". Tenant shall not carry separate or additional insurance, concurrent in form or contributing, in the event of any loss or damage, with any insurance required to be obtained by Tenant under this Lease.

SECTION C. The parties hereto shall procure an appropriate clause in, or endorsement on, any „all risk" or fire or extended coverage insurance covering the Premises, the Building, the personal property, fixtures or equipment located thereon or therein, pursuant to which the insurance companies waive subrogation or consent to a waiver of right of recovery by the insured prior to any loss. The waiver of subrogation or permission for waiver of the right of recovery in favor of Tenant shall also extend to all other persons or entities occupying or using the Premises in accordance with the terms of the Lease. If the payment of an additional premium is required for the inclusion of such waiver of subrogation provisions or consent to a waiver of right of recovery, each party shall advise the other of the amount of any such additional premiums by written notice and the other party shall pay the same or shall be deemed to have agreed that the party obtaining the insurance coverage in question shall be free of any further obligations under the provisions hereof relating to such waiver or consent. It is expressly understood and agreed that Landlord will not be obligated to carry insurance on Tenant's Property or Tenant's Work or insurance against interruption of Tenant's business.

SECTION D. As to each party hereto, provided such party's right of full recovery under the applicable policy is not adversely affected, such party hereby releases the other (its servants, agents, employees and invitees) with respect to any claim (including a claim for negligence) which it might otherwise have against the other party for loss, damages or destruction with respect to its property by fire or other casualty i. e. in the case of Landlord, as to the Building, and, in the case of Tenant, as to Tenant's Property and Tenant's Work (including rental value or business interruption, as the case may be) occurring during the Term of this Lease.

ARTICLE XIII

DESTRUCTION OF THE PREMISES; PROPERTY LOSS OR DAMAGE

SECTION A. If the Building or the Premises shall be partially or totally damaged or destroyed by fire or other cause, then, whether or not the damage or destruction shall have resulted from the fault or neglect of Tenant, or its employees, agents or visitors (and if this Lease shall not have been terminated as in this Article 13 hereinafter provided), Landlord shall repair the damage and restore and rebuild the Building and/or the Premises, at its expense, with reasonable dispatch after notice to Landlord of the damage or destruction, subject to Force Majeure; *provided, however,* that Landlord shall not be required to repair or replace any of Tenant's Property or Tenant's Work. Tenant shall repair Tenant's Property and Tenant's Work promptly and with due diligence.

SECTION B. If the Building or the Premises shall be partially damaged or partially destroyed by fire or other cause, the Rent and Additional Rent payable hereunder shall be abated in the proportion which the untenantable area of the Premises bears to the total area of the Premises and for the period from the date of such damage or destruction to the date the damage required to be repaired by Landlord shall be substantially repaired or restored. If the Premises or a major part thereof shall be totally (which shall be deemed to include substantially totally) damaged or destroyed or rendered completely (which shall be deemed to include substantially completely) untenantable on account of fire or other cause, the Rent and Additional Rent shall abate as of the date of the damage or destruction and until Landlord shall substantially repair, restore and rebuild the Building and the Premises; *provided, however,* that should Tenant reoccupy a portion of the Premises during the period the restoration work is taking place and prior to the date that the same are made completely tenantable, Rent and Additional Rent allocable to such portion shall be payable by Tenant from the date of such occupancy.

SECTION C. (a) If the Building or the Premises shall be totally damaged or destroyed by fire or other cause, or if the Building shall be so damaged or destroyed by fire or other cause (whether or not the Premises are damaged or destroyed) that, in Landlord's opinion, substantial alteration, demolition or reconstruction of the Building shall be required, then in either such case Landlord may terminate this Lease by giving Tenant notice to such effect within ninety (90) days after the date of such damage or destruction, in which event, this Lease shall terminate ten (10) days after the giving of Landlord's notice to Tenant, and Tenant shall vacate the Premises and surrender same to Landlord. The Rent and Additional Rent shall be apportioned and shall be paid up to and including the date of such damage or destruction.

(a) If the Premises are totally damaged by fire or other casualty and are rendered wholly untenantable thereby, and if Landlord shall elect to restore the Premises, Landlord shall, within the aforesaid ninety (90) day period, cause a contractor or architect selected by Landlord to give notice to Tenant of the date by which such contractor or architect believes the restoration of the Premises shall be substantially completed (*"Restoration Date"*). If such notice shall indicate that such restoration shall not be completed on or before a date which shall be nine (9) months following the date of such damage or destruction, then Tenant shall have the right to terminate this Lease by giving notice to Landlord not later than thirty (30) days after receiving such notice. If Tenant shall not so elect to terminate this Lease, but Landlord shall thereafter fail to substantially complete the restoration of the Premises on or before the Restoration Date, Tenant shall have the right to terminate this Lease by giving written notice to Landlord not later than five (5) days following the Restoration Date and if Landlord shall fail to so complete such restoration within five (5) days following Landlord's receipt of such Tenant's termination notice, this Lease shall be deemed canceled and terminated as of the date of the giving of such termination notice as if such date were the Expiration Date.

(a) If the Premises are materially damaged by fire or other casualty during the last two (2) years of the Term, then Tenant may, at Tenant's option, terminate this Lease upon notice to Landlord given within thirty (30) days following such damage and destruction.

SECTION D. No damages, compensation or claims shall be payable by Landlord for inconvenience, loss of business or annoyance arising from any repair or restoration of any portion of the Premises or of the Building pursuant to this Article.

SECTION E. Notwithstanding any of the foregoing provisions of this Article, if Landlord or the lessor of any Superior Lease or the holder of any Mortgage shall be unable to collect all of the insurance proceeds (including rent insurance proceeds) applicable to damage or destruction of the Premises or the Building by fire or other cause, by reason of some

4. Form of Agreement of Lease

action or inaction on the part of Tenant or any of its invitees, employees, agents or contractors, then, without prejudice to any other remedies which may be available against Tenant, there shall be no abatement of Rent or Additional Rent, but the total amount of such Rent and Additional Rent not abated (which would otherwise have been abated) shall not exceed the amount of the uncollected insurance proceeds.

SECTION F. The provisions of this Article shall be considered an express agreement governing any case of damage or destruction of the Premises by fire or other casualty, and Section 227 of the Real Property Law of the State of new York, providing for such a contingency in the absence of an express agreement, and any other law of like import, now or hereafter in force, shall have no application in such case.

SECTION G. Tenant shall give immediate notice to Landlord in case of fire or accident in the Premises or in the Building.

SECTION H. Any Building employee to whom any property shall be entrusted by or on behalf of Tenant shall be deemed to be acting as Tenant's agent with respect to such property and neither Landlord nor its agents shall be liable for any damage to property of Tenant or of others entrusted to employees of the Building, nor for the loss of or damage to any property of Tenant by theft or otherwise. Neither Landlord nor its agents shall be liable for any injury or damage to persons or property or interruption of Tenant's business resulting from fire, explosion, falling plaster, steam, gas, electricity, water, rain or snow or leaks from any part of the Building or from the pipes, appliances or plumbing works or from the roof, street or subsurface or from any other place or by dampness or by any other cause of whatsoever nature; nor shall Landlord or its agents be liable for any such damage caused by other tenants or persons in the Building or caused by construction of any private, public or quasi-public work; nor shall Landlord be liable for any latent defect in the Premises or in the Building. Anything in this Article 13 to the contrary notwithstanding, nothing in this Lease shall be construed to relieve Landlord from responsibility directly to Tenant for any loss or damage caused directly to Tenant wholly or in part by the gross negligence or willful misconduct of Landlord; *provided, however*, that Landlord shall in no event be liable to Tenant for any loss, damage, liability, cost or expense incurred by Tenant in connection with or arising from, any security system implemented or installed by Landlord for or at Building. Nothing in the foregoing sentence shall affect any right of Landlord to the indemnity from Tenant to which Landlord may be entitled under Article

37 hereof in order to recoup for payments made to compensate for losses of third parties.

SECTION I. If, at any time or from time to time, any windows of the Premises are temporarily closed or darkened for any reason whatsoever, including, but not limited to, Landlord's own acts, or any of such windows are permanently closed or darkened or bricked up if required by law or related to any construction upon property adjacent to the Real Property by any party other than Landlord, Landlord shall not be liable for any damage Tenant may sustain thereby and Tenant shall not be entitled to any compensation therefor nor abatement of Rent or Additional Rent nor shall the same release Tenant from its obligations hereunder nor constitute an eviction. Landlord will use all reasonable efforts to minimize any disruption to Tenant, which efforts shall not include any obligation on the part of Landlord to employ labor at overtime rates.

ARTICLE XIV

EMINENT DOMAIN

SECTION A. If the whole of the Real Property, the Building or the Premises shall be acquired or condemned for any public or quasi-public use or purpose, this Lease and the Term shall end as of the date of the vesting of title with the same effect as if said date were the Expiration Date, and the Rent and Additional Rent payable hereunder shall be prorated and adjusted as of such date.

SECTION B. If only a part of the Real Property shall be so acquired or condemned then, except as hereinafter provided in this Article, this Lease and the Term shall continue in force and effect. If a part of the Premises shall be so acquired or condemned and this Lease and the Term shall not be terminated, Landlord, at Landlord's expense, shall restore that part of the Premises not so acquired or condemned so as to constitute tenantable Premises. If a part of the Premises is included in the part of the Real Property so acquired or condemned, from and after the date of the vesting of title, the Rent and Additional Rent shall be reduced in the proportion which the area of the part of the Premises so acquired or condemned bears to the total area of the Premises immediately prior to such acquisition or condemnation.

SECTION C. Whether or not the Premises shall be affected thereby, Landlord, at Landlord's sole option, may give to Tenant, within

4. Form of Agreement of Lease

sixty (60) days next following the date upon which Landlord shall have received notice of vesting of title, a thirty (30) days' notice of termination of this Lease. If the part of the Real Property so acquired or condemned shall contain more than thirty percent (30%) of the total area of the Premises immediately prior to such acquisition or condemnation, or if, by reason of such acquisition or condemnation, Tenant no longer has reasonable means of access to the Premises, Tenant, at Tenant's sole option, may give to Landlord, within thirty (30) days next following the date upon which Tenant shall have received notice of vesting of title, a thirty (30) days' notice of termination of this Lease. If any such thirty (30) days' notice of termination is given by Landlord or Tenant, as the case may be, this Lease and the Term shall come to an end and expire upon the expiration of said thirty (30) days with the same effect as if the date of expiration of said thirty (30) days were the Expiration Date. In the event of any termination of this Lease and the Term pursuant to the provisions of this Section, the Rent and Additional Rent shall be apportioned as of the date of sooner termination and any prepaid portion of Rent or Additional Rent for any period after such date shall be refunded by Landlord to Tenant.

SECTION D. In the event of any such acquisition or condemnation of all or any part of the Real Property, Landlord shall be entitled to receive the entire award for any such acquisition or condemnation, Tenant shall have no claim against Landlord or the condemning authority for the value of any unexpired portion of the Term and Tenant hereby expressly assigns to Landlord all of its right in and to any such award. Nothing contained in this Section 14.04 shall be deemed to prevent Tenant from making a claim in any condemnation proceedings for moving expenses or the then value of Tenant's Property and Tenant's Work included in such taking which does not become part of the Building; *provided, however,* that such award shall in no event reduce the amount of the award otherwise payable to Landlord.

SECTION E. The terms „condemnation" and „acquisition" as used herein shall include any agreement in lieu of or in anticipation of the exercise of the power of eminent domain between the lessor under a Superior Lease or Landlord and any governmental authority authorized to exercise the power of eminent domain.

SECTION F. If the temporary use or occupancy of all or any part of the Premises shall be lawfully taken by condemnation or in any other manner for any public or quasi-public use or purpose during the Term of this Lease, Tenant shall be entitled, except as hereinafter set forth, to receive that portion of the award for such taking which represents compensation for the use and occupancy of the Premises and, if so awarded, for the taking of Tenant's personal property and for moving expenses, and Landlord shall be entitled to receive that portion which represents reimbursement for the cost of restoration for the Premises. This Lease shall be and remain unaffected by such taking and Tenant shall continue to be responsible for all of its obligations hereunder insofar as such obligations are not affected by such taking and shall continue to pay in full the Rent and Additional Rent when due. If the period of temporary use or occupancy shall extend beyond the Expiration Date, that part of the award which represents compensation for the use or occupancy of the Premises (or a part thereof) shall be divided between Landlord and Tenant so that Tenant shall receive so much thereof as represents the period prior to the Expiration Date and Landlord shall receive so much thereof as represents the period subsequent to the Expiration Date. All moneys received by Tenant as, or as part of, an award for temporary use and occupancy for a period beyond the date to which the Rent and Additional Rent hereunder have been paid by Tenant shall be received, held and applied by Tenant as a trust fund for payment of the Rent and Additional Rent falling due hereunder.

ARTICLE XV

ASSIGNMENT AND SUBLETTING

SECTION A. Tenant, for itself, its heirs, distributees, executors, administrators, legal representatives, successors and assigns, expressly covenants that it shall not assign, mortgage, pledge, encumber, or otherwise transfer this Lease, nor sublet (nor underlet), nor suffer, nor permit the Premises or any part thereof to be used or occupied by others (whether for desk space, mailing privileges or otherwise), without the prior written consent of Landlord in each instance. If this Lease be assigned, or if the Premises or any part thereof be sublet or occupied by anybody other than Tenant, or if this Lease or the Premises or Tenant's personal property shall be encumbered (whether by operation of law or otherwise) without Landlord's consent, then Landlord may, after default by Tenant, collect rent from the assignee, subtenant or occupant, and apply the net amount collected to the Rent and Additional Rent herein reserved, but no assignment, subletting, occupancy or collection shall be deemed a waiver of the provisions hereof, the acceptance of the assignee, subtenant or oc-

4. Form of Agreement of Lease

cupant as tenant, or a release of Tenant from the further performance by Tenant of covenants on the part of Tenant herein contained and Tenant shall remain fully liable for the obligations of Tenant under this Lease. The consent by Landlord to an assignment or subletting shall not in any way be construed to relieve Tenant from obtaining the express consent in writing of Landlord to any further assignment or subletting. In no event shall any permitted subtenant assign or encumber its sublease or further sublet all or any portion of its sublet space, or otherwise suffer or permit the sublet space or any part thereof to be used or occupied by others, without Landlord's prior written consent in each instance. Any assignment, sublease, mortgage, pledge, encumbrance or transfer in contravention of the provisions of this Article 15 shall be void.

SECTION B. If Tenant shall, at any time or from time to time, during the Term desire to assign this Lease or sublet all or part of the Premises, Tenant shall give notice thereof to Landlord, which notice shall be accompanied by (a) a conformed or photostatic copy of the proposed assignment or sublease, the effective or commencement date of which shall be not less than sixty (60) nor more than one hundred and eighty (180) days after the giving of such notice (b) a statement setting forth in reasonable detail the identity of the proposed assignee or subtenant, the nature of its business and its proposed use of the Premises, (c) current financial information with respect to the proposed assignee or subtenant, including, without limitation, its most recent financial report, and (d) an agreement by Tenant to indemnify Landlord against liability resulting from any claims that may be made against Landlord by the proposed assignee or subtenant or by any brokers or other persons claiming a commission or similar compensation in connection with the proposed assignment or sublease. The aforesaid notice shall be deemed an offer from Tenant to Landlord whereby Landlord (or Landlord's designee) may, at its option, (i) sublease such space (or terminate the Lease with respect to only such space) (hereinafter called the „Leaseback Space") from Tenant upon the terms and conditions hereinafter set forth, or (ii) if the proposed transaction is an assignment of this Lease or a subletting of fifty percent (50%) or more of the rentable square footage contained in the Premises, terminate this Lease. Said options may be exercised by Landlord by notice to Tenant at any time within sixty (60) days after the aforesaid notice has been given by Tenant to Landlord, and during such sixty (60) day period Tenant shall not assign this Lease nor sublet such space to any person other than Landlord.

SECTION C. If Landlord exercises its option to terminate this Lease with respect to all or a portion of the Premises, pursuant to Section 15.02 hereof, then this Lease shall end and expire on the date that such assignment or sublease was to be effective or commence, as the case may be, and the Rent and Additional Rent due hereunder shall be paid and apportioned to such date. In such event, Tenant, upon request of Landlord, shall enter into an amendment of this Lease ratifying and confirming such total or partial termination, and setting forth appropriate modifications, if any, to the terms and provisions hereof.

SECTION D. If Landlord exercises its option to terminate this Lease with respect to all or a portion of the Premises, pursuant to Section 15.02 hereof, Landlord shall be free to and shall have no liability to Tenant if Landlord should lease the Premises (or any part thereof) to Tenant's prospective assignee or subtenant.

SECTION E. If Landlord exercises its option to sublet the Leaseback Space, such sublease to Landlord or its designee (as subtenant) shall be at a rental rate equal to the product of (a) the lesser of (i) the rental rate per rentable square foot of Rent and Additional Rent then payable pursuant to this Lease, and (ii) the rental rate per rentable square foot of rent and additional rent set forth in the proposed sublease, multiplied by (a) the number of rentable square

feet of the Leaseback Space, and shall be for the same term as that of the proposed subletting, and such sublease shall:

(a) be expressly subject to all of the covenants, agreements, terms, provisions and conditions of this Lease except such as are irrelevant or inapplicable, and except as expressly set forth in this Article 15 to the contrary;

(b) be upon the same terms and conditions as those contained in the proposed sublease, except such as are irrelevant or inapplicable and except as expressly set forth in this Article 15 to the contrary;

(c) give the subtenant the unqualified and unrestricted right, without Tenants permission, to assign such sublease or any interest therein and/or to sublet the space covered by such sublease or any part or parts of such space and to make any and all changes, alterations and improvements in the space covered by such sublease, and if the proposed sublease will result in all or substantially all of the Premises being sublet, grant Landlord or its designee the option to extend the term of such sublease for the balance of the Term of this Lease less one day;

4. Form of Agreement of Lease

(d) provide that any assignee or further subtenant of Landlord or may, at Landlord's option, be permitted to make alterations, decorations and in such space or any part thereof and shall also provide in substance that any alterations, decorations and installations in such space therein made by any subtenant of Landlord or its designee may be removed, in whole or in part, assignee or subtenant, at its option, prior to or upon the expiration or other such sublease; provided, however, that such assignee or subtenant shall, at and expense, repair any damage and injury caused by such removal; and its designee, installations such assignee or by such termination of its sole cost and expense, repair any damage and injury caused by such removal; and

(e) provide that (i) the parties to such sublease expressly negate any intention that any estate created under such sublease be merged with any other estate held by either of said parties, (ii) any assignment or sublease by Landlord or its designee (as the subtenant) may be for any purpose or purposes that Landlord, in Landlords uncontrolled discretion, shall deem suitable or appropriate, (iii) Tenant shall, at Tenant's sole cost and expense, at all times provide and permit reasonably appropriate means of ingress to and egress from such space so sublet by Tenant to Landlord or its designee, (iv) Landlord may, at Tenant's sole cost and expense, make such alterations as may be required or deemed necessary by Landlord to physically separate the subleased space from the balance of the Premises and to comply with any legal or insurance requirements relating to such separation, and (v) that at the expiration of the term of such sublease, Tenant will accept the space covered by such sublease in its then existing condition, subject to the obligations of the subtenant to make such repairs thereto as may be necessary to preserve the premises demised by such sublease in good order and condition.

SECTION F.

(a) If Landlord exercises its option to sublet the Leaseback Space, Landlord shall indemnify and save Tenant harmless from all obligations under this Lease as to the Leaseback Space during the period of time it is so sublet to Landlord, except as to any obligation which arises out of or results from the negligence or willful misconduct of Tenant, or any of its agents, servants or employees.

(b) Performance by Landlord, or its designee, under a sublease of the Leaseback Space shall be deemed performance by Tenant of any similar obligation under this Lease and any default under any such sublease shall not give rise to a default under a similar obligation contained in this Lease nor shall Tenant be liable for any default under this Lease or deemed to be in default hereunder if such default is occasioned by or arises from any act or omission of the tenant under such sublease or is occasioned by or arises from any act or omission of any occupant holding under or pursuant to any such sublease.

(c) Tenant shall have no obligation, at the expiration or earlier termination of the Term, to remove any alteration, installation or improvement made in the Leaseback Space by Landlord (or Landlord's designee).

(d) Any consent required of Tenant, as Landlord under the sublease, shall be deemed granted if consent with respect thereto is granted by Landlord under this Lease, and any failure of Landlord (or its designee) to comply with the provisions of the sublease other than with respect to the payment of Rent and Additional Rent to Tenant, shall not constitute a default thereunder or hereunder if Landlord shall have consented to such noncompliance.

SECTION G. In the event Landlord does not exercise either option provided to it pursuant to Section 15.02 hereof and providing that Tenant is not in default of any of Tenants obligations under this Lease, after notice and the expiration of any applicable grace period, as of the time of Landlord's consent and as of the effective date of the proposed assignment or commencement date of the proposed sublease, Landlord's consent (which must be in writing and in form and substance satisfactory to Landlord) to the proposed assignment or sublease shall not be unreasonably withheld or delayed; provided, however, that:

(a) Tenant shall have complied with the provisions of Section 15.02 hereof and Landlord shall not have exercised any of its options under Section 15.02 hereof within the time permitted therefor;

(b) In Landlord's judgment the proposed assignee or subtenant is engaged in a business or activity, and the Premises, or the relevant part thereof, will be used in a manner, which (i) is in keeping with the then standards of the Building, (ii) is limited to the use of the Premises as general and executive offices, (iii) does not violate the restrictions set forth in Article 3 hereof, and (iv) will not violate any negative covenant as to use contained in any other lease of office or retail space in the Building;

4. Form of Agreement of Lease

(c) The proposed assignee or subtenant is a reputable person or entity of good character and with sufficient financial worth considering the responsibility involved, and Landlord has been furnished with reasonable proof thereof;

(d) Neither the proposed assignee or subtenant nor any person which, directly or indirectly, controls, is controlled by, or is under common control with, the proposed assignee or subtenant, is then an occupant of any part of the Building;

(e) The proposed assignee or subtenant is not a person or entity (or affiliate or a person or entity) with whom Landlord or Landlord's agent is then negotiating in connection with rental of space in the Building;

(f) The form of the proposed sublease or instrument of assignment shall be reasonably satisfactory to Landlord and shall comply with the applicable provisions of this Article 15;

(g) There shall not be more than two (2) subtenants (including Landlord or its designee) of the Premises;

(h) The amount of the aggregate rent to be paid by the proposed subtenant is not less than the then current market rent per rentable square foot for the Premises determined as though the Premises were vacant, and the rental and other terms and conditions of the sublease are the same as those contained in the proposed sublease furnished to Landlord pursuant to Section 15.02,

(i) Tenant shall reimburse Landlord, as Additional Rent upon demand, for (x) the greater of $1,000.00 or the costs and expenses incurred by Landlord in connection with said assignment or sublease, including, but not limited to, the costs of making investigations as to the acceptability of the proposed assignee or subtenant and the cost of receiving plans and specifications proposed to be made in connection therewith, and (y) legal costs incurred in connection with the granting of any requested consent;

(j) Tenant shall not have (i) advertised or publicized in any way the availability of the Premises without prior notice of and approval by Landlord, nor shall any advertisement state the name (as distinguished from the address) of the Building or the proposed rental, (ii) listed the Premises to be sublet or assignment with a broker, agent or otherwise at a rental rate less than the fixed rent and additional rent at which Landlord is then offering to lease other space in the Building;

(k) The proposed occupancy shall not increase the office cleaning requirements or impose an extra burden upon services to be supplied by Landlord to Tenant; and

(l) The proposed subtenant or assignee shall not be entitled, directly or indirectly, to diplomatic or sovereign immunity and shall be subject to the service of process in, and the jurisdiction of the courts of New York State.

Except for any sublease by Tenant to Landlord or its designee pursuant to this Article 15, each sublease pursuant to this Section 15.07 shall be subject to all of the covenants, agreements, terms, provisions and conditions contained in this Lease. Notwithstanding any such sublease to Landlord or any such sublease to any other subtenant and/or acceptance of Rent or Additional Rent by Landlord from any subtenant, Tenant shall and will remain fully liable for the payment of the Rent and Additional Rent due and to become due hereunder and for the performance of all the covenants, agreements, terms, provisions and conditions contained in this Lease on Tenant's part to be observed and performed and all acts and omissions of any licensee or subtenant or anyone claiming under or through any subtenant which shall be in violation of any of the obligations of this Lease, and any such violation shall be deemed to be a violation by Tenant. If Landlord shall decline to give its consent to any proposed assignment or sublease, or if Landlord shall exercise either of its options under Section 15.02 hereof, Tenant shall indemnify, defend and hold harmless Landlord against and from any and all losses, liabilities, damages, costs, and expenses (including attorneys' fees and disbursements) resulting from any claims that may be made against Landlord by the proposed assignee or subtenant or by any brokers or other persons claiming a commission or similar compensation in connection with the proposed assignment or sublease.

SECTION H. In the event that (a) Landlord fails to exercise either of its options under Section 15.02 hereof and consents to a proposed assignment or sublease, and (a) Tenant fails to execute and deliver the assignment or sublease to which Landlord consented within ninety (90) days after the giving of such consent, then, Tenant shall again comply with all of the provisions and conditions of Section 15.02 hereof before assigning this Lease or subletting all or part of the Premises.

SECTION I. With respect to each and every sublease authorized by Landlord under the provisions of this Lease, it is further agreed that:

4. Form of Agreement of Lease

(a) No sublease shall be for a term ending later than one day prior to the Expiration Date of this Lease;

(b) No sublease shall be delivered, and no subtenant shall take possession of the Premises or any part thereof, until an executed counterpart of such sublease has been delivered to Landlord and approved in writing by Landlord; and

(c) Each sublease shall be subject and subordinate to this Lease and to the matters to which this Lease is or shall be subordinate, and each subtenant by entering into a sublease is deemed to have agreed that in the event of termination, re-entry or dispossession by Landlord under this Lease, Landlord may, at its option, take over all of the right, title and interest of Tenant, as sublandlord, under such sublease, and such subtenant shall, at Landlord's option, attorn to Landlord pursuant to the then executory provisions of such sublease, except that Landlord shall not (i) be liable for any previous act or omission of Tenant under such sublease, (ii) be subject to any counterclaim, offset or defense, not expressly provided in such sublease, which theretofore accrued to such subtenant against Tenant, (iii) be bound by any previous modification of such sublease or by any previous prepayment of more than one month's Rent or Additional Rent, or (iv) be obligated to perform any work in the subleased space of the Building or to prepare them or occupancy beyond Landlord's obligations under this Lease, and the subtenant shall execute and deliver to Landlord any instruments Landlord may reasonably request to evidence and confirm such attornment. Each subtenant or licensee of Tenant shall be deemed automatically upon and as a condition of occupying or using the Premises or any part thereof, to have given a waiver of the type described in and to the extent and upon the conditions set forth in this Article 15. The provisions of this Article 15 shall be self-operative and no further instrument shall be required to give effect to this provision.

SECTION J. If Landlord shall consent to any assignment of this Lease or to any sublease or if Tenant shall enter into any other assignment or sublease permitted hereunder, Tenant shall in consideration therefor, pay to Landlord, as Additional Rent:

(a) In the case of an assignment, on the effective date of the assignment, an amount equal to all sums and other considerations paid to Tenant by the assignee for or by reason of such assignment (including, but not limited to, sums paid for Tenant's Property, less, in the case of a sale thereof, the then net unamortized or undepreciated cost thereof determined on the basis of Tenant's federal income tax returns); or

(b) In the case of a sublease, any additional charges or other consideration payable under the sublease to Tenant by the subtenant which is in excess of the Rent and Additional Rent accruing during the term of the sublease in respect of the subleased space (at the rate per square foot payable by Tenant hereunder) pursuant to the terms hereof (including, but not limited to, sums paid for the sale or rental of Tenant's Property, less, in the case of the sale thereof, the then net unamortized or undepreciated cost thereof determined on the basis of Tenant's federal income tax returns). The sums payable under this clause shall be paid by Tenant to Landlord as Additional Rent as and when paid by the subtenant to Tenant.

SECTION K.

(a) If Tenant is a corporation (but not a public corporation), the provisions of Section 15.01 hereof shall apply to a transfer (by one or more transfer(s)), of a majority of the stock of Tenant as if such transfer of a majority of the stock of Tenant were an assignment of this Lease. It is expressly understood that the term *,,transfer(s)"* shall be deemed to include the issuance of new stock which results in a majority of the stock of Tenant being held by a person or entity which does not hold a majority of the stock of Tenant on the date hereof. Said provisions shall not apply to transactions with a corporation into or with which Tenant is merged or consolidated or to which substantially all of Tenant's assets are transferred; provided, however, such transfer shall have been made for a legitimate independent business purpose and not for the principal purpose of transferring this Lease, that in any of such events, (i) the successor to Tenant has a net worth computed in accordance with generally a ccepted accounting principles at least equal to the greater of (1) the net worth of Tenant immediately prior to such merger, consolidation or transfer, or (2) the net worth of Tenant herein named on the date of this Lease, and (ii) proof satisfactory to Landlord of such net worth shall have been delivered to Landlord at least ten (10) days prior to the effective date of any such transaction.

(b) If Tenant is a partnership, the provisions of Section 15.01 hereof shall apply to a transfer (by one or more transfers) of a majority interest in the partnership, as if such transfer were an assignment of this Lease.

(c) The limitations set forth in this Section 15.11 shall be deemed

4. Form of Agreement of Lease

to apply to subtenant(s), assignee(s) and guarantor(s) of this Lease, if any, and any transfer by any such entity in violation of this Section 15.11 shall be deemed to be a transfer in violation of Section 15.01.

(d) A modification, amendment or extension of a sublease shall be deemed a sublease For the purposes of Section 15.01 hereof, and a takeover agreement shall be deemed a transfer of this Lease for the purposes of Section 15.01 hereof.

SECTION L. Tenant may, with Landlord's consent which shall not be unreasonably withheld, permit any corporations or other business entities which control, are controlled by, or are under common control with Tenant (herein referred to as ,,*related corporation*") to sublet all or part of the Premises for any Permitted Use, subject however to compliance with Tenant's obligations under this Lease. Such sublease shall not be deemed to vest in any such related corporation any right or interest in this Lease or the Premises nor shall it relieve, release, impair or discharge any of Tenant's obligations hereunder. For the purposes hereof, ,,control" shall be deemed to mean ownership of not less than 50% of all of the voting stock of such corporation or not less than 50% of all of the legal and equitable interest in any other business entities.

SECTION M. Any assignment or transfer, whether made with Landlord's consent pursuant to Section 15.01 hereof or without Landlord's consent to the extent permitted under Section 15.11 (a) hereof, shall be made only if, and shall not be effective until, the assignee shall execute, acknowledge and deliver to Landlord an agreement in form and substance satisfactory to Landlord whereby the assignee shall assume the obligations of this Lease on the part of Tenant to be performed or observed and whereby the assignee shall agree that the provisions in Section 15.01 hereof shall, notwithstanding such assignment or transfer, continue to be binding upon it in respect of all future assignments and transfers.

SECTION N. The joint and several liability of Tenant and any immediate or remote successor in interest of Tenant and the due performance of the obligations of this Lease on Tenant's part to be performed or observed shall not be discharged, released or impaired in any respect by any agreement or stipulation made by Landlord, or any grantee or assignee of Landlord by way of mortgage or otherwise, extending the time, or modifying any of the obligations of this Lease, or by any waiver or failure of Landlord, or any grantee or assignee of Landlord by way of mortgage or otherwise, to enforce any of the obligations of this Lease.

U.S. Sample Agreements

SECTION O. The listing of any name other than that of Tenant, whether on the doors of the Premises or the Building directory, or otherwise, shall not operate to vest any right or interest in this Lease or in the Premises, nor shall it be deemed to be the consent of Landlord to any assignment or transfer of this Lease or to any sublease of Premises or to the use or occupancy thereof by others. Any such listing shall constitute a privilege extended by Landlord, revocable at Landlord's will by notice to Tenant.

SECTION P. In the event that Tenant desires to sublet the Premises or assign this Lease, it shall designate Landlord or the then managing agent of the Building, at Landlord's sole option, as Tenant's exclusive agent to effect such sublease or assignment and shall pay Landlord or such managing agent, as the case may be, a reasonable brokerage commission computed in accordance with the usual rates charged by Landlord or such managing agent.

SECTION Q. In the event that, at any time after Tenant named herein may have assigned its interest in this Lease, this Lease shall be disaffirmed or rejected in any proceeding of the types described in subdivisions (f) or (g) of Section 18.01 hereof or in any similar proceeding, or in the event of termination of this Lease by reason of any such proceeding or by reason of lapse of time following notice of termination given pursuant to Article 19 hereof based upon any of the conditions of limitation set forth in said subdivisions, Tenant named herein, upon request of Landlord given within thirty (30) days after such disaffirmance, rejection or termination (and actual notice thereof to Landlord in the event of a disaffirmance or rejection or in the event of termination other than by act of Landlord), shall (a) pay to Landlord all Additional Rent and other charges due and owing by the assignee to Landlord under this Lease to and including the date of such disaffirmance, rejection or termination, and (a) as *„tenant"*, enter into a new lease with Landlord of the Premises for a term commencing on the effective date of such disaffirmance, rejection or termination and ending on the Expiration Date, unless sooner terminated as in such lease provided, at the same Rent and upon the then executory terms, covenants and conditions as are contained in this Lease, except that (i) the rights of Tenant named herein under the new lease shall be subject to the possessory rights of the assignee under this Lease and the possessory rights of any persons claiming through or under such assignee or by virtue of any statute or of any order of and court, (ii) such new lease shall require all defaults existing under this Lease to be cured by Tenant named herein with due diligence, and (iii) such new lease shall require Tenant named herein to pay all Additional Rent which, had this Lease not been so disaffirmed, rejected or terminated, would have become due under the provisions of Article 28 hereof after the date of such disaffirmance, rejection or termination with respect to any period prior thereto. In the event Tenant named herein shall default for a period often (10) days after Landlord's request in its obligations to enter into said new lease then, in addition to all other rights and remedies by reason of default, either at law or in equity, Landlord shall have the same rights and remedies against Tenant named herein as if it had entered into such new lease and such new lease had thereafter been terminated as at the commencement date thereof by reason of the default thereunder of Tenant named herein.

ARTICLE XVI

ACCESS TO PREMISES

SECTION A. Tenant shall permit Landlord, Landlord's agents and any agents or employees of any public utility servicing the Building access to the Property and the Premises to erect, use, maintain and replace ducts pipes and conduits in and through the Premises and Landlord shall repair, at Landlord's sole cost and expense, and indemnify Tenant against, any damage to the Premises, Tenant's Work or Tenant's Property resulting therefrom.

SECTION B. Landlord or Landlord's agents shall have the right to enter the Premises at all reasonable times upon notice, except in an emergency, in which case no notice shall be required, for any of the purposes specified in this Article 16, (a) to examine the same, (a) to show them to prospective purchasers, mortgagees or lessees of the Building or space therein, (a) to make such repairs, alterations, improvements or additions as Landlord may be permitted to perform in the Premises or to any other portion of the Building, pursuant to, and in accordance with, any of the terms and provisions of this Lease, following Tenant's default in the performance thereof, (a) for the purpose of complying with laws, regulations or other requirements of government authorities, or (a) to take all material into and upon the Premises that may be required therefor, without any such entry by Landlord or Landlord's agents constituting an eviction or constructive eviction of Tenant in whole or in part, and the Rent

U.S. Sample Agreements

and Additional Rent shall in no wise abate while said decorations, repairs, alterations, improvements, or additions are being made, by reason of loss or interruption of business of Tenant, or otherwise.

SECTION C. During the one year prior to the Expiration Date or the expiration of any renewal or extended term, Landlord may exhibit the Premises to prospective tenants thereof, and if, during such period, Tenant shall have removed all or substantially all of Tenant's property therefrom, Landlord may immediately enter and alter, renovate and redecorate the Premises, without elimination or abatement of Rent or Additional Rent, or incurring liability to Tenant for any compensation, and such acts shall not be deemed an actual or constructive eviction.

SECTION D. If Tenant shall not be personally present to open and permit an entry into the Premises, at any time and from time to time, when for any reason an entry therein shall be necessary or permissible pursuant to the terms and provisions of this Lease, Landlord or Landlord's agents may enter the same by a master key, or may forcibly enter the same, without rendering Landlord or such agents liable therefor (if during such entry Landlord or Landlord's agents shall accord reasonable care to Tenant's property), and without in any manner affecting the obligations and covenants of this Lease.

SECTION E. Landlord reserves the right, at any time and from time to time, without the same constituting an actual or constructive eviction and without incurring any liability to Tenant therefor, to change the arrangement and/or location of public entrances or passageways, doors and doorways, and corridors, elevators, escalators, stairs, toilets, or other public parts of the Building; *provided, however,* that such change does not unreasonably deprive Tenant of access to the Premises, and to change the name, number, address or designation by which the Building is commonly known. In addition, Tenant expressly understands and agrees that Landlord may (but is not obligated) at any time and from time to time during the Term hereof, perform substantial alteration and renovation work in and to the public and non-public portions of the Building and the mechanical systems serving the Building (which work may include relocation of the entrance to the Building, alteration, renovation, repair, replacement and/or decoration of the Building lobby, elevators, windows, lintels, parapet walls and roof), and that Landlord shall incur no liability to Tenant, nor shall Tenant be entitled to any abatement of Rent or Additional Rent, on account of any noise, vibration, construction, temporary arrangements or other disturbance to Tenant's business

4. Form of Agreement of Lease

at the Premises; *provided, however,* that Tenant is not unreasonably deprived of access to said Premises, which shall arise out of the performance by Landlord of any such renovations at the Building.

SECTION F. Tenant understands and agrees that all parts (except surfaces facing the interior of the Premises) of all walls, and doors bounding the Premises (including exterior Building walls, core corridor walls, doors and entrances), all balconies, terraces and roofs adjacent to the Premises, all space in or adjacent to the Premises used for shafts, stacks, stairways, chutes, pipes, conduits, ducts, fan rooms, telephone rooms, heating, air cooling, plumbing and other mechanical facilities, service closets and other Building facilities are not part of the Premises, and Landlord shall have the use thereof, as well as access thereto, through the Premises, for the purposes of operation, maintenance, alteration, decoration, cleaning, safety, security and repair.

SECTION G. In the performance of any work in the Premises referred to in this Article 16, Landlord shall use all reasonable efforts to minimize interference with Tenant's use of the Premises, subject to Force Majeure, and without any obligation to employ overtime labor.

SECTION H. Landlord or Landlord's agents shall have the right to permit to the Premises, at any time and from time to time, whether or not Tenant shall be present, receiver, trustee or other person entitled to, or reasonably purporting to be entitled to, such for the purpose of taking possession of, or removing, any of Tenant's personal property or property of any other occupant of the Premises, or for any other lawful purpose, or by any representative of fire, police, building, sanitation or other department or instrumentality of the borough, city, state or federal governments. Nothing contained in, nor any action taken by Landlord under, this Section 16 shall be deemed to constitute recognition by Landlord that any person other than Tenant has any right or interest in this Lease or the Premises.

SECTION I. Landlord reserves the right, at Landlord's cost and expense, to light all or any portion of the Premises at night for display purposes.

ARTICLE XVII

LANDLORD'S LIABILITY

SECTION A. The obligations of Landlord under this Lease shall not be binding upon Landlord named herein after the sale, conveyance, assignment or transfer by such Landlord (or upon any subsequent landlord after the sale, conveyance, assignment or transfer by such subsequent landlord) of its interest (in whole or in part) in the Building or the Real Property, as the case may be, and in the event of any such sale, conveyance, assignment or transfer, Landlord shall be and hereby is entirely freed and relieved of all existing and future covenants, obligations and liabilities of Landlord hereunder (to the extent of the interest transferred), and it shall be deemed and construed without further agreement between the parties or their successors in interest or the parties and the transferees of said property that such purchaser, grantee, assignee or other transferee has assumed and agreed to carry out any and all covenants, obligations and liabilities of Landlord hereunder (to the extent of the interest transferred).

SECTION B. Neither the shareholders, directors or officers of Landlord, if Landlord is a corporation, nor the partners comprising Landlord (nor any of the shareholders, directors or officers of such partners), if Landlord is a partnership (collectively, the *„Parties"*), shall be liable for the performance of Landlord's obligations under this Lease. Tenant shall look solely to Landlord to enforce Landlord's obligations hereunder and shall not seek any damages against any of the Parties. The liability of Landlord for Landlord's obligations under this Lease shall not exceed and shall be limited to Landlord's estate and interest in the Building and the Real Property, and Tenant shall not look to any other property or assets of Landlord or the property or assets of any of the Parties in seeking either to enforce Landlord's obligations under this Lease or to satisfy ajudgment for Landlord's failure to perform such obligations. No other property or assets of Landlord or the Parties shall be subject to levy, lien, execution, attachment or other enforcement procedure.

ARTICLE XVIII

CONDITIONS OF LIMITATION

SECTION A. This Lease and the Term and estate hereby granted are subject to the limitations that:

4. Form of Agreement of Lease

(a) if, Tenant shall default in the payment when due of any installment of Rent or in the payment when due of any Additional Rent, and such default shall continue for a period of five (5) days after notice by Landlord to Tenant of such default; or

(b) if, Tenant shall default in the observance or performance of any term, covenant or condition of this Lease on Tenant's part to be observed or performed (other than the covenants for the payment of Rent and Additional Rent) and Tenant shall fail to remedy such default within twenty (20) days after notice by Landlord to Tenant of such default, or if such default is of such a nature that it cannot be completely remedied within said twenty (20) day period, if Tenant shall not commence within said twenty (20) day period and thereafter diligently prosecute to completion all steps necessary to remedy such default; or

(c) if, Tenant shall default in the observance or performance of any term, covenant or condition on Tenant's part to be observed or performed under any other lease with Landlord or Landlord's predecessor-in-interest of space in the Building and such default shall continue beyond the expiration of any applicable grace period set forth in such other lease; or

(d) if, the Premises shall become vacant, deserted or abandoned or if Tenant shall fail to take occupancy (Tenant's taking of occupancy being deemed to include the commencement of Tenant's Initial Alterations) of the Premises within sixty (60) days after the Commencement Date; or

(e) if, Tenant's interest in this Lease shall devolve upon or pass to any person, whether by operation of law or otherwise, except as may be expressly permitted under Article 15 hereof or

(f) it Tenant shall file a voluntary petition in bankruptcy or insolvency, or shall be adjudicated a bankrupt or insolvent, or shall file any petition or answer seeking any reorganization, arrangement, composition, readjustment, liquidation, dissolution or similar relief under the present or any future federal bankruptcy act or any other present or future applicable federal, state or other statute or law, or shall make an assignment for the benefit of creditors or shall seek or consent to or acquiesce in the appointment of any trustee, receiver or liquidator of Tenant or of all or any part of Tenant's property; or

(g) if, within sixty (60) days after the commencement of any proceeding against Tenant, whether by the filing of a petition or otherwise, seeking any reorganization, arrangement, composition, readjustment, liquidation, dissolution or similar relief under the present or any future federal bankruptcy act or any other present or future applicable federal, state or other statute or law, such proceeding shall not have been dismissed, or if, within sixty (60) days after the appointment of any trustee, receiver or liquidator of Tenant, or of all or any part of Tenant's property, without the consent or acquiescence of Tenant, such appointment shall not have been vacated or otherwise discharged, or if any lien, execution or attachment shall be filed or issued against Tenant or any of Tenant's property pursuant to which the Premises shall be taken or occupied or attempted to be taken or occupied by someone other than Tenant;

then upon the occurrence, at any time prior to or during the Term, of any one or more of such events, Landlord may, at any time thereafter, at Landlord's sole option, give to Tenant a five (5) days' notice of cancellation of this Lease and, in such event, this Lease and the Term shall come to an end and expire (whether or not the Term shall have commenced) upon the expiration of said five (5) day period with the same force and effect as if the date of expiration of said five (5) days were the Expiration Date stated herein and Tenant shall then quit and surrender the Premises to Landlord, but Tenant shall remain liable for damages as provided in Article 19 hereof. However, if Tenant shall default (i) in the timely payment of Rent and Additional Rent, and any such default shall continue or be repeated for two (2) consecutive months or for a total of four (4) months in any period of twelve (12) months, or (ii) more than three (3) times in any period of six (6) months, in the performance of any other term of this Lease to be performed by Tenant, then, notwithstanding that such defaults shall have each been cured within the applicable period, if any, as above provided, any further similar default shall be deemed to be deliberate and Landlord thereafter may serve the said five (5) days' notice of termination upon Tenant without affording to Tenant an opportunity to cure such further default.

SECTION B. If, at any time, (a) Tenant shall be comprised of two (2) or more persons, (a) Tenant's obligations under this Lease shall have been guaranteed by any person other than Tenant, or (a) Tenant's interest in this Lease shall have been assigned, the word *„Tenant",* as used in clauses (f) and (g) of Section 18.01 hereof, shall be deemed to mean any one or more of the persons primarily or secondarily liable for Tenant's obligations under this Lease. Any monies received by Landlord from or on behalf of Tenant during the pendency of any proceeding of the types referred to in said clauses (f) and (g) shall be deemed paid as compensation for the use and occupation of the Premises and the acceptance of any such compensation by Landlord shall not be deemed an acceptance of Rent or Additional Rent or a waiver on the part of Landlord of any rights under Section 18.01 hereof.

SECTION C. Landlord reserves the right, without liability to Tenant, to suspend furnishing to Tenant electric energy and all or any other services (including heat, ventilation and air conditioning), whenever Landlord is obligated to furnish the same after hours or otherwise at Tenant's expense, in the event that (but only for so long as) Tenant is in arrears in paying Landlord therefor:

ARTICLE XIX

RE-ENTRY BY LANDLORD; REMEDIES

SECTION A.

1. If this Lease and the Term shall expire and come to an end as provided in Article 18 hereof:

(a) Landlord and its agents may immediately, or at any time thereafter, re-enter the Premises or any part thereof, without notice, either by summary proceedings, or by any other applicable action or proceeding, or by force or otherwise (without being liable to indictment, prosecution or damages therefor), and may repossess the Premises and dispossess Tenant and any other persons from the Premises and remove any and all of their property and effects from the Premises; and

(b) Landlord, at its option, may relet the whole or any part or parts of the Premises, at any time or from time to time, either in the name of Landlord or otherwise, to such tenant or tenants, for such term or terms ending before, on or after the Expiration Date, at such rental or rentals and upon such other conditions, which may include concessions and free rent periods, as Landlord, in its sole discretion, may determine. Landlord shall have no obligation to relet the Premises or any part thereof and shall in no event be liable for refusal or failure to relet the Premises or any part thereof, or, in the event of any such reletting, for refusal or failure to collect any rent due upon any such reletting, and no such refusal or failure shall operate to relieve Tenant of any liability under this Lease or otherwise to affect any such liability. Landlord, at its option, may make such repairs, replacements, alterations, additions, improvements, decorations and other physical changes in and to the Premises as Landlord, in its sole discretion, considers advisable or necessary in connection with any such reletting or proposed reletting, without relieving Tenant of any liability under this Lease or otherwise affecting any such liability.

2. Tenant, on its own behalf and on behalf of all persons claiming through or under Tenant, including all creditors, does further hereby waive any and all rights which Tenant and all such persons might otherwise have under any present or future law to (a) the service of any notice of intention to re-enter or to institute legal proceedings to that end which may otherwise be required to be given under any present or future law, (a) redeem the Premises, or reenter or repossess the Premises, or (a) restore the operation of this Lease, after (i) Tenant shall have been dispossessed by a judgment or by warrant of any court or judge, (ii) any re-entry by Landlord, or (iii) any expiration or termination of this Lease and the Term, whether such dispossess, re-entry, expiration or termination shall be by operation of law or pursuant to the provisions of this Lease. The words „re-enter", „re-entry" and „re-entered" as used in this Lease shall not be deemed to be restricted to their technical legal meanings. The right to invoke the remedies hereinbefore set forth are cumulative and shall not preclude Landlord from invoking any other remedy allowed at law or in equity.

SECTION B. In the event of any breach or threatened breach by Tenant or any person claiming through or under Tenant, of any of the terms of this Lease (whether or not the Term shall have commenced), Landlord shall be entitled to enjoin such breach or threatened breach and shall have the right to invoke any other remedy allowed at law or in equity, by statute or otherwise, as if re-entry, summary proceedings or other specific remedies were not provided for in this Lease.

SECTION C.

1. If this Lease and the Term shall expire and come to an end as provided in Article 18 hereof, or by or under any summary proceeding or any other action or proceeding, or if Landlord shall re-enter the Premises

4. Form of Agreement of Lease

as provided in this Article 19, or by or under any summary proceeding or any other action or proceeding, then, in any of said events:

(a) Tenant shall pay to Landlord all Rent, Additional Rent and other charges payable under this Lease by Tenant to Landlord to the date upon which this Lease and the Term shall have expired and come to an end or to the date of re-entry upon the Premises by Landlord, as the case may be;

(b) Landlord shall be entitled to retain all monies, if any, paid by Tenant to Landlord, whether as advanced Rent, Additional Rent, Security Deposit or otherwise, but such monies shall be credited by Landlord against any damages payable by Tenant to Landlord;

(c) Tenant also shall be liable for and shall pay to Landlord, as damages, any deficiency (referred to as *„Deficiency"*) between the Rent and Additional Rent reserved in this Lease for the period which otherwise would have constituted the unexpired portion of the Term (conclusively presuming the Additional Rent to be the same as was payable for the year immediately preceding such termination or re-entry) and the net amount, if any, of rents collected under any reletting effected pursuant to the provisions of Section 19.01A hereof for any part of Such period (first deducting from the rents collected under any such reletting all of Landlord's expenses in connection with the termination of this Lease, and Landlord's re-entry upon the Premises and with such reletting, including, but not limited to, all repossession costs, brokerage commissions, legal expenses, attorneys' fees and disbursements, alteration costs and other expenses of preparing the Premises for such reletting). Any such Deficiency shall be paid in monthly installments by Tenant on the days specified in this Lease for payment of installments of Rent. Landlord shall be entitled to recover from Tenant each monthly Deficiency as the same shall arise, and no suit to collect the amount of the Deficiency for any month shall prejudice Landlord's right to collect the Deficiency for any subsequent month by a similar proceeding; and

(d) Whether or not Landlord shall have collected any monthly Deficiencies as aforesaid, Landlord shall be entitled to recover from Tenant, and Tenant shall pay to Landlord, on demand, in lieu of any further Deficiencies, as and for liquidated and agreed final damages and not as a penalty, a sum equal to the amount by which the sum of the Rent and Additional Rent reserved in this Lease for the period which otherwise would have constituted the unexpired portion of the Term (conclusively presuming the Additional Rent to be the same as payable for the year immediately preceding such termination or re-entry) exceeds the then fair and reasonable rental value of the Premises for the same period, less the aggregate amount of Deficiencies theretofore collected by Landlord pursuant to the provisions of clause (c) above, for the same period. Af, before presentation of proof of such liquidated damages to any court, commission or tribunal, the Premises, or any part thereof, shall have been relet by Landlord for the period which otherwise would have constituted the unexpired portion of the Term, or any part thereof, the amount of rent reserved upon such reletting shall be conclusively deemed, prima facie, to be the fair and reasonable rental value for the part or the whole of the Premises so relet during the term of the reletting.

2. If the Premises, or any part thereof, shall be relet together with other space in the Building, the rents collected or reserved under any such reletting and the expenses of any such reletting shall be equitably apportioned for the purposes of Section 19.03A hereof. In no event whatsoever, shall Tenant be entitled to any rents collected or payable under any reletting, whether or not such rents shall exceed the Rent and Additional Rent reserved in this Lease. Nothing contained in Article 18 hereof or this Article 19 shall be deemed to limit or preclude the recovery by Landlord from Tenant of the maximum amount allowed to be obtained as damages by any statute or rule of law, or of any sums or damages to which Landlord may be entitled in addition to the damages set forth in Section 19.03A hereof.

ARTICLE XX

CURING TENANT'S DEFAULTS

SECTION A. If Tenant shall default in the observance or performance of any term, covenant or condition in this Lease on Tenant's part to be observed or performed, Landlord may, without thereby waiving such default and without liability to Tenant in connection therewith, remedy such default for the account of Tenant, immediately and without notice in the case of an emergency, or in any other case, if Tenant shall fail to remedy such default after notice by Landlord and before the expiration of any applicable grace period. If Landlord makes any expenditures, incurs any obligations for the payment of money in connection therewith, or sustains or incurs any damages or fines, due to such non-observance or non-performance by Tenant, including but not limited to, reasonable attorneys' fees and disbursements in instituting, prosecuting or defending any action or proceeding, such sums paid or obligations incurred, together with interest at the Interest Rate and costs, shall be paid by Tenant to Landlord, as Additional Rent, within five (5) days of rendition of any bill or statement to Tenant therefor In the event that Tenant is in arrears in the payment of Rent or Additional Rent, Tenant hereby waives Tenant's right, if any, to designate the items against which any payments made by Tenant to Landlord are to be credited and Landlord may apply any such payments to any items Landlord sees fit.

ARTICLE XXI

NO REPRESENTATIONS BY LANDLORD; LANDLORD'S APPROVAL

SECTION A. Except as herein expressly set forth, Landlord or Landlord's agents have made no warranties, representations, statements or promises with respect to the Building, the Real Property, the Premises and no rights, easements or licenses are acquired by Tenant by implication or otherwise. All understandings and agreements previously had between the parties hereto are merged in this Lease, which alone fully and completely expresses their agreement and that the same is entered into after full investigation, neither party relying upon any statement or representation made by the other not embodied in this Lease.

SECTION B. All references in this Lease to the consent or approval of Landlord shall be deemed to mean the written consent or approval of Landlord as set forth in a written instrument executed by Landlord.

SECTION C. Wherever in this lease Landlord's consent or approval is required, if Landlord shall refuse such consent or approval, Tenant in no event shall be entitled to make, nor shall Tenant make, any claim, and Tenant hereby waives any claim, for money damages (nor shall Tenant claim any money damages by way of set-off, counterclaim or defense) based upon any claim or assertion by Tenant that Landlord unreasonably withheld or unreasonably delayed its consent or approval. Tenant's sole remedy shall be an action or proceeding to enforce any such provision, for specific performance, injunction or declaratory judgment.

SECTION D. Tenant recognizes and acknowledges that the operation of the Building equipment may cause vibration, noise, heat or cold which may be transmitted throughout the Premises. Landlord shall have no obligation to endeavor to reduce such vibration, noise, heat or cold beyond that which is prevalent in the Building.

ARTICLE XXII
END OF TERM

SECTION A. Upon the expiration or other termination of the Term, or re-entry by Landlord upon the Premises in accordance with the terms and provisions of this Lease, Tenant shall quit and surrender to Landlord the Premises, broom clean, in good order and condition, ordinary wear and tear and damage for which Tenant is not responsible under the terms of this Lease excepted, and Tenant may remove Tenant's Property and Tenant's Work to the extent permitted under and in accordance with Article S hereof. If the last day of the Term or any renewal thereof falls on a non-business day, this Lease shall expire on the business day immediately preceding such last day of the Term.

SECTION B. Tenant expressly waives, for itself and for any person claiming through or under Tenant, any rights which Tenant or any such person may have under the provisions of Section 2201 of the New York Civil Practice Law and Rules and of any successor law of like import then in force in connection with any holdover summary proceedings which Landlord may institute to enforce the foregoing provisions of this Article 22.

SECTION C. In addition, the parties recognize and agree that the damage to Landlord resulting from any failure by Tenant to timely surrender possession of the Premises as aforesaid will be substantial, will exceed the amount of the monthly installments of the Rent and Additional Rent theretofore payable hereunder, and will be impossible to accurately measure. Tenant therefore agrees that if possession of the Premises is not surrendered to Landlord within twenty-four (24) hours after the Expiration Date or sooner termination of the Term, in addition to any other rights or remedies Landlord may have hereunder or at law, Tenant shall pay to Landlord for each month and for each portion of any month during which Tenant holds over in the Premises after the Expiration Date or sooner termination of this Lease, a sum equal to the greater of (a) three (3) times the aggregate of that portion of the Rent and all Additional Rent which was payable under this Lease for the last full calendar month of the Term, and (a) the then fair market value of the Premises, as determined by Landlord. Nothing herein contained shall be deemed to permit Tenant to retain possession of the Premises after the Expiration Date or sooner termination of this Lease and no acceptance by Landlord of payments from Tenant after the Expiration Date or sooner termination of the Term shall be deemed to be other than on account of the amount to be paid by Tenant in accordance with the provisions of this Article 22. Tenant's obligations under this Article shall survive the expiration or earlier termination of this Lease.

ARTICLE XXIII

QUIET ENJOYMENT

SECTION A. Landlord covenants and agrees that upon Tenant paying the Rent and Additional Rent and observing and performing all the terms, covenants and conditions on Tenant's part to be observed or performed, Tenant may peaceably and quietly enjoy the Premises, subject, nevertheless, to (a) the terms and conditions of this Lease including, but not limited to, Article 16 hereof, and (a) all Superior Leases and Mortgages.

ARTICLE XXIV

NO WAIVER

SECTION A. The failure of either party to insist in any one or more instances upon the strict performance of any one or more of the obligations of this Lease or the Rules or Regulations, or to exercise any election herein contained, shall not be construed as a waiver or relinquishment for the future of the performance of such one or more obligations of this Lease or the Rules or Regulations or of the right to exercise such election, but the same shall continue and remain in full force and effect with respect to any subsequent breach, act or omission. No executory agreement hereafter made between Landlord and Tenant shall be effective to change, modify, waive, release, discharge, terminate or effect an abandonment of this Lease, in whole or in part, unless such executory agreement is in writing, refers expressly to this Lease and is signed by the party against whom enforcement of the change, modification, waiver, release, discharge or termination or effectuation for the abandonment is sought.

SECTION B. The following specific provisions of this Section shall not be deemed to limit the generality of any of the foregoing provisions of this Article 24:

(a) No agreement or act or thing done shall be deemed an acceptance of surrender of all or any part of the Premises unless in writing and signed by Landlord. The delivery of keys to an employee of Landlord or of its agent shall not operate as a termination of this Lease or a surrender of the Premises. If Tenant shall, at any time or from time to time, request Landlord to sublet the Premises for Tenants account, Landlord or its agent is authorized to receive said keys for such purposes without releasing Tenant from any of its obligations under this Lease, and Tenant hereby releases Landlord from any liability for loss or damage to any of Tenant's Property in connection with such subletting;

(b) The receipt by Landlord of Rent or Additional Rent with knowledge of breach of any obligation of this Lease shall not be deemed a waiver of such breach;

(c) No payment by Tenant or receipt by Landlord of a lesser amount than the correct Rent or Additional Rent due hereunder shall be deemed to be other than a payment on account, nor shall any endorsement or statement on any check or any letter accompanying any check or payment be deemed an accord and satisfaction, and Landlord may accept such check or payment without prejudice to Landlord's right to recover the balance or pursue any other remedy in this Lease or at law provided; and

(d) The existence of a right of renewal or extension of this Lease, or the exercise of such right, shall not (i) limit Landlord's right to terminate this Lease in accordance with the terms hereof, or (ii) create an option for further extension or renewal of this Lease.

ARTICLE XXV

WAIVER OF TRIAL BY JURY

SECTION A. Landlord and Tenant hereby do waive trial by jury in any action, proceeding or counterclaim brought by either of the parties hereto against the other on any matters whatsoever arising out of or in any way connected with this Lease, the relationship of Landlord and Tenant, Tenant's use or occupancy of the Premises, and/or any claim of injury or damage, or for the enforcement of any remedy under any statute, emergency or otherwise. It is further mutually agreed that in the event Landlord commences any summary proceeding for nonpayment of Rent or Additional Rent or for any holding over by Tenant following the expiration of this Lease, Tenant will not interpose (by consolidation of actions or otherwise) any counterclaim of whatever nature or description in any such proceeding. The provisions of this Article 25 shall survive the expiration or earlier termination of this Lease.

ARTICLE XXVI

INABILITY TO PERFORM

SECTION A. This Lease and the obligation of Tenant to pay Rent and Additional Rent hereunder and perform all of the other covenants and agreements hereunder on the part of Tenant to be observed and performed, shall in no wise be affected, impaired or excused because Landlord is unable to fulfill any of its obligations under this Lease expressly or impliedly to be performed by Landlord or because Landlord is unable to make, or is delayed in making any repairs, additions, alterations, improvements or decorations or is unable to supply or is delayed in supplying any equipment or fixtures if Landlord is prevented or delayed from so doing by reason of Force Majeure (as hereinafter defined). Force Majeure shall mean and include strikes oHabor troubles or by accident or by any cause whatsoever reasonably beyond Landlord's control, including but not limited to, delays caused by Tenant, other tenants, governmental restriction, regulation or control, accident, mechanical breakdown, shortages or inability to obtain labor, fuel, steam, water, electricity or materials, acts of God, enemy action, civil commotion, fire or other casualty.

ARTICLE XXVII
BILLS AND NOTICES

SECTION A. Except as otherwise expressly provided in this Lease, any bills, statements, notices, demands, requests or other communications which may or are required to be given under this Lease, or by law or governmental regulation, shall be deemed sufficiently given or rendered if in, writing, sent by registered or certified mail (return receipt requested) or by hand (provided a written receipt therefor is obtained) addressed (a) to Tenant (i) at Tenant's address set forth in this Lease if mailed prior to Tenant's taking possession of the Premises, or (ii) at the Building if mailed subsequent to Tenant's taking possession of the Premises, or (iii) at any place where Tenant or any agent or employee of Tenant may be found if mailed subsequent to Tenant's vacating, deserting, abandoning or surrendering the Premises, or (a) to Landlord at Landlord's address set forth in this Lease, with a copy to: _____, or (a) to such other address as either Landlord or Tenant may designate as its new address for such purpose by notice given to the others in accordance with the provisions of this Article 27. Any such bill, statement, demand, request or other communication shall be deemed to have been rendered or given on the date when it shall have been mailed or delivered (if delivered personally) as provided in this Article 27.

ARTICLE XXVIII
ESCALATION

SECTION A. For the purposes of this Lease (and in addition to the defined terms set forth in Article 1 hereof):

1. *"Taxes"* shall mean the aggregate amount of (a) all real estate taxes, assessments (special or otherwise), sewer and water rents, rates and charges and any other governmental levies, impositions or charges, whether general, special, ordinary, extraordinary, foreseen or unforeseen, which may be assessed, levied or imposed upon all or any part of the Real Property (including, without limitation, (i) assessments made upon or with respect to any air rights, and (ii) any assessments levied after the date of this Lease for public benefits to the Real Property or the Building (excluding an amount equal to the assessments payable in whole or in part during or for the Base Tax Year (as defined in Article I of this Lease)), and (a) any expenses (including attorneys' fees and disbursements and ex-

4. Form of Agreement of Lease

perts' and other witness' fees) incurred in contesting any of the foregoing or the Assessed Valuation of all or any part of the Real Property, but taxes shall not include any interest or penalties incurred by Landlord as a result of Landlord's late payment of Taxes, except for interest payable in connection with the installment payments of assessments pursuant to the next sentence. If by law, any assessment may be divided and paid in annual installments, then, provided the same is not prohibited under the terms of any Superior Leases or any Mortgages for the purposes of this Article 28, (i) such assessment shall be deemed to have been so divided and to be payable in the maximum number of annual installments permitted by law, and (ii) there shall be deemed included in Taxes for each Comparison Year the annual installment of such assessment becoming payable during such Comparison Year, together with interest payable during such Comparison Year on such annual installment and on all installments thereafter becoming due as provided by law, all as if such assessment had been so divided. If at any time after the date hereof the methods of taxation prevailing at the date hereof shall be altered so that in lieu of or as an addition to or as a substitute for the whole or any part of the taxes, assessments, rents, rates, charges, levies or impositions now assessed, levied or imposed upon all or any part of the Real Property, there shall be assessed, levied or imposed (1) a tax, assessment, levy, imposition or charge based on the income or rents received therefrom whether or not wholly or partially as a capital levy or otherwise, or (2) a tax, assessment, levy, imposition or charge measured by or based in whole or in part upon all or any part of the Real Property and imposed upon Landlord, or (3) a license fee measured by the rents, or (4) any other tax, assessment, levy, imposition, charges or license fee however described or imposed, then all such taxes, assessments, levies, impositions, charges or license fees or the part thereof so measured or based shall be deemed to be Taxes; provided, however, that any tax, assessment, levy, imposition or charge imposed on income from the Real Property shall be calculated as if the Real Property is the only asset of Landlord.

2. *„Assessed Valuation"* shall mean the amount for which the Real Property is assessed pursuant to applicable provisions of the New York City Charter and of the Administrative Code of the City of New York for the purpose of imposition of Taxes.

3. *„Tax Year"* shall mean the period July 1 through June 30 (or such other period as hereinafter may be duly adopted by the City of New York as its fiscal year for real estate tax purposes).

U.S. Sample Agreements

4. **"Base Taxes"** shall mean (i) in the event the Base Tax Year shall be the fiscal year period as set forth in C above, the Taxes payable on account of the Base Tax Year, or (ii) in the event the Base Tax Year shall be a calendar year period, the sum of (x) one-half (1/2) of the Taxes payable for the fiscal Tax Year ending on June 30 of said calendar year, plus (y) one-half (1/2) of the Taxes payable for the fiscal Tax Year commencing on July 1 of said calendar year.

5. **"Tenant's Projected Share of Taxes"** shall mean Tenant's Tax Payment (as defined in Section 28.02), if any, made by Tenant for the prior Comparison Year, plus an amount equal to Landlord's estimate of the amount of increase in Tenant's Tax Payment for the then current Comparison Year, divided by twelve (12) and payable monthly by Tenant to Landlord as Additional Rent.

6. **"Comparison Year"** shall mean (a) with respect to Taxes, any Tax Year commencing subsequent to the first day of the Base Tax Year, and (a) with respect to Operating Expenses (hereinafter defined), any calendar year subsequent to the Base Expense Year (as defined in Section 1.01 of this Lease).

7. **"Operating Expenses"** shall mean the aggregate of all costs and expenses (and taxes, if any, thereon) paid or incurred by or on behalf of Landlord (whether directly or through independent contractors) in respect of the operation, maintenance, security and management of the Real Property, Building and the sidewalks and areas adjacent thereto (hereinafter called „Operation of the Property") which, in accordance with the accounting practices used by Landlord (and which is in accordance with sound management principles respecting the operation of non-institutional first class office buildings in New York City) are properly chargeable to the Operation of the Property, including, but not limited to, the financial expenses incurred in connection with the Operation of the Property such as ground rent, if any, insurance premiums, the cost of electricity, gas, oil, steam, water, air conditioning and other fuel and utilities, attorneys' fees and disbursements (exclusive of any such fees and disbursements incurred in applying for any abatement of Taxes) and auditing, management and other professional fees and expenses, but specifically excluding (a) Taxes, (a) franchise or income taxes imposed upon Landlord, (a) mortgage interest, (a) leasing commissions, (a) the cost of tenant installations and decorations incurred in connection with preparing space for a new tenant, and (a) capital improvements; provided, however, that (i) if any capital improvement results in reducing Operating Ex-

4. Form of Agreement of Lease

penses (as, for example, a labor-saving improvement), then with respect to the Comparison Year in which the improvement is made and each subsequent Comparison Year during the Term, the amount by which the Operating Expenses have been reduced shall be deemed deducted from the Base Operating Expenses (hereinafter defined), and (ii) if during all or part of the Base Expense Year (as defined in Section 1.01 of this Lease) or any Comparison Year, Landlord shall not furnish any particular item(s) of work or service (which would otherwise constitute an Operating Expense hereunder) to portions of the Building due to the fact that (1) such portions are not occupied or leased, (2) such item(s) of work or service is not required or desired by the tenant of such portion, (3) such tenant is itself obtaining and providing such item or work or service, or (4) any other reason, then, for the purposes of computing Operating Expenses for the Base Expense Year or any Comparison Year, as the case may be, the amount included in Operating Expenses for such item(s) for such period shall be deemed to be increased by an amount equal to the additional costs and expenses which would reasonably have been incurred during such period by Landlord if it had, at its own expense, furnished such item(s) of work or service to such portion of the Building. In determining the amount of Operating Expenses for the Base Expense Year or any Comparison Year, if less than ninety percent (90%) of the Building rentable area shall have been occupied by tenant(s) at any time during any such Base Expense Year or Comparison Year, Operating Expenses shall be determined for such Base Expense Year or Comparison Year to be an amount equal to the like expenses which would normally be expected to be incurred had such occupancy been ninety percent (90%) throughout such Base Expense Year or Comparison Year.

8. *„Base Operating Expenses"* shall mean the Operating Expenses for the Base Expense Year.

9. *„Landlord's Statement"* shall mean an instrument or instruments containing a comparison of (a) the Taxes payable for the Base Tax Year and for any Comparison Year, or (b) the Base Operating Expenses and the Operating Expenses payable for any Comparison Year.

SECTION B.

1. If the Taxes payable for any Comparison Year (any part or all of which falls within the Term) shall exceed the Base Taxes, Tenant shall pay to Landlord an amount („Tenant's Tax Payment"), equal to Tenant's Proportionate Share of such excess. Before or after the start of each Com-

parison Year, Landlord shall furnish to Tenant a Landlord's Statement in respect of Taxes. Tenant's Tax Payment shall be payable by Tenant to Landlord, as Additional Rent within ten (10) days after receipt of a demand from Landlord therefore, which demand shall be accompanied by Landlord's Statement, regardless of whether such Landlord's Statement is received prior to, on or after the first day of such Comparison Year. If there shall be any increase in Taxes payable for any Comparison Year, whether during or after such Comparison Year or If there shall be any decrease in the Taxes payable for any Comparison Year during such Comparison Year, Landlord may furnish a revised Landlord's Statement for such Comparison Year, and Tenant's Tax Payment for such Comparison Year shall be adjusted and, (a) within ten (10) days after Tenant's receipt of such revised Landlord's Statement, Tenant shall (with respect to any increase in Taxes payable for such Comparison Year) pay such increase in Tenant's Tax Payment to Landlord, or (a) (with respect to any decrease in Taxes payable for such Comparison Year), Landlord shall credit such decrease in Tenant's Tax Payment against the next installment of Additional Rent payable by Tenant pursuant to this Section 28.02 If during the Term, Landlord shall elect to collect Tenant's Tax Payments, in full or in quarterly or bi-annual or other installments on any other date or dates than as presently required, then following Landlord's notice to Tenant, Tenant's Tax Payments shall be correspondingly revised. The benefit of any discount for any early payment or prepayment of Taxes and of any tax exemption or abatement relating to all or any part of the Real Property shall accrue solely to the benefit of Landlord and Taxes shall be computed without subtracting such discount or taking into account any such exemption or abatement.

2. With respect to each Comparison Year, on account of which Landlord shall (or anticipates that it may) be entitled to receive Tenant's Tax Payment, Tenant shall pay to Landlord, as Additional Rent for the then Tax Year, Tenant's Projected Share of Taxes. Upon each date that a Tax Payment or an installment on account thereof shall be due from Tenant pursuant to the terms of Subsection (A) of this Section 28.02, Landlord shall apply the aggregate of the installments of Tenant's Projected Share of Taxes then on account with Landlord against Tenant's Tax Payment or installment thereof then due from Tenant. In the event that such aggregate amount shall not be sufficient to discharge such Tax Payment or installment, Landlord shall so notify Tenant in a demand served upon Tenant pursuant to the terms of Subsection (A) hereof, and the amount of

4. Form of Agreement of Lease

Tenant's payment obligation with respect to such Tax Payment or installment pursuant to Subsection (A) hereof, shall be equal to the amount of the insufficiency. If, however, such aggregate amount shall be greater than the Tax Payment or installment, Landlord shall forthwith either (a) pay the amount of excess directly to Tenant concurrently with the notice or (a) permit Tenant to credit the amount of such excess against the next payment of Tenant's Projected Share of Taxes due hereunder and, if the credit of such payment is insufficient to liquidate the entire amount of such excess, Landlord shall then pay the amount of any difference to Tenant.

3. If the real estate tax fiscal year of the City of New York shall be changed, at any time or from time to time, after the date hereof, any Taxes for such fiscal year, a part of which is included within a particular Comparison Year and a part of which is not so included, shall be apportioned on the basis of the number of days in such fiscal year included in the particular Comparison Year for the purpose of making the computation under this Section 28.02

4. Only Landlord shall be eligible to institute tax reduction or other proceedings to reduce the Assessed Valuation of the Real Property and the filings of any such proceeding by Tenant without Landlord's prior written consent shall constitute a default hereunder. If the Taxes payable for the Base Tax Year are reduced by final determination of legal proceedings, settlement or otherwise, then, the Base Taxes shall be correspondingly revised, the Additional Rent theretofore paid or payable on account of tenant's Tax Payment hereunder for all Comparison Years shall be recomputed on the basis of such reduction, and Tenant shall pay to Landlord, as Additional Rent within ten (10) days after being billed therefor, any deficiency between the amount of such Additional Rent theretofore computed and paid by Tenant to Landlord and the amount thereof due as a result of such recomputations. If the Taxes payable for the Base Tax Year are increased by such final determination of legal proceedings, settlement or otherwise, then, Landlord shall either pay to Tenant, or at Landlord's election, credit against subsequent payments under this Section 28.02 or Section 28.03 hereof, an amount equal to the excess of the amounts of such Additional Rent theretofore paid by Tenant over the amount thereof actually due as a result of such recomputations. If Landlord shall receive a refund of Taxes for any Comparison Year, Landlord shall either pay to Tenant, or, at Landlord's election, credit against subsequent payments under this Section 28.02 or Section 28.03 hereof, an

amount equal to Tenant's Proportionate Share of the refund, but which amount shall not exceed Tenant's Tax Payment paid for such Comparison Year. Nothing herein contained shall obligate Landlord to file any application or institute any proceeding seeking a reduction in Taxes or Assessed Valuation.

5. Tenant's Tax Payment and any credits with respect thereto as provided in this Section 28.02 shall be made as provided in this Section 28.02 regardless of the fact that Tenant may be exempt, in whole or in part, from the payment of any taxes by reason of Tenant's diplomatic or other tax exempt status or for any other reason whatsoever.

6. Tenant shall pay to Landlord, as Additional Rent upon demand, any occupancy tax or rent tax now in effect or hereafter enacted, if payable by Landlord in the first instance or hereafter required to be paid by Landlord.

7. If the Commencement Date or the Expiration Date shall occur on a date other than July 1 or June 30, respectively, any Additional Rent payable by Tenant to Landlord under this Section 28.02 for the Comparison Year in which such Commencement Date or Expiration Date shall occur, shall be apportioned in that percentage which the number of days in the period from the Commencement Date to June 30 or from July 1 to the Expiration Date, as the case may be, both inclusive, shall bear to the total number of days in such Comparison Year. In the event of a termination of this Lease, any Additional Rent under this Section 28.02 shall be paid or adjusted within thirty (30) days after submission of Landlord's Statement. In no event shall Rent ever be reduced by operation of this Section 28. 02 and the rights and obligations of Landlord and Tenant under the provisions of this Section 28.02 with respect to any Additional Rent shall survive the expiration or earlier termination of this Lease.

SECTION C.

1. Tenant shall pay to Landlord, as Additional Rent for each Comparison Year, an amount („Tenant's Operating Payment"), calculated as follows:

(a) In the case of the first Comparison Year, a sum equal to Tenant's Proportionate Share of the amount by which Operating Expenses for such Comparison Year exceed the Base Operating Expenses;

(b) In the case of each Comparison Year subsequent to the first Comparison Year, the sum of Tenant's Operating Payment for the im-

4. Form of Agreement of Lease

mediately preceding Comparison Year, plus a sum equal to Tenant's Proportionate Share of the amount by which Operating Expenses for such Comparison Year exceed the Operating Expenses for the immediately preceding Comparison Year.

2. Landlord may furnish to Tenant, with respect to each Comparison Year, a written statement setting forth Landlord's estimate of Tenant's Operating Payment for such Comparison Year. Tenant shall pay to Landlord on the first day of each month during such Comparison Year an amount equal to one-twelfth of Landlord's estimate of Tenant's Operating Payment for such Comparison Year. If, however, Landlord shall furnish any such estimate for a Comparison Year subsequent to the commencement thereof, then (a) until the first day of the month following the month in which such estimate is furnished to Tenant, Tenant shall pay to Landlord on the first day of each month an amount equal to the monthly sum payable by Tenant to Landlord under this Section 28.03 in respect of the last month of the preceding Comparison Year, (a) promptly after such estimate is furnished to Tenant or together therewith, Landlord shall give notice to Tenant stating whether the installments of Tenant's Operating Payment previously made for such Comparison Year were greater or less than the installments of Tenant's Operating Payment to be made for such Comparison Year in accordance with such estimate, and (i) if there shall be a deficiency, Tenant shall pay the amount thereof within ten (10) days after demand therefor, or (ii) if there shall have been an overpayment, Landlord shall either refund to Tenant the amount thereof or, at Landlord's election, credit the amount thereof against subsequent payments under this Section 28.03 or Section 28.02 hereof, and (a) on the first day of the month following the month in which such estimate is furnished to Tenant, and monthly thereafter throughout the remainder of such Comparison Year, Tenant shall pay to Landlord an amount equal to one-twelfth of Tenant's Operating Payment shown on such estimate. Landlord may, at any time or from time to time (but not more than twice with respect to any Comparison Year) furnish to Tenant a revised statement of Landlord's estimate of Tenant's Operating Payment *for* such Comparison Year, and in such case, Tenant's Operating Payment for such Comparison Year shall be adjusted and paid or refunded, or, at Landlord's election, credited, as the case may be, substantially in the same manner as provided in the immediately preceding sentence.

3. After the end of each Comparison Year, Landlord shall furnish to Tenant a Landlord's Statement for such Comparison Year. Each such

year-end Landlord's Statement for any Comparison Year in which Tenant's Operating Payment is based upon Operating Expenses shall be accompanied by a computation of Operating Expenses for the Building prepared by an independent managing agent designated by Landlord from which Landlord shall make the computation of Operating Expenses hereunder. In making computations of Operating Expenses, the managing agent may rely on Landlord's estimates and allocations whenever said estimates and allocations are needed for this Article 28. If the Landlord's Statement shall show that the sums paid by Tenant under Section 28.03 C hereof exceeded the actual amount of Tenant's Operating Payment required to be paid by Tenant for such Comparison Year, Landlord shall either refund to Tenant the amount of such excess or, at Landlord's election, credit the amount of such excess against subsequent payments under this Section 28.03 or Section 28.02 hereof and if the Landlord's Statement for such Comparison Year shall show that the sums so paid by Tenant were less than Tenant's Operating Payment payable by Tenant for such Comparison Year, Tenant shall pay the amount of such deficiency within ten (10) days after demand therefor.

4. If the Commencement Date or the Expiration Date shall occur on a date other than January 1 or December 31, respectively, any Additional Rent under this Section 28.03 for the Comparison Year in which such Commencement Date or Expiration Date shall occur shall be apportioned in that percentage which the number of days in the period from the Commencement Date to December 31 or from January 1 to the Expiration Date, as the case may be, both inclusive, shall bear to the total number of days in such Comparison Year. In the event of a termination of this Lease, any Additional Rent under this Schedule D shall be paid or adjusted within thirty (30) days after submission of a Landlord's Statement. In no event shall Rent ever be reduced by operation of this Section 28.03 and the rights and obligations of Landlord and Tenant under the provisions of this Schedule with respect to any Additional Rent shall survive the expiration or earlier termination of this Lease.

SECTION D.

1. Landlord's failure to render Landlord's Statements with respect to any Comparison Year shall not prejudice Landlord's right to thereafter render a Landlord's Statement with respect thereto or with respect to any subsequent Comparison Year, nor shall the rendering of a Landlord's Statement prejudice Landlord's right to thereafter render a corrected Landlord's Statement for that Comparison Year. Nothing herein con-

tained shall restrict Landlord from issuing a Landlord's Statement at any time there is an increase in Taxes or Operating Expenses during any Comparison Year or any time thereafter.

2. Each Landlord's Statement sent to Tenant shall be conclusively binding upon Tenant unless, within thirty (30) days after such statement is sent, Tenant shall (a) pay to Landlord the amount set forth in such statement, without prejudice to Tenant's right to dispute the same, and (a) send a written notice to Landlord objecting to such statement and specifying the respects in which such statement is claimed to be incorrect. If such notice is sent, the parties recognize the unavailability of Landlord's books and records because of the confidential nature thereof and hence agree that either party may refer the decision of the issues raised to a reputable independent firm of certified public accountants selected by Landlord and reasonably acceptable to Tenant, and the decision of such accountants shall be conclusively binding upon the parties. The fees and expenses involved in such decision shall be borne by the unsuccessful party (and if both parties are partially unsuccessful, the accountants shall apportion the fees and expenses between the parties based on the degree of success of each party)

3. If any capital improvement is made during any Comparison Year in compliance with requirements of any federal, state or local law or governmental regulation, whether or not such law or regulation is valid or mandatory, then Tenant shall pay to Landlord, as Additional Rent upon demand, Tenant's Proportionate Share of the reasonable annual amortization, with interest at the Interest Rate, of the cost of such improvements in each Comparison Year during the Term during which such amortization occurs.

ARTICLE XXIX

SERVICES

SECTION A. Landlord shall provide passenger elevator facilities in the Building on business days from 8:00 A.M. to 6:00 P.M. and freight elevator facilities 8:00 A.M. to 4:45 P.M. and shall have one elevator in the bank of elevators servicing the Premises available at all other times. At Landlord's option, the elevators shall be operated by automatic or by manual control, or by a combination of both such methods. Landlord will provide Tenant with after hours freight elevator service pursuant

U.S. Sample Agreements

to Landlord's Rules and Regulations and at Landlord's then established rates in the Building for the same, payable as Additional Rent on demand. Landlord shall have the right to change the operation or manner of operation of any of the elevators in the Building and shall have the right to discontinue, temporarily or permanently, the use of any one or more cars in any of the banks; *provided, however,* that reasonable elevator service is provided to the Premises. Landlord acknowledges that the elevator system is designed to permit individual tenants' floors, including the floor on which the Premises are located, to be „locked off" between the hours of 6:00 P. M. and 8:00 A. M. and Landlord hereby agrees to cause same to be done at Tenant's request with respect to said Tenant's floor, *provided, however,* that in no event shall Landlord be liable to Tenant, or anyone claiming through or under Tenant, as a result of Landlord's failure to so „lock off" the floor on which the Premises are located.

SECTION B. Landlord shall furnish heat to the Premises when and as required by law, on business days from 8:00 A. M. to 6:00 P. M. Landlord does not represent the adequacy of, nor is Landlord responsible for, the heat distribution system, its design or capacity.

SECTION C. Tenant shall have the privilege of using the „package" air-cooling system currently servicing the Premises, *provided* that Tenant shall pay for all electricity (or other requisite power service), water and refrigerants used in connection with such system, and *provided, further,* that Tenant shall not alter, modify or replace such system without the prior written consent of Landlord in each instance. Landlord, at its sole cost and expense, shall make all repairs required to maintain the air-cooling system in good working order. Tenant covenants that its use of such air-cooling system at all times shall be in compliance with all applicable orders, rules or regulations with respect to the days or hours of operation of such system, or the volume or capacity of such system, as may be imposed from time to time by all governmental agencies and instrumentalities having jurisdiction over the same. Anything in this Section 29.03 to the contrary notwithstanding, Landlord shall not be responsible if the normal operation of such air-cooling system shall fail to provide cooled air at reasonable temperatures, pressures or degrees of humidity or any reasonable volumes or velocities in any parts of the Premises (a) which, by reason of any machinery or equipment installed by or on behalf of Tenant or any person claiming through or under Tenant, shall have an electrical load in excess of the average electrical load and human occupancy factors for such air-cooling system as designed, or (a) because of

4. Form of Agreement of Lease

any rearrangement of partitioning or other Alterations made or performed by or on behalf of Tenant or any person claiming through or under Tenant. Tenant shall keep and cause to be kept closed all of the windows in the Premises whenever the air-cooling system is in operation and shall lower and close the blinds when necessary because of the sun's position whenever the air-cooling system is in operation. Tenant at all times shall cooperate frilly with Landlord and abide by the regulations and requirements which Landlord may prescribe for the proper functioning and protection of the air-cooling system. Landlord, throughout the Term, shall have free access to the Premises for the purpose of repairing and maintaining the air-cooling system, as well as any and all mechanical installations of Landlord, including, but not limited to, air-cooling, fan, ventilating machine rooms and electrical closets.

SECTION D. The Rent does not reflect or include any charge to Tenant for the furnishing or distributing of any necessary elevator facilities, heat, cooled air or mechanical ventilation to the Premises during periods other than the hours and days set forth in this Article 29 for the furnishing and distributing of such services (hereinafter *„Overtime Periods"*). Landlord shall not be required to furnish any such services during Overtime Periods unless Landlord has received advance written notice from Tenant requesting such services not less than forty-eight (48) hours prior to the time when such services shall be required. Accordingly, if Landlord shall furnish any such elevator facilities, heat, cooled air or mechanical ventilation to the Premises at the request of Tenant during Overtime Periods, Tenant shall pay to Landlord, as Additional Rent upon demand, for such services at the standard rates then fixed by Landlord for the Building. Landlord shall supply all condenser water used in connection with Tenant's use of cooled air during Overtime Periods and Tenant shall pay to Landlord's then established rates therefor, as Additional Rent upon demand. If Tenant fails to give Landlord such advance notice requesting such services during any Overtime Periods, then, whether or not the Premises are inliabitable during such Periods, failure by Landlord to furnish or distribute any such services during such Periods shall not constitute an actual or constructive eviction, in whole or in part, or entitle Tenant to any abatement or diminution of Rent or Additional Rent, or relieve Tenant from any of its obligations under this Lease, or impose any liability upon Landlord or its agents by reason of inconvenience or annoyance to Tenant, or injury to or interruption of Tenant's business or otherwise.

U.S. Sample Agreements

SECTION E. Provided this Lease is then in full force and effect, without any defaults by Tenant hereunder, Landlord, at Landlord's expense, shall cause the Premises (excluding any portion of the Premises used for the storage, preparation, service or consumption of food or beverages), to be cleaned, substantially in accordance with the standard set forth in Exhibit 2. Tenant shall pay to Landlord as Additional Rent upon demand, Landlord's charges for (a) cleaning work in the Premises or the Building required because of (i) misuse or neglect on the part of Tenant or its agents, employees, contractors licensees or invitees, (ii) use of portions of the Premises for the storage, preparation, or consumption of food or beverages, reproduction, data processing or computer operations, private lavatories or toilets or other special purposes requiring greater or more difficult cleaning work than office areas, (iii) interior glass surfaces, (iv) non–Building Standard materials or finishes installed by Tenant or at its request, (v) increases in frequency or scope in any of the items set forth in Exhibit 2 as shall have been requested by Tenant, and (a) additional cleaning work in the Premises or the Building required because of the use of the Premises by Tenant after hours. Landlord and its cleaning contractor and their employees shall have access to the Premises at all times except between 8:00 A. M. and 5:30 P. M. on business days and shall have the use of Tenant's light, power and water in the Premises, without charge therefor, as may reasonably be required for the purposes of cleaning the Premises. If, however, the Premises are to be kept clean by Tenant, it shall be done at Tenant's sole cost and expense, in a manner satisfactory to Landlord and no one other than persons approved by Landlord shall be permitted to enter the Premises or the Building for such purpose. Tenant shall pay to Landlord the cost of removal of any of tenant's refuse and rubbish from the Premises and the Building to the extent that the same exceeds the refuse and rubbish usually attendant upon the use of such Premises as offices, as Additional Rent upon rendition of bills therefor.

SECTION F. Landlord shall supply reasonably adequate quantities of hot and cold water to a point or points on the floor of which the Premises are a part, for ordinary drinking, cleaning or lavatory purposes. If Tenant requires, uses or consumes water for any other purpose, Landlord may install a water meter and measure Tenant's water consumption for all purposes. In such event, Tenant shall (a) pay Landlord for the cost of the meter and its installation thereof, as Additional Rent upon rendition of bills, (a) keep said meter and installation equipment in good working order and repair, at Tenant's sole cost and expense, in default of which

4. Form of Agreement of Lease

Landlord may cause such meter and equipment to be replaced or repaired and collect the cost thereof from Tenant, as Additional Rent upon rendition of bills and invoices therefor, and (a) pay to Landlord for water consumed, as shown on said meter, together with a reasonable charge for any required pumping or heating thereof, all sewer rents, charges or any other taxes, rents, levies or charges which now or hereafter are assessed, imposed or shall become a lien upon the Premises or the Real Property pursuant to law, order or regulation made or issued in connection with any such metered use, consumption, maintenance or supply of water, water system, or sewage or sewage connection or system, as Additional Rent upon rendition of bills, and in default in making such payment Landlord may pay such charges and collect the same from Tenant. Independently of and in addition to, any of the remedies reserved to Landlord hereinabove or elsewhere in this Lease, Landlord may sue for and collect any monies to be paid by Tenant or paid by Landlord for any of the reasons or purposes hereinabove set forth.

SECTION G. Only Landlord or one or more persons approved by Landlord will be permitted to furnish laundry, linen, towels, drinking water, ice, food, beverages, bootblacking, barbering and other similar supplies and services to tenants. Landlord may fix the hours during which and the regulations under which said supplies and services are to be furnished. Landlord expressly reserves the right to act as or to designate, at any time and from time to time, the exclusive supplier of all or any or one or more of said supplies and services; *provided, however* that the quality thereof and the charges therefor are reasonably comparable to that of other suppliers. Landlord furthermore expressly reserves the right to exclude from the Building any person attempting to furnish any of said supplies or services but not so designated by Landlord. Notwithstanding the foregoing, Tenant, its regular office employees, or invitees may bring food or beverages into the Building for consumption within the Premises solely by Tenant, its regular office employees or invitees. In all events, all food and beverages shall be carried in closed containers.

SECTION H. Only Landlord or one or more persons approved by Landlord shall be permitted to act as maintenance contractor for all waxing, polishing, lamp replacement, cleaning and maintenance work in the Premises; *provided, however,* that the quality thereof and the charges therefor are reasonably comparable to that of other contractors servicing a first class office building with retail space. Landlord may fix the hours during which and regulations under which such services are to be furnished.

Landlord expressly reserves the right to act as or to designate, at any time and from time to time, the exclusive contractor for all or any one or more of said services; *provided, however,* that the quality thereof and the charges therefor are reasonably comparable to that of other contractors. Landlord furthermore expressly reserves the right to exclude from the Building any person attempting to furnish any of said services but not so designated by Landlord.

SECTION I. Landlord shall not be required to furnish any services, including other cleaning services, except as otherwise expressly provided in this Article 29.

SECTION J.

1. Landlord, at Landlord's expense, shall redistribute or furnish electrical energy to or for the use of Tenant in the Premises for the operation of the lighting fixtures and the electrical receptacles installed in the Premises on the Commencement Date. Tenant shall pay to Landlord, as additional rent, on demand, at any time and from time to time, but no more frequently than monthly, for its consumption of electrical energy at the Premises, based upon Landlord's then applicable rate for sub-metered electrical energy, such payment by Tenant to be calculated on the basis of the rate schedule applicable to Landlord's purchase of electrical energy, plus Landlord's reasonable charge for overhead and supervision. All sub-meters and all additional panel boards, feeders, risers, wiring and other conductors and equipment which may be required to obtain electricity, of substantially the same quantity, quality and character, shall be installed by Tenant, at Tenant's sole cost and expense. Where more than one meter measures the electric service to Tenant, the electric service rendered through each meter shall be computed and billed separately in accordance with the provisions herein above set forth. Bills for such amounts shall be rendered to Tenant at such time as Landlord may elect. The rate to be paid by Tenant for sub-metered electrical energy shall include any taxes or other charges in connection therewith. If any tax shall be imposed upon Landlord's receipts from the sale or resale of electrical energy to Tenant, the pro rata share of such tax allocable to the electrical energy service received by Tenant shall be passed on to, included in the bill of, and paid by, Tenant if and to the extent permitted by law. If either the quantity or character of electrical service is changed by the public utility or other company supplying electrical service to the Building or is no longer available or suitable for Tenant's requirements, no such change, unavailability or unsuitability shall constitute an actual or constructive

4. Form of Agreement of Lease

eviction, in whole or in part, or entitle Tenant to any abatement or diminution of Rent, or relieve Tenant from any of its obligations under this Lease, or impose any liability upon Landlord, or its agents, by reason of inconvenience or annoyance to Tenant, or injury to or interruption of Tenant's business, or otherwise.

2. Tenant's use of electrical energy in the Premises shall not at any time exceed four (4) watts per square foot. Any additional feeders or risers, whether new or existing, to be installed to supply Tenant's additional electrical requirements, and all other equipment proper and necessary in connection with such feeders or risers, shall be provided and installed by Landlord upon Tenant's request, at the sole cost and expense of Tenant; *provided, however,* that, in Landlord's judgment, such additional feeders or risers are necessary and are permissible under applicable laws and insurance regulations and the installation of such feeders or risers will not cause permanent damage or injury to the Building or the Premises or cause or create a dangerous or hazardous condition or entail excessive or unreasonable alterations or interfere with or disturb other tenants or occupants of the Building. In the event that Landlord shall install any such additional feeder, riser or other equipment pursuant to this Section 29.10 B, Tenant shall pay to Landlord Landlord's then established charge therefor, as Additional Rent, upon demand. In the event that Tenant's use of electrical energy in the Premises shall exceed four (4) watts per square foot and the power risers existing on the Commencement Date are sufficient to handle the requested additional electrical needs of Tenant and Landlord expressly consents in writing to Tenant's connection thereto, Tenant shall pay to Landlord its pro rata share of the total cost of connection and installation of said power riser in addition to the increase in Rent effective pursuant to Section 29.10 A. Tenant covenants that at no time shall the use of electrical energy in the Premises exceed the capacity of the existing feeders or wiring installations then serving the Premises. Tenant shall not make or perform, or permit the making or performance of, any Alterations to wiring installations or other electrical facilities in or serving the Premises or any additions to the business machines, office equipment or other appliances in the Premises which utilize electrical energy without the prior written consent of Landlord in each instance. Any such Alterations, additions or consent by Landlord shall be subject to the provisions of this subsection, as well as to other provisions of this Lease, including, but not limited to, the provisions of Article 5 hereof.

3. Landlord reserves the right to discontinue furnishing electricity to

U.S. Sample Agreements

Tenant in the Premises on not less than thirty (30) days' notice to Tenant. If Landlord exercises such right to discontinue, or is compelled to discontinue furnishing electricity to Tenant, this Lease shall continue in full force and effect and shall be unaffected thereby, except only that from and after the effective date of such discontinuance, Landlord shall not be obligated to furnish electricity to Tenant. If Landlord so discontinues furnishing electricity to Tenant, Tenant shall arrange to obtain electricity directly from the public utility or other company servicing the
Building. Such electricity may be furnished to Tenant by means of the then existing electrical facilities serving the Premises to the extent that the same are available, suitable and safe for such purposes. All meters and all additional panel boards, feeders, risers, wiring and other conductors and equipment which may be required to obtain electricity, of substantially the same quantity, quality and character, shall be installed by Landlord, at Tenant's sole cost and expense.

4. Landlord shall not be liable to Tenant in any way for any interruption, curtailment, failure, or defect in the supply or character of electricity furnished to the Premises by reason of any requirement, act or omission of Landlord or of any public utility or other company servicing the Building with electricity or for any other reason except Landlord's gross negligence or willful misconduct.

SECTION K. Landlord reserves the right to stop, interrupt or reduce service of the heating, ventilation or air conditioning systems, elevator, electrical energy or plumbing or any other service or systems, during any period of a violation or breach by Tenant of the provisions of this Article 29 and to stop any service when necessary by reason of Force Majeure, or for repairs, additions, alterations, replacements, decorations or improvements which are, in the judgment of Landlord, desirable or necessary to be made, until said repairs, alterations, replacements or improvements shall have been completed. The exercise of such right or such failure by Landlord shall not (a) constitute an actual or constructive eviction, in whole or in part, (b) entitle Tenant to any compensation or to any abatement or diminution of Rent, (c) relieve Tenant from any of its obligations under this Lease, or (d) impose any responsibility or liability upon Landlord or its agents by reason of inconvenience or annoyance to Tenant, or injury to or interruption of Tenant's business, or otherwise.

SECTION L. Landlord shall provide Tenant with Tenant's Proportionate Share of lobby directory listings, but in no event greater than eight (8) such listings.

4. Form of Agreement of Lease

ARTICLE XXX

STATUS OF TENANT

SECTION A. If Tenant, or a permitted assignee of this Lease pursuant to Article 15 hereof, is a partnership, or is comprised of two (2) or more persons, individually and as copartners of a partnership (any such partnership and such persons are referred to in this Article 30 as ,,Partnership Tenant"), then: (a) the liability of each of the parties comprising Partnership Tenant shall be joint and several, (b) each of the parties comprising Partnership Tenant hereby consents in advance to, and agrees to be bound by, any written instrument which may hereafter be executed, changing, modifying or discharging this Lease, in whole or in part, or surrendering all or any part of the Premises to Landlord, (c) any bills, statements, notices, demands, requests or other communications given or rendered by or to Partnership Tenant and/or any of the parties comprising Partnership Tenant shall be binding upon all of the parties comprising Partnership Tenant, (d) if Partnership Tenant shall admit new partners, all of such new partners shall, by their admission to Partnership Tenant, be deemed to have assumed performance of all of the terms, covenants and conditions of this Lease on Tenant's part to be observed and performed, and (e) Partnership Tenant shall give prompt notice to Landlord of the admission of any such new partners, and upon demand of Landlord, shall cause each such new partner to execute and deliver to Landlord an agreement in form and content satisfactory to Landlord, wherein each such new partner shall assume performance of all the terms, covenants and conditions of this Lease on Tenant's part to be observed and performed (but neither Landlord's failure to request any such agreement or the failure of any such new partner to execute or deliver any such agreement to Landlord shall vitiate the provisions of subdivision (d) of this Section 30.01). Notwithstanding anything to the contrary contained in this Lease, in the event of any default by Partnership Tenant, Landlord agrees to look solely to the partnership assets of Partnership Tenant and on to the non-partnership assets of the parties comprising the Partnership Tenant.

SECTION B. If Tenant is a corporation, each person executing this Lease on behalf of Tenant hereby covenants, represents and warrants that Tenant is a duly incorporated or duly qualified (if foreign) corporation and is authorized to do business in the State of New York (a copy of evidence thereof to be supplied to Landlord upon request); and that each person executing this Lease on behalf of Tenant is an officer of Tenant and that he is duly authorized to execute, acknowledge and deliver this Lease to Landlord (a copy of a resolution to that effect to be supplied to Landlord upon request).

ARTICLE XXXI
VAULT SPACE

SECTION A. Notwithstanding anything contained in this Lease or indicated on any sketch, blueprint or to print to the contrary, any vaults, vault space or other space outside the boundaries of the Real Property are not included in the Premises. Landlord makes no representation as to the location of the boundaries of the Real Property. All vaults and vault space an all other space outside the boundaries of the Real Property which Tenant may be permitted to use or occupy, shall be used and/or occupied under a license revocable by Landlord on ten (10) days' prior written notice to Tenant. If any such license shall be revoked by Landlord, or if the amount of any such vaults, vault space or other space shall be diminished as required by any federal, state or municipal authority or by any public utility company, such revocation, diminution or requisition shall not (a) constitute an actual or constructive eviction, in whole or in part, (a) entitle Tenant to any abatement or diminution of Rent or Additional Rent, (a) relieve Tenant from any of its obligations under this Lease, or (a) impose any liability upon Landlord. Any fee, tax or charge imposed by any governmental authority for any such vault, vault space or other space shall be paid by Tenant, as Additional Rent within five (5) days after Landlord's demand therefor.

ARTICLE XXXII
SECURITY DEPOSIT

SECTION A.

1. Tenant shall deposit with Landlord upon the execution of this Lease the Security Deposit in cash as security for the faithful performance and observance by Tenant of the terms, conditions, covenants and provisions of this Lease, including without limitation the surrender of possession of the Premises to Landlord as herein provided.

2. In lieu of a cash deposit, Tenant may deliver to Landlord a clean,

4. Form of Agreement of Lease

irrevocable, non-documentary and unconditional Letter of Credit issued by and drawn upon any commercial bank (hereinafter referred to as the *„Issuing Bank"*) with offices for banking purposes, or a correspondent bank, in the City of New York an having a net worth of not less than One Hundred Million and 00/100 Dollars ($ 100,000,000.00), which Letter of Credit shall have a term of not less than one year, be in form and content satisfactory to Landlord, be for the account of Landlord, be in the amount of the Security Deposit and be fully transferable by Landlord without the payment of any fees or charges, it being agreed that if any such fees or charges shall be so imposed, then such fees or charges shall be paid by Tenant. The Letter of Credit shall provide that it shall be deemed automatically renewed, without amendment, for consecutive periods of one year each thereafter during the term of this Lease, unless the Issuing Bank sends notice (the *„Non-Renewal Notice"*) to Landlord by certified mail, return receipt requested, not less than thirty (30) days next preceding the then expiration date of the Letter of Credit that it elects not to have such Letter of Credit renewed. Additionally, the Letter of Credit shall provide that Landlord shall have the right, exercisable within twenty (20) days of its receipt of the Non-Renewal Notice, by sight draft on the Issuing Bank, to receive the monies represented by the exiting Letter of Credit and to hold such proceeds pursuant to the terms of this Article 32 as a cash security pending the replacement of such Letter of Credit. In the event that Tenant defaults in respect of any of the terms, provisions, covenants or conditions of this Lease, including, but not limited to, the payment of Rent and Additional Rent, Landlord may apply or retain the whole or nay part of the cash security so deposited or may notify the Issuing Bank and thereupon receive the monies represented by the Letter of Credit and use, apply, or retain the whole or nay part of such proceeds, as the case may be, to the extent required for the payment of any Rent or Additional Rent or any other sum as to which Tenant is in default tor for any sum which Landlord may expend or may be required to expend by reason of Tenant's default in respect of any of the terms, provisions, covenants or conditions of this Lease, including, but not limited to, any damages or deficiency in the reletting of the Premises, whether such damages or deficiency accrue or accrues before or after summary proceedings or other reentry by Landlord. If Landlord applies or retains any part of the cash security or proceeds of the letter of Credit, as the case may be, Tenant, upon demand, shall deposit with Landlord the amount so applied or retained so that Landlord shall have the full deposit on hand at all times during the Term. If Tenant shall fully and faithfully comply with all of the terms, provisions, covenants and conditions of this Lease, the cash security or Letter of Credit, as the case may be, shall be returned to Tenant after the Expiration Date and after delivery of the entire possession of the Premises to Landlord. In the event of a sale of the Real Property or the Building or leasing of the Building, Landlord shall have the right to transfer the cash security to the vendee or lessee and with respect to the Letter of Credit, within thirty (30) days of notice of such sale or leasing, Tenant, at Tenant's sole costs and expense, shall arrange for the transfer of the Letter of Credit to the new landlord, as designated by Landlord in the foregoing notice or have the Letter of Credit reissued in the name of the new landlord and Landlord shall thereupon be released by Tenant from all liability for the return of such security. Tenant shall look solely to the new landlord for the return of such cash security or Letter of Credit and the provisions hereof shall apply to every transfer or assignment made of the security to a new landlord. Tenant further covenants and agrees that it shall not assign or encumber or attempt to assign or encumber the monies or Letter of Credit deposited herein as security and that neither Landlord nor its successors or assigns shall be bound by any such assignment, encumbrance, attempted assignment or attempted encumbrance.

ARTICLE XXXIII

CAPTIONS

SECTION A. The Captions are inserted only as a matter of convenience and for reference and in no way define, limit or describe the scope of this Lease or the intent of any provision thereof.

ARTICLE XXXIV

ADDITIONAL DEFINITIONS

SECTION A.

1. The term „office" or „offices", wherever used in this Lease, shall not be construed to mean premises used as a store or stores, for the sale or display, at any time, of goods, wares or merchandise, of any kind, or as a restaurant, shop, booth, bootblack or other stand, barber shop, o for other similar purposes or for manufacturing.

2. The words „reenter" and „reentry" as used in this Lease are not restricted to their technical legal meaning.

3. The term „rent" as used in this Lease shall mean and be deemed to include Rent, Additional Rent and any increases in Rent,

4. The term „business days", if and when used in this Lease, shall exclude Saturdays, Sundays, and all days observed by either Local 32B-32J or the State or Federal Government as legal holidays.

5. The term „person" when used in this Lease shall mean an individual, a corporation, a partnership, an association, a joint venture, an estate, a trust or any other legal entity.

ARTICLE XXXV
PARTIES BOUND

SECTION A. The terms, covenants, conditions and agreements contained in this Lease shall bind and inure to the benefit of Landlord and Tenant and their respective heirs, distributees, executors, administrators, successors, and, except as otherwise provided in this Lease, their assigns.

ARTICLE XXXVI
BROKER

SECTION A. Tenant represents and warrants that Tenant has dealt directly with (and only with), the Broker (as defined in Article 1 hereof) herein a broker in connection with this Lease, and that insofar as Tenant knows, no other broker negotiated this Lease or is entitled to any fee or brokerage commission in connection herewith, and the execution and delivery of this Lease by Landlord shall be conclusive evidence that Landlord has relied upon the foregoing representation and warranty of Tenant. Tenant shall indemnify, defend and save Landlord harmless from and against all claims for fees or brokerage commissions from anyone other than the Broker with whom Tenant has dealt in connection with the Premises or this Lease. Landlord agrees to pay a brokerage commission to the Broker pursuant to a separate agreement and this Lease is fully executed and delivered to Landlord. Landlord shall have no liability for fees or brokerage commissions arising out of an assignment of this Lease or a sublease of all or a portion of the Premises by Tenant and Tenant shall indemnify, defend and save Landlord harmless from and against all liability for fees or brokerage commissions arising out of any such assignment or sublease. The covenants, representations and agreements of Tenant set forth in this Section 36.01 shall survive the expiration or earlier termination of this Lease.

ARTICLE XXXVII

INDEMNITY

SECTION A. Tenant shall not do or permit any act or thing to be done upon the Premises which may subject Landlord to any liability or responsibility for injury, damages to persons or property or to any liability by reason of any violation of law or of any legal requirement of public authority, but shall exercise such control over the Premises as to fully protect Landlord against any such liability. Tenant agrees to indemnify and save Landlord and its agents harmless from and against (a) all claims of whatever nature against Landlord arising from any act, omission or negligence of Tenant, its contractors, licensees, agents, servants, employees, invitees or visitors, including any claims arising from any act (including, without limitation, any thing whatsoever done or any condition created), omission or negligence of Landlord and Tenant, (a) all claims against Landlord arising from any accident, injury or damage whatsoever caused to any person or to the property of any person and occurring prior to, during or (if Tenant shall continue to use and occupy the Premises) after the expiration of the Term, in or about the Premises, (a) all claims against Landlord arising from any accident, injury or damage occurring outside of the Premises but anywhere within or about the Real Property, where such accident, injury or damage results or is claimed to have resulted from an act or omission of Tenant or Tenant's agents, employees, invitees or visitors, including any claims arising from any act, omission or negligence of Landlord and Tenant, and (a) any breach, violation or non-performance of any covenant, condition or agreement in this Lease set forth and contained on the part of Tenant to be fulfilled, kept, observed and performed. This indemnity and hold harmless agreement shall include indemnity from and against any and all liability, fines, suits, damages, losses, demands, costs and expenses of any king or nature incurred in or in connection with any such claim or proceeding brought thereon, and the defense thereof with counsel approved by Landlord in writing, which

4. Form of Agreement of Lease

approval shall not be unreasonably withheld or delayed. Landlord shall indemnify Tenant against all claims of whatever nature against Tenant arising from any accident, injury or damage whatsoever caused to any person or to the property of any person which shall occur in the public areas of the Building. This Article shall survive the expiration or earlier termination of this Lease.

ARTICLE XXXIII
ADJACENT EXCAVATION-SHORING

SECTION A. If an excavation or other substructure work shall be made upon land adjacent to the Building, or shall be authorized to be made, Tenant shall afford to the person causing or authorized to cause such excavation or other substructure work, license to enter upon the Premises for the purpose of doing such work as said person shall deem necessary to preserve the wall or the building from injury or damage and to support the same by proper foundations without any claim for damages or indemnity against Landlord, or diminution or abatement of Rent or Additional Rent.

ARTICLE XXXIX
MISCELLANEOUS

SECTION A.

1. This Lease is submitted to Tenant on the understanding that it shall not be considered an offer and shall not bind Landlord in any way whatsoever until (a) Tenant has duly executed and delivered duplicate originals to Landlord, and (a) Landlord has executed and delivered one of said fully executed originals to Tenant.

SECTION B. If more than one person executes this Lease as Tenant, each of them understands and hereby agrees that the obligations of each of them under this Lease are and shall be joint and several, that the term „Tenant" as used in this Lease shall mean and include each of them jointly and severally and that the act of or notice from, or notice or refund to, or the signature of, any one or more of them, with respect to the tenancy and/or this Lease, including, but not limited to, any renewal, extension, expiration, termination or modification of this Lease, shall be binding upon each and all of the persons executing this Lease as Tenant with the same force and effect as if each and all of them had so acted or so given or received such notice or refund or so signed.

SECTION C. All Exhibits to this Lease and any and all Rider provisions attached to this Lease are hereby incorporated into this Lease. If any provision contained in any Rider hereto is inconsistent or in conflict with any printed provision of this Lease, the provision contained in such Rider shall supersede said printed provision and shall control.

SECTION D. From time to time, within seven (7) days next following Landlord's request, Tenant shall deliver to Landlord a written statement executed and acknowledged by Tenant, in form satisfactory to Landlord, (a) stating that this Lease is then in full force and effect and has not been modified (or if modified, setting forth all modifications), (a) setting forth the date to which the Rent, Additional Rent and other charges hereunder have been paid, together with the amount of fixed base monthly Rent then payable, (a) stating whether or not, to the best knowledge of Tenant, Landlord is in default under this Lease, and, if Landlord is in default, setting forth the specific nature of all such defaults, (a) stating the amount of the security deposit under this Lease, (a) stating whether there are any subleases affecting the Premises, (a) stating the address of Tenant to which all notices and communication under the Lease shall be sent, the Commencement Date and the Expiration Date, and (a) as to any other matters requested by Landlord. Tenant acknowledges that any statement delivered pursuant to this Section 39.04 may be relied upon by any purchaser or owner of the Real Property or the Building, or Landlord's interest in the Real Property or the Building or any Superior Lease, or by any mortgagee of a Mortgage, or by an assignee of any mortgagee of a Mortgage, or by any lessor under any Superior Lease.

4. Form of Agreement of Lease

IN WITNESS WHEREOF, Landlord and Tenant have respectively executed this Lease as of the day and year first above written.

LANDLORD: _____

_____   By: _____
                                   Name:
                                   Title:

TENANT: _____

_____   By: _____
                                   Name:
                                   Title:

Tenant's Federal Tax Identification Number _____
(or Social Security Number)

U.S. Sample Agreements

Anmerkung des Herausgebers/Editor's Note

Der vorgehende Büromietvertrag entspricht in Umfang und Detail heutigem Standard. Die nachfolgende Kurzform desselben Vertrages enthält *de facto sämtliche* Regelungen und Details des langen Vertrages und hat dennoch nur ein Drittel des Umfangs. Dies wird *ausschließlich* durch Streichung von Wiederholungen und logisch zwingenden Aussagen erreicht. Selbst die folgende Kurzform ist noch zu umfangreich und könnte durch Auslassung von Selbstverständlichkeiten und exotischen Details nochmals um mindestens 25% gestrafft werden, ohne an Präzision und Brauchbarkeit zu verlieren.

Mandanten wissen oder ahnen es meist, wenn Verträge unnötig lang sind. Sie lassen dies jedoch als „kulturellen" Brauch über sich ergehen.

Length and detail of the preceding office lease agreement represent today's standard. The following abbreviated version of this agreement, however, contains precisely the same number of provisions, statements or details as the long version. It is shrunk to one third of the volume solely by eliminating repetitive or logically evident statements. Even the short form could be reduced by at least another 25% simply by deleting „obvious" rules and some exotic detail.

Clients often know when agreements are unnecessarily long, but will accept them as customary practice.

5. FORM OF AGREEMENT OF LEASE
– Basic Version –

(Gewerblicher Mietvertrag, einfache Fassung)

Between

_____

Landlord

AND

_____

Tenant

New York, New York

Dated: _____, 199__

5. Form of Agreement of Lease

TABLE OF CONTENTS

ARTICLE I – DEFINITIONS 307

ARTICLE II – PREMISES, TERM, RENT 308

ARTICLE III – USE AND OCCUPANCY 308

ARTICLE IV – CONDITION OF THE PREMISES 309

ARTICLE V – ALTERATIONS AND INSTALLATIONS 309

ARTICLE VI – FLOOR LOAD 311

ARTICLE VII – REPAIRS AND MAINTENANCE......... 311

ARTICLE VIII – COMPLIANCE BY TENANT; INSURANCE 312

ARTICLE IX – SUBORDINATION 314

ARTICLE X – DAMAGE TO PROPERTY OR PREMISES... 315

ARTICLE XI – EMINENT DOMAIN 317

ARTICLE XII – ASSIGNMENT AND SUBLETTING....... 318

ARTICLE XIII – ACCESS TO PREMISES................ 321

ARTICLE XIV – LANDLORD'S LIABILITY.............. 322

ARTICLE XV – DEFAULT BY TENANT 323

ARTICLE XVI – RE-ENTRY BY LANDLORD; REMEDIES..................................... 324

ARTICLE XVII – CURING TENANT'S DEFAULTS 324

ARTICLE XVIII – NO REPRESENTATIONS; LANDLORD'S APPROVAL 325

ARTICLE XIX – END OF TERM 325

ARTICLE XX – NO WAIVER 326

ARTICLE XXI – WAIVER OF TRIAL BY JURY 326

ARTICLE XXII – BILLS AND NOTICES 326

U.S. Sample Agreements

ARTICLE XXIII – ESCALATIONS 326
ARTICLE XXIV – SERVICES........................ 330
ARTICLE XXV – STATUS OF TENANT 332
ARTICLE XXVI – VAULT SPACE 333
ARTICLE XXVII – SECURITY DEPOSIT 333
ARTICLE XXVIII – BROKER........................ 334
ARTICLE XXIX – INDEMNITY...................... 334
ARTICLE XXX – MISCELLANEOUS 334

5. Form of Agreement of Lease

AGREEMENT OF LEASE,

dated _____, 199__, between _____, having an office at _____, New York, New York _____ (,,*Landlord*") and _____, having an office at _____, New York, New York _____ (,,*Tenant*").

ARTICLE I

DEFINITIONS AND GENERAL PROVISIONS

The definitions and provisions of this Article are subject to, and may be superseded, by the provisions following this Article.

,,*Additional Rent*" shall mean all sums other than Base Rent payable by Tenant under this Lease. Unless otherwise provided herein, Additional Rent shall be paid by Tenant within 10 days after demand therefor by Landlord.

,,*Base Rent*" shall mean (vi) $_____ per annum beginning on the Commencement Date and ending on the day preceding the fourth anniversary of the Commencement Date, and (vii) $_____ for the _____ -year period following thereafter; the beginning and ending days always inclusive.

,,*Business Days*" shall exclude Saturdays, Sundays, and all days observed by either Local 32B-32J or the State or Federal Government as legal holidays.

,,*Interest*" shall mean interest at the lesser of 2% p. a. above the then current prime rate charged by Citibank, N. A. or its successor, or the maximum rate permitted by applicable law.

,,*Premises*" shall mean the entire _____ floor of the Property, as shown on Exhibit 1 hereto, together with all fixtures and equipment which are attached thereto.

,,*Property*" shall mean the building and land located at _____, in the Borough of Manhattan, City, County and State of New York.

,,*Rent*" shall mean Base Rent plus Additional Rent.

ARTICLE II

PREMISES, TERM, RENT

1. Landlord hereby leases to Tenant the Premises for a term (the „*Term*") which shall commence on _____, 199__ (the „Commencement Date") and shall expire on _____, 199__, or on the last business day of the Term if this Lease is sooner terminated or extended (the „Expiration Date").

2. Tenant expressly waives any right to rescind this Lease, or extend its Term, or to recover any damages if Landlord fails to deliver possession of the Premises on the Commencement Date. Rent shall not commence until the Premises are available for occupancy by Tenant. If Tenant takes occupancy of any premises in the Property prior to the Commencement Date, such occupancy shall be subject to all the terms of this Lease.

3. Tenant shall pay to Landlord, without notice, in lawful money of the United States of America, by check drawn on a member of the New York Clearinghouse Association, Base Rent in advance on the first day of each month, and Additional Rent as set forth in this Lease. If Tenant shall fail to pay Rent within ten days after the due date, Interest shall accrue from such due date to and including the day of payment. There shall be no deduction from or set-off against Rent except as otherwise provided herein. Tenant shall pay $ _____ on account of Rent upon the execution of this Lease, which shall be credited toward the first payment of Rent. If the Commmencement Date is not on the first day of a month, Rent for such month shall be pro-rated on a per diem basis.

4. If the Rent shall become uncollectible, be reduced or required to be refunded due to regulation or action of any entity having jurisdiction, Landlord may terminate this Lease upon 30 days notice.

ARTICLE III

USE AND OCCUPANCY

Tenant may use the Premises as executive offices only, and not as a banking, broker-dealer or any other business. Tenant's use of the Premises shall not violate the certificate of occupancy or adversely affect services to, or the use by, other tenants, or the appearance of the Property as a first-class office building. Landlord represents that the certificate of occupancy permits the use of the Premises as executive offices, but does not

5. Form of Agreement of Lease

represent that such use is legal. Upon request, Landlord shall provide such certificate to Tenant. If any governmental authority declares that Tenant's use is in violation of the certificate, Tenant shall, within 5 days notice from Landlord, discontinue such use.

ARTICLE IV

CONDITION OF THE PREMISES

1. Tenant has examined the Premises and accepts possession on the Commencement Date „as is" and vacant, and further agrees that, except as otherwise provided herein, Landlord shall have no obligation to perform or order any work in the Premises. The taking of possession of the Premises by Tenant shall be conclusive evidence that the Premises and the Property are in good condition.

2. Landlord at its own cost will remove asbestos, if any, in the Premises in accordance with applicable law. Landlord and Tenant shall cooperate so that the asbestos removal and the alterations made in connection with Tenant's initial occupancy *(„Tenant's Initial Alterations")* shall not unreasonably interfere with each other. If Tenant's Initial Alterations cause a modification of any existing asbestos containing material, Landlord shall not be responsible for restoring the pre-existing condition of such materials.

ARTICLE V

ALTERATIONS AND INSTALLATIONS

1. Tenant shall not make any alterations or installations in the Premises *(„Alterations")* without Landlord's prior consent. Landlord shall not unreasonably withhold its consent to any Alterations which are non-structural and do not affect other parts or the value or utility of the Property, or the rendition of services to other tenants; *provided,* such Alterations are performed only by contractors approved by Landlord. Tenant shall not employ any contractor or laborer in the Premises if, in Landlord's sole discretion, such employment may interfere with other contractors or laborers performing work in the Property.

2. All Alterations shall be done at Tenant's cost and at such times and in such manner as Landlord may designate. Prior to any Alterations Ten-

U.S. Sample Agreements

ant shall submit to Landlord detailed plans, obtain all required governmental permits with the cooperation, if reasonably requested, by Landlord, and furnish to Landlord duplicate original policies of worker's compensation covering all persons to be employed as well as comprehensive public liability (including property damage and completed operations/ product liability) insurance in such form as Landlord may reasonably require, naming Landlord as additional insured. Landlord shall give its approval or its specific reasons for disapproval of Tenant's plans within twenty-one business days of their submission, or within 10 business days after the submission of revised plans. Tenant shall reimburse Landlord for any out-of-pocket expenses incurred by Landlord in reviewing Tenant's plans. Landlord's approval shall not relieve Tenant of responsibility for the legal sufficiency and technical competence of the plans. Upon completion of such Alterations, Tenant shall obtain any required governmental certificates of final approval and shall furnish Landlord with copies thereof together with copies of final „as built" plans. All Alterations shall be made and performed in accordance with the Rules and Regulations, all materials and equipment to be incorporated in the Premises shall be new and first quality, and no such materials or equipment shall be subject to any lien or security agreement. For any Alterations costing more than $ 10,000.00, Tenant shall pay to Landlord 10% of the cost of all Alterations, other than Tenant's Initial Alterations, on account of Landlord's indirect costs, field supervision and coordination.

3. All personal property, movable fixtures and partitions installed by Tenant at its cost *(„ Tenant's Property")* and all Alterations in the Premises made by Tenant at its cost *(„ Tenant's Work"),* shall remain the property of Tenant and may, upon the termination of this Lease, be removed, *provided,* that Tenant shall repair any damage caused by such removal. Any property of Tenant not so removed shall become Landlord's property.

4. Tenant shall discharge any mechanic's lien filed for work or materials claimed to have been furnished to Tenant, within 10 days after the filing.

5. Tenant shall not move any safe, heavy equipment or bulky fixtures into or out of the Property without Landlord's prior consent, and shall only employ persons holding a Master Rigger's License if special handling is required.

6. Landlord agrees to contribute toward the out-of-pocket cost of

5. Form of Agreement of Lease

Tenant's Initial Alterations a sum which shall not exceed $_____. Provided Tenant shall not be in default hereunder, Landlord and Tenant, pro-rata to their respective contribution, shall make progress payments for Tenant's Initial Alterations for work performed or materials delivered, less a retainer of not less than 10%. Landlord's initial progress payment shall not be greater than $_____. Such progress payments shall be made within 30 days after requisition by contractor. Each requisition shall set forth the names of, and the amount due to, each subcontractor and, with the exception of the first requisition, shall be accompanied by waivers of lien from all contractors or materialmen relating to the required progress payment and certification of satisfactory completion from Tenant's architect.

ARTICLE VI

FLOOR LOAD

Landlord reserves the right to prescribe the weight and position of all heavy equipment and installations in the Premises and no load shall exceed the prescribed or legal floor load. Business machines and mechanical equipment shall be placed and maintained by Tenant in such manner that vibration, noise and inconvenience to Landlord and other tenants shall be prevented.

ARTICLE VII

REPAIRS AND MAINTENANCE

1. Tenant shall take good care of the Premises. Tenant shall, at its cost, promptly make all required non-structural repairs to the Premises, including to scratched or damaged doors, signs, glass (including exterior windows), walls, floors, ceilings and other items, reasonable wear and tear excepted. Any repairs shall be of a quality at least equal to the original work. Tenant shall pay Landlord for all repairs or replacements of lighting fixtures in the Premises, at Landlord's then established rates. Tenant shall give Landlord prompt notice of any defective condition in any plumbing, electrical, air-cooling or heating system, which defects are known or should reasonably be known to Tenant. If at any time the Premises shall become infested with vermin, Tenant shall, at its cost, cause the same to be exterminated and shall employ such exterminators as are

approved by Landlord. Landlord represents that, to the best of its knowledge, the Premises are not invested with vermin. The closets, mechanical rooms, fire stairs and plumbing fixtures shall only be used for their designated purposes and no sweepings, rubbish, rags, acids or other substances shall be deposited therein. Tenant shall not allow the cleaning of any window in the Premises from the outside unless the legally prescribed equipment is used, or allow the cleaning of the outside of any window from within the Premises except by persons employed by Landlord. If any sprinkler system shall not be in proper working order because of any act or omission of Tenant, Tenant shall promptly restore the same. If any changes to the sprinkler system are recommended to be made because of Tenant's use of, or Alterations to, the Premises, Tenant shall, at its cost, promptly make such changes.

ARTICLE VIII

COMPLIANCE BY TENANT; INSURANCE

1. Tenant shall comply with all laws, including fire regulations with respect to the Premises, and with the Rules and Regulations annexed hereto, as amended from time to time, unless they are in conflict with this Lease. Notwithstanding the foregoing, Tenant shall be under no obligation to make any alterations to the Premises unless such obligation shall arise as a result of the use thereof by Tenant for any purpose not authorized under this Agreement. If Tenant disputes any change in the Rules or Regulations the dispute shall be submitted for decision to the Chairman of the Management Division of The Real Estate Board of New York, Inc., or to such impartial person as said Chairman may designate, whose determination shall be final and conclusive. During the pendency of any such arbitration, Tenant shall comply with all Rules and Regulations. Tenant must dispute the change in Rules and Regulations by notice to Landlord within 10 days after receipt of notice of the change.

2. No sign, advertisement or other object which is visible outside the Property shall be exhibited by Tenant without the prior consent of Landlord. Any signs or similar objects shall conform to Property standard and shall be at the expense of Tenant. Landlord may remove same and charge the expense of such removal to Tenant.

3. Landlord shall have no obligation to enforce the Rules and Regulations against other tenants and shall not be liable for violation of the

5. Form of Agreement of Lease

same by other tenants. Landlord agrees not to discriminate against Tenant in the enforcement of the Rules and Regulations.

4. Tenant shall obtain and keep, at its sole cost, in effect during the Term:

(a) policy of comprehensive general public liability and property damage insurance with a board form contractual liability endorsement, protecting Tenant, Landlord, and any mortgagees or lessors, as insureds, against claims for personal injury, death and/or property damage, and under which the insurer agrees to indemnify Landlord against all cost, expense and/or liability. Such policy shall contain a provision that no act or omission of Tenant shall affect the payment obligation of the insurance company. The minimum limits shall be a combined single limit for each occurrence of not less than $ 3,000,000, or of any increased amount reasonably required by Landlord; and

(b) insurance against damage by fire and other risks (including theft) and, if the Premises are located at or below street level, broad form flood insurance, as are insurable under available standard „all risk" insurance, to Tenant's Property and Tenant's Work for the full replacement cost thereof (including an „agreed amount" endorsement), protecting Tenant, Landlord and any mortgagees or lessors having an interest in the Property; and

(c) business interruption insurance in an amount sufficient to prevent Landlord and Tenant from becoming co-insurers.

5. Tenant agrees to deliver to Landlord evidence of payment together with certificates evidencing such insurance and its coverage of Landlord and the other required insureds, which insurance shall not be subject to cancelation or modification except upon 30 days' notice to Landlord by certified mail, return receipt requested. Tenant's failure to keep in force the aforementioned insurance shall be regarded as a material default under this Lease. All insurance policies required of Tenant under this Lease shall be issued by reputable and independent insurers permitted to do business in the State of New York, and rate in Best's Insurance Guide, or any successor thereto (or if there be none, an organization having a national reputation) as having a general policy-holder rating of „A" and a financial rating of at least „13". Tenant shall not carry separate insurance, concurrent in form, with any insurance required of Tenant under this Lease.

6. The parties hereto shall procure „all risk" or fire or extended coverage insurance, pursuant to which the insurer waives subrogation or consents to a waiver of right of recovery by the insured prior to any loss. The waivers shall also extend to all other persons or entities occupying or using the Premises. If an additional premium is required for the inclusion of such waivers, each party shall advise the other of the amount of such additional premiums and the other party shall pay the same or shall be deemed to have released the party obtaining insurance from its duty to obtain such waivers. It is expressly agreed that Landlord will not be obligated to carry insurance on Tenant's Property or Tenant's Work or insurance against interruption of Tenant's business.

7. Each party hereby releases the other (its employees and invitees) from any claim (including a claim for negligence) which it might have for damage by fire or other casualty, provided the releasing party's right of full recovery under the applicable policy is not adversely affected.

8. Tenant shall not do or allow anything which is in conflict with any insurance policies covering the Property or property therein, or which may increase the rate of fire insurance over that in similar buildings or over the rate in effect prior to this Lease. If Tenant shall cause fire insurance rates to exceed otherwise applicable rates, Tenant shall reimburse Landlord for such excess. In any proceeding wherein Landlord and Tenant are parties, a schedule of rates issued by the body fixing fire insurance rates shall be conclusive evidence of the rates then applicable to the Premises.

ARTICLE IX

SUBORDINATION

1. This Lease is subordinate to every ground or other overriding lease of the Property (the *„Superior Leases"*) and to every trust indenture and mortgage (the *„Mortgages"*) affecting the Property or any Superior Leases, and to all renewals, modifications or replacements thereof. This Section shall be self-operative and no further instruments of subordination shall be required. Tenant shall, however, within 5 days upon Landlord's request, execute a certificate confirming such subordination, and Tenant hereby irrevocably appoints Landlord as attorney-in-fact to execute any such certificate if Tenant shall fail to do so within said 5 day period.

5. Form of Agreement of Lease

2. Tenant shall not do, or omit to do, anything which would cause Landlord to be in default under any Superior Lease or Mortgage. If, in connection with any financing of the Property, any lender shall request reasonable modifications of this Lease that do not increase the obligations or affect the rights of Tenant in a material way, Tenant agrees to promptly consent to such modifications.

3. If any act or omission of Landlord would give Tenant the right to terminate or amend this Lease, Tenant shall not exercise such right until it has given notice to each holder of any Superior Lease or Mortgage whose name shall have been furnished to Tenant, and until a reasonable period for remedying such act or omission by Landlord or by such holder shall have elapsed, unless it is not capable of so being remedied.

4. If any person shall succeed to the rights of Landlord under this Lease, Tenant, upon such successor's request, shall attorn to and recognize such successor as Landlord under this Lease. The foregoing provision shall be self-operative; *provided,* that Tenant shall promptly execute any instrument that such successor may reasonably request to evidence such attornment. Upon attornment this Lease shall continue in full force except that the successor landlord shall not (i) be liable for any acts or omissions of Landlord; (ii) be subject to any offset previously accrued to Tenant, which is not expressly provided for in this Lease and promply asserted; (iii) be bound by any previous modification of this Lease, not expressly provided for in this Lease, or by any previous prepayment of more than one month's Rent, unless such modification or prepayment shall have been expressly approved by the holder of a Superior Lease or Mortgage; (iv) be obligated to perform any alteration of the Premises; (v) be obligated to repair any part of the Property in the event of damage or condemnation which cannot reasonably be restored or compensated from the proceeds of insurance or condemnation award available to successor landlord.

ARTICLE X

DAMAGE TO PROPERTY OR PREMISES

1. Tenant shall give immediate notice to Landlord of any fire or other damage to the Property. If the Property shall be so damaged and this Lease shall not, as a consequence, have been terminated, Landlord shall repair the damage with reasonable dispatch; *provided,* that Tenant, and not

U.S. Sample Agreements

Landlord, shall be required to repair Tenant's Property or Tenant's Work. Rent shall be abated proportionate to the untenantable area of the Premises until the damage required to be repaired by Landlord shall have been substantially repaired or, if earlier, until Tenant reoccupies the damaged portion of the Premises. If, through some action or inaction of Tenant, not all of the insurance proceeds applicable to the damage can be collected, then, in addition to any other remedies, there shall be no abatement of Rent to the extent of the uncollected insurance amount.

2. Tenant shall not be entitled to any compensation or abatement of Rent if any windows of the Premises are temporarily closed or darkened for any reason, including Landlord's own acts, or any such windows are permanently closed or darkened due to any construction upon adjacent property by any party unrelated to Landlord. Landlord will use all reasonable efforts to minimize any disruption to Tenant, which shall not include any obligation of Landlord to employ labor at overtime rates.

3. If the Property or the Premises shall be so damaged that, in Landlord's opinion, substantial alteration or reconstruction shall be required, Landlord may terminate this Lease by giving Tenant notice within 90 days after such damage. The Lease shall terminate 10 days after such notice by Landlord. If the Premises are totally damaged and rendered wholly untenantable thereby, and if Landlord elects to restore the Premises, Landlord shall, within said 90 day period, cause a contractor or architect to give notice to Tenant of the date by which the restoration shall be substantially completed (the *„Estimated Restoration Date"*). If such notice indicates that the Estimated Restoration Date will be not less than 9 months after the date of damage, Tenant may terminate this Lease by giving notice within 30 days after receiving notice of the Estimated Restoration Date. If Tenant elects not to terminate this Lease, but Landlord thereafter fails to substantially complete the restoration on or before the Estimated Restoration Date, Tenant may terminate this Lease by giving notice not later than 5 days after the Estimated Restoration Date and if Landlord shall fail to substantially complete restoration within 5 days following Tenant's termination notice, this Lease shall be deemed terminated as of the date of Tenant's termination notice. If the Premises are materially damaged by fire or other casualty during the last 2 years of the Term, Tenant may terminate this Lease by giving notice within 30 days after such damage.

4. Landlord shall not be liable for loss or injury to persons or property resulting from fire or any other casualty, or for acts of other tenants or

persons, or for latent defects, or for loss or damage to property Tenant has entrusted to any employee of the Property, unless any such loss, damage or injury results from gross negligence or willful misconduct of Landlord; *provided*, that Landlord shall in no event be liable for any damage arising from any security system installed by Landlord.

ARTICLE XI

EMINENT DOMAIN

1. If the Property or the Premisis shall be acquired or condemned for any public or semi-public use *(„ Condemnation"),* this Lease shall end as of the date title vests. If only a part of the Property or Premises shall be condemned this Lease shall continue, provided that Landlord, at its expense, shall restore to tenantable condition that part of the Premises not so condemned, and provided that Rent shall be reduced proportionately. The term Condemnation shall include any agreement in lieu of eminent domain with the respective governmental authority.

2. Whether or not the Premises shall be affected thereby, Landlord may, within 60 days after receiving notice of vesting of title, give Tenant 30 days notice of termination. If the Condemnation covers more than 30% of the total area of the Premises or deprives Tenant of reasonable access to the Premises, Tenant may, within 30 days after receiving notice of vesting of title, give Landlord 30 days notice of termination.

3. Tenant shall not be entitled to any part of a Condemnation award and hereby assigns any such right to Landlord. Tenant may, however, make a claim in any Condemnation proceedings for moving expenses or the value of Tenant's Property and Tenant's Work; *provided,* such claim does not reduce the award otherwise payable to Landlord. If a Condemnation results in the temporary use of all or part of the Premises, this Lease shall continue and Tenant shall be entitled to receive that portion of the Condemnation award which represents compensation for the partial or interrupted use of the Premises. Any such award shall be held by Tenant as a trust fund for the future payment of Rent.

ARTICLE XII

ASSIGNMENT AND SUBLETTING

1. Tenant shall not assign, encumber or otherwise transfer this Lease or personal property in the Premises, nor sublet or permit any part of the Premises to be used by others, without the prior consent of Landlord in each instance. If Landlord has not given its consent and Tenant is in default hereunder, Landlord may collect rent from the assignee, subtenant or occupant and apply the net amount collected to the Rent. Such collection shall not be deemed the acceptance of the assignee, subtenant or occupant as tenant, or a release of Tenant from its obligations under this Lease.

2. Tenant shall give notice of a proposed assignment or sublease at least 60 days and not more than 6 months before the commencement date of such assignment or sublease, accompanied by (a) a copy of the proposed assignment or sublease (b) information regarding the identity, business, current financial information, including the most recent financial report, of the assignee or subtenant and (c) an agreement by Tenant indemnifying Landlord against claims by any persons for commissions or fees in connection with the proposed assignment or sublease. Within 60 days of receiving Tenant's notice, Landlord may, at its option, (i) consent or withhold consent to the proposed transaction, or (ii) sublet such space from Tenant or terminate the Lease with respect to such space (the „Leaseback Space"), or (iii) if the proposed transaction involves 50 % or more of the rentable area in the Premises, terminate this Lease. Said options shall take effect on the commencement date that the proposed assignment or sublease. If Landlord elects to terminate this Lease with respect to all or part of the Premises, Landlord shall be free to lease the vacant space to Tenant's prospective assignee or subtenant.

3. If Landlord sublets the Leaseback Space from Tenant, such sublease shall be at a rental rate equal to the lesser of the going Rent or the rental rate of the proposed sublease. Such sublease shall be subject to all of the terms of this Lease and the proposed sublease, except as are irrelevant or expressly excluded herein. It shall give subtenant the right, without Tenants permission, to further assign or sublet part or all of the space and to make alterations therein. If the proposed sublease concerns substantially all of the Premises, Landlord may extend the term of such sublease for the balance of the Term of this Lease less one day. The sublease shall provide that (i) the parties to such sublease shall expressly negate any inten-

5. Form of Agreement of Lease

tion that any estate created under such sublease be merged with any other estate, (ii) Tenant shall, at its cost, at all times permit reasonable ingress to and egress from the sublet space, (iii) Landlord may, at Tenant's cost, make such alterations as Landlord deems necessary to physically separate the subleased space, and that (iv) at the expiration of such sublease, Tenant will accept the space in its then condition, subject to the obligation of subtenant to make required repairs, except for reasonable wear and tear. Landlord shall indemnify Tenant against all obligations under this Lease as to the Leaseback Space, except for willful misconduct or negligence of Tenant. Any default by the subtenant shall not be deemed to be a default of Tenant under this Lease. Tenant shall have no obligation, at the end of the Term, to remove any alterations made in the Leaseback Space by Landlord or subtenant. Any consent required of Tenant, as landlord under the sublease, shall be deemed granted if consent with respect thereto is granted by Landlord under this Lease.

4. If Landlord does not exercise its option to terminate the Lease or sublet space from Tenant, and if Tenant is not in default hereunder, Landlord's consent to the proposed assignment or sublease shall not be unreasonably withheld; provided that (i) in Landlord's judgment the assignee's or subtenant's business and use of the Premises will be in keeping with Property standards and the restrictions hereunder, and be limited to the previous use of the Premises as executive offices; (ii) Landlord has reasonable proof that the assignee or subtenant is reputable and with sufficient financial worth; (iii) neither the assignee or subtenant nor any person directly or indirectly controlled, controlling or in any way affiliated with assignee or subtenant is an occupant of any part of the Property or is in negotiations with Landlord for the rental of space in the Property; (iv) there shall not be more than two subtenants (which may include Landlord) of the Premises; (v) the aggregate rent under the sublease shall not be less than the then current market rent as though the Premises were vacant; (vi) Tenant shall reimburse Landlord the greater of $1,000.00 or the costs incurred by Landlord in connection with reviewing the proposed transaction, including legal costs; (vii) Tenant shall not have advertised the availability of the Premises without prior approval by Landlord, nor shall any advertisement state the name (as distinguished from the address) of the Property, or list the Premises at a lower rental rate than offered by Landlord at such time for other space in the Property; (viii) the occupancy shall not increase cleaning or services requirements of Landlord; (ix) the sublease shall be subject to all the terms of this Lease; (x)

U.S. Sample Agreements

notwithstanding Landlord's consent to the sublease or its acceptance of rent from subtenant, Tenant will remain fully liable under this Lease for any violation of it; (xi) Tenant will execute and deliver the assignment or sublease within 90 days of Landlord's consent; (xii) the assignee has delivered an agreement satisfactory to Landlord in which assignee assumes all obligations of this Lease, including the restrictions regarding further assignments or subleases; and (xiii) the subtenant or assignee shall not be entitled to immunity, and shall be subject to service of process in of New York State.

5. If Landlord declines to give its consent to the proposed transaction or exercises its option to terminate the Lease or sublet space from Tenant, Tenant shall indemnify Landlord against any liabilities and costs (including legal fees) resulting from claims made by the proposed assignee or subtenant or by any brokers or similar persons.

6. With respect to any sublease, it is further agreed that (i) its term shall end not later than one day prior to the Expiration Date; (ii) it shall not be delivered and no subtenant shall take possession of space, until an executed counterpart of such sublease has been approved by Landlord; and (iii) it shall be subject to this Lease and each subtenant shall agree that it will attorn to Landlord should Landlord terminate this Lease, except that Landlord shall not be liable for any acts or omissions of Tenant or be bound by any previous modification of such sublease or any previous prepayment of more than one month's Rent or be obligated to perform any work in the subleased space, and the subtenant shall execute any instruments Landlord may reasonably request to evidence such attornment.

7. If Tenant enters into an assignment or sublease permitted hereunder, Tenant shall pay to Landlord, as Additional Rent (i) in the case of an assignment, any considerations received by Tenant for the assignment (including for Tenant's Property, less, in a sale thereof, the original cost thereof); or (ii) in the case of a sublease, any rent and charges payable to Tenant (including for Tenant's Property, less, in a sale thereof, the original cost thereof), which are in excess of the Rent allocable to the subleased space. The sums payable under this clause shall be paid to Landlord as and when received by Tenant.

8. If Tenant is a privately held corporation, the transfer or transfers, through issuance of new stock or otherwise, of a majority of the stock of Tenant shall be deemed an assignment of this Lease, unless such transfer is made to a corporation (through merger or asset sale) for a legitimate

5. Form of Agreement of Lease

business purpose and not for the principal purpose of transferring this Lease and Landlord, at least 10 days prior to the effective date or such transaction, has obtained proof that the successor to Tenant has a net worth at least equal to Tenant's net worth at the date of this Lease or at the date of such merger or acquisition, whichever net worth is greater. If Tenant is a partnership, the above provisions shall equally apply to the transfer or transfers, through issuance of new interests or otherwise, of a majority interest in the partnership. Tenant may, with Landlord's consent which shall not be unreasonably withheld, permit any business entities affiliated with Tenant to sublet or use the Premises. An entity shall be deemed affiliated if there exists direct or indirect ownership of at least 50% of the voting stock or equity interests by or in Tenant.

9. Tenant shall not be discharged of its joint and several liability with its successors in interest under this Lease if Landlord modifies or waives any of the provisions of this Lease.

10. The listing in the Property of any name other than Tenant's shall not be deemed to be the consent of Landlord to an assignment or sublease or occupancy.

11. If Tenant desires to sublet the Premises or to assign this Lease, it shall designate Landlord as exclusive agent to effect the sublease or assignment and shall pay to Landlord a reasonable and customary commission.

12. If, after an assignment of this Lease, this Lease shall be disaffirmed in any proceeding or terminated, Tenant, upon request of Landlord given within 30 days after Landlord received notice of such disaffirmance or termination, shall pay to Landlord all Additional Rent accrued to and including the date of such disaffirmance or termination, and shall enter into a new lease with Landlord of the Premises for the balance of the Term, if any, at the same Rent and terms as are contained in this Lease, subject, however, to the possessory rights of the assignee.

ARTICLE XIII

ACCESS TO PREMISES

1. Landlord, its employees, contractors or agents, and any public utility persons servicing the Property may enter the Premises at all reasonable times, upon notice, or without notice in an emergency, to examine the same, to show them to prospective purchasers, mortgagees or lessees

of the Property and to make such repairs or alterations required or permitted to be done by Landlord, or to protect the Property from imminent damage. During the one year period prior to the end of the Term, Landlord may show the Premises to prospective tenants, and if, during such period, Tenant shall have removed substantially all of Tenant's property, Landlord may alter and renovate the Premises.

2. If Tenant shall not be present to open the Premises for a permissible entry, Landlord or its agents may open the same forcibly or otherwise, provided reasonable care shall be accorded to Tenant's property.

3. Landlord reserves the right to substantially change or renovate, from time to time, entrances, corridors, elevators, stairs, toilets, mechanical systems or any other parts of the Property, and to change the name or address of the Property. Tenant agrees that all exterior walls or doors bounding the Premises, all balconies, terraces and roofs adjacent to the Premises, all space in or adjacent to the Premises used by Landlord for shafts, stairs, ducts, heating, ventilation, telephone, closets, plumbing and other similar facilities are not part of the Premises. In the performance of any work Landlord shall use all reasonable efforts to minimize interference with Tenant's use of the Premises, without any obligation to employ overtime labor. Landlord shall be liable for damage to Tenant's Work or Tenant's Property resulting from any such work. Landlord may, at its own cost, light the Premises at night for display purposes.

ARTICLE XIV

LANDLORD'S LIABILITY

1. No shareholder, partner, director or officer of Landlord shall be personally liable for Landlord's obligations or for damages under this Lease. The liability of Landlord shall be limited to Landlord's estate in the Property, and Tenant shall not look to any other assets of Landlord. Tenant's obligations shall not be excused if Landlord shall be unable, for any reason beyond Landlord's control, to perform its obligations under this Lease. Landlord shall be released from his obligations hereunder upon the sale or transfer of its interest (in whole or in part) in the Property, and the purchaser or transferee shall be deemed to have assumed all obligations of Landlord hereunder (to the extent of the interest transferred).

ARTICLE XV
DEFAULT BY TENANT

If Tenant shall (i) default in the payment of Rent, and such default shall continue for 5 days after notice by Landlord; or (ii) default in the performance of any other term of this Lease and shall fail to remedy or diligently attempt to remedy such default within 20 days after notice by Landlord; or (iii) default under any other lease with Landlord and such default shall continue beyond any grace period in such other lease; or (iv) within 60 days after the Commencement Date, fail to take occupancy or begin Tenant's Initial Alterations or allow the Premises to become vacant; or (v) allow its interest in this Lease to pass to any other person except as expressly permitted in this Agreement; or (vi) file a petition in bankruptcy, insolvency or reorganization or make an assignment for the benefit of creditors or seek or consent to the appointment of a trustee, receiver or liquidator of its property; or (vii) within 60 days after the commencement of any such insolvency, reorganization, assignment or receivership proceeding on an involuntary basis, such proceeding shall not have been dismissed or such trusteeship or receivership shall not have been vacated; or (viii) any lien or attachment shall be filed against Tenant pursuant to which the Premises may be taken by creditor of Tenant;

then, Landlord may at any time and at its option, give Tenant 5 days' notice of cancellation of this Lease. Tenant shall then surrender the Premises but shall remain liable for damages. However, if Tenant shall default in the timely payment of Rent in 2 consecutive months or in a total of 4 months within any twelve months' period, or if Tenant shall default in the performance of any other term hereunder more than 3 times within any 6-months' period, then, notwithstanding that each such default shall have been cured within the applicable period, any further similar default shall be deemed deliberate and Landlord thereafter may serve the 5 days' termination notice without any further grace period. Any monies received by Landlord from Tenant during the pendency of any insolvency or reorganization proceeding shall be deemed paid as compensation for the use of the Premises and not an acceptance of Rent or a waiver by Landlord of any rights hereunder. Landlord may suspend furnishing electric energy and any other services if such services are payable by Tenant's so long as Tenant is in arrears paying therefor.

ARTICLE XVI

RE-ENTRY BY LANDLORD; REMEDIES

1. If this Lease shall expire, Landlord may re-possess the Premises, without notice, and dispossess Tenant from the Premises. Landlord shall have no obligation to relet the Premises. Tenant waives any right it might have to restore the operation of this Lease after such dispossession. The word „re-entry" shall not be restricted to its technical legal meanings. Landlord may enjoin any threatened breach of this Lease and invoke any other remedy allowed.

2. Tenant shall also pay any deficiency between the Rent reserved for the unexpired portion of the Term (Additional Rent to be the same as for the 12 preceding months), and the rents collected under any reletting, net after Landlord's expenses in connection with the termination and reletting, including renovation costs, brokers' and legal fees. Such deficiency shall be paid in monthly installments on the days specified for the payment of Rent. Landlord may at any time at its election, in lieu of collecting further monthly deficiencies, demand as final damages the payment by Tenant of an amount equal to the excess of the Rent such reserved in this Lease from the date of such election to the end of the Term, over the then fair rental value of the Premises. If Landlord shall have relet the Premises rent payable under such reletting shall be conclusively deemed to the the fair rental value. In no event shall Tenant be entitled to any rents payable under such reletting, whether or not they exceed the Rent reserved in this Lease. Nothing contained herein shall preclude Landlord from recovering any other or greater damages he may be entitled to under this Agreement or applicable law.

ARTICLE XVII

CURING TENANT'S DEFAULTS

1. If Tenant shall be in default under this Lease or otherwise fail to perform any of its obligations after notice by Landlord, Landlord may, without thereby waiving the default, remedy such default, without notice in an emergency, or after the applicable grace period has expired. Landlord may request reimbursement by Tenant for any expenses or damages incurred, together with Interest, within 5 days after Landlord received the respective bill therefor.

5. Form of Agreement of Lease

ARTICLE XVIII

NO REPRESENTATIONS; LANDLORD'S APPROVAL

1. Landlord has made no warranties or promises, and no rights are acquired by Tenant, other than as expressly stated in this Lease. All previous understandings are merged in this Lease. Tenant acknowledges that the operation of the Property equipment may produce a certain level of vibration, noise or temperature, and shall accept such level as is prevalent in the Property.

2. The terms „consent", „approve" or „notice", whereever used herein, shall mean written consent, approval or notice. Landlord shall in no instance withhold its consent unreasonably. If Tenant claims that Landlord unreasonably withheld its consent, Tenant shall waive any claims for damages, and shall be restricted to pursue specific performance or similar remedies.

ARTICLE XIX

END OF TERM

1. Upon the expiration of the Term or re-entry by Landlord, Tenant shall surrender the Premises broom clean and in good order, ordinary wear and tear excepted. At any termination date, Rent shall be apportioned and pre-paid Rent applicable to any period after the termination date shall be reimbursed, except that Landlord may retain all monies, including advanced Rent or security deposit to the extent Landlord claims damages against Tenant. Tenant expressly waives any special rights it might have under New York civil practice law in connection with any holdover summary proceedings Landlord may institute.

2. The parties acknowledge that the damage to Landlord resulting from any failure by Tenant to timely surrender the Premises will be substantial and impossible to accurately measure. Tenant therefore agrees that if possession of the Premises is not surrendered on the day after the Expiration Date, in addition to any other remedies Landlord may have, Tenant shall pay for each hold-over period, a sum equal to the greater of (i) 3 times the Rent which was payable for the same period immediately before the end of the Term or (ii) the then fair rental value of the Premises, as determined by Landlord.

ARTICLE XX

NO WAIVER

The failure of either party, in any one instance, to insist upon strict performance of this Lease, or to exercise any election, shall not be deemed a waiver or failure to elect for future instances. No agreement or act, including an acceptance of Tenant's keys by Landlord, hereafter made shall effectively modify or terminate this Lease unless it is in writing and expressly refers to this Lease and its modification or termination.

ARTICLE XXI

WAIVER OF JURY TRIAL

Landlord and Tenant hereby waive trial by jury in any action arising out of this Lease, including any tort action. It is agreed that, if Landlord commences any proceeding for nonpayment of Rent or for any holdover, Tenant will not interpose any counterclaim in any such proceeding.

ARTICLE XXII

BILLS AND NOTICES

SECTION E. Any statements, demands or notices shall be deemed delivered if, and when, sent by registered or certified mail (return receipt requested) or by hand against written receipt, if to Tenant, at its address at the Property or its other address, and if to Landlord, at Landlord's address, with a copy to: _____.

ARTICLE XXIII

ESCALATIONS

1. For purposes of this Lease:

,,Base Expense Year" shall mean the calendar year 199__.

,,Base Operating Expenses" shall mean the Operating Expenses for the Base Expense Year.

,,Base Taxes" shall mean the Taxes payable on account of the Base Tax Year.

5. Form of Agreement of Lease

„*Base Tax Year*" shall mean the calendar year 199__ Tax Year.

„*Comparison Year*" shall mean (a) with respect to Taxes, any Tax Year commencing subsequent to the first day of the Base Tax Year, and (a) with respect to Operating Expenses (hereinafter defined), any calendar year subsequent to the Base Expense Year.

„*Landlord's Statement*" shall mean an instrument or instruments containing a comparison of (a) the Taxes payable for the Base Tax Year and for any Comparison Year, or (b) the Base Operating Expenses and the Operating Expenses payable for any Comparison Year.

„*Operating Expenses*" shall mean all expenses incurred by Landlord in the operation and management of the Property and the areas adjacent thereto which, in accordance with sound management principles for the operation of non-institutional first class office buildings, are properly chargeable to the operation of the Property, including financial expenses, ground rent, insurance premiums, electricity, gas, oil, water, air conditioning and other utilities, legal cost, auditing, management and other fees and expenses; but excluding items defined as Taxes above and general income taxes imposed upon Landlord, mortgage interest, leasing commissions, installations and expenses incurred in preparing space for tenants, and capital improvements, provided, that if any capital improvement results in reducing Operating Expenses the savings in Operating Expenses shall be deemed deducted from the Base Operating Expenses. If, however, such capital improvement was made pursuant to applicable law, whether or not such law is valid or mandatory, Tenant shall pay its Proportionate Share of the reasonable annual amortization, with Interest, of such improvement. If Landlord, for any reason, shall not furnish certain services (which would otherwise constitute Operating Expenses hereunder) to any portion of the Property, then, for purposes of computing Operating Expenses, the estimated cost of such non-furnished services shall be added to the actual Operating Expenses. If less than 90% of the Property rentable area shall have been occupied by tenant(s) at any time during the year, Operating Expenses shall be reasonably determined as if such occupancy had been 90% throughout such year.

„*Proportionate Share*" shall mean _____ %.

„*Taxes*" shall mean all real estate taxes, sewer and water charges, occupancy or rent taxes, and any other special or general governmental levies which may be imposed upon the Property, including on its air rights, if any, and any expenses incurred in contesting any of the foregoing, and in any Comparison Year any installments of Taxes including interest which under the law are payable in installment, but Taxes shall not include any interest or penalties charged for late filing or late payment by Landlord. Taxes shall also include any possible future levy based partly or wholly on income or rents received from the Property; provided, that any such levy shall be calculated as if the Property was the only asset of Landlord.

„*Tax Year*" shall mean the period July 1 through June 30 or such other period as may be adopted by the tax authority.

1. Tenant shall pay its Proportionate Share of any increase in Taxes payable for any Comparison Year over the Base Taxes (Tax Payments). Such payment shall be made irrespective of whether Tenant may be exempt from taxes because of diplomatic status or otherwise. Before or during each Comparison Year, Landlord shall furnish to Tenant Landlord's Statement, or any revised statement if Taxes shall have been increased or reduced during or after such Comparison Year. Any decrease in Taxes shall be credited against the next installment of Tenant's Tax Payment. Landlord may elect at any time to collect Tenant's Tax Payments in full or in periodic installments. The benefit of any discount for prepayment of Taxes and of any exemption or abatement of Taxes shall accrue solely to the benefit of Landlord and shall not be deducted from Taxes for purposes of determining Tenant's Tax Payments.

2. Landlord may request Tenant to add to each Tax Payment the projected increase of Taxes for the current year, as estimated by Landlord. If such added payments exceed the actual increase in Taxes for such year, Landlord must directly reimburse the excess if a credit against Tenant's next Tax Payment is insufficient to liquidate the entire amount of the excess payment.

3. Only Landlord shall be entitled, but shall not be obligated, to institute tax reduction or similar proceedings. If the Taxes payable for the Base Tax Year are definitely and finally reduced by legal proceedings or otherwise, the Base Taxes shall be correspondingly revised and Tenant's Tax Payments for prior Comparison Years shall be recomputed, any deficiencies being payable by Tenant. If the Taxes payable for the Base Tax Year are increased by such final determination or Landlord receives a refund of Taxes for any Comparison Year, Landlord, at its election, shall either pay or credit to Tenant any excess Tax Payments, provided that the amount of any refund allocable to Tenant shall not exceed Tenant's Tax Payment for such Comparison Year.

4. Tenant shall pay for each Comparison Year its Proportionate Share

5. Form of Agreement of Lease

of any increase in Operating Expenses over the Base Operating Expenses (Tenant's Operating Payment). Landlord may furnish to Tenant Landlord's estimate of Tenant's Operating Payment for each Comparison Year. Until receipt of such estimate or revised estimate, Tenant shall continue paying, in equal monthly installments on the first day of each month, its Operating Payment at the same rate as paid for the last month of the preceding Comparison Year. Upon receipt of Landlord's estimate, Tenant's future Operating Payment shall be adjusted accordingly, and Tenant shall pay any deficiency accrued during the previous months of such Comparison Year or, in case of any overpayment for such previous months, Landlord shall, at its election, refund or credit such overpayment to Tenant. Landlord may revise its estimate at any time, but not more than twice for any Comparison Year.

5. After each Comparison Year, Tenant shall be furnished Landlord's Statement of Operating Expenses for such Comparison Year prepared by an independent managing agent designated by Landlord. If Landlord's Statement shall show that the sums paid by Tenant hereunder hereof exceeded the actual amount of Tenant's Operating Payment required to be paid by Tenant for such Comparison Year, Landlord shall either refund to Tenant the amount of such excess or, at Landlord's election, credit the amount of such excess against subsequent payments under this Section, and if Landlord's Statement for such Comparison Year shall show that the sums so paid by Tenant were less than Tenant's Operating Payment payable by Tenant for such Comparison Year, Tenant shall pay the amount of such deficiency within 10 days after demand therefor.

6. Each Landlord's Statement shall be conclusively binding unless, within 30 days after it was sent, Tenant shall pay the amount due under such statement and include a notice objecting with specificity to the correctness of such statement. The parties recognize the confidential nature of Landlord's books and records, and hence agree that either party may refer the issue to the binding decision of a reputable independent accounting firm selected by Landlord and acceptable to Tenant. The expenses involved in such decision shall be borne by the unsuccessful party, or be apportioned by the accountants equitably between the parties in case of partial success. Landlord's failure to timely render Landlord's Statements shall not prejudice Landlord's right to thereafter render or correct Landlord's Statement for any Comparison Year. A Landlord's Statement may also be issued at any time there is an increase in Taxes or Operating Expenses during any Comparison Year.

U.S. Sample Agreements

7. In no event shall Base Rent ever be reduced by operation of this Article.

ARTICLE XXIV

SERVICES

1. Passenger elevator service shall be provided on business days from 8:00 A. M. to 6:00 P. M., freight elevator service from 8:00 A. M. to 4:45 P. M. One elevator shall be available to service the Premises at all times. The elevators shall be operated by automatic or by manual control. Landlord may change or discontinue the operation of any elevators or elevator banks; *provided,* that reasonable elevator service is provided to the Premises. Landlord acknowledges that the elevator system permits individual tenants' floors to be „locked off" during after hours and Landlord agrees to lock off Tenant's floor at Tenant's request, *provided,* that in no event shall Landlord be liable for its failure to so „lock off" Tenant's floor.

2. Heat shall be furnished to the Premises when and as required by law, on business days from 8:00 A. M. to 6:00 P. M. Landlord shall not be responsible for the design or adequacy of the heat distribution system.

3. Tenant shall have the privilege of using the „package" air-cooling system currently servicing the Premises, *provided* that Tenant shall pay for all power, water and refrigerants used in such system, and that Tenant shall not alter such system. Landlord, at its cost, shall maintain the air-cooling system in good repair. Tenant covenants that its use of such system shall be in compliance with all applicable Rules or Regulations regarding the times, volume and operation of such system. Landlord shall not be responsible if the air-cooling system fails to provide air at reasonable temperatures or degrees of humidity, to the extent such failure results from the installation or rearrangement of equipment or fixtures by Tenant that have electrical loads in excess of the average load. Tenant shall keep closed the windows in the Premises, and shall lower and close the blinds when necessary because of the sun's position, whenever air-cooling is in operation.

4. The Rent does not include any charge to Tenant for the furnishing of elevator facilities, heat, cooled air, condenser water or ventilation during regular office hours. Landlord shall not be required to furnish any such services outside regular hours unless it has received Tenant's request

5. Form of Agreement of Lease

therefor not less than 48 hours in advance and unless Tenant pays for such services at the rates then fixed by Landlord.

5. If Tenant is not in default hereunder, Landlord, at its own expense, shall cause the Premises to be cleaned substantially in accordance with the standard set forth in Exhibit 2. Tenant shall pay for cleaning work in the Premises or in the Property required because of Tenant's neglect, or performed in space used for food storage or consumption, computer operations, private toilets or other space requiring more difficult cleaning work than office areas, or performed on interior glass surfaces or non-Property Standard materials or finishes installed by Tenant, or performed with increased frequency or scope at the request of Tenant or because of Tenant's use of the Premises after hours. Cleaning personell shall have access to the Premises at all times except between 8:00 A. M. and 5:30 P. M. on business days and may reasonably use Tenant's light, power and water without charge therefor. Tenant shall pay for the cost of removal of refuse to the extent it exceeds the amount of refuse usual for offices.

6. Landlord shall supply adequate quantities of hot and cold water to the floor of which the Premises are a part, for drinking, cleaning or lavatory purposes. If Tenant requires water for any other purpose, Landlord may install a water meter and charge Tenant for all of its water and/or sewage use and for the cost of the meter, its installation and maintenance.

7. Maintenance, cleaning, repair, laundry, food, beverage, barbering and other similar services may be furnished to Tenant only by persons, and at the times, approved by Landlord. Landlord reserves the right to act as or designate the exclusive supplier of any such services, which must be at rates and at a quality comparable to that of other suppliers. Tenant, its employees or invitees may bring food or beverages into the Property for their own consumption. All food and beverages shall be carried in closed containers.

8. Landlord, at its expense, shall furnish power lines to the Premises and Tenant shall pay, not more frequently than monthly, for Tenant's consumption of electrical energy at the then applicable rate for sub-metered energy. Such rate shall be based on the rate schedule for Landlord's purchase of energy plus a reasonable charge for Landlord's overhead and taxes, including taxes imposed on Landlord's resale of electricity. All submeters and additional panel boards, feeders, wiring and other equipment required to obtain electricity of a similar or greater quantity and quality shall be installed at Tenant's cost. Tenant's use of energy shall generally not ex-

ceed 4 watts per square foot and must in no event exceed the capacity of existing feeders and risers. If such use exceeds 4 watts per sq. ft. at certain times and the existing power risers are sufficient to handle the additional need, Tenant shall pay its pro rata share of the total cost of connection and installation of said power riser. Tenant shall not alter any electrical facilities serving the Premises or add business machines and equipment which utilize electrical energy without the Landlord's consent.

9. Landlord may discontinue furnishing electricity to Tenant on not less than 30 days' notice. If Landlord exercises such right to discontinue, this Lease shall be unaffected thereby and Tenant shall arrange to obtain electricity directly from the public utility servicing the Property. Such electricity may be furnished to Tenant by means of the then existing electrical facilities to the extent the same are suitable for such purposes. All meters, feeders and other electrical equipment required to obtain such electricity shall be installed by Landlord, at Tenant's cost.

10. Landlord may stop, interrupt or reduce service of the heating, ventilation or air conditioning systems, electricity, elevators or any other service or systems, if Tenant violates the provisions of this Article, or by reason of Force Majeure, or during any repairs or alterations which are, in Landlord's judgment, desirable to be made.

11. Landlord shall provide Tenant with Tenant's Proportionate Share of lobby directory listings, but in no event more than 8 such listings.

ARTICLE XXV

STATUS OF TENANT

If Tenant is an entity, each person executing this Lease on behalf of Tenant hereby represents that Tenant is in good standing and duly qualified or authorized to do business in the State of New York, and that such person is an officer of Tenant or otherwise authorized to execute and deliver this Lease. Landlord may request from Tenant certificates or resolutions to such effect. If Tenant is a partnership or is comprised of 2 or more persons, each such person or partner, existing or newly admitted, shall be liable under this Lease as it may be amended and shall be considered an agent of all other persons or partners for the service of any statements or notices by or to the Tenant. However, Landlord agrees to look solely to the partnership assets of Tenant and not to the assets of any individual partner.

5. Form of Agreement of Lease

ARTICLE XXVI

VAULT SPACE

Landlord makes no representation as to the boundaries of the Property. Notwithstanding any sketch or blueprint indicating otherwise, any vaults or other space outside the Property boundaries are not included in the Premises. Such space may only be used under a license revocable at will by Landlord on 10 days' notice. Tenant shall be liable to pay any governmental charge or tax imposed for any such space.

ARTICLE XXVII

SECURITY DEPOSIT

1. Upon the execution of this Lease, Tenant shall make a deposit *(,, Security Deposit")* with Landlord in the amount of $\$\_\_\_\_$, to be held as security for the faithful observance by Tenant of all the terms hereunder. In lieu of a cash deposit, Tenant may deliver as Security Deposit an irrevocable, non-documentary and unconditional Letter of Credit *(,, LC"),* satisfactory to Landlord, and issued by a commercial bank with offices or a correspondent bank in the City of New York and having a net worth of not less than One Hundred Million Dollars (\$100,000,000). The LC shall have a term of at least one year and be transferable by Landlord without the payment of any fees. The LC shall provide that it shall be deemed automatically renewed for consecutive one-year periods during the term of this Lease, unless the issuing bank sends a notice of non-renewal to Landlord by certified mail, return receipt requested, not less than 30 days prior to the then expiration date of the LC. Additionally, the LC shall provide that Landlord may, within 20 days of its receipt of the non-renewal notice, draft the full amount of the LC by sight draft on the issuing bank and to hold the proceeds as Security Deposit hereunder pending the replacement of such LC.

2. If Tenant defaults under this Lease beyond the applicable grace period, Landlord may apply or retain the Security Deposit for the payment of Rent or any other sum owed or expected to be owed by Tenant. If Landlord so applies or retains the Security Deposit, Tenant shall, upon demand, restore the full amount of the Security Deposit at all times during the Term. If Tenant is not in default under this Lease, the Security Deposit shall be returned after the Expiration Date and after delivery of

the possession of the Premises to Landlord. If Landlord wishes to transfer the Security Deposit to a purchaser or lessee of the Property, Tenant shall cooperate in such transfer and shall release Landlord from its obligation to return the Security Deposit at the end of the Term. Tenant may not encumber or assign the Security Deposit and Landlord shall not be bound by any such encumbrance or assignment.

ARTICLE XXVIII

BROKER

Tenant represents that it has only dealt with_____ (the „*Broker*") and that to the best of Tenant's knowledge, no other broker or person is entitled to any commission in connection with this Lease. Landlord shall pay the commission to Broker pursuant to a separate agreement after this Lease has been fully executed and delivered to Landlord. Tenant indemnifies Landlord against all claims for fees or commissions from anyone other than the Broker with whom Tenant has dealt in connection with this Lease. Landlord shall have no liability for, and shall be indemnified by Tenant against, any fees or commissions in connection with an assignment of this Lease or a sublease.

ARTICLE XXIX

INDEMNITY

Tenant shall indemnify Landlord against all claims of whatever nature against Landlord, including fines, suits, costs and legal fees, arising or claimed to arise from any act or omission of Tenant or arising from any accident or injury occurring within the Premises. Landlord shall similarly indemnify Tenant against all claims of whatever nature arising from any accident or injury occurring in the public areas of the Property, except if caused by Tenant.

ARTICLE XXX

MISCELLANEOUS

1. The terms of this Lease shall bind and inure to the benefit of the parties and their respective heirs, distributees, executors, administrators, successors and permitted assigns.

5. Form of Agreement of Lease

2. Tenant shall not be entitled to compensation or termination of the Lease or to an abatement of Rent if any act of Landlord or of any other person shall cause business interference, noise, vibration, or any other nuisance to Tenant, or diminish access to or the use of the Premises, unless such act represents a material breach of this Lease.

3. This Lease is submitted to Tenant not as a binding offer. It shall be binding only after both parties have executed and delivered originals thereof.

4. All Exhibits and Riders attached to this Lease are hereby incorporated into this Lease. If any provisions therein conflict with any printed provisions of this Lease, the provisions of this Lease shall be superseded.

5. From time to time, within 7 days after Landlord's request, Tenant shall deliver and acknowledge a statement which shall (i) state that this Lease is then in full force and effect and has not been modified or, if modified, set forth any modifications, (ii) set forth the date to which the Rent has been paid, (iii) state whether or not, to the best knowledge of Tenant, Landlord is in default under the Lease, (iv) state the amount of the Security Deposit, (v) state whether there are any subleases affecting the Premises, (vi) state the address of Tenant to which any notices shall be sent as well as the Commencement and Expiration Date, and (vii) address any other matters requested by Landlord. Tenant acknowledges that any such statement may be relied upon by any purchaser of the Property, or of any lessee or mortgagee.

6. The term Landlord shall include, if and when reasonably requested by Landlord, any holders of Senior Leases or Mortgages on the Property, as well as any successors in interest to Landlord. Any acts or obligations of Tenant shall be deemed to also be acts or obligations of Tenant's successors in interest and, if applicable, of Tenant's employees, agents, contractors, invitees and similar persons.

7. The Captions are inserted only as a matter of convenience and for reference and in no way define, limit or describe the scope of this Lease or the intent of any provision thereof.

U.S. Sample Agreements

IN WITNESS WHEREOF, Landlord and Tenant have executed this Lease as of the day and year first above written.

LANDLORD   TENANT

By:_____   By:_____
    Name, Title   Name, Title
                                             Tenant's Federal Tax

Identification Number
(or Social Security Number)